Best Vacation Rentals

Caribbean

Produced by The Philip Lief Group, Inc.

Managing Editor, Richard Eastman

Edited by Constance Jones

Written and Researched by:

Julia Banks
Scott Corngold
Luz Cruz
Loren Elmaleh
Josh Eppinger
Robyn Feller
Fiona Gilsenan
Catherine Henningsen
Robert Hernandez
Robin Hohman
Mitsy Campbell Kovacs
Lisa Schwartzburg
Willy Spain
Paula Stelzner
Susan Wells
Denise Wydra

Design by Margaret Davis
Maps by Myra Klockenbrink and Charlie Williams

Best Vacation Rentals

Caribbean

A Traveler's Guide to Cottages, Condos, and Castles

Prentice Hall Press
New York

The information in this book is the most up-to-date available at the time of publication. However, specifics can change and we recommend that you confirm all details before making reservations. In addition, many states are currently reviewing and changing policies on the right of accommodations to refuse children as guests, and if a child-free environment is important, you should check with the establishment about its current policy.

 Published by Prentice Hall Press
A division of Simon & Schuster Inc.
15 Columbus Circle
New York, NY 10023

Produced by The Philip Lief Group, Inc.
6 West 20th Street
New York, NY 10011

ISBN 0-13-928-227-0

ISSN 1054-9757

Manufactured in the United States of America

First Edition   10 9 8 7 6 5 4 3 2 1

Contents

Introduction: A World of Homes Away from Home

Journey in your mind's eye to a villa you've rented for a week on Virgin Gorda, its stucco walls as dazzlingly white as its private beach. You lounge on the shady terrace watching your children play tennis as the Caribbean surf rolls gently in. Stepping through French doors to prepare another pina colada, you pause to admire the tropical flowers adorning the immaculate interior.

Or instead, envision a weathered wooden cottage set amid a cluster of palm trees on Saba. You've opened the louvered shutters to let the breeze sweep through your two spare rooms. Gathering up your flippers and mask from their resting place on the deck, you toss them into your Jeep and head for a secluded cove where you've heard the snorkeling is great.

Perhaps you'd rather dream of a sleek modern condominium overlooking a charming harbor in the Bahamas. From your balcony you can watch private yachts glide between the mighty cruise ships anchored offshore. As the sun sets, you admire the spoils of an afternoon spent in the town's quaint shopping district; your mouth waters as your traveling companion prepares the catch of the day, bought straight off a fishing boat.

Each of these vacation fantasies can come true once the secrets of the self-catered getaway are revealed. People seeking an extra element of privacy, comfort, adventure and economy on vacation have begun to discover the advantages of renting houses, cabins and apartments when they travel. Instead of settling for a cramped, nondescript room in a hotel or an inn and paying for three expensive restaurant meals a day, you can enjoy the convenience and independence of homes away from home. Today, a whole world of vacation rental options—from fully staffed mansions to compact studios, from lavish resort bungalows to rustic lodges—lies open to the savvy, adventurous traveler.

Best Vacation Rentals: Caribbean introduces you to the unique pleasures of self-sufficient travel. The properties presented in the pages that follow offer stunning locales and delightful features unavailable in traditional arrangements, creating an exciting and intimate environment seemingly designed just for you. Gardens, Jacuzzis or balconies; historic surroundings, breathtaking views or fireplaces; a taste for local color or seclusion off the beaten path—this unique option lets you choose the best setting for your next trip. The personalized touch you can get in planning a vacation of this kind allows you to indulge all of your specific needs and interests more completely than simply registering at the best local hotel. For instance, couples can enjoy the privacy, peace and solitude offered by a romantic and secluded place of their own while senior citizens may appreciate the services, comfort and convenience of self-contained units at fully staffed resort condos.

Families appreciate the extra indoor and outdoor space, savings on food and lodging and access to kitchen and laundry room facilities.

Best Vacation Rentals: Caribbean presents a whole spectrum of self-catering accommodations. In its pages you will find vacation rental properties in every region of the Caribbean, to suit every desire and budget. This array of self-sufficient lodgings is available through several types of businesses and organizations:

- Vacation rental agencies that rent out vacation houses, apartments and condominiums owned by individuals who use them only during certain seasons.
- Hotel and resort complexes that include bungalows and apartments.
- Private owners who offer their homes for rent at certain times of the year.
- Historical societies and government agencies that manage unusual properties maintained by foundations or municipalities.

This broad spectrum of sources gives you access to every type of vacation rental—whether you seek a restored plantation, a contemporary home or a simple beach house—and to every vacation destination, from the most popular to the most secluded. An appendix at the end of the book directs you to tourism boards that can provide you with further information on self-catered travel in the Caribbean.

Before you turn to the listings, take a moment to read "Travel Tips." It covers the nuts and bolts of self-sufficient travel and outlines exactly what to look for and what to expect when planning a self-catered vacation. As you read, you will find valuable information on selecting the appropriate type of lodging, making reservations and determining what to bring. You'll learn how to research the differences among rentals, such as frequency of housekeeping service, provision of kitchen equipment and linens and requirements for minimum stays. Specific suggestions relating to Caribbean travel are featured in a special section. A short "How to Use This Guide" follows and describes how the book is organized and how to read the listings. A quick glance at these guides will help you make the most of this invaluable source book, no matter which kind of getaway you choose.

Welcome to the exciting world of *Best Vacation Rentals: Caribbean*—and have a great island vacation!

Travel Tips:
Making Yourself at Home

Congratulations on selecting a travel option that will make your trip more fascinating, relaxing and fun! Experienced vacation renters have found that a little preparation can go a long way toward making your vacation rental a smashing success. And with that in mind, this section shows you both what to look for and what to expect when renting a vacation home. A little research will help you get the most from your home away from home.

What kind of vacation home is right for me?

Although many American travelers are new to self-catering vacations—those where you make a rental home your own for the length of your stay—a dizzying array of possibilities lies open to the traveler who knows where to look, especially in the Caribbean. The travel-wise have been vacationing this way for decades, and the incredible abundance of vacation rentals available throughout the islands will astound you: Secluded bungalows overlooking thriving reefs; luxurious mini-estates with mountaintop vistas—whatever your dream destination, you can rent it there. Many different sources, each of which has distinct advantages, are available, and all are represented in this guide.

North American or Caribbean-based vacation rental agencies often represent dozens, hundreds or even thousands of rental homes and apartments on one or more islands, giving you an almost endless selection of properties to choose from. Many of the listings that appear in this book are handled by such agencies, most of which also offer scores more rentals than could be listed here—so when you call or write to request information on a property, inquire as well about other rentals that might be of interest. Leasing through an agency can make the job a lot easier: This arrangement ensures that your selection has met stringent quality requirements; and they handle all the financial and scheduling arrangements and any problems that may arise during your stay. You may find dealing with a Caribbean agency the easiest solution to selecting a vacation rental, because differences in language, currency and customs are eliminated.

Hotel and resort complexes with bungalows or condominiums on the grounds offer less variety in lodging type but provide all of the amenities expected from a standard hotel or motel. Swimming pools, complimentary breakfasts, housekeeping/linen service and child care are only a few comforts offered in this category. And because self-catering suites or apartments in such establishments may cost no more than an ordinary hotel room, they represent a real bargain. The level of luxury often far exceeds what you might expect for the price, so resorts are guaranteed to appeal to vacationers who want to be pampered. Generally located near the action—in downtown areas or popular tourist destinations—resort condos have the added advantage of easy access to all the local attractions.

Private owners provide wonderfully personal vacation lodgings— where personal libraries, video collections, gourmet kitchens or even cars or boats are often at your disposal. And because owners may have only one property for rent, they can give undivided attention to your questions, requests and needs. Ask the owners for advice on shopping, dining, sightseeing and local traditions; or have them put you in touch with neighbors who can ease you into a foreign setting. Private owners may not be equipped to accept your credit cards, but they'll often leave a trail of personal touches and amenities seldom found in more formal arrangements.

Historical societies and government agencies offer unique vacation rental possibilities. If you want to stay in a perfectly preserved sugar baron's mansion or a converted landmark rum distillery, these sources are for you. Maintained through private donations or public funds, such historic properties frequently rent for absurdly low rates. Many agencies are interested only in covering the cost of your stay, not in making a profit. For an unforgettable cultural experience, renting from these organizations can't be beat. Time spent in this truly special kind of setting could prove unforgettable, and make your vacation stay a lifelong treasured memory.

Regardless of the self-catering alternative you select, you are guaranteed to derive tremendous benefits from this kind of vacation. If you managed to locate comparable accommodations in a traditional hotel, they would likely be far more expensive. While squeezing into a good hotel room for a week on St. John strains the finances of many families, a spacious two-bedroom self-catered flat—with a kitchen and maybe a fireplace or washing machine—can be quite affordable. Self-caterers save even more by eating some meals (particularly breakfasts, which are often light but expensive) at "home" instead of in restaurants.

Even when money is not an issue, the extra space and increased privacy of a house or an apartment makes any vacation more pleasurable. Good-bye paper-thin walls and postage-stamp rooms! These become a thing of the past when you leave hotels behind for rentals. The freedom to whip up a midnight snack or a secret family recipe for finicky children can also be a boon to weary tourists. A place to keep your beer cold, a machine to wash your socks or a grassy yard to nap in removes that great stress of traveling: the need to compromise on comfort.

But it's up to *you* to tap the potential of your vacation rental to the fullest. Maybe you prefer to travel with friends, and need separate bedrooms at night in addition to common areas for group activities. Perhaps your family can't live without at least two bathrooms. A private yard for your children to play in; a secluded haven miles away from the next neighbor; a wide porch to view spectacular sunsets: Renting a vacation home can secure any creature comforts you require while traveling. Even if no one in your party wants to be the cook, self-catering still makes sense: You'll save money while enjoying more space, greater privacy and personalized comforts not found in traditional inns or hotels.

Be sure to reserve far in advance, because the demand for these appealing properties is high among travel aficionados. Many travelers return again and again to a favorite rental, sometimes booking their time slot a year in advance. Don't worry, however, that you won't be able to find something you like: The sheer number of vacation rentals on the market almost ensures a suitable property will be available wherever you're going—and whenever you're going there. But remember that the most attractive lodgings and those that represent the best value go quickly, especially in peak seasons.

The various rental sources offer a wide array of vacation homes, from compact studio apartments to modern condominiums and from rustic cottages to lavish estates. When deciding among these vacation rental options, consider your traveling needs, desires and budget and make sure your lodging meets them. The location, setting, design and decor should satisfy your tastes and enhance your vacation experience. For instance: Do health problems preclude an isolated setting far from town? Would you prefer the excitement of the city? Do condominium complexes offend you? Have you always wanted to live on your own private island?

The Comforts of Home—and More

Each traveler has a unique notion of the ideal vacation lodging. (Indeed, self-catering is not for everyone.) But travelers who appreciate the advantages of renting a home away from home can expect their vacation rentals to offer certain amenities. The rentals included in this book all have kitchen facilities, living areas and at least one comfortable bed, but beyond that vary widely. As you set out to find your dream flat or cottage from among the listings that follow, keep these few pointers in mind to help you determine how potential rentals rate.

Each listing includes information on the special features most important to travelers. Look for a mention of balconies, decks, porches or patios if you like to lounge outdoors, or of yards, gardens or extensive acreage if you long to stretch out. Imagine the perfect setting, then scour the listings for properties with water frontage, views or unusual architectural or design features. Indoors, you'll make decisions about telephones, televisions, VCRs, fireplaces, Jacuzzis, hot tubs and saunas. Many rentals come complete with barbecues, while others offer swimming pools or private beaches. Decide which items will make your vacation complete and mark the listings that meet your requirements.

Basic services are at least as important to a rental's appeal as its location is, and the listings present comprehensive information that will help you narrow your selection of possibilities. Is central air conditioning important to you? Will you need a parking space? Are linens and blankets provided, and are they changed on a daily or weekly basis? Is housekeeping service included? Is it offered daily, weekly or between tenants only? Will you have the assistance of a full- or part-time maid or other staff member? Other diverse service possibilities include: Complimentary breakfast, lunch, dinner or cocktails and babysitting or other child care services.

You can expect the kitchen to come equipped with a refrigerator, stove, cooking and eating utensils and plates and glassware (listings generally do not make specific mention of these items). Look for references to items you require in addition to the basics—such as a microwave—to help narrow your field of choices. For those who want to rent but don't plan to cook, many listings mention bars or restaurants on the premises or close by. Some rentals offer private cooks who can prepare your favorite meals without your having to lift a finger.

Having established this basic information, the listings go on to describe a colorful array of optional amenities. You'll come across everything from stereos, pianos and wet bars to security systems, valet service and meeting rooms. Some listings mention free use of bicycles, docking facilities or country club privileges, while others make note of playgrounds and tennis courts. Don't despair if your dream rental seems to be missing one key element: It might be there; we just couldn't fit it all in. If a rental sounds tempting, investigate it further by calling or writing the contact listed to learn more.

Clearly, *Best Vacation Rentals: Caribbean* is only meant to be a starting point—the variety of features offered in vacation rental homes couldn't be contained in these pages. But the abundance of features described in the listings proves that, whatever your travel desires, self-catering can fulfill them.

Check it Out

Once you've targeted some possible properties, take the first step in planning a self-catered trip: Request brochures with photographs of those that interest you; and ask for local maps and any other available materials. If you're contacting an agency, ask for information on its rules and regulations and inquire about other properties in the area you will visit. Agencies publish extensive catalogues containing data on many more vacation rentals than *Best Vacation Rentals: Caribbean* could accommodate; and their listings change periodically.

The agents, resorts, private owners and historical societies will provide complete details, in writing, about the properties listed in this book and let you know if anything has changed since publication. Additionally, we recommend that you speak with someone by telephone to confirm everything. As you review the material and prepare to make your final choice, be sure none of your questions are left unanswered.

Take the time to formulate a complete picture of your potential rental. If something you require is not mentioned—Fax service, for example, or a kitchen with an automatic coffee maker—ask if it is available. An on-site owner or manager to set your mind at ease or a game room to help keep the kids busy while you sunbathe are other considerations that may apply to your individual travel situation. The athletic vacationer might ask if there's a gym on the premises, or if golf, boating, fishing, hiking or riding are available nearby.

Confirm that the property is open and available on the dates you plan to visit. Find out if your visit will fall in peak season, and if the proprietor will book a reservation as far in advance as is practical to avoid disappointment. If a minimum stay is required (many vacation rentals are offered on a weekly basis only), see if it applies to your off-season stay. When you are not renting an individual house, you may want to find out how many units the building, resort or restoration you've chosen encompasses. Some travelers prefer the security of large complexes; others like the intimacy of smaller establishments.

Is the unit you want to rent the right size for your needs? Make sure it can accommodate at least the number of guests in your party and determine if the number of bedrooms included provides adequate privacy. You may wish to confirm that the beds are the size you prefer. (If you and your mate like to share a double bed, for instance, don't risk ending up with two twins.) Get a sense of the overall size of the unit, including any common areas, the kitchen and outdoor space.

Ask about any restrictions placed on guests: Are pets allowed? What about St. Bernards? Can you smoke indoors? Even if you smoke a pipe or cigar? Is the unit accessible to the handicapped? Are there steep stairs or a wheelchair ramp? Some older rentals—reached by rugged footpaths, equipped with steep stairs or built with narrow doorways—may be particularly problematic for the infirm.

Request precise rate information on the dates of your intended stay. Most rates fluctuate on a seasonal or even a weekly basis. Find out what is included in the rate quoted and what sorts of extra charges might apply. You may or may not, for instance, be charged extra for heat, for the use of certain resort facilities, for daily instead of weekly housekeeping or linen service, for extra guests or for a pet.

On the other hand, some establishments offer discounts to senior citizens, groups or guests who pay in advance. Check to see if you can take advantage of any price breaks. You may also discover tantalizing package deals, in which extra amenities or privileges are included at cut rates. Historic restorations sometimes offer packages that include the price of a unit rental plus golf or fishing privileges, tours of historic sites, cocktail parties and other bonuses.

Confirm the forms of payment accepted, and determine what kind of deposit is required to guarantee a reservation. Many properties ask for a deposit equal to one night's charge; others may request half or even all of the total rental fee up front. In some cases, the deposit may be charged by phone to a credit card, but most renters require a bank draft in the currency of the country in which the rental is located, and will hold your reservation for seven days to receive it. Agencies and individuals will also often ask you to sign a rental agreement (like a short-term lease agreement) and pay a security deposit against possible damage. The deposit is refunded to you after your stay, when it is determined you have not damaged the property.

Finally, check to see if check-in and check-out times fit your itinerary and if you must follow any special procedures when arriving or departing.

Make sure you understand the renter's cancellation policy before putting down a deposit: You can lose the entire amount if you need to cancel and don't give enough notice. This is also a good time to find out who is responsible for assisting you if something goes wrong with your rental while you are on vacation. And read any contracts carefully before you sign. Then, once you are satisfied with the details, go ahead and make your reservation. When you do, ask for a receipt or other confirmation that your deposit has been received and your reservation finalized.

Some carefree travelers, of course, can't be tied down by reservations, or prefer to experiment with new locations once their trip is well underway. Upon arrival in some irresistibly tempting locale, adventurers can usually find self-catering accommodations through local travel information bureaus, newspaper or real estate agents. In popular tourist destinations, rentals are sometimes found simply by walking or driving around with an eye out for "vacancy" or "for rent" signs. When a charming vacant property is spied, rent it on the spot—often for a favorable rate and no minimum stay requirement. Using this method, savvy self-caterers who don't require the security of advance planning can find wonderful lodgings at great rates. *But if you're traveling on-season, reservations are strongly recommended.*

Be Prepared

Do you need to pack any differently for a self-catered vacation than you would for a traditional one? Not really. If the unit, especially the kitchen, does not provide some item or convenience you absolutely require, think about bringing it along. Of course, if you must pack light and the missing element—a television or microwave—is not easily transportable, you might consider either doing without or renting a different property.

Those whose rentals include access to laundry facilities may choose to pack fewer clothes than usual. You may want to add a flashlight or some candles to your luggage if it will help you feel safer in a strange house. Or if you have a favorite cook's knife or corkscrew, toss it in with your toothbrush and swimsuit.

Some self-caterers pack a few non-perishable necessities—herbal tea, a pound of decaffeinated coffee, a special spice—if they suspect the items might be difficult to find in local stores. Others surrender entirely to their destination, savoring the adventure of shopping and eating like a local resident. Experienced international self-caterers agree it is impractical and unnecessary to carry more than the smallest food items with you.

Beyond these few minor points, making arrangements for your self-catered trip should be no different from preparing for a traditional vacation. Pack as you normally would, and get ready to have a great time!

At Home on the Road

The travel experience is distinctly different when you choose a home away from home instead of lodging in a hotel. The extra space, comfort, independence and privacy are a luxury, but those who are first-timers may wonder if it involves more work. After all, who wants to do housework on vacation? A little planning goes a long way toward making your self-catered trip carefree.

The most obvious difference between self-catered and hotel accommodations is access to a kitchen. But remember: You can make as much or as little use of it as you like. Some self-caterers prepare every meal, but others only enter the kitchen to enjoy a midnight snack in their pajamas. Whatever your preference, a few simple rules will help you minimize shopping and cooking time.

Plan your basic weekly menu before leaving home. Find out from guidebooks, your property's management or neighbors what kinds of foods and shopping facilities are available. Take into account the number of meals you are likely to eat out and design a menu based on as few ingredients as possible to avoid wasted staples and uneaten leftovers at departure time.

You'll find breakfast will be the time when you make best use of your rented kitchen, and you'll love the freedom of having an early-morning fruit salad in your bathrobe and slippers. So shop to make your vacation breakfasts special. Go ahead and buy the kinds of foods you normally don't indulge in.

For lunch and dinner, simple dishes requiring little advance preparation are best. Cooks who love to experiment with regional cuisines, however, have an exciting opportunity to cut loose when they travel the self-catered way—prowling the farmers' markets, fishermen's stalls and specialty shops in search of delectable local ingredients to bring home and cook up to their heart's delight.

Don't despair if you want to self-cater and can't stand the prospect of doing even minimal housework on vacation. As the listings in *Best Vacation Rentals: Caribbean* show, plenty of Caribbean vacation rentals include daily or weekly housekeeping service (this may or may not include dishwashing)—or even a full-time staff. And for those that do not include maid service during your stay, we've found that a small amount of housework on a daily basis goes a long way toward saving you from a laborious clean-up on the day of departure. It's all in choosing your dream rental and taking the time to make the simple preparations and inquiries about services necessary to insure your comfort and happiness.

Island Life

Renting a vacation home in the Caribbean involves only slight adjustments for visitors from the United States. Various differences in currency, language and culture face all U.S. travelers in the Caribbean; and all must observe customs and immigration formalities when crossing international borders. We will not cover most of these points here, as you've probably found that information already in your travel guide to the Caribbean. Certain points, however, are of particular interest to self-caterers from up north.

- Given the high cost of dining out in the Caribbean, self-catering in the islands is an exceptional bargain. Groceries can cost up to 50 percent more than they do in the U.S., but preparing your own meals will still be far cheaper than eating out.

- For those who hate housework—and who doesn't?—Caribbean self-catering offers another tremendous advantage: Most rentals come either with daily maid service or with a staff that might include a cook, a maid and a gardener. Rates for staffed rentals are surprisingly reasonable, so go ahead and treat yourself to the ultimate in island luxury.

- A number of U.S.-based agencies offer substantial discounts (up to 50 percent) on rental properties in the Caribbean. You may get the best price by renting through them.

- Other companies specialize in package rentals that include accommodations, a car and airfare. Using such an agency can make planning your Caribbean vacation easier, and can keep costs predictable. See the back of the book for more information.

- Don't drink the water. In many Caribbean regions the water contains bacteria that can cause dysentery or diarrhea in visitors. Use bottled, purified water when you wash produce, make ice cubes and beverages, cook food and brush your teeth.

- Milk in the Caribbean is often unpasteurized, so avoid it and all uncooked dairy products.

- Resist the temptation to eat unpeeled fruit, uncooked vegetables and food prepared by street vendors.

- The often rough terrain of Caribbean islands frequently makes Jeeps, motorbikes and motorcycles more practical modes of transportation than ordinary rental cars. Be prepared for some challenging motoring that on some islands also calls for driving on the left-hand side of the road. The faint of heart might prefer to walk, take taxis or hire a private driver.

- A few of the islands—notably Aruba, Bonaire and Curacao—have converted to the metric system. Bring your metric conversion table and be prepared to do a little arithmetic in the market.

- Most islands use the same 110 volts, 60 amps AC electricity as the United States, but check to be sure.

- In general, transporting pets across international borders involves an array of immunization and quarantine procedures that may make taking your pet on vacation impractical. Nonetheless, if you're determined to bring Rover or Fluffy along, check to see what requirements your pet must meet in order to enter the island you plan to visit.

- Peak season for travel in the Caribbean is the wintertime. Reserve your rental well in advance—six months or so—if you plan to visit during the cooler months.

- Enjoy!

How to Use This Guide

The listings in this guide appear alphabetically by island or island group, city and lodging name, in that order. A list of tourist boards appears at the end of the book; contact them as a valuable source of information and ideas to enhance your self-catered vacation.

Each listing contains the following information:

Rates:
Instead of quoting actual figures, prices are divided into categories. Rates change too often to be quoted exactly, but the price range provided in the listings will give you a reliable impression of the cost of a unit. More than one rate category in a listing generally reflects the difference between on-season and off-season rents. Be sure to ask specific questions about rate changes when planning your vacation to get the best possible deal. Prices are quoted per unit, not per person, and reflect conversion into American dollars. The categories are as follows:

budget	up to $75/night or $600/week
inexpensive	$76-125/night or $601-850/week
moderate	$126-175/night or $851-1,200/week
expensive	$176-250/night or $1,201-1,750/week
deluxe	$251 and up/night or $1,751 and up/week

Open:
Indicates the dates when the property is open.

Minimum Stay:
Information on the length of stay required is provided here. Minimum stay requirements may differ between the high and low tourist seasons.

Descriptive text:
This paragraph describes the highlights of the property. Outstanding features and furnishings of the unit, amenities and services available on the premises, and characteristics of the surrounding region are included. If something is not mentioned in this paragraph, do not assume it is unavailable: The description is not comprehensive and provides only an introduction to the property. For your convenience, agency listings often include a reference number for particular rentals. Use this number when you contact the agency to find out more.

Children (Yes or No):
Indicates if children are permitted.

Pets (Yes or No):
Indicates if pets are permitted. (Be sure to check the quarantine policies of your particular destination well in advance.)

Smoking (Yes or No):
Indicates if cigarette smoking is permitted. Restrictions on pipes and cigars should be confirmed with the rental proprietor.

Handicap Access (Yes or No):
Some properties, such as ground-floor units, represent themselves as partially accessible to the handicapped. Unless it has been determined, however, that the property is fully accessible, we have indicated "no" accessibility.

Payment:
Indicates the forms of payment accepted:

C	Cash
P	Personal check
T	Travelers check
A	American Express
V	Visa
M	MasterCard
O	Other credit cards
All	All forms of payment

Shoal
Bay

Sandy
Ground● *Katouche* ★ **The Valley**
Bay
Blowing
Point Sea Feathers
● *Little* *Bay*
Harbor
Rendezvous
Maundays *Bay*
Bay

Caribbean Sea

Anguilla

BLOWING POINT

CUL DE SAC *Rates: moderate*
Open: year-round *Minimum Stay: none*
Sun, sea and tranquility are yours in these handsome studio apartments
perched on the water at pretty Blowing Point. All six apartments feature
a bedroom/sitting room, kitchen and dining room opening onto a large
terrace with sea views. You can swim in the private pool with views of
the mountains of St. Maarten in the background, or sunbathe on a private beach with jetty, where you can also find good snorkeling. For a
truly memorable dining experience, have a champagne and lobster picnic at one of the offshore cays. Guests at Cul de Sac can also use the
resort facilities at nearby Malliouhana. Contact: Cul de Sac, Blowing
Point, Anguilla, British West Indies. Call 809-497-6461.
Children: Y Pets: N Smoking: Y Handicap Access: N Payment: C, T, V, M

KATOUCHE BAY

MASARA RESORT *Rates: inexpensive-expensive*
Open: year-round *Minimum Stay: one week*
For years, Mac and Sara Brooks dreamed about creating a quiet island
getaway where people could enjoy the beauty of Anguilla without the
crowds and hassles so common at the large resorts. They've created
Masara Resort with that in mind, and have included maid service six
days a week to leave guests time to soak up the sun or get their tennis
game in shape. Choose from one-bedroom apartments or two-bedroom

villas, both featuring sparkling tile floors, comfortable furnishings and fully equipped kitchens. There's plenty of room to eat inside, but a better choice would be to enjoy your meals on the private patio while drinking in magnificent views of golden sunsets across the Caribbean. Contact: Rent A Home International, Inc., 7200 34th Ave. N.W., Seattle, WA 98117. Call 206-545-6963. Ref. ANG/002.

Children: Y Pets: N Smoking: Y Handicap Access: N Payment: C, P, T, V, M

LITTLE HARBOR

CINNAMON REEF BEACH CLUB   *Rates: inexpensive-deluxe*
Open: year-round   *Minimum Stay: none*

Large archways lead onto private terraces at these modern white stucco villas, enhancing the air of luxury and privacy. Choose from a garden suite, beach suite or villa, each of which features several steps up to tastefully decorated bedrooms and dressing rooms overlooking the spacious and comfortable living room. A freshwater swimming pool, two championship tennis courts, free sailboats, snorkeling equipment and other water sports equipment are available to guests. From the dining rooms and bar areas of the club, you can view the reef-sheltered harbor and the boats moored in the calm waters. Live entertainment and dancing will fill your nights with ample entertainment. Contact: Cinnamon Reef Beach Club, Little Harbor, Anguilla, British West Indies. Call 1-800-223-1108.

Children: N Pets: N Smoking: Y Handicap Access: N Payment: C, T, V, M

MAUNDAYS BAY

CAP JULUCA   *Rates: expensive-deluxe*
Open: November 1 - August 31   *Minimum Stay: one week*

Cap Juluca's graceful domes form the skyline at Maundays Bay, creating a tropical oasis in spectacular Moorish style. Set on 170 acres along miles of white sandy beaches, this sophisticated retreat features oversized rooms and large suites for supreme comfort. Cool white tile floors, ceiling fans, louvered doors and windows and a fully stocked bar and ice maker keep you as cool as the gentle sea breezes. Eighteen units may be divided into deluxe doubles, one- and two-bedroom suites, or rented whole. Among the many luxurious features here are the palatial bathrooms appointed with imported travertine marble and glass-walled showers, some opening onto private sunbathing terraces. Room service and a variety of water sports as well as a good restaurant round out the offerings for guests. Contact: Nicola Lindsay, Cap Juluca, Maundays Bay Management, Ltd., P.O. Box 240, Anguilla, British West Indies. Call 1-800-323-0139.

Children: Y Pets: N Smoking: Y Handicap Access: N Payment: C, P, T, A

MEADS BAY

CARIMAR BEACH CLUB   *Rates: inexpensive-deluxe*
Open: year-round   *Minimum Stay: five nights*

Both the privacy of apartment living and the amenities of hotel service are available at Carimar Beach Club on beautiful Meads Bay on the northwest side of the island. Four to six guests can stay comfortably in two- or three-bedroom units, all with spacious patios or balconies, fully equipped kitchens and living/dining rooms. Some of the units offer excellent water views. Two all-weather tennis courts, snorkeling, sailing, fishing and swimming allow for plenty of healthy exercise. For a pleasant diversion, experience the casino nightlife at neighboring St. Maarten, only 15 minutes away by ferry. Contact: Pamela Berry, Carimar Beach Club, P.O. Box 327, Anguilla, British West Indies. Call 809-497-6881.

Children: Y Pets: N Smoking: Y Handicap Access: N Payment: C, T, A, V, M

MALLIOUHANA   *Rates: expensive-deluxe*
Open: year-round   *Minimum Stay: none*

Malliouhana is the Carib Indian word for Anguilla, but this splendidly luxurious modern hotel is far removed from the island's humble beginnings. Set on 25 acres and two miles of white sandy beaches, everything here is geared to the pampered traveler. Villas can be rented singly or divided into three units, each with a private veranda, cool tropical decor and marble bathrooms. You'll find burnished mahogany throughout Malliouhana, creating a warm and cozy setting. Three tennis courts, water sports facilities and a fine restaurant on-site give you plenty to do day and night. Contact: Malliouhana, P.O. Box 173, Meads Bay, Anguilla, British West Indies. Call 809-497-6111.

Children: Y Pets: N Smoking: Y Handicap Access: N Payment: C, T, A, V, M

VILLA DEL MAR AT LA SIRENA   *Rates: moderate-deluxe*
Open: year-round   *Minimum Stay: none*

You won't find expensive furnishings, exotic decor or celebrity guests at La Sirena, but you'll get spacious, clean, comfortable villas with good sea views and easy access to the beach, all at truly moderate prices. Villa del Mar, a two-bedroom villa, features a full kitchen, lounge veranda and private patio off the bedrooms. A ceiling fan cools the rooms with sweet ocean breezes, and a telephone and minibar provide extra comfort. Barbecue equipment and a freshwater swimming pool provide an alternative to the kitchen and the beach. Maid service is available daily, and you can even have your dishes washed for an extra fee. Or, if you prefer, you can take advantage of a meal plan and simply relax and enjoy. Contact: La Sirena, P.O. Box 200, Meads Bay, Anguilla, British West Indies. Call 1-800-331-9358.

Children: Y Pets: N Smoking: Y Handicap Access: N Payment: C, T, A, V, M

RENDEZVOUS BAY

ANGUILLA GREAT HOUSE   *Rates: inexpensive-deluxe*
Open: year-round   *Minimum Stay: one week*

Gingerbread trim and painted shutters adorn resort buildings in the whimsical style typical of Anguilla, luxuriously modernized for comfort. An air of gracious informality created by Victorian reproduction furnishings permeates the Great House, where all rentals open onto private verandas for outdoor comfort. You can rent simple accommodations for two as a base for exploring the beautiful beaches at Rendezvous Bay and the nearby resorts. Families of four may want to try the two-bedroom suites, some with living and dining rooms and kitchenettes for meals. West Indian and Continental cuisine may be enjoyed at the Great House Beach Bar and Restaurant on the premises. Contact: Anguilla Great House, P.O. Box 157, Rendezvous Bay, Anguilla, British West Indies. Call 809-497-6061.

Children: Y Pets: N Smoking: Y Handicap Access: N Payment: C, T, A, V, M

CHINABERRY   *Rates: expensive-deluxe*
Open: year-round   *Minimum Stay: one week*
Chinaberry commands an inspiring view over lovely Rendezvous Bay toward the hills of St. Maarten, and offers guests luxury and elegance with many unusual amenities. You'll find the house enclosed in a completely secluded courtyard brimming with seagrape and coconut palms around a beautiful waterfall. The sounds of the water echo up to the huge master bedroom with a king-sized bed and several comfortable chairs. Take a long bath in the exotic sunken tub while planning the week's activities. A breakfast bar allows for quick, simple meals in the morning, and there are also full cooking facilities for more elaborate dinners. The living room features a small collection of fine Haitian art and a stereo and VCR for entertainment. Contact: Island Hideaways, 1317 Rhode Island Ave., N.W., Suite 503, Washington, D.C. 20005. Call 1-800-832-2302 (in Washington, D.C., 202-667-9652).

Children: Y   Pets: N   Smoking: Y   Handicap Access: N   Payment: C, P, T

CUL DE SAC   *Rates: moderate*
Open: year-round   *Minimum Stay: one week*
You'll find this villa tucked into a gentle hillside only minutes from two beautiful beaches on Rendezvous Bay, one of the prettiest areas on Anguilla. Six can sleep comfortably in three bedrooms, all equipped with ceiling fans to make the most of cooling sea breezes. A fully screened, three-sided wraparound deck on the top floor offers breathtaking views of the bay and St. Maarten on the horizon. Newly tiled floors and wicker furniture throughout create a cool and comfortable ambiance, and daily maid service helps keep the villa clean. Tennis, snorkeling, and swimming are a short drive away. Contact: Villa Holidays, Inc., 13100 Wayzata Blvd., Suite 150, Minneapolis, MN 55343. Call 1-800-328-6262 (in Minneapolis, 612-591-0076).

Children: Y Pets: N Smoking: Y Handicap Access: N Payment: C, P, T, V, M

KENWORTHY   *Rates: expensive-deluxe*
Open: year-round   *Minimum Stay: one week*
Set right on the water's edge, Kenworthy stands just a few feet from protected reefs superb for snorkeling. It offers panoramic views of the ferry traffic crossing the channel to and from St. Maarten. Designed by its architect owner, this three-bedroom villa is built with comfort in mind. Each bedroom features a private bath, and all rooms are luxuriously and elegantly furnished. An open-plan kitchen, living and dining room allows for leisurely meals and relaxation. The rooms lead to

a huge wooden sun deck with a separate bar alcove and a sheltered courtyard, where you can sip cocktails, catch a nap or read in the shade of a palm tree before deciding where to spend your day. Contact: Island Hideaways, 1317 Rhode Island Ave., N.W., Suite 503, Washington, D.C. 20005. Call 1-800-832-2302 (in Washington, D.C., 202-667-9652).

Children: Y   Pets: N   Smoking: Y   Handicap Access: N   Payment: C, P, T

THE SEAHORSE *Rates: budget-inexpensive*
Open: year-round *Minimum Stay: none*
Set right on Rendezvous Bay, one of the most enticing beaches on Anguilla, the Seahorse boasts dazzling views of the blue-green sea as it laps at the powdery white sands. These spacious one-bedroom apartments surround a barbecue area at the water's edge, where you can grill dinner while sipping a cocktail as the sun sets over the bay. If you prefer, you can prepare dinner in your fully equipped kitchen, then bring the meal outdoors to the private gallery. Maid service leaves you free to enjoy pleasant day trips to neighboring St. Maarten, which is just a short ferry ride away. Contact: Joe Maiorino, The Seahorse, P.O. Box 17, Anguilla, British West Indies. Call 809-497-6751.

Children: Y   Pets: N   Smoking: Y   Handicap Access: N   Payment: C, T

SANDY GROUND

SYDANS APARTMENTS HOTEL *Rates: budget-inexpensive*
Open: year-round *Minimum Stay: none*
Set only 60 feet from a beautiful beach, Sydans Apartments offer inexpensive accommodations with easy access to all the water sports a vacationer could desire. Built in Spanish style, the apartments are self-contained units set around a common courtyard with a pond. There are plenty of resorts in the area, but not so many that they overwhelm the natural beauty of Sandy Ground. Bird lovers can walk the beaches and watch the gulls and pelicans take their evening meals as the sun sets over the Caribbean. There are abundant opportunities for snorkeling, sailing, diving, waterskiing and other water sports at the many beautiful bays on the north shore. Contact: Anne Edwards, Sydans Apartments Hotel, Sandy Ground, Anguilla, British West Indies. Call 809-756-7764.

Children: Y   Pets: N   Smoking: Y   Handicap Access: N   Payment: C, T, A, V

THE MARINERS *Rates: inexpensive-expensive*
Open: year-round *Minimum Stay: none*
These cheerful West Indian-style beachfront cottages are tucked into the cliffside overlooking colorful Road Bay Harbor amid island palms and seagrape trees. Set on nearly nine private acres, the cottages feature handcrafted lattice and gingerbread trim, with high ceilings and wooden shutters that close at night for privacy. Studios and one- and two-bedroom suites sleep two to four, each featuring a refrigerator or full kitchen, ceiling fans, a veranda and a telephone for added convenience. Two tennis courts and a restaurant are available in the complex, and a multitude of water sports activities are available day and night.

Contact: The Mariners, Road Bay, P.O. Box 139, Sandy Ground, Anguilla, British West Indies. Call 809-497-2671.

Children: Y Pets: N Smoking: Y Handicap Access: N Payment: C, T, A, V, M

SEA FEATHERS BAY

BAY VILLAS   *Rates: inexpensive-moderate*
Open: year-round   *Minimum Stay: one week*

You'll find these four homes right on Sea Feathers Bay, with shared use of a modern gazebo, barbecue facilities and lounge furniture. The villas all feature two bedrooms, a living/dining area, a fully equipped kitchen for simple or elaborate meals and a large gallery boasting views of the sea and St. Maarten. Nearby, you'll be able to rent mopeds, bikes and "mini-mokes" for exploring the more remote parts of the island. Water sports enthusiasts will find the more than 12 miles of white sandy beaches perfect for swimming, snorkeling and scuba diving. Many restaurants offer up exotic island meals. Contact: Rent A Home International, Inc., 7200 34th Ave. N.W., Seattle, WA 98117. Call 206-545-6963.

Children: Y Pets: N Smoking: Y Handicap Access: N Payment: C, P, T, V, M

PALM GROVE APARTMENTS   *Rates: inexpensive-expensive*
Open: year-round   *Minimum Stay: two nights*

These charming apartments are located close to Sea Feathers Bay, a beautiful white sand beach with inspiring views of the neighboring islands and quays to the south. Comfortable living rooms and one-, two- and three-bedroom suites, each with a private bath, accommodate up to six guests. Each apartment features a large balcony and fully equipped kitchen for easy or elaborate meals, but if you prefer, you can have meals prepared for you. A maid will clean and do laundry for you, allowing you more time to take in the sun or explore nearby resorts and water activities. Contact: Palm Grove Apartments, P.O. Box 16, Sea Feathers Bay, Anguilla, British West Indies. Call 809-497-4100.

Children: Y Pets: N Smoking: Y Handicap Access: N Payment: C, T

RAINBOW REEF VILLAS   *Rates: inexpensive-moderate*
Open: year-round   *Minimum Stay: five nights*

With a gazebo set right on the beach and equipped with beach furniture and barbecue facilities, guests at Rainbow Reef Villas may decide to spend nearly all their time outdoors. Spend long days on the beach basking in the sun and catching the soft sea breezes, with the lull of gently flowing waves as a backdrop. Inside, you'll find comfort in these two-bedroom villas featuring a large kitchen, dining and living areas, with the added pleasure of a large gallery overlooking the sea and St. Maarten. Daily maid service allows you to spend all your time relaxing and soaking up the sun. Contact: Bob and Laura Smith, 611 E. 3rd St., Hinsdale, IL 60521. Call 312-325-2299.

Children: Y Pets: N Smoking: Y Handicap: N Payment: C, P, T, A, V, M

SHOAL BAY

COVE CASTLES VILLA RESORT
Rates: deluxe
Open: year-round
Minimum Stay: none

These ultra-modern beach houses and villas tucked away in a secluded cove on Shoal Bay feature luxurious and spotless interiors with access to the beach and water sports. Wake to the bright morning sun streaming through large windows and fall asleep to the murmur of the waves as they crash gently against the beach. Both the villas and beach houses accommodate two, three or four guests, with a fully equipped kitchen, dining room, living room and covered veranda directly on the beach. The villas feature an additional balcony on the second level and a bilevel living room for added luxury. Daily maid service, cable TV, snorkeling gear and a concierge are among the many amenities included. Contact: Andre de Lucinges, Cove Castles Villa Resort, P.O. Box 248, Anguilla, British West Indies. Call 1-800-223-1588.

Children: Y Pets: N Smoking: Y Handicap Access: N Payment: C, P, T, A

FOUNTAIN BEACH
Rates: inexpensive-deluxe
Open: year-round
Minimum Stay: one week

This secluded resort, nearly hidden from view by seagrape and coconut palms, is set right on Shoal Bay, one of the prettiest beaches on Anguilla. You'll find large studio and two-bedroom apartments loaded with island antiques and local artwork as well as cozy living and dining areas and fully equipped kitchens. Scuba diving and other water sports, restaurants and shops are all nearby. Located near the western tip of Anguilla, Fountain Beach is named for The Fountain, a large limestone cavern with stalagmite carvings of ancient deities. This famous archeological find is still undamaged and open to the public. Contact: Andrew Austin, Fountain Beach, Shoal Bay, Anguilla, British West Indies. Call 1-800-633-7411.

Children: Y Pets: N Smoking: Y Handicap Access: N Payment: C, P, T, V, M

VILLA LA TRADESCANTIA
Rates: deluxe
Open: year-round
Minimum Stay: one week

Spend peaceful evenings amid the quiet of an indoor garden, centrally located for optimal access. This entire villa is cleverly designed around the garden and features a large, sunny patio offering spectacular sea views. Six can relax in comfort and style in three luxurious bedrooms and two baths, while the large living room, dining room and fully equipped kitchen provide ample living space. Snorkeling and swimming in the bay are just steps from the villa, and a beach is conveniently located only five minutes away. The villa can accommodate children over ten only. Contact: Villas International, 71 West 23rd St., New York, NY 10010. Call 212-929-7585.

Children: Y Pets: N Smoking: Y Handicap Access: N Payment: C, P, T

SOUTH HILL

EASY CORNER VILLAS   *Rates: inexpensive-deluxe*
Open: year-round   *Minimum Stay: none*

Intimate surroundings with up-to-date conveniences await visitors at Easy Corner Villas. Choose a one-, two- or three-bedroom unit with quiet views of the sunset and beach from a private porch. A combination living-dining room is large and airy; the units feature ceilings fans for optimal cooling and cheerful and brightly colored rattan furnishings for comfort. Full kitchens allow for leisurely meals of local delicacies, and optional maid service will make clean-up a snap. Contact: Maurice Connor, Easy Corner Villas, P.O. Box 65, South Hill, Anguilla, British West Indies. Call 1-800-223-9815 or 809-497-6433.

Children: Y Pets: N Smoking: Y Handicap Access: N Payment: C, T, A, V, M

INTER-ISLAND GUEST HOUSE   *Rates: budget*
Open: year-round   *Minimum Stay: none*

This two-story villa features covered verandas on both floors offering inspiring views of the sea and neighboring St. Maarten. Set about three miles back from the pretty beaches at Sandy Ground, the rooms at Inter-Island Guest House are simple but clean and comfortable, with possibly the best rates on the island. One- and two-bedroom apartments are also available for larger families. Sandy Ground offers several small resort areas, boats and facilities for water sports activities and beaches and salt ponds. Nature lovers will enjoy long walks on the beach among the gulls and pelicans fishing for an early evening dinner. Contact: Inter-Island Guest House, Lower South Hill, Anguilla, British West Indies. Call 809-497-6259.

Children: Y   Pets: N   Smoking: Y   Handicap Access: N   Payment: C, T

Map labels:
Dickenson Bay, Hodges Bay, BARBUDA, 27 Miles to Antigua, St. John's, Dian Bay, Nonsuch Bay, Jolly Beach, Johnson's Point, Falmouth, English Harbor, Half Moon Bay, Marmora Bay, Caribbean Sea, Falmouth Harbor

Antigua and Barbuda

DIAN BAY

DIAN BAY RESORT	*Rates: inexpensive-expensive*
Open: year-round	*Minimum Stay: five nights*

A privately owned peninsula on the eastern side of the island is the setting for this resort, which contains just 32 exclusive suites situated on a terraced slope overlooking the beach. Contemporary and casual, the suites have ceiling fans, attractive wooden and rattan furniture and balconies that provide a wonderful view of this protected bay. The suites have either one or two bedrooms (plus fold-out couches in the living rooms), plus kitchens and bathrooms; maid and linen service is provided daily. There is a freshwater pool on the premises and free snorkeling equipment is provided. Guests can enjoy a bar and French restaurant at the resort or stock their kitchens from the commissary on the premises. Contact: International Travel and Resort Inc., 25 West 39th St., New York, NY 10018. Call 212-840-6636 or 800-223-9815.

Children: Y Pets: N Smoking: Y Handicap Access: N Payment: C, T, V, M, A

VILLA DIAN	*Rates: deluxe*
Open: year-round	*Minimum Stay: one week*

Two separate buildings comprise this villa, one with three bedrooms and two baths, the other with one bedroom and one bath; they can be rented separately or together. Overlooking a sparkling bay, the villa offers a measure of privacy that is a welcome change from busy resorts and hotels, yet offers easy access to the island's many sporting and boating facilities. Lovingly decorated and filled with tropical art pieces, the villa is cooled by the breezes that constantly bathe this island. Large furnished porches overlook the water, and a short pathway lined with flowers leads to the beach. Contact: Villa Holidays, 13100 Wayzata Blvd., Suite 150, Minneapolis, MN 55343. Call 612-591-0076 or 800-328-6262.

Children: Y Pets: N Smoking: Y Handicap Access: N Payment: C, P, T, V, M

DICKENSON BAY

ANTIGUA HOUSE *Rates: deluxe*
Open: year-round *Minimum Stay: one week*

Located on a hillside behind Dickenson Bay, this luxury villa has its own swimming pool and sun decks, as well as a patio that runs the length of the house. The grounds cover an acre of tropical greenery surrounding a pool. Indoors and out, the villa is maintained by a staff that includes a maid and cook. The master bedroom has a king-size bed, en suite bathroom and private patio; there are also two twin bedrooms. The kitchen area contains a breakfast nook and utility room, and there is a dining room and a living room with cable color TV and stereo system. This house is decorated throughout with exceptional furnishings and fine art, including Asian antiques. Contact: Rent A Home International, Inc., 7200 34th Ave. N.W., Seattle, WA 98117. Call 206-545-6963.

Children: Y Pets: N Smoking: Y Handicap Access: N Payment: C, P, T, V, M

ANTIGUA VILLAGE *Rates: inexpensive-expensive*
Open: year-round *Minimum Stay: none*

Garden paths lined with hibiscus and oleander, a stretch of sugar-white beach, a freshwater pool and complimentary water sports are all part of the vacation experience here at Antigua Village. The choice of studio, one- or two-bedroom villas is yours, each with private bathroom and kitchen, living rooms with fold-out couches and daily maid service. The rooms have tiled floors and ceiling fans; some feature soaring ceilings or balconies that serve as living rooms in this temperate climate. A few miles away lies the challenging Cedar Valley Golf Course, while sailing and fishing cruises leave daily from Dickenson Bay. St. John's, the historic capital, is a few minutes' drive away. Contact: Antigua Village, P.O. Box 649, St. John's, Antigua, West Indies.

Children: Y Pets: N Smoking: Y Handicap Access: N Payment: C, T, V, M

BARRYMORE BEACH APARTMENTS *Rates: moderate-deluxe*
Open: year-round *Minimum Stay: one week*

One- and two-bedroom apartments can be found in this complex of two-story buildings offering privacy among the palms. Each of the apartments has a separate living room and kitchenette, as well as a patio or balcony with views of the ocean. An assortment of resorts, restaurants, bars and casinos is just a few minutes away on Dickenson Bay; back at Barrymore is the "Satay Hut," a peaceful place to have a quiet drink or snack. Just 300 yards from the apartments is a water sports operator who can get you set up for windsurfing, waterskiing, sailing or snorkeling. Tennis and golf facilities are plentiful, and the island's tropical gardens and old sugar mills make daily excursions fascinating and fun. Contact: Rent A Home International, Inc., 7200 34th Ave. N.W., Seattle, WA 98117. Call 206-545-6963.

Children: Y Pets: N Smoking: Y Handicap Access: N Payment: C, P, T, V, M

PARADISE VILLA   *Rates: deluxe*
Open: year-round   *Minimum Stay: one week*
This Spanish-style villa is a marvel of design, with each room opening up through a French or sliding glass door to a terrace. Furnished in cool, contemporary colors, the villa is air-conditioned throughout, and has ceiling fans in each room, plus a radio and color TV. All three bedrooms have en suite baths, and the cook/housekeeper is at the house daily. A private swimming pool is surrounded by fragrant flowers; within five minutes is one of Antigua's many fine beaches where you can go snorkeling, windsurfing, fishing or sailing. Restaurants, casinos and resorts provide exciting nightlife for visitors, while days can be spent relaxing in the privacy of this hilltop property. Contact: Caribrep Villas, 531 East Lincoln, P.O. Box 9016, Mt. Vernon, NY 10552. Call 914-667-7275.

Children: Y Pets: N Smoking: Y Handicap Access: N Payment: C, P, T, M, A

RUNAWAY BEACH CLUB   *Rates: inexpensive-expensive*
Open: year-round   *Minimum Stay: one week*
Clustered around a swimming pool, the villas here are just steps away from the white sand of a reef-protected beach. Located on two levels, the standard apartments feature a bedroom/living space, kitchenette or kitchen, bathroom and either a balcony or dining porch. The deluxe villas have two bedrooms, two baths and separate kitchen and dining porch. Decorated in island rattan with delicately colored fabrics, the villas all have daily maid and linen service. The club offers all water sports, including certified instructors to take you scuba diving; deep-sea fishing and boating or sailing cruises are easily arranged. A restaurant on the premises serves fresh seafood and continental cuisine, and the casinos, restaurants and bars along the shore make the nightlife lively. Contact: Runaway Beach Club, 1329 Shepard Drive, Sterling, VA 22170. Call 703-450-6620.

Children: Y Pets: Y Smoking: Y Handicap Access: N Payment: C, T, V, M, A

SEA VILLA   *Rates: deluxe*
Open: year-round   *Minimum Stay: one week*
This fabulous three-bedroom, three-bath villa offers all the privacy of an exclusive home, yet is within walking distance of two fine resort hotels. The villa has a living/dining room with a sitting area for quiet moments, plus a modern kitchen and maid and cook service six days a week (the cook can prepare breakfast, a light lunch and dinner). A private swimming pool and terrace makes a wonderful place to relax

and sip tropical drinks as warm breezes bring the scent of hibiscus to you. Guests can use the owner's membership at a local tennis court. Extra amenities at the villa include cable color TV and a stereo system. Contact: Barry Shepard, At Home Abroad, Inc., 405 East 56th St. #6H, New York, NY 10022. Call 212-421-9165.

Children: Y Pets: N Smoking: Y Handicap Access: N Payment: C, P, T

SIBONEY BEACH CLUB *Rates: inexpensive-deluxe*
Open: year-round *Minimum Stay: none*

Named for a Caribbean love song, Siboney stands in a romantic setting surrounded by a lush tropical garden and waving palm fronds. Each suite is self-contained, many with fully equipped kitchenettes behind louvered panels, and has either king-size or twin beds. The arched doorways and airy design cool the rooms, but if you choose, air-conditioned suites are available. Throughout, the decor is contemporary, with splashes of color that match the brilliant flowers just outside. The apartment lounges open onto a patio or balcony surrounded by plants and providing views of the sea. The club's Coconut Grove restaurant is locally renowned and situated right on the beach; other hotels, casinos and restaurants are all nearby. Contact: Siboney Beach Club, P.O. Box 222, St. John's, Antigua, West Indies. Call 809-462-3356/0806 or 800-533-0234,

Children: Y Pets: N Smoking: Y Handicap: N Payment: C, P, T, V, M, A

TRADE WINDS HOTEL AND APARTMENTS *Rates: inexpensive-expensive*
Open: year-round *Minimum Stay: none*

You can relax by the pool or in the lounge here, but there is also plenty of opportunity for more active guests to keep busy: Scuba diving, windsurfing, parasailing, tennis and horseback riding are less than five minutes away, as are three casinos and even more nightclubs. The resort's French restaurant draws visitors from all over the island and has live music on weekends. Trade Winds offers nearly 30 elegant apartments, beautifully appointed with rattan furniture, ceiling fans, tiled floors, TV and private balconies overlooking the sea. Choose from studio apartments and one-bedroom suites; each has a private bathroom and a kitchen or kitchenette. The hotel also keeps a fleet of Jeeps in which guests can explore the island, and free bus service to any number of beaches on the island. Contact: Trade Winds Hotel and Apartments, P.O. Box 1390, St. John's, Antigua, West Indies. Call 809-462-1223.

Children: Y Pets: N Smoking: Y Handicap Access: N Payment: C, T, V, M, A

YEPTON BEACH RESORT *Rates: inexpensive-deluxe*
Open: year-round *Minimum Stay: none*

Although the trade winds keep Antiguans cool even on the hottest days, this condominium resort has air-conditioned units for additional comfort. Located beside a palm-dotted beach, with a swimming pool and outdoor restaurant, the resort is within walking distance of golf courses and the Royal Antiguan Casino Hotel. The units are serviced by a maid daily and have fully equipped kitchens and a living/dining area. Studios have a double fold-out couch; one-bedroom apartments have twin beds. Each week there is music and entertainment; tennis, windsurfing, sunfish sailing and snorkeling can all be enjoyed on the premises. Additional activities, such as boat charters or fishing trips, scuba diving in the abundant coral reefs or horseback riding on inland trails, are available nearby. Contact: Yepton Beach Resort, P.O. Box 1427, St. John's, Antigua, West Indies. Call 809-462-2520.

Children: Y   Pets: N   Smoking: Y   Handicap Access: N   Payment: C, T

ENGLISH HARBOUR

FREEMAN'S BAY ESTATE   *Rates: deluxe*
Open: year-round   *Minimum Stay: one week*
Louvered windows and sliding glass doors keep the cooling breezes flowing through this hillside villa, bringing the fragrance of tropical flowers indoors. Three bedrooms (two queen and one twin) and a fold-out couch provide spacious accommodations for up to eight guests; all of the bedrooms have en suite bathrooms. The living/dining room has a table for eight, a TV with VCR, a stereo and library. The kitchen comes complete with microwave, coffee maker and dining area, plus sliding glass doors on one side that provide breathtaking views of the ocean. Throughout the house are ceiling fans, high-beamed ceilings and the cool, rattan furniture and tropical colors so favored on the island. Contact: Rent A Home International, Inc., 7200 34th Ave. N.W., Seattle, WA 98117. Call 206-545-6963.

Children: Y Pets: N Smoking: Y Handicap Access: N Payment: C, P, T, V, M

JACARANDA   *Rates: deluxe*
Open: year-round   *Minimum Stay: one week*
You'll find this luxury villa in the English Harbour area near Nelson's Dockyard, one of the best-preserved historic sites in the Caribbean. The views from the garden and tiled terrace reach out past Freeman's Bay to Montserrat and the endless azure ocean. There are three bedrooms, one with full bathroom en suite and two with showers. The living/dining area contains a TV and stereo, and the kitchen contains a blender for mixing tropical drinks, a microwave, coffee maker and a breakfast bar for casual meals. The maid is on the premises daily and a cook is available if desired. Outside is the pool and a lovely garden. Contact: Caribrep Villas, 531 East Lincoln, P.O. Box 9016, Mt. Vernon, NY 10552. Call 914-667-7275.

Children: Y Pets: N Smoking: Y Handicap Access: N Payment: C, P, T, M, A

THE ADMIRAL'S INN   *Rates: moderate-expensive*
Open: year-round   *Minimum Stay: none*
One of the intriguing things about Antigua is that Admiral Nelson commanded the British fleet from the Naval Dockyard over two centuries ago; now Nelson's Dockyard is one of the Caribbean's most fascinating attractions. Located here is this charming red brick hotel with white-shuttered windows and beamed ceilings. An adjacent two-bedroom apartment known as the "Joiner's Loft" is available for rental;

it has a fully equipped kitchen and a large living room overlooking the bay. The bay is an active yachting center where guests can join a boating trip; there are nearly 400 beaches to choose from on this island, enough to keep you busy snorkeling, beachcombing, windsurfing or just relaxing. Contact: American Wolfe International, 1890 Palmer Ave., Suite 204, Larchmont, NY 10538. Call 914-833-3303 or 800-223-5695.

Children: **Y**   Pets: **N**   Smoking: **Y**   Handicap Access: **N**   Payment: **C, T**

FALMOUTH HARBOUR

FALMOUTH HARBOUR BEACH APARTMENTS   *Rates: budget-inexpensive*
Open: year-round   *Minimum Stay: none*

Located near historic English Harbour, these studio apartments are owned and operated by the Admiral's Inn. Guests have full access to the facilities at the inn, which is just down the road at Nelson's Dockyard. The studios are set either slightly up a wooded hillside or directly facing a private sandy beach. Either way, the beach is at your disposal—for snorkeling, swimming, sailing, sunbathing or windsurfing. Each unit has a fully equipped electric kitchen and complete maid service. A long balcony provides a comfortable and private place to sit and look out over the harbor. Contact: Ethelyn Philip, Falmouth Harbour Beach Apartments, P.O. Box 713, St. John's, Antigua, West Indies. Call 809-463-1027 or 809-463-1094 or 800-223-5695.

Children: **Y** Pets: **N** Smoking: **Y** Handicap Access: **N** Payment: **C, T, V, M, A**

HALF MOON BAY

GLENEAGLES VILLA   *Rates: deluxe*
Open: year-round   *Minimum Stay: one week*

An ocean-view villa with private pool and large outdoor terrace, Gleneagles is located one and a half miles from the sea and the golf course at Half Moon Bay Resort. Three bedrooms (two queens and one twin), two baths, a kitchen and a living/dining room make up the floor plan. You can fill the house with stereo music or settle down with an classic movie on the VCR. Guests can enjoy an evening barbecue on the terrace under the Caribbean sky, or a day of relaxation at poolside. All water sports, golf, tennis and horseback riding are available on the island; the scuba diving and fishing are both excellent. Contact: Caribrep Villas, 531 East Lincoln, P.O. Box 9016, Mt. Vernon, NY 10552. Call 914-667-7275.

Children: **Y** Pets: **N** Smoking: **Y** Handicap Access: **N** Payment: **C, P, T, M, A**

KIMBERLY HOUSE   *Rates: deluxe*
Open: year-round   *Minimum Stay: one week*

One of the finest villas on the island, Kimberly House is located on one acre of land and enjoys the cooling effects of the trade winds. A short walk brings you to a crescent-shaped mile of sparkling sand, but the villa also has its own pool surrounded with chaise lounges and a patio with low stone walls. In all, there are four bedrooms, a living/

dining room and a full kitchen. A cook, a maid and a gardener are present most of the week and a car and airport transfers are included. Island-style decor of bright prints and rattan furniture flatters the house. All the facilities of the island are within easy reach—from casinos and nightlife to scuba diving in the coral reefs. Contact: Villas International, 71 West 23rd St., New York, NY 10010. Call 212-929-7585.

Children: Y Pets: N Smoking: Y Handicap Access: N Payment: C, P, T, O

WOOD HOUSE   *Rates: deluxe*
Open: year-round   *Minimum Stay: one week*

Your hosts will greet you at the airport and show you to this private villa, starting your vacation with a taste of island hospitality. During your stay, maid and cook services are provided; special arrangements can be made for car rental, babysitting and tours of the historic and beautiful little island. Wood House has three bedrooms, two baths and a living area that opens onto the pool deck; a spiral staircase winds up to the master bedroom suite above. You can swim or lounge around the pool or venture out to one of Antigua's 365 beaches—all of them tropical gems with white sand and turquoise water. The villa overlooks the Half Moon Bay Golf Course. Contact: Paul Mermelstein, Island Hideaways, 1317 Rhode Island Ave. NW, Suite 503, Washington, DC 20005. Call 202-667-9652 or 800-832-2302.

Children: Y   Pets: N   Smoking: Y   Handicap Access: N   Payment: P, T

HODGES BAY

HODGES BAY CLUB   *Rates: moderate-deluxe*
Open: year-round   *Minimum Stay: none*

Facing Prickly Pear Island across from the mainland, Hodges Bay is within a few minutes of the airport, the capital of St. John's and the golf course. The club offers spacious apartments whose cathedral ceilings frame views of endless ocean stretching away from your private balcony. The two-bedroom apartments have a separate kitchen, a living/dining area, two bathrooms and a terrace accessible from the master bedroom and the living room. The one-bedroom apartments are similar, but feature a kitchenette, one bathroom and a twin bedroom. Ceiling fans and air conditioning supplement the cooling trade winds; cable TV and telephone, as well as complete maid service, ensure guests' comfort. Contact: Scott Calder International, Inc., 152 Madison Ave., New York, NY 10016. CAll 212-535-9530 or 800-223-5581.

Children: Y Pets: N Smoking: Y Handicap Access: N Payment: C, T, V, M, A

JOHNSON'S POINT

PELICAN ISLE   *Rates: inexpensive-deluxe*
Open: year-round   *Minimum Stay: one week*

One- and two-bedroom villas for two to four guests and a large Master House with four bedrooms can be found in this private complex on a hillside overlooking a sandy beach. Up on the hilltop is a gazebo where guests can prepare an outdoor meal under tropical evening skies; Pelican Isle will stock your fridge for your arrival if requested. All the villas have a dining/living area with sliding glass doors that lead to a patio or porch—the views from these houses stretch all the way to St. Kitts. Special requirements such as car rental or babysitting can be arranged, and daily maid service is provided. Down along the beaches, guests can windsurf or scuba dive. Venturing further afield, you can take a deep-sea fishing trip or luxury cruise. Contact: Caribbean South Ltd., 1011 High Ridge Road, Stamford, CT 06905. Call 203-329-2170 or 800-243-5237.

Children: **Y**   Pets: **N**   Smoking: **Y**   Handicap Access: **N**   Payment: **C, T**

JOLLY BEACH

CAPE COAST COTTAGES   *Rates: budget-inexpensive*
Open: year-round   *Minimum Stay: one week*

There is a beach in Antigua for every day of the year—over 365 to choose from. Inland lie tropical gardens and old sugar mills and off the coastline are rings of coral reef perfect for scuba diving and snorkeling. Here, Cape Coast Cottages beckons visitors to its one- and two-bedroom units with kitchen facilities and private baths. Included in the price of your rental are round-trip transfers from the airport; housekeeping services can be arranged for extra charge. A short drive from your home away from home are golfing and tennis facilities or historic Nelson's Dockyard, once home to the British Navy fleet. Contact: Rent A Home International, Inc., 7200 34th Ave. N.W., Seattle, WA 98117. Call 206-545-6963.

Children: **Y** Pets: **N** Smoking: **Y** Handicap Access: **N** Payment: **C, P, T, V, M**

MAMORA BAY

DUNNING VILLA (THE WHITE HOUSE)   *Rates: deluxe*
Open: year-round   *Minimum Stay: one week*

A tropical garden and cobblestone driveway lead to this magnificent villa overlooking the exclusive St. James Club. The master bedroom features a king-size bed and en suite bathroom, while two other double bedrooms also have en suite bathrooms. The living room includes a dining area and the kitchen is completely modern, with microwave, blender, toaster oven, dishwasher and all standard appliances. Daily maid service is provided and a cook can be arranged. A terrace wraps around the swimming pool, where the views out to sea are spectacular. Guests have access to the club facilities, including tennis, health club, horseback riding and all water sports, including scuba diving and sailing. Contact: Caribrep Villas, 531 East Lincoln, P.O. Box 9016, Mt. Vernon, NY 10552. Call 914-667-7275.

Children: **Y** Pets: **N** Smoking: **Y** Handicap Access: **N** Payment: **C, P, T, M, A**

GARDNER VILLA   *Rates: deluxe*
Open: year-round   *Minimum Stay: one week*

Gardner Villa is located on the southeast coast of Antigua, looking down over the Caribbean and the shoreline. Each of the three double bedrooms in the villa has an en suite bathroom and the living room and dining room are combined into one spacious area. A completely modern kitchen comes with a microwave, blender and dishwasher—a cook is available if needed. The outdoor terrace and swimming pool overlook the nearby St. James Club, where guests have access to all facilities, including horseback riding, tennis, water sports and a health club. Boating of all kinds, as well as deep-sea fishing expeditions, can be easily arranged; scuba diving around the coral reefs and sunken ships on this island is especially popular. Contact: Caribrep Villas, 531 East Lincoln, P.O. Box 9016, Mt. Vernon, NY 10552. Call 914-667-7275.

Children: Y Pets: N Smoking: Y Handicap Access: N Payment: C, P, T, M, A

ST. JAMES'S CLUB *Rates: expensive-deluxe*
Open: year-round *Minimum Stay: none*
Bayside and hillside villas and private homes are surrounded with brilliant flowers and interspersed with free-form swimming pools. With one or two bedrooms, ceiling fans and decor that features island hues and rattan furniture, the villas and homes at St. James's also have separate kitchens, bathrooms and maid service. Access to the club's many facilities means you might spend a day on the tennis courts (perhaps taking a lesson—Martina Navratilova is the touring pro), pass an afternoon in the health club or a take a morning horseback ride. Restaurant choices range from casual to elegant and an intimate casino invites you to try your luck. At the private marina, guests can try their hand at a variety of water sports or take a day trip on a luxury yacht; snorkeling and scuba diving on the nearby reef can be arranged with a guide if desired. Contact: Prime Hotels and Resorts, 800-274-0008 or 212-486-2575.

Children: Y Pets: N Smoking: Y Handicap Access: N Payment: C, T, V, M, A

NONSUCH BAY

BROWN'S BAY VILLAS *Rates: expensive-deluxe*
Open: year-round *Minimum Stay: one week*
Seven two-bedroom, two-bathroom villas are grouped here in a serene setting encircling a swimming pool and tennis courts. Inside, the villas offer island prints, charming rattan furniture, louvered windows and sliding glass doors that let in the light and the ocean breeze. You can step out onto your private patio and lounge in the sun or take a few steps down to the beach, where gleaming sand and warm water provide an irresistible combination. The kitchen is at your disposal, and if desired, a cook can be engaged; a maid tidies up daily. On more active days, visitors can keep busy with golf, sailing, scuba diving, fishing, windsurfing or visiting the historic sights in St. John's or English Harbour. Contact: Caribrep Villas, 531 East Lincoln, P.O. Box 9016, Mt. Vernon, NY 10552. Call 914-667-7275.

Children: Y Pets: N Smoking: Y Handicap Access: N Payment: C, P, T, M, A

HIGH POINT VILLA   *Rates: deluxe*
Open: year-round   *Minimum Stay: one week*

This modern villa is all clean lines, soaring ceilings, pastel shades and glass doors, a beautiful complement to the deep green forest and turquoise water in Nonsuch Bay. Three bedrooms make up the sleeping accommodations; the master bedroom has a queen-size bed and en suite bathroom. The living and dining rooms are combined and lead to a chef's kitchen and an outdoor tiled terrace and swimming pool. The house commands wonderful views over the southeast side of Antigua; Half Moon Bay Hotel is just three miles away. Daily maid service is provided and a cook's services can be arranged. Tennis, swimming, golf and all water sports can be found at Half Moon Bay. Contact: Caribrep Villas, 531 East Lincoln, P.O. Box 9016, Mt. Vernon, NY 10552. Call 914-667-7275.

Children: Y Pets: N Smoking: Y Handicap Access: N Payment: C, P, T, M, A

ST. JOHN'S

BAY VIEW VILLA   *Rates: expensive*
Open: year-round   *Minimum Stay: one week*

Connected to the Long Bay Hotel, Bay View Villa is actually a main house and separate annex with twin beds, a bathroom and a kitchen. The main house has a master bedroom with en suite bath and a living area that sleeps four guests. The living/dining room and kitchen are separated from the bedroom by a hallway and sun deck. Guests can use the hotel's dining room, bar and library/game room. Maid service is available, as is babysitting, on request. Situated between a lagoon and a beach, the hotel grounds are naturally cooled by the trade winds. A championship tennis court and all water sports, scuba facilities, sailing boats and windsurfing are among the hotel amenities. Contact: Jacques E. Lafaurie, Long Bay Hotel, P.O. Box 442, St. John's, Antigua, West Indies. Call 809-463-2005.

Children: Y Pets: N Smoking: Y Handicap Access: N Payment: C, T, V, M, A

BLUE WATERS BEACH HOTEL   *Rates: deluxe*
Open: year-round   *Minimum Stay: none*

Set in a sheltered cove, this hotel offers 14 acres of tropical gardens, white sandy beaches and activities to suit every mood. The hotel features eight deluxe villas, all air conditioned and with one to three bedrooms, living room, dining room, mini bar and a private wall safe. The master bedroom has a Jacuzzi, and each villa has its own private patio or balcony with views of the gardens and ocean. The rooms are furnished in contemporary style, with island influence reflected in the tasteful prints and rattan couches and chairs. There's a romantic feeling to this hotel in its comfortable cocktail bars, spacious grounds, decadent lawn hammocks and freshwater pool. Contact: Dawn Greene, Blue Waters Beach Hotel, P.O Box 256, St. John's, Antigua, West Indies. Call 809-462-0290/0292.

Children: Y Pets: N Smoking: Y Handicap Access: Y Payment: C, P, T, V, M, A

LONG BAY HOTEL *Rates: inexpensive-moderate*
Open: year-round *Minimum Stay: none*
Situated in a protected lagoon on a landscaped tropical estate, these six one-bedroom and studio houses contain everything visitors need for a completely relaxing vacation. All the houses are slightly different in design (the Round House is actually circular) but all contain a kitchen, bathroom, living room and dining area with beds or fold-out couches, and in some cases a separate bedroom. Maid service is provided, and a meal plan can be arranged if desired. The rooms are charming, with louvered windows and balconies that face the lagoon. A beach is close by, and there are coral reefs to explore, plus deep-sea fishing, sailing and windsurfing to enjoy. Contact: Jacques E. Lafaurie, Long Bay Hotel, P.O. Box 442, St. John's, Antigua, West Indies. Call 809-463-2005.
Children: Y Pets: N Smoking: Y Handicap Access: N Payment: C, T, V, M, A

PILLAR ROCK PAVILLIONS CONDOMINIUMS *Rates: inexpensive-deluxe*
Open: year-round *Minimum Stay: none*
Each unit of the one-bedroom villas and studio apartments at Pillar Rock has a balcony or patio overlooking Hog John Bay and the shoreline stretching into the distance. Cathedral ceilings and contemporary rattan furniture give the decor an island feel and the kitchens even come equipped with blenders and daiquiri glasses. The villas have two bathrooms, large living spaces and a separate kitchen with breakfast counter and seating, as well as a dining area. The studios have comfortable couches, a separate bathroom and a kitchenette. Tennis, golf, all kinds of water sports, fishing and boating fill the days; casinos, live music on the beach and fresh seafood in the restaurants keep the evenings busy. Contact: Pillar Rock Pavillions Condominiums, P.O. Box 1166, St. John's, Antigua, West Indies. Call 809-462-0559.
Children: Y Pets: N Smoking: Y Handicap Access: N Payment: C, T

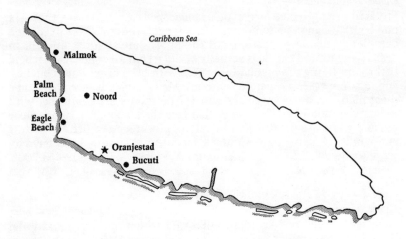

Caribbean Sea

Malmok

Palm
Beach

Eagle
Beach

Noord

★ Oranjestad
Bucuti

Aruba

BUCUTI

THE VISTALMAR
Open: year-round

Rates: budget-inexpensive
Minimum Stay: none

Especially convenient for vacationers not planning to rent a car, this
island cottage for two offers a location close to the airport and near
public transportation lines. Accommodations here include a full
kitchen, color satellite TV, a restful front porch and daily maid service.
The added feature of Vistalmar's own seaside pier with tanning deck
promises a lazy kind of stay. The southwestern exposure provides
daily natural drama with beautiful sunsets. When it comes time to
planning your days, you'll find practically every type of tropical activity on this island, from water sports to horseback riding and from
bicycling along tropical roads to people watching. Contact: The Vistalmar, Bucutiweg 28, Bucuti, Aruba, Netherlands Antilles. Call 812-
429-0075 or 011-297-8-28579.

Children: Y   Pets: N   Smoking: Y   Handicap Access: N   Payment: C, T

EAGLE BEACH

LA QUINTA
Open: year-round

Rates: budget-deluxe
Minimum Stay: two nights

Situated on glorious Eagle Beach, this white-washed, tile-roofed resort
offers air-conditioned suites. The studio, one-, two- and three-bedroom
units each come with a fully equipped kitchenette including a micro-

wave and a blender. Contemporary furnishings and a private terrace or balcony add elegance and atmosphere to these accommodations. Additional features, such as a satellite color TV with VCR, a video library, direct-dial telephone and a large swimming pool make your stay here as relaxed as can be. And the location puts you close to everything you come to Aruba for—uninterrupted miles of white sandy beaches, a wide variety of water sports, fabulous dining and lively casinos. Contact: La Quinta Beach Resort, L.G. Smith Blvd. 228, Eagle Beach, Aruba, Netherlands Antilles. Call 011-297-8-350010.

Children: Y Pets: N Smoking: Y Handicap Access: N Payment: C, T, V, M

MALMOK

WINDSURF VILLAS *Rates: budget-moderate*
Open: year-round *Minimum Stay: one week*

Windsurfing authorities say that only the Gorge and Maui rival Aruba as a windsurfer's paradise. If there's any question about Aruba's status as one of the windiest spots in the world, the wind-sculpted "Divi Divi" trees scattered throughout the island provide the answer. This resort specializes in windsurfing for vacationers who know what they want. The 35 efficiency apartments offer features such as microwaves, color TVs, private or shared decks with barbecues and kitchenettes. Adjacent to the villas and less than 100 feet from the beautiful sailing mecca at Fisherman's Huts, you'll find the Caribbean's largest and best-equipped windsurfing boardshop, where you can be outfitted with everything you need to excel, whether you're a beginner or an accomplished pro. Contact: Sailboard Vacations, L.G. Smith Blvd. 462, Malmok, Aruba, Netherlands Antilles. Call 011-297-8-22572 (in the U.S., 1-800-252-1070).

Children: Y Pets: N Smoking: Y Handicap Access: N Payment: C, T, V, M, A

NOORD

ARUBIANA INN HOTEL *Rates: budget*
Open: year-round *Minimum Stay: none*

Situated on the highly prized west end of this enchanting island, these studio apartments offer simple accommodations for two within walking distance of the high-rise hotels and gorgeous Eagle Beach. Each studio features a kitchenette, satellite TV and telephone. Guests enjoy the swimming pool, bar and colorful open-air terrace restaurant at breakfast and lunch. You can make use of the public transportation available nearby and hop on a bus to explore the landscape, or rent bicycles for a more vigorous outing. And of course, you won't want to leave the island without making a serious foray or two into the wonderful duty-free shopping area. Contact: Arubiana Inn Hotel, Bubali 74, Noord, Aruba, Netherlands Antilles. Call 011-297-8-26044/27557.

Children: Y Pets: N Smoking: Y Handicap Access: N Payment: C, T

CAMACURI APARTMENTS   *Rates: budget*
Open: year-round   *Minimum Stay: none*

Conveniently located within walking distance of the beach, supermarkets and the lively and colorful center of the small town of Oranjestad, this complex consists of one-bedroom apartments, each of which includes a kitchenette, a dining area, a color TV and maid service. Each air-conditioned unit features a private terrace or balcony; guests share a swimming pool and socialize at a charming little bar. These apartments also offer a wonderful chance to meet some of the warm and friendly local residents, who usually speak both Spanish and English as well as a native patois. For a look at the less populated end of Aruba, you can hop on a bus and head east. But the lure of the fabulous beaches, ideal for windsurfing and other water sports, is bound to draw you west as well, where you'll also find the island's famous casinos. Contact: Camacuri Apartments, Fergusonsstraat 46-B, Dakota, Aruba, Netherlands Antilles. Call 011-297-8-26805.

Children: **Y**   Pets: **N**   Smoking: **Y**   Handicap Access: **N**   Payment: **C, T**

COCONUT INN   *Rates: budget*
Open: year-round   *Minimum Stay: none*

At the Coconut Inn, you can choose from a variety of accommodations, ranging from a simply appointed room to a larger suite or a studio apartment. Each air-conditioned rental includes a TV and a kitchenette; the terraces in front of each unit face the courtyard where many tropical trees and plants sway in the sea winds. Located conveniently close to the island's glamorous high-rise hotels and casinos, the inn also situates you within walking distance of fabulous white beaches as well as the conveniences of a supermarket, several excellent restaurants, a bank and a church. For a chance to stretch and breathe deep, you can take advantage of tennis courts, a gym and spa and a swimming pool all located just a short walk from your door. Contact: Mr. A.F. Rojer, Coconut Inn, Noord 31, Noord, Aruba, Netherlands Antilles. Call 011-297-8-26288.

Children: **Y**   Pets: **N**   Smoking: **Y**   Handicap Access: **N**   Payment: **C, T**

ORANJESTAD

AMSTERDAM MANOR BEACH RESORT   *Rates: inexpensive-deluxe*
Open: year-round   *Minimum Stay: none*

Situated on a beautiful stretch of beach a short distance from the high-rise hotels, this luxurious low-rise apartment complex boasts a swimming pool with a dramatic waterfall on the terrace, complete with a bar where you can enjoy breakfast or lunch. This handsome resort invites you in with its charming, traditionally Dutch exterior of yellow walls, white trim and terra-cotta tile roofs. Apartments range in size from studios with kitchenettes to three-room suites of royal dimensions. All accommodations but the studios feature full kitchens, color TVs with VCRs, Jacuzzis and balconies offering sunset views. The Dutch management will happily arrange all your activities on Aruba, from horseback riding in the hills to a round of golf or a tour of the island on motor scooters. Contact: Amsterdam Manor Beach Resort, L.G. Smith Blvd. 252, Oranjestad, Aruba, Netherlands Antilles. Call 011-297-8-31492/34376.

Children: Y Pets: N Smoking: Y Handicap Access: N Payment: C, T, V, M, A

AULGA'S PLACE   *Rates: budget*
Open: year-round   *Minimum Stay: none*

Ideal for a big family or a group of vacationing friends, this rental consists of an air-conditioned three-room house and a completely furnished independent apartment. Each unit features a private entrance and a patio; laundry facilities and maid service are available. Located on the southwestern coast of this lovely island, the house offers a private spot for viewing the stunning sunsets, plus easy public transportation to the white sandy beaches for which Aruba is famous. Cooks both sophisticated and simple will enjoy a visit to the local markets, where the fresh seafood and produce remind you of the delightful tropical pleasures. Contact: Aulga's Place, Seroe Blanco 31, Oranjestad, Aruba, Netherlands Antilles.

Children: Y   Pets: N   Smoking: Y   Handicap Access: N   Payment: C, T

BOULEVARD VILLAS AND APARTMENTS   *Rates: moderate-deluxe*
Open: year-round   *Minimum Stay: one week*

Famous for its sunny, dry weather and immaculate beaches with warm, crystalline water, Aruba offers an ideal setting for windsurfing. Guests at the Boulevard Villas enjoy the use of a huge array of windsurfing equipment as well as time with patient instructors. When you tire of riding the wind, you can also try waterskiing, snorkeling and scuba diving in the divine turquoise waters along the shores of this Caribbean jewel. The worldlier pleasures of first-class restaurants, casino gambling and shopping await your pleasure. Each studio apartment and two-bedroom villa includes a full kitchen, maid service, an ocean view and a shared barbecue. Contact: Villas International, 71 West 23rd Street, New York, NY 10010. Call 212-929-7585.

Children: Y   Pets: N   Smoking: Y   Handicap Access: N   Payment: C, P, T

BUCATI APARTMENTS   *Rates: budget-moderate*
Open: year-round   *Minimum Stay: one week*

Located in a quiet, secluded residential neighborhood, these studio and one-bedroom apartments (a four-bedroom villa is available upon request) offer the perfect setting for sunbathing on pristine beaches, snorkeling or scuba diving in shimmering blue waters or a lovely outdoor lunch on Bucati's private dock. The apartments, which accommodate from two to four, include complete kitchens and private terraces; laundry facilities are located conveniently nearby. Large, airy and pleasantly furnished, the apartments guarantee night after night of peaceful sleep. You can make your stay here as relaxing as you like, with a stroll through the town and a drink at an oceanside lounge your most strenuous activity. Or keep yourself going constantly, with water sports and bicycling by day and casino hopping by night. Contact:

Villas International, 71 West 23rd Street, New York, NY 10010. Call 212-929-7585.

Children: Y   Pets: N   Smoking: Y   Handicap Access: N   Payment: C, P, T

CAMARI GUEST HOUSE

Rates: budget
Open: year-round
Minimum Stay: none

Conveniently located within walking distance of the ocean and many of the island's other pleasures, this guest house consists of six units ranging from a simple room to a studio with a kitchenette to an air-conditioned suite that includes a full kitchen, a bedroom and a sitting/dining room. Economically priced and versatile, this home offers a great opportunity for a group of friends who require privacy but want to be able to jump into their car or onto their bicycles to really get to know this island. Word has it that Aruba is the windsurfing capital of the Caribbean, ideal for both experts and novices. Many shops provide helpful assistance in purchasing or renting equipment, and instructors can teach you all you need to know to safely and confidently enjoy this wonderful water sport. Contact: Camari Guest House, Hospitaalstraat 10, Oranjestad, Aruba, Netherlands Antilles. Call 011-297-8-28026.

Children: Y   Pets: N   Smoking: Y   Handicap Access: N   Payment: C, T

CROES HOUSE

Rates: budget
Open: year-round
Minimum Stay: none

Aruban culture offers a distinctly international flavor, a result of the more than 40 nationalities that have influenced the island over many centuries. With one of these simple efficiency rentals for a base, you can acquaint yourself thoroughly with this rich historical and cultural island. Each air-conditioned unit includes a TV and an outdoor barbecue, and guests share a lovely swimming pool. The owner enjoys showing her island home to visitors and can act as your personal tour guide. You can explore the beautiful, clear waters atop windsurf boards, waterskis or sailboats, or go down a little deeper with snorkeling or scuba-diving gear. A day of horseback riding on the beach offers a truly memorable experience, and a night or two of trying your luck at the glamorous casinos won't be quickly forgotten either. Contact: Maria Croes, Palo di Boonchistraat 2, Oranjestad, Aruba, Netherlands Antilles. Call 011-297-8-22439.

Children: Y   Pets: N   Smoking: Y   Handicap Access: N   Payment: C, T

IN 'T VELD GUEST HOUSE

Rates: budget
Open: year-round
Minimum Stay: none

You'll find the beach, supermarkets and the downtown district of a lively and colorful Aruba town all within walking distance of this simple home for two. Accommodations here include a living room area with a fully equipped kitchen and an air-conditioned bedroom with a color TV. A separate storage area offers the added convenience of a washing machine; maid service can be provided upon request. You can use this home away from home as your base for developing vacation skills such as scuba diving, shopping, snorkeling, dining out, windsurfing and gambling at the casinos! Contact: In 'T Veld Guest House, Stadionweg 18-a, Dakota, Aruba, Netherlands Antilles. Call 011-297-8-21368.

Children: Y   Pets: N   Smoking: Y   Handicap Access: N   Payment: C, T

SUNSET VILLAS   *Rates: expensive-deluxe*
Open: year-round   *Minimum Stay: one week*
Ideally located in this island paradise, these studio, one- and two-bedroom apartments situate you just a three-minute walk from Aruba's famed seven-mile stretch of beach. In a setting that offers privacy and luxury, each rental features tasteful and comfortable furnishings, a TV, a telephone and a kitchenette. Amenities include a private swimming pool, a Jacuzzi and tropical garden settings. Enjoy the sun and the water all day long, and walk to one of the fine restaurants or exciting casinos in the evening. Contact: Villas International, 71 West 23rd Street, New York, NY 10010. Call 212-929-7585.

Children: Y   Pets: N   Smoking: Y   Handicap Access: N   Payment: C, P, T

PALM BEACH

PLAYA LINDA BEACH RESORT   *Rates: inexpensive-deluxe*
Open: year-round   *Minimum Stay: two nights*
Situated on Aruba's favored Palm Beach, this elegant resort overlooks six miles of unspoiled sand kissed by the soft, turquoise Caribbean. Each of the plush, new air-conditioned studio, one- and two-bedroom suites features queen-size beds, a large balcony or terrace with a fabulous ocean view, kitchenettes or full kitchens and color TV with in-house movies. This resort offers all the services that will make your vacation truly restful: babysitting, a professional masseuse on call and laundromats. Take advantage of the shopping arcade with a sports and beachwear shop, tennis courts, free-form pool, outdoor tropical bar and restaurant and several whirlpools. You'll find such activities as snorkeling, windsurfing and waterskiing as well as five casinos and nightclubs within walking distance. Contact: International Hotel Representatives. Call 1-800-617-8877 (in New Jersey, 201-617-7579).

Children: Y   Pets: N   Smoking: Y   Handicap Access: Y   Payment: C, T, V, M

THE MILL RESORT   *Rates: inexpensive-deluxe*
Open: year-round   *Minimum Stay: none*
Beautifully situated only steps from the white beach and sparkling waters of the Caribbean, this gracious and elegant resort offers accommodations ranging in size from studios to two-bedroom suites. Your apartment features satellite TV, a bright and airy sitting area, a patio and either a kitchenette with a microwave or a full kitchen with a dishwasher. Resort amenities such as two free-form swimming pools, a children's pool, a large marble Jacuzzi, poolside breakfast and lunch service and tennis and racquetball courts for night play assure you the kind of holiday you're seeking. Honeymooners,

families and mature couples will find this resort to their liking, with all the tropical beauty of this lush island—the sailing, scuba diving, deep-sea fishing and beachcombing—yours for the taking. Contact: The Mill Resort—U.S./Canada, 343 Neponset Street, Canton, MA 02021. Call 617-821-1568.

Children: Y   Pets: N   Smoking: Y   Handicap Access: N   Payment: C, T

Bahamas

ABACO

Great Guana Cay

BAY VIEW APARTMENTS *Rates: budget*
Open: November-August *Minimum Stay: none*

Located on Great Guana Cay overlooking the bay, you have your choice of a one- or two-bedroom apartment. A short three blocks away you can swim, fish or just lounge on a six-mile-long white sand beach. Charter a boat and go deep-sea fishing for the day or rent a small boat to take the kids out. One-bedroom apartments have a double bed in the bedroom and two single pull-out beds in the lovely living room, while two-bedroom units can sleep seven people. Visit nearby Marsh Harbor to buy fresh vegetables and fruit; purchase your groceries for dinner in Guana. Your kitchen is fully equipped; your linens and towels will be restocked each week. Contact: Bay View Apartments, Great Guana Cay, Abaco, Bahamas. Call 809-367-2207.

Children: Y Pets: N Smoking: Y Handicap Access: N Payment: C, T

CAT ISLAND

Fernandez Bay

FERNANDEZ BAY VILLAGE *Rates: inexpensive-expensive*
Open: summer *Minimum Stay: none*

Open the sliding glass door to your patio overlooking the sea and let the overhead fans invite the gentle trade winds indoors. Perfect for one or the whole gang, you'll find studios, one-, two- and three-bedroom accommodations here, all with direct waterfront views. The island is accessible by private plane and an occasional flight of Bahamasair, which makes this the perfect place for a quiet getaway. Relax in the spacious but cozy living room and cook in the fully equipped kitchen. Some units have elegant dining areas with water views, and you'll find garden paths and lush island plants right outside your door. You can water-ski, play tennis, bicycle around the island or just watch the kids on the playground by the beach. Daily maid and linen service are available; the on-site restaurant offers some of the finest fare in the Bahamas. Contact: Fernandez Bay Village, 5260 S.W. 6 Street, Plantation, FL 33317. Call 305-729-1905.

Children: Y Pets: N Smoking: Y Handicap Access: N Payment: C, P, T, A

ELEUTHERA

Governor's Harbor

LAUGHING BIRD APARTMENTS *Rates: budget-inexpensive*
Open: year-round *Minimum Stay: none*

Endless beaches, pineapple farms and the shimmering blue of the Caribbean coastline will surround you when you rent the air-conditioned units here. Studio, one- and three-bedroom apartments are available; each has a separate dining room, living room and kitchen. A separate three-bedroom house can accommodate six guests, with a spacious living room, dining room and large kitchen, where you can cook for the whole crew. A two-minute walk from town, this lovely complex boasts a landscaped garden. You can lounge on the dazzling beach all day, or play tennis, go boating, fishing or hiking nearby. All accommodations include telephones and some have decks as well. Maid service is available upon request. Contact: Laughing Bird Apartments, P.O. Box 76, Governor's Harbor, Eleuthera, Bahamas. Call 809-332-2012 or 809-332-2029.

Children: Y Pets: N Smoking: Y Handicap Access: N Payment: C, P, T, V, M

Governor's Harbor

RAINBOW BAY *Rates: moderate-expensive*
Open: year-round *Minimum Stay: one week*

Situated on a hill overlooking the ocean, this charming stone and stucco three-bedroom, two-bath villa sleeps six in one queen-sized bed and four twins. A crib is also available for that first-time traveler in your family. Terra cotta floors, a cathedral ceiling in the comfortably furnished living room, a dining room for family meals and a fully equipped kitchen with handcrafted pine cabinets will invite you to relax in luxury. The coral and stone beach is perfect for snorkeling, diving or fishing, and you're just a mile away from beautiful white sand swimming beaches. Charter boats are available at many spots on the island; grocery shopping, gift shops and a lovely selection of restaurants are just a few minutes away. This home includes a private dance studio with an oak floor, mirror and ballet barre. Contact: VHR

Worldwide, 235 Kensington Avenue, Norwood, New Jersey, 07648. Call 800-633-3284. Ref. #BH105.

Children: **Y** Pets: **N** Smoking: **Y** Handicap Access: **N** Payment: **C, P, T**

Hatchet Bay

RAINBOW INN   *Rates: budget-inexpensive*
Open: November 16-August 31   *Minimum Stay: none*

You can walk for miles on the pristine beach and bask in unforgettable sunsets here. Snorkel, swim or fish right from the beach or enjoy a seaside game of tennis followed by a refreshing dip in the pool. Poolside studios and one-, two- and three-bedroom villas are available, where you can flip on the air-conditioning, mix your drinks at the wet bar before dinner, and retire to the sun deck to sip in peace. Kitchenettes and kitchens allow you the option of cooking or grazing for a midnight snack. Or you can wine and dine with the other guests at the restaurant on the premises. Maid service keeps things in order so that all you need to do is relax and enjoy. Contact: Rainbow Inn, P.O. Box 53, Governor's Harbor, Eleuthera, Bahamas. Call 809-332-0294.

Children: **Y** Pets: **N** Smoking: **Y** Handicap Access: **N** Payment: **C, T, V, M**

North Eleuthera

SAND CASTLE COTTAGES   *Rates: budget*
Open: year-round   *Minimum Stay: none*

Relax under a thatched umbrella on the beautiful expanse of oceanfront beach. Go snorkeling, rent a boat or go diving. Even if all you want to do is float in the crystal-clear water, the sea will beckon you from sunup to sundown. These one- and two-bedroom cottages are situated beneath palm and shade trees, and you can crank open the jalousie windows to let the ocean breeze cool you. Cottages are equipped with full kitchens complete with all utensils and tableware, so you can stir up dinner in your bikini after a leisurely day at the beach. Hike around the island, go fishing or bicycling, and eat out whenever you wish. Laundry service is available on the premises. Contact: Sand Castle Cottages, Current, Eleuthera, Bahamas. Call 809-333-0264

Children: **Y** Pets: **N** Smoking: **Y** Handicap Access: **N** Payment: **C, P, T**

Palmetto Shores

VILLA PALMETTO   *Rates: moderate-deluxe*
Open: year-round   *Minimum Stay: one week*

Once you step into this magnificent contemporary villa you won't want to leave it for a second. Sliding glass doors running the full length of the house lead to a private pool. The elegantly furnished living room and dining area are perfect for entertaining; you can serve meals or cocktails at the spacious breakfast bar in the kitchen, which is equipped with everything you'll need. Two bedrooms with king-sized beds and baths also have sliding glass doors leading to the pool. Bring your tennis racquets for a game at the private tennis court just a quarter of a mile down the road. Of course, you can play golf on either of the islands's 18-hole golf courses, charter a boat, fish or swim in the ocean nearby. Contact: Villas International, 71 West 23rd Street, New York, NY 10010. Call 212-929-7585.

Children: Y   Pets: N   Smoking: Y   Handicap Access: N   Payment: C, P, T

EXUMA

George Town
REGATTA POINT

Rates: budget-moderate

Open: year-round

Minimum Stay: one week

Borrow one of the free sunfish or windsurfers here and sail out into sparkling Elizabeth Harbor. Go snorkeling and let the colors of the saltwater fish awe you. There's tennis, boating, fishing, bicycling and water-skiing for the active set, and guided tours of the island—including famous Kidd Cove and the spot where Ponce de Leon once landed. Studio, one- and two-bedroom units all have high ceilings and spacious rooms to take full advantage of the cooling trade winds. Studios with queen-sized beds comfortably sleep two; one-bedrooms have two twins and the large two-bedrooms offer two double beds and one queen-sized bed. All units have full kitchens; your maid will do as much or as little as you wish, leaving you free to laze in the hammock or let your feet dangle over the dock. Contact: Regatta Point, P.O. Box 6, George Town, Exuma, Bahamas. Call 809-336-2206.

Children: Y Pets: N Smoking: Y Handicap Access: N Payment: C, P, T, V, M

GRAND BAHAMA

Freeport—Lucaya
WATER'S EDGE RESORT AND MARINA

Rates: budget-moderate

Open: year-round

Minimum Stay: none

Step out onto the terrace of your waterfront condominium and breathe in the salt air. Dive into the gorgeous freshwater pool directly over-looking the marina and then flop into a lounge chair on the spacious deck to enjoy the sun. Six beautiful golf courses allow you to tee off whenever you like, and you can play tennis by sunlight or by flood-light. Your studio condominium sleeps two in style. A large living room and separate dining room are right off your private porch, and a full kitchen, complete with utensils and tableware, is perfect for nights when you'd rather eat in. A spacious dressing room and walk-in closet make it easy to slip in and out of those island fashions, while maid service will keep your apartment in good order. Contact: Water's Edge Resort and Marina, P.O. Box F2727, Freeport, Grand Bahama. Call 203-852-9300.

Children: Y   Pets: N   Smoking: Y   Handicap Access: N   Payment: C, T

GREAT ABACO

Green Turtle Cay

BLUFF HOUSE CLUB AND MARINA   *Rates: inexpensive-expensive*
Open: year-round   *Minimum Stay: three nights*

Explore the underwater sea gardens and gaze at the colorful fish swimming past you in the warm, crystal-clear waters of the ocean. Stroll down to the marina and charter a boat for deep-sea fishing. Sail all day long here in the "Sailing Capital of the World." Catch some sailfin tuna for dinner and cook it up in the kitchen of your villa. You can choose an air-conditioned split-level suite for two, a one-, two- or three-bedroom villa or a "Treehouse" able to house two to six people in comfort. Some villas have sofa beds for extra guests as well as lounge and deck areas to work on that tan. When you don't feel up to cooking, you can elect the MAP plan and have your breakfast and dinner right on the premises. Contact: Abaco Vacation Res. Inc., 120 Chandler St., Worcester, MA 01609. Call 508-791-1300 or 800-633-9197.

Children: Y   Pets: N   Smoking: Y   Handicap Access: N   Payment: C, T

Green Turtle Cay

GREEN STAR   *Rates: inexpensive-moderate*
Open: year-round   *Minimum Stay: three nights*

When it's time to come ashore for a bit, you can cruise into Black Sound and moor your boat at the deep water dock that comes with this newly renovated two-bedroom cottage. Lounge on the partially covered deck with its spectacular water view or put your feet up in the living/dining area. A double bed in the first bedroom and two twins in the second will sleep four, and two day beds—perfect for the kids—let you raise the head count to six. Water sports enthusiasts will love snorkeling, diving and windsurfing here, while those who prefer quieter activities can beachcomb for hours. The town is just a quarter of a mile from your door too, making it easy to pick up groceries or explore. Contact: Abaco Vacation Res. Inc., 120 Chandler St., Worcester, MA 01609. Call 800-633-9197 or 508-791-1300.

Children: Y   Pets: N   Smoking: Y   Handicap Access: N   Payment: C, T

Green Turtle Cay

JAMAICA   *Rates: moderate*
Open: year-round   *Minimum Stay: three nights*

Beachcombers will be in heaven with a choice of two beaches for shelling here. This lovely two-bedroom cottage for four people offers you the Atlantic Ocean on one side of the house and the Green Turtle Bay beach on the other. Go snorkeling along the reef just offshore on the Atlantic Ocean side or try windsurfing on the calm crystal-clear waters of the bay. When it's time to take a break or just change bathing suits, relax for a few moments on the wraparound deck of the cottage or fix a quick lunch in the beautiful modern kitchen with all new appliances and all of the cookware, bakeware and utensils you'll need.

Pluck your dessert or a snack off any one of the luscious fruit trees surrounding the cottage before heading back to the beach. Contact: Abaco Vacation Res. Inc., 120 Chandler St., Worcester, MA 01609. Call 800-633-9197 or 508-791-1300.

Children: Y   Pets: N   Smoking: Y   Handicap Access: N   Payment: C, T

Green Turtle Cay

PINK *Rates: inexpensive*

Open: year-round *Minimum Stay: three nights*

Located on the narrowest part of Green Turtle Cay, this two-bedroom housekeeping cottage has the bay on one side and the ocean on the other. A perfect spot for snorkelers, divers or windsurfers, the Atlantic side of the cottage offers a sea garden reef, while the bay offers windsurfers smooth sailing all the way. Curl up in the rattan furniture when it's time to come indoors, or sunbathe on the wraparound deck of the cottage. The fully modern kitchen makes it easy to eat in. At bedtime, five people can sleep to the sound of the ocean in two lovely bedrooms fully supplied with all your linens and towels. Make sure to check out the fruit trees before you shop for groceries, as you're welcome to pick all you can eat. Contact: Abaco Vacation Res. Inc., 120 Chandler St., Worcester, MA 01609. Call 800-633-9197 or 508-791-1300.

Children: Y   Pets: N   Smoking: Y   Handicap Access: N   Payment: C, T

Mariner's Cove

MARINER'S COVE APARTMENTS *Rates: inexpensive-expensive*

Open: year-round *Minimum Stay: three nights*

Water lovers will have their choice of poolside or waterfront accommodations here, where air-conditioned studio, one- and two-bedroom apartments all have patios or terraces and fully equipped kitchens. Island rattan furniture with bright cushions in the lovely living/dining area invites you to curl up for an afternoon siesta after a morning spent swimming, snorkeling, diving or fishing. You can play tennis nearby or barbecue dinner and then eat it at the picnic tables under the stars. Golf carts can be rented for the course or just for bopping around the island; you won't need a car with the island's taxi service. Perfect for two to four adults, some of these units have pull-out sofa beds to accommodate an extra guest. Maid service can be arranged once you're on the island, leaving you free to play the day away. Contact: VHR Worldwide, 235 Kensington Avenue, Norwood, NJ 07648. Call 800-NEED-A-VILLA or 800-633-3284.

Children: Y   Pets: N   Smoking: Y   Handicap Access: Y   Payment: C, P, T

Marsh Harbor

COCONUT PALM *Rates: moderate*

Open: year-round *Minimum Stay: one week*

A little bit of heaven awaits you in this glorious two-bedroom villa situated on six acres, with a quarter of a mile of pristine beach for your private enjoyment. Walk through the sliding glass doors in either the dining room or living room and slip into the Jacuzzi on the deck overlooking the ocean. Enjoy perfect solitude, as there isn't a single phone in the entire area to disturb you. Two bedrooms, one with a queen-sized bed and the other with two twins, invite you to catch up on your z's. A gleaming modern bath stands waiting for you, and the fully equipped kitchen with microwave lets you take your meals in utter privacy whenever you feel like it. The villa comes with a VW van for touring around the island with the whole gang. A TV and VCR complete the comforts. Contact: Abaco Vacation Res. Inc., 120 Chandler St., Worcester, MA 01609. Call 800-633-9197 or 508-791-1300.

Children: Y   Pets: N   Smoking: Y   Handicap Access: N   Payment: C, T

Treasure Cay

BEACH VILLAS   *Rates: expensive*
Open: year-round   *Minimum Stay: none*

Walk through the exquisitely maintained garden outside your door and into a glorious villa just steps away from three and a half miles of pristine beach. These two-bedroom, two-bath homes have spacious, open living/dining areas where you can relax on comfortable island furniture. Large windows face the ocean, letting you drink in the sparkling views. Ceiling fans coax the trade winds in and air-conditioning is just a flick of a button away. Sneak out to one of the two patios located off the living room and one of the bedrooms and breathe in the salt air. A fully modern kitchen makes it easy to whip up dinner in your bathing suit; or arrange for a babysitter and go out on the town. In the morning, you can arrange for full maid service if you want it and then take off for a dip in the pool. Contact: VHR Worldwide, 235 Kensington Avenue, Norwood, NJ 07648. Call 800-NEED-A-VILLA or 800-633-3284.

Children: Y   Pets: N   Smoking: Y   Handicap Access: Y   Payment: C, P, T

Treasure Cay

BRIGANTINE BEACH   *Rates: expensive*
Open: year-round   *Minimum Stay: none*

Stick a hibiscus blossom behind your ear on your way down to the white sand beach just 100 yards from your door. Swim, snorkel, fish or play tennis or golf by day when you're not out exploring this litle gem of an island. No need to climb the stairs when it comes time to dress for dinner: Your centrally air-conditioned home has its two bedrooms and two baths on one level. Have cocktails in the spacious living room or walk through the sliding glass doors onto the deck to view the gardens and the ocean. Eating in is easy, with a modern kitchen and lovely dining area right off the living room. A sofa bed in the living room lets you add an extra guest or two for a total of up to six. Maid service is available and laundry facilities and a swimming pool are just another 100 yards away in the villa section. Contact: VHR Worldwide, 235 Kensington Avenue, Norwood, NJ 07648. Call 800-NEED-A-VILLA or 800-633-3284.

Children: N   Pets: N   Smoking: Y   Handicap Access: N   Payment: C, P, T

Treasure Cay

ROYAL POINCIANA   *Rates: expensive-deluxe*
Open: year-round   *Minimum Stay: one week*

Surrounded by the turquoise water and white sand beaches of Treasure Cay, you can enjoy the ultimate combination of privacy and modern convenience in these cheerful two-bedroom condominiums. They feature full kitchens with microwaves, food processors and dishwashers to make eating in a delight. Laundry rooms and spacious, airy living rooms with dining areas decorated in rattan and bright island prints are added attractions. Lower-level units with patios and upper-level units with balconies both offer gorgeous ocean views while you sip your morning coffee. Choose between upper-level accommodations with two bedrooms and two baths downstairs, and a sofa bed in the living room, or lower-level units with two bedrooms, three baths and a sleeping loft that contains an extra two twin beds. You can play tennis on the private courts or dive into the central swimming pool. Contact: VHR Worldwide, 235 Kensington Ave., Norwood, NJ 07648. Call 800-NEED-A-VILLA or 800-633-3284.

Children: Y   Pets: N   Smoking: Y   Handicap Access: Y   Payment: C, P, T

Treasure Cay

SNOWMASS   *Rates: deluxe*
Open: year-round   *Minimum Stay: one week*

Just an hour's flight from Florida's Atlantic Coast, Treasure Cay's three and a half miles of pink sand and sparkling turquoise water will make you want to stay forever. Drive up a long, palm-lined driveway and walk into the marble-paved foyer of this beautiful two-story villa. Inside, the open floor plan and glass walls will pull the ocean view into every room. On the second level you'll find a spacious dining/living area with sliding glass doors at both ends and a kitchen equipped for all the cooking you feel like doing. A master suite with private bath, dressing room and walk-in closets has an iron-railed balcony. Downstairs are an oversized family room and two more bedrooms, each with a separate bath and one with its own private seaside patio. Contact: VHR Worldwide, 235 Kensington Avenue, Norwood, NJ 07648. Call 800-NEED-A-VILLA or 800-633-3284. Ref. #BH219.

Children: Y   Pets: N   Smoking: Y   Handicap Access: N   Payment: C, P, T

Treasure Cay

TREBANYAN ESTATES   *Rates: deluxe*
Open: year-round   *Minimum Stay: none*

Wake to views of the ocean from every window of this two-bedroom, two-bath air-conditioned villa. Make breakfast for the family in the fully modern kitchen with microwave before walking the few feet to the beach to swim, fish, snorkel and frolic in the pristine white sand. In the evening, feel free to kick your sandals off and put your feet up in the large living/dining area furnished with tropical island prints. A pull-out bed in the living area sleeps two, allowing you to house six people in this lovely unit. At night, you can flick on the color TV or the stereo to unwind; you can arrange for frequent maid service and be truly pampered. Contact: VHR Worldwide, 235 Kensington Ave., Norwood, NJ 07648. Call 800-NEED-A-VILLA or 800-633-3284.

Children: Y   Pets: N   Smoking: Y   Handicap Access: N   Payment: C, P, T

Treasure Cay

TURQUOISE SEAS   *Rates: deluxe*
Open: year-round   *Minimum Stay: one week*

Water sports enthusiasts have never had it better: They've got fishing, sailing, scuba diving, snorkeling, waterskiing and swimming in the crystal blue ocean water here. Ideal for a large family or group, this secluded beachfront house has three bedrooms and can easily accommodate 12 people. It has a king-sized bed in the master suite, a queen-sized bed in the second, and a third dormitory-style bedroom with one double bed and four twins. Both the spectacular master suite and the spacious living room open onto a deck that runs the length of the house. The dining room has sliding glass doors on both ends and is just a few steps from the fully modern kitchen with dishwasher, ice maker and laundry room. Ceiling fans, central air, color cable TV and stereo are other features here. Contact: VHR, Worldwide, 235 Kensington Ave., Norwood, NJ 07648. Call 800-NEED-A-VILLA or 800-633-3284.

Children: Y   Pets: N   Smoking: Y   Handicap Access: Y   Payment: C, P, T

LONG ISLAND

Stella Maris

STELLA MARIS INN   *Rates: inexpensive-expensive*
Open: year-round   *Minimum Stay: none*

Stella Maris is the angler's delight, boasting year-round fishing in the North Equatorial Current. Reel in everything from blue marlin to dorado dolphins, and bring your spinning and fly rods for inland fishing, too. Private boaters are welcome at the Stella Maris Marina, the only boating facility in the Southern Bahamas. Studio, one- and two-bedroom accommodations are available here; some units offer kitchenettes or full kitchens. All rooms have air-conditioning and are elegantly modern with tile floors, bright curtains, bedspreads and dining areas. The resort offers a lounge and an on-site restaurant; child care is available for nights when it's time for some grown-up fun. Daily maid and linen service will keep you from lifting a finger. Contact: Stella Maris, 702 SW 34th Street, Ft. Lauderdale, FL 33315. Call 305-359-8236 or 800-426-0466.

Children: Y Pets: N Smoking: Y Handicap Access: N Payment: C, T, A, V, M

NASSAU

Cable Beach

CASUARINAS OF CABLE BEACH   *Rates: budget-moderate*
Open: year-round   *Minimum Stay: three nights*

Eat your lunch beneath a palm tree on a beautiful tiled terrace. After a nap, take your swim in either the freshwater or saltwater pools—and then enjoy a tall cool drink poolside beneath an umbrella. A private beach invites you into the warm aquamarine sea, where you can swim and float the day away. At this resort you can choose from an efficiency studio or a one- or two-bedroom apartment sleeping three to six, all decorated in cheery color schemes. Golf, waterskiing, and tennis are all within a short distance, and babysitting for the children can easily be arranged. Room telephones, air conditioning and color TV are all part of this luxury package. Contact: Casuarinas of Cable Beach, Cable Beach, West Bay St., Nassau, Bahamas. Call 809-327-8153 or 809-327-7921/22.

Children: Y Pets: N Smoking: Y Handicap Access: N Payment: C, T, A, V, M

Paradise Island

PARADISE RIDGE RESIDENCE *Rates: expensive-deluxe*
Open: year-round *Minimum Stay: one week*

You'll be just a short walk from the white sands and sparkling blue waters of the ocean when you choose any one of these luxurious accommodations. Relax in your air-conditioned living room before starting dinner in the fully equipped modern kitchen with dishwasher. You can arrange for a full-time maid and cook, leaving you free to spend your time in the water, on a nearby golf course or enjoying the famous nightclubs. Dive into any one of the three solar-heated swimming pools on the property for quick refreshment after a game of tennis. At night, your one- to three-bedroom villa stands so close to the water you'll fall asleep to the gentle sound of the waves. Contact: Villas International, 71 West 23rd St., NY, NY 10010. Call 212-929-7585.

Children: Y Pets: N Smoking: Y Handicap Access: N Payment: C, P, T

Paradise Island

VILLAS IN PARADISE *Rates: budget-deluxe*
Open: year-round *Minimum Stay: one week*

You'll only be a four-minute walk from the Resorts Casino complex and just 50 yards from beautiful Paradise Beach where you choose a studio or one-, two-, three- or four-bedroom private villa here. Spacious modern rooms with cheery fabrics in the living room, dining area and bedrooms echo the island's intoxicating ambiance. Serve a quick meal at the breakfast bar in the kitchen before heading to the beach or cook up a full dinner in the kitchen. Most of these villas have private pools out back, so dive in and swim at midnight if you wish. The pool is serviced daily and maid service will look after every detail of your villa. Rates include one day's free car rental and a bottle of Bacardi rum. The units have air-conditioning and satellite TV. Contact: Villa Holidays, 13911 Ridgedale Dr., Suite 399, Minneapolis, MN 55343. Call 800-328-6262 or 612-545-8101.

Children: Y Pets: N Smoking: Y Handicap Access: N Payment: C, P, T, V, M

ST. LUCY

Atlantic Ocean

Treasure Bay — ST. PETER

ST. JAMES

ST. THOMAS   ST. JOHN

ST. PHILIP

ST. MICHAEL
★ Bridgetown

CHRIST
CHURCH

Barbados

CHRIST CHURCH

BLYTHWOOD BEACH APARTMENTS

Rates: budget-moderate

Open: year-round

Minimum Stay: three nights

Situated on the unspoiled white sandy beach at Worthing, four miles from Bridgetown, Blythwood is an elegant yet surprisingly affordable vacation apartment building. Each of the 15 studio, one- and two-bedroom units contains a well-equipped kitchen and commands a splendid ocean view. There's also a luxurious one-bedroom penthouse apartment with a private sun deck. The ocean swimming here is excellent year-round and the snorkeling and diving opportunities, with equipment rental facilities within easy walking distance, are superb as well. Cycling and tennis are just two of the land-based recreational pursuits visitors can enjoy in the area, which also offers an assortment of fine shops and restaurants. Contact: Blythwood Beach Apartments, Worthing, Christ Church, Barbados, British West Indies. Call 809-435-7712.

Children: Y   Pets: N   Smoking: Y   Handicap Access: N   Payment: C, T

CACRABANK BEACH APARTMENT HOTEL

Rates: budget-inexpensive

Open: year-round

Minimum Stay: three days

The 21 studio, one- and two-bedroom units of the Cacrabank Beach Apartment Hotel, each containing complete kitchen facilities, make terrific home bases for a stay on the dramatic southeastern coast of Barbados. The sea here kicks up a healthy surf that's ideal for board sailing and makes for some exhilarating waterskiing, while those who prefer gentler waters can swim in the private pool. Golf and tennis are also within easy reach, and there are plenty of scenic wonders and historic spots of interest to visit nearby. Don't miss a trip out to the Ragged Point Lighthouse, built in 1885 on a rugged cliff to aid ships navigating the treacherous Cobbler's Reef. Contact: Cacrabank Beach Apartment Hotel, #18 Worthing, Christ Church, Barbados, British West Indies. Call 809-435-8057/8060.

Children: Y Pets: N Smoking: Y Handicap Access: N Payment: C, T, V, M

MAGIC ISLE BEACH APARTMENTS
Rates: inexpensive-moderate
Open: year-round
Minimum Stay: none

All 30 of the flats available at this affable apartment complex, located on gorgeous and uncrowded Rockley Beach, offer a far-reaching view of the Caribbean. Accented with rich tropical vegetation and towering palm trees, the grounds include a freshwater swimming pool. The one- and two-bedroom apartments each feature a fully equipped kitchen, comfortable living/dining room and a private balcony. Whether guests prefer golf or deep-sea fishing, boating or tennis, arrangements can be made right at the front office for partaking in any of the island's vast recreational resources. Contact: Michaelin Dulal, Magic Isle Beach Apartments, Rockley Beach, Christ Church, Barbados, British West Indies. Call 809-435-6760/8558.

Children: Y Pets: N Smoking: Y Handicap Access: N Payment: C, T

MERIDIAN INN
Rates: budget
Open: year round
Minimum Stay: one week

Just steps from the beach, the Meridian Inn is a superb choice for vacationers seeking budget housekeeping accommodations on the southern coast of Barbados. Twelve self-contained studio units are available, each featuring a well-equipped kitchenette and a private balcony. Nearby, the gentle Caribbean shores to the west provide the best spots for swimming, snorkeling and other water sports and the rugged Atlantic coastline to the east offers dramatic seascapes only minutes away. Rent a bike at one of the facilities near the residence for a refreshing ride in either direction. Contact: Lolita Khan, Meridian Inn, Dover, Christ Church, Barbados, British West Indies. Call 809-428-4051/2.

Children: Y Pets: N Smoking: Y Handicap Access: N Payment: C, T

ROMAN BEACH APARTMENTS
Rates: budget-inexpensive
Open: year-round
Minimum Stay: three nights

The Roman Beach Apartments, fully equipped studios containing complete kitchen facilities, offer a central location for enjoying Barbados's bountiful recreational opportunities, sightseeing pleasures and fine restaurants and shops. Right outside is a clean and safe swimming beach where windsurfing, snorkeling and a variety of other water sports can be pursued. Here, too, freshly caught seafood is available daily right out of the fishermen's nets. Try some fishing of your own from a charter boat or off the cliffs about a half mile away. Or take a five-minute walk down to the South Point Lighthouse, site of the island's best surfing. To see the rest of Barbados, why not rent a motorbike for an invigorating ride along its charming lanes and twisting coastal byways? Contact: Francis Roman, Roman Beach Apartments, Enterprise-on-Sea Road, Oisintown, Christ Church, Barbados, British West Indies. Call 809-428-7635/2510.

Children: Y   Pets: N   Smoking: Y   Handicap Access: N   Payment: C, T

ROUND ROCK APARTMENTS ON SEA

Rates: budget-inexpensive
Open: year-round
Minimum Stay: none

Situated on Silver Sands Beach along Barbados's southeast Caribbean coast, the Round Rock Apartment complex features seven studio, one- and two-bedroom units, each equipped with complete kitchen facilities. The area is delightfully uncrowded, the atmosphere casual and intimate, making a superb spot for enjoying a rejuvenating sun and sports holiday. With a five- to 15-foot surf and trade winds blowing from 12 to 25 knots, this part of the coast offers what many experts consider to be the finest windsurfing this side of Maui; there's also excellent deep-sea fishing opportunities as well as tennis and other recreational activities available nearby. Contact: Willie B. Thompson, Round Rock Apartments, Silver Sands, Christ Church, Barbados, British West Indies. Call 809-428-7500/7970.

Children: Y Pets: N Smoking: Y Handicap Access: N Payment: C, T, V, M

SOUTHERN SURF APARTMENTS

Rates: budget
Open: October-April
Minimum Stay: three nights

The 12 apartments of Southern Surf are situated on the eastern end of Rockley Beach, where the swells are hefty enough for exceptional surfing but the water is sufficiently gentle to allow for bathing. Guests may also enjoy swimming in the private pool or resting under the brilliant Caribbean sun on the poolside patio. Other recreational facilities, plus exciting dining and colorful nighttime entertainment opportunities, are also close by. Each studio unit here is self-contained and features comfortable furnishings, complete kitchen facilities and a private balcony. Contact: Harold Worme, Manager, Southern Surf, Rockley Beach, Christ Church, Barbados, British West Indies. Call 809-435-6672.

Children: N Pets: N Smoking: Y Handicap Access: N Payment: C, T, V, M

SUMMERSET APARTMENTS

Rates: budget-inexpensive
Open: year-round
Minimum Stay: one week

Located in Dover, one of Barbados's most popular resort areas, Summerset Apartments offers seven one- and two-bedroom units, each containing a fully equipped kitchenette and several featuring large, private garden patios. The beach is only about 300 yards away, superb for swimming and particularly fine for windsurfing. From nearby Worthing, escorted snorkeling and scuba cruises take divers to fascinating coral reefs and shipwrecks in both deep and shallow water off the coast. Contact: Lorna Austin, Summerset Apartments, Dover, Christ Church, Barbados, British West Indies. Call 809-428-7936.

Children: Y   Pets: N   Smoking: Y   Handicap Access: Y   Payment: C, T

THE NOOK APARTMENTS
Open: year-round

Rates: budget-inexpensive
Minimum Stay: one week

Located in the gardens of "The Nook," a graceful Colonial-style bungalow in Rockley, these four charming apartments are built alongside a private swimming pool. The units each contain two bedrooms, a living room and kitchen area and feature a private patio that makes a terrific spot for dining. Three miles away, Bridgetown offers many historic sites of interest and a host of fine dining, shopping and nightlife opportunities. Embark from there for a relaxing day or evening cruise along the coast; enjoy food, drinks and entertainment on board and stop for swimming and snorkeling on the way. Contact: Mr. Harold Clarke, The Nook Apartments, Dayrells Road, Rockley, Christ Church, Barbados, British West Indies. Call 809-427-6502/436-9697.

Children: Y   Pets: N   Smoking: Y   Handicap Access: N   Payment: C, T

ST. JAMES

ANGLER APARTMENTS
Open: year-round

Rates: budget-inexpensive
Minimum Stay: one week

Angler Apartments, situated on the west coast only a few yards from the beach, offers superior one- and two-bedroom units. Each flat contains a sitting room, dining area and fully equipped kitchen and features a private patio or balcony. Ceiling fans waft the refreshing sea air throughout the residences. Golf, tennis and a full variety of water sports opportunities are all less than five minutes away; superb duty-free shopping is within easy reach as well. Contact: Chandra or Roger Gosain, Angler Apartments, Clarke's Rd. #1, Derricks, St. James, Barbados, British West Indies. Call 1-800-223-5608 or 809-432-0817.

Children: Y   Pets: N   Smoking: Y   Handicap Access: N   Payment: C, T, V, M

AUJOURD'HUI
Open: year-round

Rates: deluxe
Minimum Stay: one week

This enchanting holiday home stands on an acre of exquisitely landscaped grounds 150 yards from beautiful St. James Beach. Offering the services of a cook, two maids, a laundress and a gardener, the two-story residence contains three bedroom suites, a kitchen and pantry area with excellent amenities. The formal living room leads onto a sunny patio; the dining room and casual sitting area open onto the verdant lawn. Recreational opportunities are plentiful both on the beach—reached by a private path—and inland. Nearby Holetown, Speightstown and the Glitter Bay Resort provide a number of exciting dining and entertainment options. Contact: Villas and Apartments Abroad, Ltd., 420 Madison Avenue, New York, NY 10017. Call 1-800-433-3020 or 212-759-1025.

Children: Y   Pets: N   Smoking: Y   Handicap Access: N   Payment: C, P, T

BAGGYWRINKLE
Open: year-round

Rates: deluxe
Minimum Stay: one week

This modern and comfortably furnished coral stone villa with complete household staff is ideally situated on St. James Beach, one of the finest spots for swimming and other water sports on the entire island.

Featuring a luxurious master suite that contains a king-sized bed, the house also includes two other bedrooms—both with quaint ceiling fans—that share a large bathroom, plus a spacious living and dining area that opens onto inviting shaded patios. There, guests can relax in idyllic surroundings, savoring the balmy sea breezes and spying far-reaching views across the Caribbean through the casurina trees. Contact: Villas International, 71 West 23rd Street, New York, NY 10010. Call 212-929-7585.

Children: **Y**   Pets: **N**   Smoking: **Y**   Handicap Access: **N**   Payment: **C, P, T**

BALI BALI   *Rates: deluxe*
Open: year-round   *Minimum Stay: one week*

Days of idyllic rest and recreation by the water, capped by spectacular Caribbean sunsets—that's what awaits guests staying in this lovely duplex-style home ideally located on the unspoiled beach of Paynes Bay. Complete with a maid and gardener taking care of all housekeeping duties, this splendid two-bedroom residence is fully equipped and self-sufficient. The lower of two flats offers access to an adjoining terrace, while the upper unit commands sweeping views of the sand and ocean; both are graced with such enticing features as tiled floors and huge floor-to-ceiling windows. Contact: LaCure Villas, 11661 San Vicente Blvd., Suite 1010, Los Angeles, CA 90049. Call 1-800-387-2726.

Children: **Y**   Pets: **N**   Smoking: **Y**   Handicap Access: **N**   Payment: **C, P, T**

BEACH AVIARY   *Rates: deluxe*
Open: year-round   *Minimum Stay: one week*

A staff that includes a housekeeper and laundress, butler, maids and a gardener guarantees that large parties staying at this majestic beach home receive truly regal treatment. Built in Colonial style, the house is filled with fine examples of traditional Barbadian furniture that lend an air of grandeur. The four-bedroom house is constructed on two levels, both opening onto spacious covered terraces that overlook the grounds. And such lovely grounds, too, where lush tropical gardens envelop a sparkling swimming pool and a mesmerizing aviary houses a striking assortment of local bird life. Contact: LaCure Villas, 11661 San Vicente Blvd., Suite 1010, Los Angeles, CA 90049. Call 1-800-387-2726.

Children: **Y**   Pets: **N**   Smoking: **Y**   Handicap Access: **N**   Payment: **C, P, T**

FOC'SL   *Rates: deluxe*
Open: year-round   *Minimum Stay: one week*

Some of the finest swimming and warmest, gentlest water to be found along Barbados's famed "Platinum Coast" is right at the doorstep of this delightfully secluded beach cottage. The two-bedroom residence features a bright open-plan living/dining area that looks out across the sunny patio to the azure Caribbean. The owner's expert staff takes care of guests' every need, leaving them all the time in the world to pursue the recreational activities of their choice and to enjoy the island's manifold scenic delights and places of interest.

Contact: Villas International, 71 West 23rd Street, New York, NY 10010. Call 212-929-7585.

Children: Y   Pets: N   Smoking: Y   Handicap Access: N   Payment: C, P, T

HOLDERS   *Rates: deluxe*
Open: year-round   *Minimum Stay: one week*

Set on vast grounds that offer a private swimming pool, enchanting gardens and lovely views of the sea, this plantation villa exhibits a provocative blend of period and contemporary characteristics. The main house features a noble foyer and formal living room, a very well-equipped kitchen, three bedrooms—two opening onto a terrace— a large covered patio for casual lounging and a covered outdoor dining area. Adjacent to this is an annex that contains two additional bedrooms, both with king-sized beds. The beach is a five-minute drive away; an array of other recreational opportunities are also within easy reach. Contact: At Home Abroad, Inc., 405 East 56th Street, 6H, New York, NY 10022. Call 212-421-9165. Ref. 9988.

Children: Y   Pets: N   Smoking: Y   Handicap Access: N   Payment: C, P, T

LINDSAY RIDGE   *Rates: deluxe*
Open: year-round   *Minimum Stay: one week*

Commanding a breathtaking 160-degree view of the Caribbean coast and a nearby polo field, Lindsay Ridge is a majestic private compound clustered around a radiant pool and patio area. The residence offers some 6,000 square feet of living space, including four plush bedrooms—the master suite has a bay window looking out over the pool—a formal living room, den, circular dining room opening onto the patio and a fantastic kitchen with a storeroom and pantry. There's also a separate annex, whose entertainment pavilion features a sunken cocktail and dining area. A complete staff takes care of the house and keeps the two acres of beautiful, flourishing gardens meticulously tended. Contact: Villas and Apartments Abroad, Ltd., 420 Madison Avenue, New York, NY 10017. Call 1-800-433-3020 or 212-759-1025.

Children: Y   Pets: N   Smoking: Y   Handicap Access: N   Payment: C, P, T

MOORE HOUSE   *Rates: deluxe*
Open: year-round   *Minimum Stay: one week*

Moore House is an authentic Barbadian plantation home sumptuously decorated with superior antique furniture. It contains two bedrooms, a living room, den and fully equipped kitchen. The hilltop estate commands breathtaking views of both the Atlantic and the Caribbean and features marvelously landscaped grounds that encompass a large swimming pool surrounded by a vast lawn and ravishing gardens. To make unforgettable excursions throughout the island even more convenient, a car comes with the property. While guests enjoy their adventures, the estate's staff takes care of cooking and every other household chore. Contact: LaCure Villas, 11661 San Vicente Blvd., Suite 1010, Los Angeles, CA 90049. Call 1-800-387-2726.

Children: Y   Pets: N   Smoking: Y   Handicap Access: N   Payment: C, P, T

THE GARDEN *Rates: deluxe*
Open: year-round *Minimum Stay: one week*
This recently built group of eight luxurious townhouses, exquisitely designed with Spanish flair, is located right on St. James Beach. Featuring whitewashed walls, red-tiled roofs and individual plunge pools, each residence contains three bedrooms with ceiling fans, three baths, a fully equipped kitchen and a living and dining area that opens onto a large shared pool and patio area. A maid and cook are there to handle housekeeping chores, while guests pursue water sports, sightseeing or a host of other leisure activities. Contact: At Home Abroad, Inc., 405 East 56th Street, 6H, New York, NY 10022. Call 212-421-9165. Ref. 9985.
Children: N   Pets: N   Smoking: Y   Handicap Access: N   Payment: C, P, T

TRAVELLER'S PALM *Rates: budget*
Open: year-round *Minimum Stay: one week*
A stone's throw from Holetown and a five-minute walk from a beautiful white beach, Traveller's Palm offers 16 quality apartments, each containing a walk-in closet, full kitchen and large living room and dining room. But guests won't want to take all their meals in their flats—join the inn hosts for their weekly barbecue and buffet and sample a complimentary rum punch concocted from local fruits and spirits. Or try out one of the many fine restaurants in the area, perhaps a lattice-ceilinged island house offering exotic Bajan cuisine. And to work off all that food, enjoy swimming or snorkeling, jet skiing or waterskiing, sailing or parasailing, golf or tennis, all available within easy reach. Contact: Marilyn and Keith Rippingham, Traveller's Palm, 265 Palm Avenue, St. James, Barbados, British West Indies. Call 809-432-7722.
Children: Y   Pets: N   Smoking: Y   Handicap Access: N   Payment: C, T

VILLA LANDMARK *Rates: deluxe*
Open: year-round *Minimum Stay: one week*
Positioned on the northern end of Sandy Lane Beach, a superb area for swimming, snorkeling and other water sports, this striking home commands sweeping views of the entire bay. The two-floor residence, built primarily of local coral stone, is tended by a four-person staff and contains four bedroom suites that sleep eight comfortably, a well-equipped kitchen, a spacious open-plan living room and a charming separate dining pagoda. Comfortable furnishings of the highest quality have been carefully chosen to complement the traditional Barbadian beach house ambiance. Contact: Rent A Home International, Inc., 7200 34th Avenue NW, Seattle, WA 98117. Call 206-545-6963.
Children: Y Pets: N Smoking: Y Handicap Access: N Payment: C, P, T, V, M

WHITE GATES *Rates: deluxe*
Open: year-round *Minimum Stay: one week*
Offering a particularly lovely private pool area, this attractive coastal villa sits high atop a coral cliff commanding stunning views of the Caribbean. It features a luxurious master suite, containing a king-sized

bed, and three other bedrooms plus a casual sitting area. The formal dining/living room—bedecked with a delightful row of tall, arched windows—opens onto the outdoor dining terrace. There, guests can enjoy relaxed meals prepared and served by the staff, while looking out over the pool and the shimmering blue waters. Then, when the last bite is eaten, they can head right down the stairway to the small, secluded and seductive cove below. Contact: Villa Holidays, Inc., 13100 Wayzata Blvd., Suite 150, Minneapolis, MN 55343. Call 1-800-328-6262 or 612-591-0076.

Children: Y Pets: N Smoking: Y Handicap Access: N Payment: C, P, T, V, M

ST. JOHN

ON THE BEACH   *Rates: expensive-deluxe*
Open: year-round   *Minimum Stay: one week*

Only 50 yards from the beach on Barbados's dramatic Atlantic coast, this quality two-story villa can accommodate large parties of up to ten. Three bedrooms are located on the upper level, two on the lower. Both floors are self-contained and equipped with a kitchen, making the residence an ideal choice for two families vacationing together. There are a number of recreational opportunities and many sites of interest within easy reach. Guest won't want to miss Harrison Cave, an extraordinary natural underground marvel viewed aboard an electric tram. Visit Sam Lord's Castle, an opulent Georgian mansion built in 1820 that's now a luxury hotel. Contact: Rent A Home International, Inc., 7200 34th Ave NW, Seattle, WA 98117. Call 206-545-6963.

Children: Y Pets: N Smoking: Y Handicap Access: N Payment: C, P, T, V, M

ST. LUCY

FREYERS WELL BAY HOUSE   *Rates: deluxe*
Open: year-round   *Minimum Stay: one week*

Perched atop a lofty coral cliff along the St. Lucy coastline, Freyers Well Bay House overlooks the Caribbean and has a pathway leading down to the beach below. The interior features a large living and dining room with vaulted cathedral ceilings of mortar and coral dust, a very well-equipped kitchen and a wing with an enclosed balcony, which contains three bedrooms. Outside, there's over an acre of walled gardens, a wrought-iron enclosed patio and a swimming pool facing the sea and surrounded by an expansive lawn. The property is nicely secluded at the end of a private road and is impeccably tended by a complete household staff. Contact: Villa Holidays, Inc., 13100 Wayzata Blvd., Suite 150, Minneapolis, MN 55343. Call 1-800-328-6262 or 612-591-0076.

Children: Y Pets: N Smoking: Y Handicap Access: N Payment: C, P, T, V, M

MESSEL HOUSE   *Rates: deluxe*
Open: year-round   *Minimum Stay: one week*

Situated on a private estate only a bit inland from Barbados' breathtaking northern Caribbean coast, Messel house is a sumptuous villa offering privacy and luxury; it's cared for by a staff who see to guests' cooking, housekeeping and laundry needs. The beautifully landscaped grounds feature a large, sparkling swimming pool surrounded by lush gardens. Inside, the house is elegantly furnished with some exquisite antique pieces, and each room receives soothing island breezes from the graceful, sunny terraces and shaded balconies that wrap around the entire residence. Contact: LaCure Villas, 11661 San Vicente Blvd., Suite 1010, Los Angeles, CA 90049. Call 1-800-387-2726.

Children: **Y**   Pets: **N**   Smoking: **Y**   Handicap Access: **N**   Payment: **C, P, T**

ST. MICHAEL

SANDRIFT APARTMENT HOTEL   *Rates: budget-inexpensive*
Open: year-round   *Minimum Stay: three nights*

Nestled in a lush tropical setting on aptly named Paradise Beach, this friendly apartment hotel offers 14 self-contained studio, one- and two-bedroom flats, most featuring a private balcony with a table and chairs for blissful outdoor dining. A complete range of water sports facilities are available practically right outside the front door, and the staff will help guests arrange for other recreational activities nearby, from tennis and squash to golf and horseback riding. For a truly distinctive perspective of the island, head to Bridgeport, three miles away, for a trip aboard the Atlantis II, a sightseeing submarine that treats riders to an unforgettable glimpse of Barbados's underwater world. Contact: Sandrift Apartments, Paradise Drive, St. Michael, Barbados, British West Indies. Call 809-424-2062/3.

Children: **Y**   Pets: **N**   Smoking: **Y**   Handicap Access: **N**   Payment: **C, T, A**

WALMER LODGE APARTMENTS   *Rates: budget*
Open: year-round   *Minimum Stay: three nights*

Just north of Bridgetown in the beach area of Black Rock, Walmer Lodge offers studio, one- and two-bedroom apartments, each with a well-equipped kitchenette and private balcony. The Caribbean waters here are warm and gentle enough to encourage swimming year-round as well as other aquatic sports; plentiful recreational opportunities are available on shore. This is also a superb central location for traveling to some of the island's key historic landmarks. Go inland to Welchman Hall Gully, a rich tropical garden run by the Barbados National Trust, which has superb specimens of local vegetation, including breadfruit trees believed to be descended from seedlings brought here by the Bounty's Captain Bligh. Contact: Keith Basil Worrell, Walmer Lodge, Black Rock, St. Michael, Barbados, British West Indies. Call 809-425-1026.

Children: **Y**   Pets: **N**   Smoking: **Y**   Handicap Access: **N**   Payment: **C, T**

ST. PETER

AQUA HAVEN   *Rates: budget-inexpensive*
Open: year-round   *Minimum Stay: one week*

Aqua Haven is a comfortable two-story guest house located right on the beach in St. Peter, with a self-contained flat on both floors. Both units feature a fully equipped kitchen, living room, two bedrooms and a terrace overlooking the water. Some of the finest snorkeling on the entire western Barbadian coast is available a mere three minutes away at the Heywoods Beach area. Fascinating banana boat rides and glass-bottomed boat excursions, providing a matchless peek at the exotic sea life of the Caribbean, are also offered nearby. There's a golf course and fine shopping and restaurants within easy walking distance as well. Contact: David and Margaret Gartrelle, 109-15 Liverpool Street, Jamaica, NY 11435. Call 718-523-1932.

Children: Y   Pets: N   Smoking: N   Handicap Access: N   Payment: C, T

COBBLERS COVE HOTEL   *Rates: expensive-deluxe*
Open: year-round   *Minimum Stay: none*

The lovely pink and white buildings of Cobblers Cove sit beside the palm-fringed beach of St. Peters. Extending onto private patios, each one- and two-bedroom suite at this posh holiday complex offers a homey sitting room, handy kitchenette and fully stocked mini bar. For the extravagant, there's also the sumptuous Camelot Suite on the top floor, featuring such luxuries as an exquisite four-poster bed and private rooftop pool. But all guests at the Cove are treated like kings and provided, free of charge, with tennis, sailing, waterskiing, windsurfing and snorkeling facilities and equipment, as well as complimentary trips aboard a delightful glass-bottomed boat. Contact: Hamish Watson, Cobblers Cove Hotel, Road View, St. Peter, Barbados, British West Indies. Call 1-800-223-6510 or 809-422-2291.

Children: N Pets: N Smoking: Y Handicap Access: N Payment: C, T, A, V, M

DUDLEY WOOD BEACH HOUSE   *Rates: expensive-deluxe*
Open: year-round   *Minimum Stay: one week*

Offering a large terrace right on the sand, with a barbecue pit and a dining pagoda, here is a beach house that truly takes advantage of its idyllic setting. Savor a romantic dinner for two or boisterous group cookout, depending on your mood, while watching a spectacular Caribbean sunset that bathes the entire coastline in a soft, golden glow. There's plenty to enjoy inside the chalet-style, split-level house, which is tended by a cook and housekeeper and contains four bedroom suites along with a fully equipped kitchen, dining room, large living room and informal sitting area. Contact: Villa Holidays, Inc., 13100 Wayzata Blvd., Suite 150, Minneapolis, MN 55343. Call 1-800-328-6262 or 612-591-0076.

Children: Y Pets: N Smoking: Y Handicap Access: N Payment: C, P, T, V, M

EASTWINDS   *Rates: deluxe*
Open: year-round   *Minimum Stay: one week*

With its rich red-tiled roofs and stately open courtyards, this spacious villa conveys an authentic Spanish ambiance. Cool Caribbean breezes waft throughout the interior, which includes five bedrooms and airy living and dining rooms. Reached by a spiral staircase, two of the bedrooms are contained within a small tower overlooking the palm speckled central courtyard. Leave the housework to the staff, which consists of a cook, maid, laundress and gardener, and go out to enjoy a refreshing day at the beach or unforgettable Barbados adventures inland. Contact: LaCure Villas, 11661 San Vicente Blvd., Suite 1010, Los Angeles, CA 90049. Call 1-800-387-2726.

Children: Y   Pets: N   Smoking: Y   Handicap Access: N   Payment: C, P, T

LA CASITA   *Rates: moderate-deluxe*
Open: year-round   *Minimum Stay: one week*
Located just outside Speightstown, which was founded in 1635 by some of the island's first British settlers and rebuilt almost entirely after a devastating hurricane in 1831, La Casita is a sumptuous vacation villa. It contains three comfortable bedrooms, a superb kitchen and casual living area, and features a glimmering pool. The superb location gives guests easy access to unspoiled beaches as well as Barbados's premiere historical areas, where august buildings, friendly neighborhoods, intriguing museums and exotic restaurants celebrate the island's rich heritage and provocative mixture of European, African and East Indian cultures. Contact: Lauren Keys, Exclusive Luxury Villas, "Rose Bank", Derricks, St. James, Barbados, British West Indies. Call 1-800-223-1108.

Children: Y   Pets: N   Smoking: Y   Handicap Access: N   Payment: C, P, T, A

LITTLE SEASCAPE   *Rates: moderate*
Open: year-round   *Minimum Stay: one week*
Little Seascape is a charming, compact hideaway positioned right on immaculate Gibbs Beach, midway between Speightstown and Holetown. Nestled amid tropical greenery, the cottage contains a bedroom suite with a queen-sized bed and a spacious kitchen. Meals may be taken on the covered patio or the open deck; either way, the cool sea breezes, redolent scents of local blossoms, beautiful coastal scenery and brilliant star-speckled evening skies make sensational dining companions. Guests can spend their entire stay engaging in recreational and leisure activities by the water. But you might want to make time to travel to nearby landmarks and sites of historic interest, like the obelisk at Holetown, which denotes the spot where the island's first English settlers landed back in 1627. Contact: Villas International, 71 West 23rd Street, New York, NY 10010. Call 212-929-7585.

Children: Y   Pets: N   Smoking: Y   Handicap Access: N   Payment: C, P, T

MULLINS MILL   *Rates: deluxe*
Open: year-round   *Minimum Stay: one week*
This is a truly top-of-the-line plantation house, sitting by the sea and surrounded by five acres of flourishing gardens. One wing is a converted sugar mill dating from 1690, and the entire interior is sumptuously decorated. A captivating open dining veranda looks out onto the Caribbean, a particular joy at sunset, when the deep-blue island sky transforms into a blazing array of hues. There's a large swimming pool with a Jacuzzi and gazebo and a flood-lit tennis court on the grounds. Two guest cottages complete the estate, making a total of six bedrooms and five baths. Small or large parties renting the property are assured of flawless service from the extensive household staff. Con-

tact: LaCure Villas, 11661 San Vicente Blvd., Suite 1010, Los Angeles, CA 90049. Call 1-800-387-2726.

Children: Y   Pets: N   Smoking: Y   Handicap Access: N   Payment: C, P, T

POINTER'S REACH
Open: year-round

Rates: moderate-deluxe
Minimum Stay: one week

Available to be rented separately or together, two winning cottages with casual resort elegance sit side by side overlooking the crystal-clear water at Mullins Beach. Each contains two bedrooms, a fully equipped kitchen and a lovely living room that opens onto a covered seaside terrace ideal for relaxing, outdoor dining or watching the bright red sun setting over the Caribbean. A housekeeper is provided who will prepare delicious examples of traditional island fair: Exotic Bajan dishes are a bewitching blend of British, West Indian and African cookery. Contact: LaCure Villas, 11661 San Vicente Blvd., Suite 1010, Los Angeles, CA 90049. Call 1-800-387-2726.

Children: Y   Pets: N   Smoking: Y   Handicap Access: N   Payment: C, P, T

SEA BREEZE
Open: year-round

Rates: deluxe
Minimum Stay: one week

This charming villa is surrounded by luxuriant tropical plants and palms on Gibbs Beach, a perfect place to enjoy swimming in calm, translucent Caribbean waters. Containing two bedrooms, the house features a very comfy living area that opens onto a large covered terrace offering a bar, plus an area where relaxing meals can be savored alfresco. Ask the cook to prepare some of the island specialties—like succulent flying fish or sea urchin, called "sea eggs" by the Bajans—topped off by a dessert made up of an assortment of luscious Barbadian papayas, mangoes and passion fruit. Contact: LaCure Villas, 11661 San Vicente Blvd., Suite 1010, Los Angeles, CA 90049. Call 1-800-387-2726.

Children: Y   Pets: N   Smoking: Y   Handicap Access: N   Payment: C, P, T

THE GREAT HOUSE
Open: year-round

Rates: deluxe
Minimum Stay: one week

A nine-person staff ensures that parties of up to 16 staying at this stately beachfront plantation villa have the time of their lives. You'll love the lavish features offered here—like a swimming pool and Jacuzzi with a poolside bar and changing room, a game room, flawlessly landscaped gardens dotted with 60 majestic coconut palms, a fountain and a gazebo perfect for sipping cocktails. Then there's the house itself, with its spacious reception areas and verandas, a music room with grand piano, alfresco dining area and four bedroom suites with baths. Four more bedrooms are provided in neighboring cottages. To top this all off, an 18-foot speed boat, 16-foot catamaran, sunfish and two windsurfers, plus additional water sports equipment, are available for guests' use. Contact: At Home Abroad, Inc., 405 East 56th Street, 6H, New York, NY 10022. Call 212-421-9165. Ref. 9937.

Children: Y   Pets: N   Smoking: Y   Handicap Access: N   Payment: C, P, T

TREASURE BAY   *Rates: expensive-deluxe*
Open: year-round   *Minimum Stay: one week*

Built in traditional island style and made of wood and coral, this handsome St. Peter beach cottage is a duplex offering self-contained upper and lower two-bedroom units. Both residences are tended by a maid/cook and feature spacious living and dining areas tastefully furnished in a casual style that open onto wide verandas overlooking a meticulously kept lawn area and a magnificent stretch of sandy shoreline. It's the perfect spot to enjoy sunning and swimming, perhaps a bit of snorkeling, too, in one of the best sections of the Barbados northwest coast. Contact: LaCure Villas, 11661 San Vicente Blvd., Suite 1010, Los Angeles, CA 90049. Call 1-800-387-2726.

Children: Y   Pets: N   Smoking: Y   Handicap Access: N   Payment: C, P, T

WESTWARD   *Rates: expensive-deluxe*
Open: year-round   *Minimum Stay: one week*

Resting by the golden sands of Gibbs Beach, this likeable cottage is a superb holiday home for visitors to West Barbados's "Platinum Coast," a stretch of Caribbean coastline where the warm tropical waters are at their most inviting, perfect for swimming and a host of other recreational opportunities that can be enjoyed any season of the year. The house contains two bedrooms, both right off the comfortable and spacious living room, which opens onto a bright terrace. A full set of garden furniture allows for outdoor lounging; with a staff to prepare and serve meals, guests barely have to lift a finger to enjoy a delicious feast alfresco. Contact: LaCure Villas, 11661 San Vicente Blvd., Suite 1010, Los Angeles, CA 90049. Call 1-800-387-2726.

Children: Y   Pets: N   Smoking: Y   Handicap Access: N   Payment: C, P, T

WHITEWOODS   *Rates: moderate-deluxe*
Open: year-round   *Minimum Stay: one week*

Positioned next to a picturesque ravine, Whitewoods is a delightful Moroccan-style villa overlooking the renowned Heywoods resort and beach. The two-bedroom, two-bath main house features an airy living area accented with ferns and other tropical plants, and an adjacent dining terrace that opens onto the pool deck. A short distance away, surrounded by the lovely garden area, is a small guest cottage that provides an additional bedroom and bath, with a charming patio area of its own. Both units are cared for by an expert three-person staff. The beach is about a mile away and golf and tennis facilities are also nearby. Contact: Villa Holidays, Inc., 13100 Wayzata Blvd., Suite 150, Minneapolis, MN 55343. Call 1-800-328-6262 or 612-591-0076.

Children: Y Pets: N Smoking: Y Handicap Access: N Payment: C, P, T, V, M

ST. PHILIP

CORAL POINT 1, 2 AND 3   *Rates: deluxe*
Open: year-round   *Minimum Stay: one week*

These three brand-new villas share a large swimming pool and patio area, as well as an attentive household staff, yet offer guests total privacy and comfort. Sitting by an uncrowded and unspoiled white coral beach that positively gleams in the sun and glows in the haunting Caribbean moonlight, the units each contain three bedrooms. All have a complete kitchen and a living/dining area that opens onto a seaside terrace offering far-reaching views of the bright blue waters and quiet coastline. The interiors are handsomely furnished in white rattan and cheery tropical pastels. Contact: LaCure Villas, 11661 San Vicente Blvd., Suite 1010, Los Angeles, CA 90049. Call 1-800-387-2726.

Children: Y   Pets: N   Smoking: Y   Handicap Access: N   Payment: C, P, T

St. Thomas

ALAN BAY HOUSE   *Rates: deluxe*
Open: year-round   *Minimum Stay: one week*

Constructed of local coral stone and resting under tall palms on an acre of beautifully landscaped grounds, Alan Bay House is one of the finest properties in the prestigious Sandy Lane Beach area. The residence contains four sumptuous double bedroom suites—each with its own bathroom and dressing area—a fully equipped kitchen, large living room and a separate formal dining area that can seat up to 15, plus an enticing open patio. Tennis is available nearby and a superb 18-hole golf course is practically next door. At home, the owner's very professional staff, consisting of a butler, cook, maid, laundress and gardener, sees to it that the house is kept in tiptop shape and the guests have everything they desire. Contact: Villas International, 71 West 23rd Street, New York, NY 10010. Call 212-929-7585.

Children: Y   Pets: N   Smoking: Y   Handicap Access: N   Payment: C, P, T

BLUE MOON   *Rates: deluxe*
Open: year-round   *Minimum Stay: one week*

Containing five bedrooms to accommodate a large party of Barbados vacationers, this luxurious villa offers such exceptional features as a grand piano in the formal living room. A melange of sunny terraces surrounds the house; the dining room and a beguiling breakfast deck overlook the garden, which borders a swimming pool and gazebo. The household staff takes care of the cooking, cleaning, laundry and meal service, but guests have to supply the piano player from their own circle. Contact: LaCure Villas, 11661 San Vicente Blvd., Suite 1010, Los Angeles, CA 90049. Call 1-800-387-2726.

Children: Y   Pets: N   Smoking: Y   Handicap Access: N   Payment: C, P, T

BON VIVANT   *Rates: deluxe*
Open: year-round   *Minimum Stay: one week*

Bon Vivant is not only a palatial vacation home—it's an entire private resort for your party...and your party alone. A 50-foot swimming pool, large Jacuzzi, floodlit tennis court, basketball court, indoor racquetball court, fully equipped gymnasium, billiard room and shuffleboard area are included. One of Barbados's finest beaches, where you'll enjoy a private cabana, is only a short walk away. The accommodations are truly top drawer, with a friendly and expert staff to make your stay even more comfortable. The ten-room main house contains four bedroom suites, an open coral stone living room, kitchen and a formal dining room. A deluxe two-bedroom guest villa has a living room, dining room and kitchen of its own. Contact: Villas and Apartments Abroad, Ltd., 420 Madison Ave, New York, NY 10017. Call 1-800-433-3020 or 212-759-1025.

Children: Y   Pets: N   Smoking: Y   Handicap Access: N   Payment: C, P, T

CAMELOT *Rates: deluxe*
Open: year-round *Minimum Stay: one week*

Resting on the Sandy Lanes Estate and Golf Course, five minutes by foot from the beach, this posh villa is tended by the owner's three-person staff and offers such tempting amenities as a private floodlit tennis court, an oversized pool and patio with a Jacuzzi and sunken bar and a wide-screen satellite TV with VCR and an extensive video library. The main part of the residence features a master suite that includes a king-sized bed and a sunken whirlpool tub, two other bedrooms, a complete kitchen and spacious and airy living and dining areas that look out onto the pool and across to the golf course. A self-contained annex provides two additional bedrooms plus a sitting area and kitchenette. Contact: Vacation Home Rentals Worldwide, 235 Kensington Ave., Norwood, NJ, 07648. Call 1-800-633-3284 or 201-767-9393.

Children: Y   Pets: N   Smoking: Y   Handicap Access: N   Payment: C, P, T

CORAL STONE COTTAGE *Rates: deluxe*
Open: year-round *Minimum Stay: one week*

This quality cottage enjoys a delightfully secluded location that also happens to lie by magnificent St. James Beach in the heart of Barbados's "Platinum Coast," which offers the clearest, gentlest water and most unspoiled shoreline on the island. Visitors never seem to tire of the recreational opportunities available here, from swimming, sailing and windsurfing to scuba diving and snorkeling. Active guests truly appreciate the total relaxation provided at the house encircled by tropical trees and shrubs, which features two bedrooms, a living and dining room that open onto a beachside patio, plus a staff that tends to all domestic chores. Contact: LaCure Villas, 11661 San Vicente Blvd., Suite 1010, Los Angeles, CA 90049. Call 1-800-387-2726.

Children: Y   Pets: N   Smoking: Y   Handicap Access: N   Payment: C, P, T

CORAL STONE HOUSE *Rates: deluxe*
Open: year-round *Minimum Stay: one week*

Positioned on St. James Beach, where there are some of the gentlest waters and finest aquatic sport facilities available in the entire Caribbean, this traditional coral stone house contains three bedrooms and baths, a complete kitchen and a large parlor and dining room. A roomy and plushly furnished patio adjacent to the living areas commands wonderful views of the ocean and coastline. Tended by a cook, maid, laundress and gardener, the residence combines the casual ease of home living with the convenience and indulgence of a full-service vacation accommodation. Contact: LaCure Villas, 11661 San Vicente Blvd., Suite 1010, Los Angeles, CA 90049. Call 1-800-387-2726.

Children: Y   Pets: N   Smoking: Y   Handicap Access: N   Payment: C, P, T

ELBA   *Rates: deluxe*
Open: year-round   *Minimum Stay: one week*

Guests staying at this outstanding home have private use of a cabana—provided with deck chairs, a refrigerator and other handy amenities—at the Property Owner's Beach adjacent to the Sandy Lane Hotel. The residence itself, just a few minutes' walk from the shore on the seventh tee of the resort's celebrated golf course, is maintained by a full housekeeping staff. It includes four bedrooms and a complete kitchen. The spacious living room and den area lead out onto a large, bright deck and swimming pool bordered by expertly tended gardens. The excellent view is of the island's picturesque west coast. Contact: Villas International, 71 West 23rd Street, New York, NY 10010. Call 212-929-7585.

Children: Y   Pets: N   Smoking: Y   Handicap Access: N   Payment: C, P, T

FAIRWAYS   *Rates: deluxe*
Open: year-round   *Minimum Stay: one week*

Located at the seventh tee of the Sandy Lane Golf Course, Barbados's premiere golfing facility, this choice single-story home is also close to a wide variety of other land and sea recreational opportunities. The three-bedroom residence featuring stylish rattan furniture includes a spacious living room that opens onto a beautiful patio, where there's a furnished gazebo beside the swimming pool. While a cook, along with a housekeeper, comes with the property to prepare meals in the very well-equipped kitchen, guests may certainly fix a bite for themselves. Better yet, try out one of the terrific restaurants in the area that specialize in characteristic Bajan cuisine specialties, like flying fish and Barbadian lobster, known as langouste. Contact: LaCure Villas, 11661 San Vicente Blvd., Suite 1010, Los Angeles, CA 90049. Call 1-800-387-2726.

Children: Y   Pets: N   Smoking: Y   Handicap Access: N   Payment: C, P, T

LA VISTA   *Rates: deluxe*
Open: year-round   *Minimum Stay: one week*

This two-floor Colonial villa is ideally situated in an area that features some of the best recreational facilities on Barbados. Golf, tennis, biking, hiking and, of course, a full array of water sports—swimming, fishing, sailing, diving and snorkeling, to mention a few—are all available nearby. Decorated in traditional island resort style and surrounded by meticulously maintained grounds, the house contains three bedrooms, a very well-appointed kitchen and a spacious living room that adjoins a patio by a shimmering swimming pool. Contact: LaCure Villas, 11661 San Vicente Blvd., Suite 1010, Los Angeles, CA 90049. Call 1-800-387-2726.

Children: Y   Pets: N   Smoking: Y   Handicap Access: N   Payment: C, P, T

LANDOVERY *Rates: deluxe*
Open: year-round *Minimum Stay: one week*
Providing a large family or group of friends the opportunity to savor a Caribbean holiday in high style, this regal villa contains five attractively furnished bedrooms, each with a private bath. The highlight of the interior is a magnificent foyer featuring a lush indoor garden and a tiny brook. Outside, the pool is a perfect place for the whole gang to gather and get a little sun and exercise, while the covered patio and several inviting open terraces offer panoramic views of the ocean and vibrant Caribbean sunsets. The staff, including a cook, maid, laundress and gardener, see to the house while guests enjoy the grounds and the matchless recreational opportunities and scenic pleasures of Barbados. Contact: LaCure Villas, 11661 San Vicente Blvd., Suite 1010, Los Angeles, CA 90049. Call 1-800-387-2726.
Children: **Y**   Pets: **N**   Smoking: **Y**   Handicap Access: **N**   Payment: **C, P, T**

LEAMINGTON PAVILION AND BEACH COTTAGE *Rates: deluxe*
Open: year-round *Minimum Stay: one week*
Available to be rented separately or together, these two beach residences offer palatial accommodations for up to ten, served by a skillful staff that includes a butler, maid, cook, gardener and laundress. The classical-style pavilion, recently extended and completely refurbished, features four bedrooms—each with its own newly fitted marble bath— a complete kitchen, baroque formal dining room and a large drawing room that opens onto a dazzling pergola and terrace. In addition, there's a roof deck that commands fantastic views of the Caribbean coastline and a garden parlor flanking the sparkling pool. The garden leads directly onto the pristine sand beach, where, behind a private gate, a one-bedroom cottage is situated, surrounded by enticing terraces of its own. Contact: Villas International, 71 West 23rd Street, New York, NY 10010. Call 212-929-7585.
Children: **Y**   Pets: **N**   Smoking: **Y**   Handicap Access: **N**   Payment: **C, P, T**

MOONSTRUCK *Rates: expensive-deluxe*
Open: year-round *Minimum Stay: one week*
Constructed out of island coral stone, this engaging seaside house contains such delightful and distinctive features as golden pickled pine floors and ceilings and an indoor garden that brings the gorgeous foliage and the scents of Barbados's sublime tropical vegetation right into the home. The residence consists of two comfortable bedrooms and baths, a well-equipped kitchen where the housekeeper will prepare all meals and a pleasant living and dining area located next to the garden. Both the living room and master suite open onto a dazzling sun deck that leads right out to the white sands of the immaculate beach. Contact: LaCure Villas, 11661 San Vicente Blvd., Suite 1010, Los Angeles, CA 90049. Call 1-800-387-2726.
Children: **Y**   Pets: **N**   Smoking: **Y**   Handicap Access: **N**   Payment: **C, P, T**

SANDY LANE BEACHFRONT ESTATE   *Rates: deluxe*
Open: year-round   *Minimum Stay: one week*

Four handsome buildings tended by a staff of five make up this striking
beachfront estate located in the prestigious Sandy Lane area. The main
villa features three deluxe bedroom suites, a fully equipped kitchen
and a formal living room and dining room, both containing exquisite
furnishings. A lovely arcade terrace and bar area sit next to the pool
and gardens, which are dotted with graceful sculpture. Set apart from
the main house, there's a modest two-bedroom, two-bath cottage perfect for the kids. Excellent golf and tennis are within a quarter mile,
while a host of recreational activities on the Caribbean can be pursued
practically right at the doorstep. Contact: Patti Slavin, Prestige Villa,
1140 Post Road, Fairfield, CT 06430. Call 1-800-336-0080 or 203-254-
1302. Ref. B217.

Children: Y   Pets: N   Smoking: Y   Handicap Access: Y   Payment: C, P, T

WINDRUSH   *Rates: deluxe*
Open: year-round   *Minimum Stay: one week*

Windrush is a bright, open-plan two-story villa that lies by one of the
rich emerald fairways of the Sandy Lane Golf Course. Containing a
master suite on the second floor and two other bedrooms downstairs,
the coral stone house features a nicely furnished living room, separate
dining room and a large, inviting patio area that overlooks the pool.
The owner's staff handles cooking and other housekeeping chores and,
as a seductive extra feature, a private cabana equipped with lounge
chairs and a refrigerator is also included with the property at the nearby
beach facility. Contact: Rent A Home International, Inc., 7200 34th
Avenue NW, Seattle, WA 98117. Call 206-545-6963.

Children: Y Pets: N Smoking: Y Handicap Access: N Payment: C, P, T, V, M

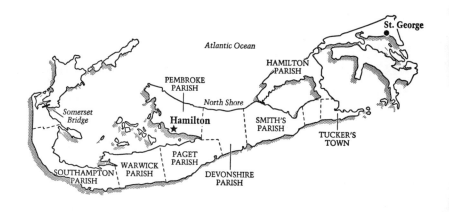

St. George

Atlantic Ocean

HAMILTON
PARISH

PEMBROKE
PARISH

North Shore

Somerset
Bridge

Hamilton
★

SMITH'S
PARISH

TUCKER'S
TOWN

PAGET
PARISH

WARWICK
PARISH

SOUTHAMPTON
PARISH

DEVONSHIRE
PARISH

Bermuda

DEVONSHIRE PARISH

CONNEMARA   *Rates: deluxe*
Open: year-round   *Minimum Stay: one week*

The green, gentle scenery in Bermuda is reminiscent of parts of
Ireland—perhaps that accounts for the name of this three-bedroom
house in the center of Bermuda. But the sunshine and semi-tropical
greenery are unique to this island. The air-conditioned master bedroom has an en suite bathroom; one of two twin bedrooms is also
air-conditioned. There is a well-equipped kitchen, an additional guest
bathroom, and maid and laundry service is provided. The living room
opens onto a patio, a perfect place to sunbathe or take morning coffee,
and there is a separate dining room. With easy access to Hamilton and
to golf and tennis clubs, visitors will find plenty to keep the days and
nights full. Contact: L.P. Gutteridge Ltd., P.O. Box HM 1024, Hamilton, Bermuda HM DX. Call 809-295-4545.

Children: Y   Pets: N   Smoking: Y   Handicap Access: N   Payment: C, T

OLD HOMESTEAD APARTMENT   *Rates: inexpensive*
Open: year-round   *Minimum Stay: one week*

Just five minutes by bus from the capital city of Hamilton and fifteen
minutes from the beaches, this charming, private apartment has its
own entrance and a garden filled with semi-tropical plants. The
kitchen is extra large, and there is a separate living room. The entrance
foyer leads to a terrace where guests can relax and sunbathe. The

bedroom has twin beds and the bathroom is equipped with a luxurious Jacuzzi tub. Air conditioned throughout, the house comes with house-keeping, although electricity is extra. Contact: Shirley B. Collier, Sherwood Building, 63 Pitts Bay Rd., Hamilton, Bermuda HM 08. Call 809-295-5487.

Children: Y   Pets: N   Smoking: Y   Handicap Access: N   Payment: C, T

SEVEN CEDARS   *Rates: expensive*
Open: year-round   *Minimum Stay: one week*

Centrally located in Devonshire, Seven Cedars is equidistant from both the north and south shores, making it central for swimming, scuba diving, windsurfing, boating and fishing. The house can sleep up to six guests in three double bedrooms and two bathrooms. The living room is attractive and comfortable; the dining room is separate. The kitchen is fully equipped, including a washing machine and dryer (a maid will do household laundry and cleaning). Contact: L.P. Gutteridge Ltd., P.O. Box HM 1024, Hamilton, Bermuda HM DX. Call 809-295-4545.

Children: Y   Pets: N   Smoking: Y   Handicap Access: N   Payment: C, T

HAMILTON PARISH

CLEAR VIEW   *Rates: inexpensive-expensive*
Open: year-round   *Minimum Stay: none*

Deep, thick carpets, homey furnishings and large glass doors facing the ocean will greet you here at the Clear View suites, each located in a multi-unit villa at the water's edge. Facilities for guests are extensive—babysitting, meal service, conference rooms, a tennis court, snorkeling equipment, washing machines and daily maid service. Special services include honeymoon holidays and unique "painting holidays" with instruction, workshops and tours. Refresh yourself in one of the two pools or down at the lovely Shelley Bay Beach, or create an informal dinner at the barbecue. The suites have full kitchen facilities, air conditioning, telephone, radio and television. Contact: Ruth Paynter or Carol Lee, Clear View, Sandy Lane, Hamilton Parish CR 02, Bermuda. Call 809-293-0484 or 800-468-9600.

Children: Y   Pets: N   Smoking: Y   Handicap Access: N   Payment: All

PAGET PARISH

BACKGAMMON   *Rates: deluxe*
Open: year-round   *Minimum Stay: one week*

This huge house is suitable for a large group or family, since it can accommodate up to ten guests. The swimming pool is surrounded by a welcoming patio, a pool room, bathroom and showers. A set of French doors lead inside to a large family room with a fireplace and hidden bar; a separate living room also has a fireplace and large windows with a view of the grounds and the pool. The dining room makes a wonderful place to entertain. In addition to the five bedrooms and five bathrooms, there is a fully equipped kitchen and a private den for quiet moments. Maid service is provided, as are pool and garden maintenance. Located near Hamilton Harbour, the house gives guests easy access to the ferry that takes them to shopping or dining. There is boating and swimming in the harbor as well as a few miles south on the shore. Contact: L.P. Gutteridge Ltd., P.O. Box HM 1024, Hamilton, Bermuda HM DX. Call 809-295-4545.

Children: Y   Pets: N   Smoking: Y   Handicap Access: N   Payment: C, T

FOURWAYS INN *Rates: expensive-deluxe*
Open: year-round *Minimum Stay: four nights*

Shades of pastel highlighted with the brilliant hues of subtropical flowers characterize this lovely inn, originally built in 1727. Now a collection of buildings on a private estate, the inn offers double and deluxe suites as well as two-bedroom cottages set in a garden hillside. Each climate-controlled accommodation is furnished in contemporary rattan, with beamed ceilings and sliding doors that open onto private furnished terraces. The inn's hospitality includes fresh flowers, complimentary robes and slippers, hair dryers, a TV and mini-kitchens; each day fresh croissants, pastries and coffee are delivered to your doorstep. The premises house a freshwater pool, a terrace bar and restaurants serving afternoon tea and gourmet meals. Contact: Olympia Corrent, Fourways Inn, P.O. Box PG 294, Paget PG BX, Bermuda. Call 809-236-6517 or 800-962-7654.

Children: N   Pets: N   Smoking: Y   Handicap Access: N   Payment: All

GREENBANK GUEST HOUSE *Rates: budget-inexpensive*
Open: year-round *Minimum Stay: none*

The main house at Greenbank is more than two hundred years old and contains cedar beams once used as ballast in sailing ships. The cottages and apartments here are quiet and relaxing, with fully equipped kitchenettes and porches that overlook the Great Sound and the city of Hamilton, which can be reached by the ferry just steps away. The furnishings are elegant and reflect the quaint charm so characteristic of Bermuda. You can choose from waterside or gardenside cottages, and there is a yacht charter and boat rental facility on the premises. Great Sound is ideal for boating and swimming, and Greenbank has its own swimming dock. A comfortable common sitting room with TV is provided for the guests' use, and there are barbecue facilities if you care to cook a casual meal. Maid and linen service is provided daily. Contact: Cindy Ashton, Greenback Guest House, Salt Kettle Road, P.O. Box PG 201, Paget PG BX, Bermuda. Call 809-236-3615.

Children: Y   Pets: N   Smoking: Y   Handicap: N   Payment: C, P, T, V, M, A

HORIZONS AND COTTAGES *Rates: expensive-deluxe*
Open: year-round *Minimum Stay: five nights*

A traditional 25-acre estate is the location of these eleven cottages, ranging in size from one to four bedrooms. The beautifully decorated cottages are secluded amid the terrace gardens, yet have full access to the estate pool, golf course, putting green and tennis courts. Maid service includes breakfast on your own private terrace. If you decide not to cook, barbecues and restaurant meals are available either on the estate or ten minutes away in Hamilton. Special events at the estate include live entertainment, calypso music and dancing by the pool. The staff will gladly arrange sailing, waterskiing, scuba diving and fishing expeditions and direct you to the beach that best suits your preference—whether lively or private. Contact: Horizons and Cottages, P.O. Box PG 198, Paget PG BX, Bermuda. Call 809-236-0048 or 800-468-0022.

Children: Y   Pets: N   Smoking: Y   Handicap Access: N   Payment: C, T

SALT KETTLE HOUSE   *Rates: inexpensive*
Open: year-round   *Minimum Stay: none*

Studio apartments and one- and two-bedroom cottages are available here in a pleasant collection of green-shuttered white buildings. The cottages are on the waterfront and all have kitchens, although many guests choose to dine in the guest dining room and lounge; a breakfast plan can also be arranged. Maid and linen service is provided, and there are beautiful shaded grounds, balconies and patios on which to relax and sunbathe. Boating and swimming facilities are located on the premises, and golf and tennis can be arranged. The ferry to Hamilton is just a two-minute walk; in this captial city you'll find shopping, historic buildings and fine restaurants. Contact: Hazel Lowe, Salt Kettle House, Paget 6-10, Bermuda. Call 809-236-0407.

Children: Y   Pets: N   Smoking: Y   Handicap Access: N   Payment: C, P, T

SKY TOP COTTAGES   *Rates: budget-inexpensive*
Open: year-round   *Minimum Stay: none*

A lush emerald hilltop high above Paget's shoreline houses these English-style cottages named after garden flowers—Pink Coralita, Morning Glory and Allamanda, to name just a few. The apartments range from one-bedroom units with kitchens and sitting rooms to studios with minimal but sufficient kitchen facilities. Each apartment is air-conditioned and decorated in an exceptionally tasteful manner, with thick carpets and comfortable chairs and couches. Daily maid service and frequent linen service keep the apartments clean and bright. The gardens stretch out in each direction, and a citrus grove offers ripe oranges and grapefruits in winter months for guests to pick themselves. Contact: Marion Stubbs, Sky Top Cottages, P.O. Box PG 227, Paget PG BX, Bermuda. Call 809-236-7984.

Children: Y   Pets: N   Smoking: Y   Handicap Access: N   Payment: C, T, V, M

SUN TRAP   *Rates: expensive*
Open: year-round   *Minimum Stay: one week*

Some of Bermuda's most striking pink beaches are located along the south shore of Paget's Parish, just ten minutes from this two-bedroom, two-bathroom house. Within easy access of Hamilton and its harbor, the house is also close to the botanical gardens, Paget Marsh Nature Reserve and Hungry Bay, popular with fishermen and naturalists alike. It has a living room with a fireplace, a separate dining room, two bedrooms and a kitchen and laundry room. One bedroom has a spacious king-size bed; the other is a twin bedroom, making Sun Trap a good family choice. Air conditioning keeps the house cool; the housekeeper comes by on a weekly basis. There are several golf and tennis clubs close by, and the south shore waters are ideal for snorkeling and swimming. Contact: Shirley B. Collier, Sherwood Building, 63 Pitts Bay Rd., Hamilton, Bermuda HM 08. Call 809-295-5487.

Children: Y   Pets: N   Smoking: Y   Handicap Access: N   Payment: C, T

THE PARAQUET   *Rates: inexpensive*
Open: year-round   *Minimum Stay: none*
The four efficiency units here can accommodate up to four guests in modern surroundings. Each unit has a small kitchenette, a bathroom and a living room/bedroom with a TV, plus a shared courtyard with lounge chairs, umbrellas and barbecue facilities. Daily maid and linen service is provided, and there are nearby supermarkets to meet your shopping needs. Golf, tennis, water sports and boating facilities are available on the island, and a bus stops right in front of the hotel restaurant. The south shore beaches are within walking or cycling distance, as is a swimming pool. Contact: Jean D. Rego, The Paraquet, South Shore Rd., P.O. Box PG 173, Paget PG BX, Bermuda. Call 809-236-5842.

Children: Y   Pets: N   Smoking: Y   Handicap Access: N   Payment: C, T

WHITE SANDS   *Rates: expensive-deluxe*
Open: March-January   *Minimum Stay: three nights*
Stone walls lined with pink blossoms lead up from the pool area to a white-shuttered pink building that houses the main hotel. For those who prefer more privacy, there are cottages for either four or six guests that can be rented with or without a meal plan at the hotel. The two- and three-bedroom cottages are air conditioned; maid and linen service is provided. The hotel offers a variety of entertainment, including festive island barbecues, evening buffets, live shows and a cozy Old English pub, as well as a dining room that serves continental and American cuisine. Golf, tennis and all water sports are minutes away, as are the beaches of the south shore. Hamilton can be reached by bus, motor scooter or taxi. Contact: Elaine M. Wragg, White Sands, P.O. Box PG 174, Paget PG BX, Bermuda. Call 809-236-2023 or 800-548-0547.

Children: Y Pets: N Smoking: Y Handicap Access: N Payment: C, T, V, M, A

PEMBROKE PARISH

MARULA GUEST APARTMENTS   *Rates: budget-moderate*
Open: year-round   *Minimum Stay: none*
Louise and Henry DeSilva are your hosts at this small, informal guest hotel created from a traditional waterside Bermudian home. The main house is divided into one- and two-bedroom apartments, and there is a separate two-bedroom cottage for extra privacy. Ceiling fans and ocean breezes cool the apartments, and each one has a telephone, TV and daily maid service (except Sunday). Spacious grounds, barbecue

facilities and a swimming pool are yours to enjoy at will, and there is a dock just steps away. For tennis and golf enthusiasts, there are good facilities nearby; windsurfing, sailing and fishing are all easily accessible. Hamilton, a busy capital with British charm, is a five-minute ride from Marula, and a little swimming cove that's sure to delight visitors is within walking distance. Contact: Louise DeSilva, Marula Guest Apartments, 17 Mariners Lane, Pembroke W. HM CX, Bermuda. Call 809-295-2893.

Children: Y Pets: N Smoking: Y Handicap Access: N Payment: C, P, T, V, M

PLEASANT VIEW GUEST HOUSE *Rates: budget-inexpensive*
Open: year-round *Minimum Stay: one week*
This contemporary house is located on the north shore within fifteen minutes of Hamilton. From the lawn and the patio, guests can enjoy good ocean views; the beach is within walking distance. Inside are several studio apartments and twin guest rooms, all carpeted throughout and cooled by air conditioning as well as ceiling fans, each with private bathroom and access to a communal kitchen. There is a common lounge overlooking the ocean, where guests can relax with a book or watch TV; each bedroom also has a TV, clock radio and telephone. Just outside the door is a heated swimming pool; all meal plans can be arranged, including weekly summer barbecues. Contact: Robert Reid Assoc., Inc., Reservation Center, 10606 Burt Circle, Omaha, NE 68114. Call 800-223-6510 or 402-498-4307.

Children: Y   Pets: N   Smoking: Y   Handicap Access: N   Payment: C, T

ROBIN'S NEST *Rates: inexpensive*
Open: year-round *Minimum Stay: two nights*
Robin's Nest is a casual group of apartments in a quiet residential area on the North Shore Road, about five minutes from the city of Hamilton. Nestled in a valley and surrounded by greenery, each one-bedroom apartment has its own yard. Decorated in warm tones and wicker or wooden furniture, with tiled floors and ceiling fans, the apartments are air conditioned and have cable TV and telephone. The outdoor area makes a quiet place to sit, and a recently built fresh-washer pool invites you to take a plunge. Maid and linen service are included. On the beaches of the nearby shore are snorkeling in calm, clear waters, waterskiing and sailing. Golf and tennis are extremely popular on the island and the facilities are good. Contact: Milt and Terri Robinson, Robin's Nest, 10 Vale Close, Pembroke West HM 04, Bermuda. Call 809-292-4347 or 800-292-4347.

Children: Y   Pets: N   Smoking: Y   Handicap Access: N   Payment: C, T

ROSEMONT *Rates: inexpensive-moderate*
Open: year-round *Minimum Stay: none*
You'll find this collection of garden and poolside units on the crest of a hill overlooking Hamilton Harbour toward the Great Sound. The capital city, with its shops, historic sites and restaurants, is just a ten-minute walk away. Each air-conditioned unit has a bedroom, a living area, a kitchenette and private bathroom; daily maid service is

included. The poolside units are arranged on two stories, each with a private balcony or patio—some are designed to accommodate wheelchairs. The garden units are sunny semi-detached cottages, each with a private entrance. The decor is colorful and each unit has cable TV; deliveries of groceries can be arranged with the local supermarket. Contact: Scott Calder International, 152 Madison Ave., New York, NY 10016. Call 212-889-0761 or 800-221-2335.

Children: **Y**   Pets: **N**   Smoking: **Y**   Handicap Access: **N**   Payment: **C, T**

SMITHS PARISH

ANGEL'S GROTTO   *Rates: budget-inexpensive*
Open: year-round   *Minimum Stay: one week*

Nestled on the shore of Harrington Sound with a walled patio that overlooks the sea, this cluster of traditional Bermudian cottages contains one- and two-bedroom apartments. Each apartment has its own kitchenette and bathroom, and a private quiet setting with access to the house's main facilities. A barbecue and swimming area are for all to enjoy, as are the wonderful views from the patio facing the turquoise water. Guests can indulge in snorkeling and fishing; not far away is the Castle Harbour Hotel, Golf and Country Club for golf and tennis. Among the beaches within walking distance are John Smiths Bay and Devil's Hole, where sharks and turtles swim side by side. Explore the limestone caves of Harrington Sound. Contact: Daisy Hart, Butterfield Travel Ltd., 75 Front Street, Hamilton HM 12, Bermuda. Call 809-295-6437.

Children: **Y** Pets: **N** Smoking: **Y** Handicap Access: **N** Payment: **C, T, V, M, A**

BEAU SOLEIL   *Rates: budget-inexpensive*
Open: year-round   *Minimum Stay: one week*

A charming house between Harrington Sound and the south coast, Beau Soleil is perfect for a honeymoon or a romantic getaway. A high-raftered living room connects through sliding glass doors to an outdoor dining terrace. The kitchen is small but well equipped with all major appliances and a toaster/broiler. The bedroom is cooled by air conditioning and has a queen-size bed; there is also a bath with shower. All utilities, daily maid service and household laundry service are included. With Harrington Sound to one side of the parish and the pink sands of Bermuda's beaches to the south, visitors will find endless opportunities for swimming, boating, windsurfing and waterskiing. Contact: L.P. Gutteridge Ltd., P.O. Box HM 1024, Hamilton, Bermuda HM DX. Call 809-295-4545.

Children: **Y**   Pets: **N**   Smoking: **Y**   Handicap Access: **N**   Payment: **C, T**

CABANA   *Rates: inexpensive*
Open: year-round   *Minimum Stay: four nights*

A gracious old home built 200 years ago by a Bermudian fisherman and farmer, Cabana has been transformed into private guest apartments without losing many of its original details. Sid or Annette will pick you up from the airport and perhaps give you a little tour to show you how Cabana is central both to Hamilton, the aquarium, Flatts Village and the pink beaches of the south shore. This personal attention continues throughout your stay, in the form of advice and arrangements for barbecues, motor scooters, golf, tennis and water sports. The apartments are air conditioned and have ceiling fans in the double bedrooms; the kitchens are stocked with all necessary appliances and utensils. A maid comes daily to tidy up and change the linens. A coral-walled common room has a TV and games, and there is a freshwater swimming pool on the grounds. Contact: Sid Rumbelow, Cabana, P.O. Box FL 40, Smiths FL BX, Bermuda. Call 809-236-6964.

Children: Y Pets: N Smoking: Y Handicap Access: N Payment: C, T, V, M, A

HOLLY ACRES   *Rates: deluxe*
Open: year-round   *Minimum Stay: one week*

This private house in Smiths Parish is an equal distance from the north shore and Harrington Sound, with access to tennis and golf as well as fishing, boating and water sports in the sound and open sea. The modern kitchen is extra large and well equipped and features a breakfast nook. Games galore are stocked in the family room, along with a bar and a cozy fireplace—families will find this house exceptionally well suited to their needs. In total, there are four double bedrooms and four bathrooms; the living room has an additional fireplace and windows that overlook the water. A swimming pool on the grounds means that guests can swim or relax without going down to the beach. Contact: L.P. Gutteridge Ltd., P.O. Box HM 1024, Hamilton, Bermuda HM DX. Call 809-295-4545.

Children: Y   Pets: N   Smoking: Y   Handicap Access: N   Payment: C, T

LANGKASUKA   *Rates: deluxe*
Open: year-round   *Minimum Stay: one week*

Huge windows in the living areas and bedrooms of this spacious air-conditioned house provide views of Harrington Sound, just minutes from the south shore's pink bathing beaches and turquoise waters so ideal for snorkeling and scuba diving. The formal dining room makes a wonderful place to entertain, leading onto an extensive veranda carefully furnished for outdoor living. The living room opens off the dining room, and there is a big kitchen, a laundry room and separate bathroom for the maid (whose service is included). The master bedroom has a bathroom en suite, and there is another bathroom and two more double bedrooms. Contact: L.P. Gutteridge Ltd., P.O. Box HM 1024, Hamilton, Bermuda HM DX. Call 809-295-4545.

Children: Y   Pets: N   Smoking: Y   Handicap Access: N   Payment: C, T

MELROSE   *Rates: expensive*
Open: year-round   *Minimum Stay: one week*

Located on the South Shore Road high above the dazzling ocean, this house offers views that will take your breath away. The master bedroom has a king-size bed; it and the twin bedroom have en suite bathrooms and are air conditioned. The sun room makes a perfectly charming place to sit and read the local paper (which actually has a section entitled "Bermuda Shorts"), and the living room has the wonderful luxury of a fireplace. The kitchen and laundry room are modern, and the housekeeper comes by once a week (cooking can be arranged separately). The clifftop grounds are extensive and private, cooled by breezes that come in off the ocean, and the pink beaches of the south shore are a ten-minute ride away. Contact: Shirley B. Collier, Sherwood Building, 63 Pitts Bay Rd., Hamilton, Bermuda HM 08. Call 809-295-5487.

Children: Y   Pets: N   Smoking: Y   Handicap Access: N   Payment: C, T

POUND FOOLISH   *Rates: deluxe*
Open: year-round   *Minimum Stay: one week*
This long, low house is set on a hillside overlooking Tuckers Town and Smiths Shore. It faces to the southeast and is well protected from northerly winds, making swimming in the spacious pool and sunbathing on the lawn a year-round pleasure. Centrally heated for cooler months and air conditioned for the hot days of summer, there is also a toasty fireplace inside. Four double bedrooms, four bathrooms, a large living room, a sunny dining room, a den and a kitchen complete the floor plan; there is a porch adjacent to the dining room for outdoor meals. A maid comes daily to clean and to order food and liquor, both of which are delivered. Two miles away is the Mid Ocean Club, and four miles away is the bustling capital of Hamilton. Contact: Villas International, 71 West 23rd St., New York, NY 10010. Call 212-929-7585.

Children: Y   Pets: N   Smoking: Y   Handicap Access: N   Payment: C, P, T

SEA VIEW   *Rates: deluxe*
Open: year-round   *Minimum Stay: one week*
The carefully tended garden is just one of the exceptional features you'll enjoy at this hillside villa. Floor-length windows and a door of glass provide fabulous views from the formal dining room, and connect the living room to a patio with its swimming pool. Two upstairs double bedrooms and one downstairs by the pool terrace are all air conditioned; there is also a den and a kitchen upstairs. The marble floors and the furnishings—antique pieces graciously interspersed with glass and chrome—are exquisite. Central heating warms the hallways and main rooms, and a fireplace graces the living room. Maid service is provided on weekdays, and the gardens and pool are carefully maintained. From the house the views stretch out over Harrington Sound and the south shore. Contact: Villas International, 71 West 23rd St., New York, NY 10010. Call 212-929-7585.

Children: Y   Pets: N   Smoking: Y   Handicap Access: N   Payment: C, P, T

TOP OF THE MARKET   *Rates: deluxe*
Open: year-round   *Minimum Stay: one week*
The swimming pool here is kidney-shaped and makes a wonderful place to sit next to and relax. Close to Harrington Sound and the south shore, Top of the Market is an inland house that provides good views, especially from the living room. The formal dining room and fully equipped kitchen make this house well suited for entertaining or for-

mal dinner parties—a maid will do the washing up and household laundry for you. Like the rest of the house, the four double bedrooms are air conditioned, and there is a total of three full bathrooms. Pool maintenance is included in your rates; golf and tennis are available at local clubs, some of which accept nonmembers. Contact: L.P. Gutteridge Ltd., P.O. Box HM 1024, Hamilton, Bermuda HM DX. Call 809-295-4545.

Children: Y   Pets: N   Smoking: Y   Handicap Access: N   Payment: C, T

SOMERSET BRIDGE

SOMERSET BRIDGE HOTEL   *Rates: inexpensive-expensive*
Open: year round   *Minimum Stay: none*

Within view of the world's smallest drawbridge, this hotel is tucked away on the southwestern part of the island on 250 feet of waterfront. The bay is dotted with pleasure and fishing boats, and glass-bottomed tour boats are available to take guests to the Sea Gardens or coral reefs. Hundreds of shipwrecks can be seen by scuba divers, and the hotel has a dive shop and scuba-diving instructors. The units have a kitchenette, bathroom, private balconies, carpeting throughout and air conditioning for your comfort. Daily maid and linen service is provided, and babysitting can be arranged. The hotel has a good-sized swimming pool and a recently built spa on the premises; sailing, windsurfing, tennis and golf are all readily available. Contact: Karen Roberts-Ray, Somerset Bridge Hotel, P.O. Box SB 149, Sandys SB BX, Bermuda. Call 809-234-1042 or 800-468-5501.

Children: Y   Pets: N   Smoking: Y   Handicap: N   Payment: C, T, V, M, A, O

SOUTHAMPTON PARISH

CHANCE IT COTTAGES   *Rates: inexpensive-expensive*
Open: year-round   *Minimum Stay: none*

Each of these private cottages has its own name and character—among them Quiet Waters, Moonrise, Whale Watch and Moonglow. Each has its own entrance, kitchenette and bathroom, and maid and linen service is provided daily. A saltwater whirlpool spa is perched on the hillside looking out over the ocean; there is also a sun deck, exercise room and shuffleboard on the premises. Your hosts will be happy to arrange barbecues, tennis, sailing, snorkeling or boat cruises for you on the island. Golf and tennis can be arranged at the Port Royal Club, and transportation in taxis, on motor scooters or via horse and buggy will ensure you can tour the island and visit the beaches at your leisure. Contact: Mrs. Sheila Carey, Chance It Cottages, 43 Granaway Heights Rd., P.O. Box SN 75, Southampton SN BX, Bermuda. Call 809-238-0372.

Children: Y Pets: N Smoking: Y Handicap Access: N Payment: C, T, V, M, A

LAURALI   *Rates: deluxe*
Open: year-round   *Minimum Stay: one week*

Close to Bermuda's most popular beach (Horseshoe Bay) as well as several fine resorts, golf courses and restaurants, Laurali is an exclu sive home commanding views in all directions. The two master bedrooms have private baths—one has a queen-size bed and a whirlpool; the other has twin beds. There are two other twin bedrooms and a bathroom upstairs; all four bedrooms have private balconies. Downstairs is a living room with a fireplace and comfortable couches, a dining room, an eat-in kitchen, a den with TV and a pool room with a fourth bathroom. The patio and free-form pool are surrounded by a low stone railing, beyond which are uninterrupted views over the ocean. Maid service is included, and the grounds are tended by a gardener. One hundred steps lead down to a secluded little beach in Cross Bay Cove. Contact: Villas International, 71 West 23rd St., New York, NY 10010. Call 212-929-7585

Children: Y   Pets: N   Smoking: Y   Handicap Access: N   Payment: C, P, T

WINDGAGE   *Rates: deluxe*
Open: year-round   *Minimum Stay: one week*

This large three-bedroom house includes a separate cottage with a twin bedroom and bath. The raised dining room has good views of the ocean, and there is a large living room with a fireplace for cozy and comfortable evenings spent at home. The master bedroom, a second double bedroom and a twin bedroom each have private baths. A fully equipped kitchen and laundry room complete the house. Located near the beaches of the south shore and Devil's Hole in Harrington Sound, the house situates guests near plenty of scenic spots and little coves for swimming and sunbathing. Contact: L.P. Gutteridge Ltd., P.O. Box HM 1024, Hamilton, Bermuda HM DX. Call 809-295-4545.

Children: Y   Pets: N   Smoking: Y   Handicap Access: N   Payment: C, T

St. George's

ST. GEORGE'S CLUB   *Rates: moderate-deluxe*
Open: year-round   *Minimum Stay: none*

This award-winning club is situated just outside the town of St. George's on the eastern part of the island, facing St. George's Harbour. The club's golf course covers a large area stretching up to Achilles Bay and historic Fort St. Catherine on the north shore. A selection of luxury one- and two-bedroom cottages are available here for up to six persons, with full kitchen, private bathrooms and lovely wooden balconies and patios. Barbecue facilities, TV and telephone are included, as is efficient daily maid service. The club is located in a lovely setting, carefully designed with staircases, terraces and gardens that lead down to several swimming pools and tennis courts. A private beach club offers swimming and water sports, and two delightful restaurants and a bar are on the premises. Contact: Michelle Williams or Ella Mills, Rose Hill, St. George's Club, P.O. Box GE 92, St. George's, Bermuda. Call 809-297-1200.

Children: Y Pets: N Smoking: Y Handicap Access: N Payment: C, T, V, M, A

TUCKERS TOWN

AIRBORNE *Rates: deluxe*

Open: year-round *Minimum Stay: one week*

Located near the famous Mid Ocean Club and Golf Course, Airborne is a private villa that can accommodate up to six guests. There are a total of three bedrooms—the master bedroom has an en suite bathroom and two twin bedrooms share another bathroom. A spacious living/dining area is surrounded by sliding glass doors that lead out to a shady tiled patio and lawn area—a perfect spot for late afternoon cocktails. The kitchen is fully equipped and there is an additional laundry room and maid's bathroom. The garden is carefully kept, and the maid service and normal household laundry are included. Castle Harbour is just a few minutes away, and bus or taxi service can easily transport you around the harbor to St. George's. Beaches, tennis and golf are all within easy reach. Contact: L.P. Gutteridge Ltd., P.O. Box HM 1024, Hamilton, Bermuda HM DX. Call 809-295-4545.

Children: **Y** Pets: **N** Smoking: **Y** Handicap Access: **N** Payment: **C, T**

CAREFREE *Rates: deluxe*

Open: year-round *Minimum Stay: one week*

A short walk across the road from this scenic house lies a private beach at Rock Merrell, an ideal spot for ocean swimming and snorkeling. This two-story home has four twin bedrooms and three bathrooms and is air conditioned. Carefree has a modern kitchen and laundry room, and the housekeeper is included in your rate. On cooler nights you can curl up on a comfortable couch in front of the living room fireplace or admire the crystal-clear sky studded with stars from the roof deck outside. A spacious sun room opens out onto an outdoor terrace, perfect for casual dining if you choose not to eat in the dining room. Rent some mopeds to explore Castle Harbour and St. George's, an interesting town with buildings and sites that date back hundreds of years. Contact: Shirley B. Collier, Sherwood Building, 63 Pitts Bay Rd., Hamilton, Bermuda HM 08. Call 809-295-5487.

Children: **Y** Pets: **N** Smoking: **Y** Handicap Access: **N** Payment: **C, T**

CORAL SEA *Rates: deluxe*

Open: year-round *Minimum Stay: one week*

Beside this magnificent house is a thin line of dune grass; beyond that is a coral-pink private beach and the turquoise ocean. Adjoining the Mid Ocean Club, Coral Sea offers exclusivity and comfort. Four double bedrooms, all with en suite baths, are cooled by air conditioning and overlook the sea. A sun room opens onto one of the terraces, where guests can enjoy privacy and fabulous views. An Olympic-size swimming pool and lovely grounds are carefully maintained; there is also a pool house with a barbecue for outdoor dining. The living room features a cozy brick fireplace and the bedrooms are sunny and individually decorated with charming throw rugs, divans and bedside lamps. Contact: Shirley B. Collier, Sherwood Building, 63 Pitts Bay Rd., Hamilton, Bermuda HM 08. Call 809-295-5487.

Children: **Y** Pets: **N** Smoking: **Y** Handicap Access: **N** Payment: **C, T**

GREENSLEEVES   *Rates: deluxe*
Open: year-round   *Minimum Stay: one week*

Located on Castle Harbour, not far from the Mid Ocean Club and Golf Course, this bayside home comes with a dock. Inside are three bedrooms and three bathrooms, making it perfect for three couples. The living room and the dining room are both formal and beautifully furnished; in addition, there is a bar and a separate pantry. The kitchen and laundry room are equipped with modern appliances, and maid service is included in the weekly rate. A private den provides a place for catching up on some reading, and there is a sun porch on which guests can relax and sunbathe. Tennis and golf facilities on this part of the island are excellent, and swimming and all water sports can be enjoyed on the southern shore's many beaches. Contact: L.P. Gutteridge Ltd., P.O. Box HM 1024, Hamilton, Bermuda HM DX. Call 809-295-4545.

Children: N   Pets: N   Smoking: Y   Handicap Access: N   Payment: C, T

LITTLE ROCK MERRELL   *Rates: expensive*
Open: year-round   *Minimum Stay: one week*

You'll find coral-pink sand right outside the doorstep of this charming two-bedroom cottage. Located on the South Shore Road near the best beaches in Bermuda, the cottage has an outdoor terrace that leads into the living/dining room. There are two bathrooms, and the bedrooms both have double beds; the furnishings and all kitchen appliances are modern. Ceiling fans and breezes that come directly off the ocean keep the house cool, and the housekeeper comes in weekly to straighten up. Close to the Mid Ocean Club and Bermuda's most stunning scenic wonder—the natural arches—the cottage is on the bus route within reach of several golf and tennis clubs. Contact: Shirley B. Collier, Sherwood Building, 63 Pitts Bay Rd., Hamilton, Bermuda HM 08. Call 809-295-5487.

Children: Y   Pets: N   Smoking: Y   Handicap Access: N   Payment: C, T

OLD HOUSE   *Rates: deluxe*
Open: year-round   *Minimum Stay: one week*

This two-story period house was the original Mid Ocean Club building until the club's current structure was built during the 1920s. Now it has been renovated but retains its Old World ambiance. Located on what is now the third fairway of the club's golf course, the house provides some of the wonderful views for which this course is renowned. A small private cove with a sandy beach is perfect for sunbathing and swimming. The master bedroom has a king-size bed and en suite bathroom; the two twin and one single bedrooms also have private baths. Downstairs is a refurbished modern kitchen with a breakfast nook, a cedar dining room, a formal dining room for parties and a living room with a fireplace. The housekeeper comes in twice weekly. Contact: Shirley B. Collier, Sherwood Building, 63 Pitts Bay Rd., Hamilton, Bermuda HM 08. Call 809-295-5487.

Children: Y   Pets: N   Smoking: Y   Handicap Access: N   Payment: C, T

PLAYHOUSE   *Rates: inexpensive*
Open: year-round   *Minimum Stay: one week*

A charming studio cottage with twin beds, this little house is located near the Mid Ocean Club and Golf Course on the south shore of the peninsula. There is a kitchenette for preparing meals and drinks, plus a full bathroom. The cottage is fully air conditioned, and maid service is included. Located on a hill above the club, the house puts you within easy reach of the beaches and natural arches, either on foot or by rented bicycle or motor scooter, which is the island's favorite mode of transportation. Tennis and golf facilities are located nearby, and visitors might want to watch a local game of cricket or soccer at one of the nearby sports clubs. Contact: L.P. Gutteridge Ltd., P.O. Box HM 1024, Hamilton, Bermuda HM DX. Call 809-295-4545.

Children: Y   Pets: N   Smoking: Y   Handicap Access: N   Payment: C, T

ROCK MERRELL   *Rates: deluxe*
Open: year-round   *Minimum Stay: one week*

A spacious beach house that can accommodate up to ten guests, Rock Merrell is perfect for a casual sun and surf vacation. With its own private beach and within easy reach of golf, tennis and boating facilities, the house appeals to the active, but a spacious living room and outdoor terrace tempt others to relax and enjoy the temperate weather. The sleeping accommodations consist of four twin bedrooms and one double bedroom. Five bathrooms and a full kitchen and laundry keep the housekeeper busy five days a week. There is a separate dining room that, like the living room, opens onto the terrace, so cooling ocean breezes can supplement the ceiling fans. Contact: Shirley B. Collier, Sherwood Building, 63 Pitts Bay Rd., Hamilton, Bermuda HM 08. Call 809-295-5487.

Children: Y   Pets: N   Smoking: Y   Handicap Access: N   Payment: C, T

SEASCAPE   *Rates: deluxe*
Open: year-round   *Minimum Stay: one week*

A period home with plenty of room, Seascape can sleep up to ten guests in its five bedrooms with en suite baths. Most of the windows face a pink beach and the ocean. Both the dining room and the living room open onto a terrace, and the grounds and grassy terraces are pleasant and inviting. The kitchen is modern and large, with laundry facilities and a separate pantry, which you'll need, since the house can accommodate up to ten guests. A housekeeper is on duty five days a week. Just a few minutes away is Bermuda's most striking natural wonder, the arches. Tuckers Town houses the famous Mid Ocean Club, which has one of the area's many golf courses. Contact: Shirley B. Collier, Sherwood Building, 63 Pitts Bay Rd., Hamilton, Bermuda HM 08. Call 809-295-5487.

Children: Y   Pets: N   Smoking: Y   Handicap Access: N   Payment: C, T

TREE TOPS *Rates: deluxe*
Open: year-round *Minimum Stay: one week*
Located on the south shore of Tuckers Town, this four-bedroom house is a truly luxurious vacation accommodation. The entrance hallway leads to a formal drawing room and dining room; there is also a writing room, a den and a powder room. The master bedroom has a dressing room and an en suite bathroom, and there are three other bedrooms, all with private baths. Maid service is included and there is a separate maid's sleeping quarters. The kitchen is fully equipped, and there are laundry facilities. The Mid Ocean Club and Golf Course is located in the south part of nearby Castle Harbour; to the north lie St. George's and the Castle Harbour Golf Club. Swimming, scuba diving and boating facilities are all within easy reach. Contact: L.P. Gutteridge Ltd., P.O. Box HM 1024, Hamilton, Bermuda HM DX. Call 809-295-4545.
Children: Y   Pets: N   Smoking: Y   Handicap Access: N   Payment: C, T

WHITE HOUSE *Rates: deluxe*
Open: year-round *Minimum Stay: one week*
The south shore of Bermuda is famous for its rose-colored beaches, and visitors to the White House will find their own private pink beach for sunbathing, swimming and snorkeling. All the rooms face the ocean in this house; a charming sun room makes the perfect breakfast spot. Two bedrooms have king-size beds and the third has twin beds; all have en suite bathrooms and are open to the sea, bringing warm ocean breezes directly to you. In addition to the living room, there is a formal dining room and a kitchen (maid service is provided). A tiled patio and covered veranda are surrounded by benches, and there is a barbecue for casual dining. Contact: L.P. Gutteridge Ltd., P.O. Box HM 1024, Hamilton, Bermuda HM DX. Call 809-295-4545.
Children: Y   Pets: N   Smoking: Y   Handicap Access: N   Payment: C, T

WARWICK PARISH

ASTWOOD COVE *Rates: inexpensive*
Open: year-round *Minimum Stay: none*
A group of white buildings with balconies and patios surrounds the swimming pool at Astwood Cove, encircled by sloping landscaped grounds. The original house was built in 1710; the grounds have recently been expanded to include several one- and two-story buildings. Near Hamilton Harbour, just a ferry ride away from the captial city, these self-contained apartments offer easy access to restaurants, buses, shops and bicycle and motor scooter rentals. The apartments consist of studios and suites, all air conditioned with well-equipped kitchens that provide bone china and wine glasses. Two or three guests can sleep comfortably (in some cases on fold-out couches) and the apartments are serviced by a maid daily. Contact: Nicky Lewin, Astwood Cove, 49 South Rd., Warwick WK 07, Bermuda. Call 809-236-0984 (in the U.S., 800-225-2230).
Children: Y   Pets: N   Smoking: Y   Handicap Access: N   Payment: C, T

HIGHLANDS   *Rates: deluxe*
Open: year-round   *Minimum Stay: one week*

Situated on the Belmont Estate, two-story Highlands is near the Belmont Hotel and Golf Club, where golf and tennis are available to nonmembers. The Belmont ferry takes you quickly to Hamilton, where visitors can admire the historic buildings and choose from the greatest concentration of restaurants on the island. The house has views over the Great Sound, Hamilton Harbour and the city itself. An outdoor swimming pool and dining terrace make a wonderful place to relax or dine casually. There are three twin bedrooms and three bathrooms, a separate den with bathroom, a living room, dining room and a modern kitchen and laundry. The housekeeper is included and comes in twice a week. Contact: Shirley B. Collier, Sherwood Building, 63 Pitts Bay Rd., Hamilton, Bermuda HM 08. Call 809-295-5487.

Children: Y   Pets: N   Smoking: Y   Handicap Access: N   Payment: C, T

LONGTAIL CLIFFS   *Rates: inexpensive-expensive*
Open: year-round   *Minimum Stay: two nights*

Located high above the pounding surf, yet within easy reach of the pink sand beaches, these two-bedroom apartments are private and well equipped. Air conditioning, wall safes, telephones, TVs, radios, daily maid service and full kitchens are some of the amenities to be found here. And that's just the beginning—many apartments have beamed ceilings and some have fireplaces, the bedrooms are carpeted and the living/dining areas have Italian tiled floors with rugs. Guests are welcome to take a dip in the swimming pool or wander around the rock garden carved out of the cliffside; there is also a special area in which children can play. Tennis, golf and evening entertainment are all within easy reach, and bicycle rental is available right on the premises. Contact: Doris Werner or Rochelle Gibbons, Longtail Cliffs, P.O. Box HM 836, Hamilton HM CX, Bermuda. Call 809-236-2822 or 809-736-2864.

Children: Y Pets: N Smoking: Y Handicap Access: N Payment: C, P, T, V, M, A

MAINSAIL APARTMENT   *Rates: inexpensive*
Open: year-round   *Minimum Stay: one week*

This clean, attractive one-bedroom apartment for two overlooks the Great Sound. There are twin beds in the bedroom, a living/dining area, a kitchen and bathroom. Regular housekeeping is provided, and a portable air-conditioning unit can be supplied during the summer months. Guests can plunge off the dock into the water or play a round on nearby Riddell's Bay Golf Course. Up the road is a ferry landing from which visitors can travel into Hamilton for shopping, sightseeing or dining. To the south are many pink beaches where scuba diving and swimming are both excellent. Contact: Shirley B. Collier, Sherwood Building, 63 Pitts Bay Rd., Hamilton, Bermuda HM 08. Call 809-295-5487.

Children: Y   Pets: N   Smoking: Y   Handicap Access: N   Payment: C, T

SOUTH VIEW GUEST APARTMENTS   *Rates: budget-moderate*
Open: year-round   *Minimum Stay: three nights*

Contemporary self-contained apartments can be found at this coral-pink guest house south of the Great Sound. Just a few minutes from the south shore beaches, including protected Jobson Cove and Long Bay Beach, South View is close to snorkeling, swimming, sailing and sunbathing. Guests have easy access to bus stops, bicycle rentals, golf and tennis. Gardens and lawns make inviting places to relax or barbecue, and each unit has its own private balcony or patio. Each apartment has a telephone, TV, private bath and maid and linen service; a choice of one-bedroom and studio apartments is available. Contact: Raymond Lauder, South View Guest Apartments, Box 515 HM CX, Hamilton 5, Bermuda. Call 809-236-5257.

Children: Y Pets: N Smoking: Y Handicap Access: N Payment: C, T, V, M

SURF SIDE BEACH CLUB   *Rates: inexpensive-moderate*
Open: year-round   *Minimum Stay: five nights*

The studio, one- and two-bedroom apartments and cottages here have been designed with the vacationer in mind. Each room is carpeted and furnished in an attractive modern style, with a fully equipped kitchen and air conditioning for comfort. A sliding glass door leads from the living room to a private balcony or patio overlooking the ocean to the south. An intriguing set of walkways, terraces and stairs leads down toward a private pink beach, with the unique coral sand of the island. The swimming pool offers poolside service for tea or breakfast and is surrounded by flowers and shrubs. Motor scooters are available on the premises, and a bus passes directly by the hotel. Golf, tennis, scuba diving, horseback riding and water sports are all advantageously located and can easily be arranged. Contact: B.B. Harvey, Surf Side Beach Club, 90 South Shore, Warwick WX BX, Bermuda. Call 809-236-7100 or 800-553-9990.

Children: Y Pets: N Smoking: Y Handicap Access: N Payment: C, P, T

THE SANDPIPER   *Rates: inexpensive-expensive*
Open: year-round   *Minimum Stay: none*

The Sandpiper offers fourteen studio and one-bedroom apartments capable of accommodating up to four guests each. Each unit has a fanciful name—Robin's Song, Angel's Loft, Longtail's Perch—a reflection of the surrounding gardens, flowers and colorful birds. A swimming pool with a separate children's area is located just outside the apartments, and a whirlpool bath is available for guests to relax in. Each air-conditioned unit is fully carpeted, with private entrances and balconies where you can watch the sun rise and set. Each apartment has a full kitchen, a dining area and a bathroom with shower; the larger ones have a separate living room with TV. Maid and linen service is provided daily, and there are barbecue facilities. Contact: Lynne Rayner, The Sandpiper, P.O. Box HM 685, Hamilton HM CX, Bermuda. Call 809-236-7093.

Children: Y Pets: N Smoking: Y Handicap Access: N Payment: C, T, V, M, A

Caribbean Sea

Bronswinkel

Boven Bolivia

KLEIN
BONAIRE

★ Kralendijk

Lac
Bay

Cai

Sorobon

Pink Beach

Bonaire

KRALENDIJK

BONAIRE BEACH BUNGALOWS   *Rates: budget-inexpensive*
Open: year-round   *Minimum Stay: one week*

These compact and charming oceanfront bungalows offer first-class
accommodations only 15 feet from the astounding blue sea. Each two-
bedroom rental features a large thatched-roof patio facing one of Bonaire's finest scuba sites; the management is affiliated with the island's
newest dive shop. Here you can learn or perfect your diving skills, rent
equipment, join a guided tour and learn the latest from the profession-
als who spend all year in the wonder-filled waters surrounding this
island. Only three minutes' drive from the airport and four minutes
from town, this convenient address on the least populated but second
largest of the islands in the Dutch Caribbean will help you claim a
little piece of tropical paradise. Contact: Villa Holidays, Inc., 13100
Wayzata Blvd., Suite 150, Minneapolis, MN 55343. Call 1-800-328-
6262 or 612-591-0076.

Children: Y Pets: N Smoking: Y Handicap Access: N Payment: C, P, T, V, M

BONAIRE SUNSET VILLAS   *Rates: moderate-deluxe*
Open: year-round   *Minimum Stay: one week*

Glass-bottomed boat tours of the coral reef, sailboat cruises at sunset
and deep-sea fishing charters—is this any way to spend your Caribbean
vacation? Absolutely. And with accommodations in your choice of
these oceanside villas with one to six bedrooms, you'll find the won-

ders of these turquoise waters just minutes from your door. Each villa features air-conditioned bedrooms and a 12-channel remote-control cable TV. Families, especially those with babies, will be glad to know about daily maid service and babysitting arrangements. All of the marvels of this island are yours to explore—the glamour of discotheques and casinos, the quiet splendor of the underwater world surrounding the island, the rich history and the fabulously varied natural environment protected by the Bonairean government. Contact: Rent A Home International, 7200 34th Avenue N.W., Seattle, WA 98117. Call 206-545-6963.

Children: Y Pets: N Smoking: Y Handicap Access: N Payment: C, P, T, V, M

CAPTAIN DON'S HABITAT *Rates: moderate-deluxe*
Open: year-round *Minimum Stay: three nights*
Scuba divers and lovers of marine life, hear this: The entire island of Bonaire is a completely protected marine sanctuary. What better place, then, for the scuba-diving vacation you've been dreaming of? Here at this southern Caribbean resort located on over a half-mile stretch of coral bluff, you'll find oceanfront villas, junior suites and two-bedroom cottages for up to six, each of which features a lovely and gracious outdoor balcony or patio with ocean or garden views. The resort can arrange island sightseeing, horseback riding and cave exploring, but the real attraction here is the scuba diving, with diving instruction for every level of ability; diving and camera equipment rental; and special courses for night dives and exploring nearby underwater wreckage and reefs. Contact: Habitat North American Office, 1080 Port Boulevard, Suite 100, Miami, FL 33132. Call 1-800-327-6709.

Children: Y Pets: N Smoking: Y Handicap Access: N Payment: C, T, V, M, A

CARIB INN *Rates: budget-inexpensive*
Open: year-round *Minimum Stay: three nights*
The calm, protected waters of Bonaire's leeward side provide some of the safest spots in the Caribbean for diving, snorkeling and swimming. This beach resort offers diving instruction for beginners by certified instructors as well as facilities for the most advanced diver. When you think you're getting water-logged, you'll find plenty of land activities, too, like scenic tours of the south of the island, where you'll find the Solar Salt Works and the huts that once housed the slaves who worked the salt pans. Accommodations here range from poolside studios to deluxe two-bedroom seaside apartments. Each air-conditioned rental includes cable TV as well as daily maid service. Contact: The Dive Resort of Bonaire. P.O. Box 68, Bonaire, Netherlands Antilles. Call 011-599-7-8819 or 1-800-223-9815.

Children: Y Pets: N Smoking: Y Handicap Access: N Payment: C, T, V, M, A

CORAL REGENCY RESORT *Rates: moderate-deluxe*
Open: year-round *Minimum Stay: three nights*
Located right on the waterfront of Bonaire's northern coast, each uniquely spacious and luxuriously decorated one- or two-bedroom suite of this resort features a stately living room leading to a private balcony or terrace. Each kitchen includes the basics as well as a dish-

washer, a coffee maker and a microwave. Right outside your door, you can enjoy the open-air waterfront pavilion offering inspiring views of the ocean and sunset. The island of Bonaire offers tremendous natural beauty; Washington National Park, a 13,500-acre game preserve, encompasses beautiful hills, miles of bays and beaches, gorgeous flora and fascinating fauna and makes an ideal walking and picnicking location. Here, you'll also find the largest sanctuary for pink flamingoes in the Caribbean. Contact: Michael Wilson, Coral Regency Resort, Kaya Gobernador N. Derrot 90, P.O. Box 380, Bonaire, Netherlands Antilles. Call 011-599-7-8065.

Children: Y Pets: N Smoking: Y Handicap Access: N Payment: C, T, V, M, A

PILOT FISH VILLAS   *Rates: budget-inexpensive*

Open: year-round   *Minimum Stay: none*

With the reef as your backyard, you'll find these two- and three-bedroom villas and efficiency apartments the perfect base for immersing yourself in the wonders of some of the Caribbean's best scuba diving. Each rental includes a full kitchen with a microwave. Situated right at the Bonaire Scuba Center, this resort offers several diving-program options but leaves it up to you to choose the best for you. Exciting diving opportunities here include instruction, guided tours, instructor certification and equipment rental. On this island, where the coral reef is protected by Bonairean law and the entire coastline has been incorporated into the Bonaire Marine Park, you'll find a uniquely spectacular view of underwater beauty. Contact: Black Durgon Properties, c/o Bonaire Scuba Ctr., P.O. Box 106, Bonaire, Netherlands Antilles. Call 011-599-7-8978 (in the U.S., 1-800-526-2370).

Children: Y   Pets: N   Smoking: Y   Handicap Access: N   Payment: C, T

SAND DOLLAR CONDOMINIUMS   *Rates: moderate-expensive*

Open: year-round   *Minimum Stay: none*

One of the newest and most luxurious resorts on Bonaire, this waterfront retreat features beautifully furnished accommodations ranging in size from studios to three-bedroom apartments, each with a balcony or terrace facing the sparkling sea. The modern kitchens include dishwashers, wine racks and many small appliances. The resort boasts a seeming infinity of amenities, including a freshwater pool, tennis courts for day or night use, a terrific restaurant where you can enjoy an occasional meal or arrange for a full meal program and the Sand Penny Club for the children. It's no secret that Bonaire enjoys a reputation as one of the Caribbean's most stellar diving sites, and the Sand Dollar offers a dive and photo operation with rentals, tours and instruction in six languages. Contact: Sand Dollar Condominiums, 52 Georgetown Road, Bordentown, NJ 08505. Call 1-800-345-0805 (in New Jersey, 609-298-3844).

Children: Y Pets: N Smoking: Y Handicap Access: N Payment: C, T, V, M, A

THE SUNSET INN   *Rates: budget-inexpensive*

Open: year-round   *Minimum Stay: none*

Appealingly situated just 60 feet from the beach, this recently renovated resort offers a lovely suite of rooms with a private entrance off a large furnished terrace. The rooms of the suite include three bedrooms with accommodations for six, a sitting area with remote-control cable TV, two bathrooms, a kitchenette and a large terrace dining area. Conveniently adjacent to the PADI Training Facility at the Dive Inn, this location also offers easy access to the Flamingo Beach Hotel and Casino; the town is just an eight-minute walk away. Naturalists will find themselves in a wonderland of beauty on Bonaire, which offers a large national park, a marine park that includes the reef surrounding the island and neighboring Klein Bonaire and many facilities for the protection of endangered species, such as sea turtles and flamingos. Contact: The Sunset Inn, P.O. Box 115, Bonaire, Netherlands Antilles. Call 011-599-7-8291.

Children: Y   Pets: N   Smoking: Y   Handicap Access: N   Payment: C, T

KRALENDIJK/YACHT HARBOR

BUDDY DIVE RESORT   *Rates: inexpensive*
Open: year-round   *Minimum Stay: none*

This diving resort on Bonaire's west coast, amid some of the Caribbean's most exquisite coral reefs, offers two locations with two types of one- and two-bedroom accommodations. Choose from the air-conditioned Carabela Bungalows across from the marina or the ocean-front apartments, each with full kitchens and airy patios. The resort offers a full diving program for divers of every level, from beginners to instructors. Land excursions to the Solar Salt Works, the former slave huts and an obelisk at the southern tip of the island promise relief to the landlubbers in your family. And if being on the water instead of in the water appeals to you, you can enjoy a romantic sunset sail aboard a 43-foot sailing vessel. Contact: Buddy Dive Resort, P.O. Box 231, Bonaire, Netherlands Antilles. Call 011-599-7-8647 or 1-800-359-0747.

Children: Y Pets: N Smoking: Y Handicap Access: N Payment: C, T, V, M, A

SOROBON

SOROBON BEACH RESORT   *Rates: inexpensive*
Open: year-round   *Minimum Stay: none*

Located on an island thought to be one of the five top diving spots in all the world, this resort offers a bar, a restaurant, a library, a volleyball court, table tennis, a telescope for star-gazing and the only government-approved nude beach in the Caribbean. You can dress or not for all your activities in the sun—snorkeling, sailing, windsurfing. At this family-oriented resort cooled by the trade winds, you'll stay in a one-bedroom beach chalet. With the beach at your doorstep, you'll enjoy the tidy kitchenette and the open and spacious living/dining area. Maid, shopping and laundry service are provided. Contact: Sorobon Beach Resort, P.O. Box 14, Bonaire, Netherlands Antilles. Call 011-599-7-8080.

Children: Y Pets: N Smoking: Y Handicap Access: N Payment: C, T, V, M, A

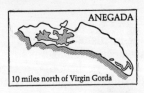

ANEGADA

10 miles north of Virgin Gorda

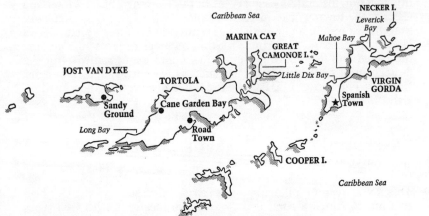

Caribbean Sea

NECKER I.

Leverick Bay

MARINA CAY

Mahoe Bay

GREAT CAMONOE I.

JOST VAN DYKE

TORTOLA

Little Dix Bay

VIRGIN GORDA

Sandy Ground

Cane Garden Bay

Spanish Town

Long Bay

Road Town

COOPER I.

Caribbean Sea

British Virgin Islands

GREAT CAMANOE
Privateers' Bay
THE PORTHOLE *Rates: inexpensive-moderate*
Open: year-round *Minimum Stay: one week*

You can only reach the house on this island by boat, and then driving down a steep and rocky road by Land Rover. But if you're in the mood for adventure, you'll find seclusion and beauty unmatched on the more populated islands. Located on four and a half acres rising 450 feet above the community dock, the Porthole offers virtually private, spectacular views of the British Virgin Islands. Built from native stone and concrete block, this three-bedroom house can sleep seven guests. A resident caretaker will pick up your provisions, leaving you to enjoy the fabulous scuba diving in this true island paradise. Contact: Babette S. Whipple, 35 Elizabeth Road, Belmont, MA 01278. Call 617-484-0988.

Children: Y Pets: N Smoking: Y Handicap Access: N Payment: C, P, T

JOST VAN DYKE
Sandy Ground
CAYVIEW *Rates: moderate-expensive*
Open: year-round *Minimum Stay: one week*

The lofty ceilings and the tower bedroom give this luxury villa the nickname, "The Castle." Fanciful decor enlightens the house and en

livens your vacation, with antique Chinese urns, stained-glass windows and a carved elephant table that is rumored to have once belonged to author Ernest Hemingway. The air is filled with the fragrant scent of bougainvillea, and with views of the cay and hills, Sandy Ground Estates strikes a responsive chord in residents and guests. With two bedrooms and two baths, up to four people can enjoy private accommodations here. Contact: West Indies Management Company, 28 Pelham St., Newport, RI 02840. Call 1-800-932-3222 (in Rhode Island, 401-849-8012). Ref. SG-CAY.
Children: **Y**   Pets: **N**   Smoking: **Y**   Handicap Access: **N**   Payment: **P, T, A**

GENIP TREE HOUSE   *Rates: moderate-expensive*
Open: year-round   *Minimum Stay: one week*
Warm sunshine fills the many windows and skylights of this two-bedroom home, creating a bright and romantic atmosphere perfect for a getaway vacation. One bedroom is located on the lower level of this seaside house, and features a bath and a private terrace with panoramic views. A second bedroom is nestled into an upper sleeping loft, comfortable at night and cheerful in the morning. The circulating trade winds keep the house at a comfortable temperature. Modern furnishings create a warm, homey environment. Contact: West Indies Management Company, 28 Pelham St., Newport, RI 02840. Call 1-800-932-3222 (in Rhode Island, 401-849-8012). Ref. SG-GTH.
Children: **Y**   Pets: **N**   Smoking: **Y**   Handicap Access: **N**   Payment: **P, T, A**

GREAT HOUSE   *Rates: moderate-expensive*
Open: year-round   *Minimum Stay: one week*
Perched on a cliffside on Sandy Ground Estates, this three-bedroom house provides plenty of room for large families or groups of friends. Surrounded by palms and native plants, the house commands an excellent view of the bay. Located in a cozy sleeping loft above the living area, one bedroom features a private outside stairway. On a separate level you'll find two spacious twin bedrooms for four more guests. The living area is a comfortable place to plan the day's activities. A covered area outside allows you to dine alfresco, taking full advantage of this spectacular environment. Contact: West Indies Management Company, 28 Pelham St., Newport, RI 02840. Call 1-800-932-3222 (in Rhode Island, 401-849-8012). Ref. SG-GRE.
Children: **Y**   Pets: **N**   Smoking: **Y**   Handicap Access: **N**   Payment: **P, T, A**

HIDEAWAY   *Rates: moderate-expensive*
Open: year-round   *Minimum Stay: one week*
Tortola is known for its lush tropical and mountain greenery, and you'll find plenty of varieties to examine around the luxurious Hideaway villa. Opening onto a sunny terrace, both the living room and master bedroom boast spectacular views of palms, bougainvillea and frangipani. A cozy sleeping loft above the living room, reached by a ladder, will be perfect for the kids. Another bedroom, like the master suite, offers a private bath. A covered dining terrace allows you to choose between dining inside or arranging an outdoor buffet after an

exhilarating day at the beach. Contact: West Indies Management Company, 28 Pelham St., Newport, RI 02840. Call 1-800-932-3222 (in Rhode Island, 401-849-8012). Ref. SG-HID.

Children: Y   Pets: N   Smoking: Y   Handicap Access: N   Payment: P, T, A

SANDY GROUND ESTATES   *Rates: inexpensive-moderate*
Open: year-round   *Minimum Stay: one week*

Located on a gently rising hillside at the eastern end of sparsely populated Jost Van Dyke, Sandy Ground Estates resembles an Italian town transplanted to the tropics. Designed to take full advantage of indoor/outdoor island living, there are several villas to choose from for two or more people. With moderately equipped kitchens, these villas allow guests to "rough it" a bit in a spectacular tropical setting. Snorkeling, swimming and sunbathing are superb on the private beach at Sandy Ground. Contact: Robert or Billie Grunzinger, Sandy Ground Estates Ltd., P.O. Box 594, West End, Tortola, British Virgin Islands. Call 809-494-3391.

Children: Y   Pets: N   Smoking: Y   Handicap: N   Payment: C, P, T, A, V, M

TORTOLA

Brewer

DIAMOND APARTMENT   *Rates: budget*
Open: year-round   *Minimum Stay: one week*

Overlooking Brewers Bay, this well-equipped apartment provides you with a place to rest your weary head after a day of swimming, horseback riding or hiking. Or make the five-minute drive into Road Town where you can mingle with the locals and sample the cuisine, music and culture. This modestly furnished one-bedroom apartment includes a living room, a dining room and a well-equipped kitchen, and it accommodates two people. Contact: Ms. Ethlyn Smith, Diamond Apt., Tortola, British Virgin Islands. Call 809-494-2593 or 809-494-3164.

Children: Y   Pets: N   Smoking: Y   Handicap Access: N   Payment: C, T

Cane Garden Bay

CANE GARDEN BAY COTTAGES   *Rates: inexpensive*
Open: year-round   *Minimum Stay: one week*

On the northwest coast of Tortola, situated on a magnificent crescent-shaped beach, are the Cane Garden Bay Cottages. White sandy beaches, crystal-clear water, and the sea grape and almond trees create one of the most lush tropical settings in the Caribbean. Cottages nestled in a coconut grove adjacent to the beach contain one bedroom with twin beds, a tiled bathroom, a fully equipped kitchenette and a dining/living room that can accommodate two to four people. Each is furnished in colorful island decor, and linens, utensils and utilities are provided. Contact: Cane Garden Bay Cottages, P.O. Box 362, Sayville, NY 11782. Call 516-567-5204.

Children: Y   Pets: N   Smoking: Y   Handicap Access: N   Payment: C, P, T

CANE GARDEN VILLA   *Rates: expensive-deluxe*
Open: year-round   *Minimum Stay: one week*

Right in the middle of a coconut grove, this villa allows guests to live in style and elegance just a pebble's toss from the water. Only steps from the water's edge on a half-moon of white sandy beach, the Cane Garden Villa boasts grand arched doorways that open onto a tiled front balcony and large side terrace. Three bedrooms and two and a half baths provide room and comfort for up to six. On the beach you'll find water sports, tennis and festive beach bars where you can mix with the local folk and other vacationers. Contact: West Indies Management Company, 28 Pelham St., Newport, RI 02840. Call 1-800-932-3222 (in Rhode Island, 401-849-8012). Ref. RH-CGB.

Children: Y Pets: N Smoking: Y Handicap Access: N Payment: C, P, T, A

Fort Recovery

FORT RECOVERY VILLAS   *Rates: inexpensive-deluxe*
Open: year-round   *Minimum Stay: one week*

Set on the beach fronting the deep blue waters of the Caribbean, the eight villas at Fort Recovery offer a tropical paradise of blossoms and trees as well as superb views of neighboring St. John. The scent of bougainvillea, oleander and hibiscus fill the air and blend with the fresh sea air. Each luxury villa has a partially covered garden patio, perfect for relaxing outside while taking a break from the sun. Preparing meals is a breeze in the fully equipped modern kitchen. After dinner, relax in the tastefully decorated living room, which also serves as an extra bedroom. Air conditioning in the bedroom assures comfort, but the constant trade winds may be enough to cool you. Contact: Rent A Home International, Inc., 7200 34th Ave., N.W., Seattle, WA 98117. Call 206-545-6963.

Children: Y Pets: N Smoking: Y Handicap Access: N Payment: C, P, T, V, M

Long Bay

SUNSET HOUSE   *Rates: deluxe*
Open: year-round   *Minimum Stay: one week*

Notched into the hillside overlooking magnificent Long Bay, Sunset House boasts fabulously picturesque views amid comfort and luxury. French windows and balconies on every level catch the cooling trade winds. Fronting a wraparound balcony, the open-plan living room with sitting and dining areas is perfect for a romantic dinner under the stars, and features a TV, VCR and CD player. Three bedrooms feature their own private showers and balconies, while the Princess suite on the upper floor boasts a full bath and balcony. A fifth bedroom on the lower level brings the sleeping accommodations to 10. Outside, you'll find a kidney-shaped swimming pool with a waterfall surrounded by a sun terrace, where you can sip cocktails at the pool bar or luxuriate in the Jacuzzi. And as if all that isn't enough, a cook, butler and maid will attend to your every need. Contact: Villas International, 71 West 23rd St., New York, NY 10010. Call 212-929-7585.

Children: Y Pets: N Smoking: Y Handicap Access: N Payment: C, P, T

SUNSET VILLA   *Rates: deluxe*
Open: year-round   *Minimum Stay: one week*
The lush foliage of Long Bay Beach surrounds this elegant and spacious home, situated just steps from the water's edge, with sweeping views of the sparkling turquoise sea and a mile-long stretch of white sandy beach. Two bedrooms, each with a separate bath, feature verandas with views of the sea. Simply furnished and elegant, with cool white tiling throughout, the villa's Danish teak furniture creates an atmosphere of tropical delight. You'll find plenty of hanging vines, broadleaf mahogany and white cedar trees, as well as avocado, mango and papaya, on one of the most naturally beautiful islands in the Caribbean. Contact: West Indies Management Company, 28 Pelham St., Newport, RI 02840. Call 1-800-932-3222 (in Rhode Island, 401-849-8012). Ref. RH-LLA.
Children: Y   Pets: N   Smoking: Y   Handicap Access: N   Payment: C, P, T, A

TRANQUIL HOUSE   *Rates: deluxe*
Open: year-round   *Minimum Stay: one week*
Spacious enough for eight guests, the multilevel Tranquil House offers panoramic views of picturesque Long Bay from its many patios, balconies and decks. Three large bedrooms and baths flank the main living area, which is private enough for groups of friends to share. A fourth bedroom is a little more secluded and offers good views of Long Bay. A private swimming pool allows you the choice of sunning and bathing right outside your door on those days when you just can't make it to the beach. Contact: West Indies Management Company, 28 Pelham St., Newport, RI 02840. Call 1-800-932-3222 (in Rhode Island, 401-849-8012). Ref. RH-QUI.
Children: Y   Pets: N   Smoking: Y   Handicap Access: N   Payment: C, P, T, A

Road Town
FORT RECOVERY ESTATES   *Rates: inexpensive-deluxe*
Open: year-round   *Minimum Stay: none*
Built around the 17th-century Dutch Fort Recovery, these luxurious one- to four-bedroom villas are set on the beach, with unmatched views of sand and sea. A covered garden patio provides sunscreen outdoors, while air-conditioned rooms keep you cool indoors. Daily maid and linen service and cable TV provide the comforts of home, while yoga instructors and masseurs offer the amenities of a full-service hotel. Explore the nearby 18th-century rum distillery, or take a sightseeing boat trip to one of the many uninhabited neighboring islands. Contact: Pamelah Jills Jacobson, 222 Grand Street, Suite 2J, Hoboken, NJ 07030. Call 1-800-367-8455 (in New Jersey, 201-792-9627).
Children: Y   Pets: N   Smoking: Y   Handicap: N   Payment: C, P, T, A, V, M

JOSIAH'S BAY COTTAGES *Rates: budget-inexpensive*
Open: year-round *Minimum Stay: one week*

The woods around Josiah's Bay Cottages are lush with almond and mahogany trees and the sweet fragrance of bougainvillea and hibiscus. Comfortably furnished in the lively tropical style, efficiency suites, traditional cottages and deluxe bungalows offer sleeping accommodations for two to three people. Sun yourself by the private swimming pool, or take the five-minute walk to one of the prettiest beaches on Tortola. There you'll find plenty of underwater life to explore while you snorkel to your heart's content. Contact: Best Vacations, P.O. Box 306, Road Town, Tortola. Call 1-800-842-6260.

Children: Y Pets: N Smoking: Y Handicap: N Payment: C, P, T, A, V, M

LONG BAY HOUSE *Rates: expensive-deluxe*
Open: year-round *Minimum Stay: one week*

Overlooking the exclusive West End of Tortola, Long Bay House is set in a secluded area of private homes and sandy beaches with panoramic views of Smuggler's Cove and neighboring islands. Custom-built in 1971 by a leading architect, Long Bay House sits on three landscaped acres filled with banana palms and avocado trees. Four double bedrooms and three and a half baths provide comfort and privacy for up to eight people. One unique feature is a lookout tower, affording spectacular views of the island. Contact: Rent A Home International, Inc., 7200 34th Ave., N.W., Seattle, WA 98117. Call 206-545-6963.

Children: Y Pets: N Smoking: Y Handicap Access: N Payment: C, P, T, V, M

PROSPECT REEF RESORT, LTD. *Rates: budget-deluxe*
Open: year-round *Minimum Stay: none*

Spend the day snorkeling through Tortola's exciting underwater coral paradise, or journey by boat to the deserted beaches of nearby uninhabited islands. At the end of your day's adventures, sip refreshing cocktails at a friendly bar while the sounds of a local steel drum band serenade you. Accommodations at the Prospect Reef Resort vary from double rooms with balconies overlooking the sea to deluxe villas with open-air courtyards, living and dining rooms, fully equipped kitchens and patios with views of both the harbor and the sea. Contact: Prospect Reef Resort Ltd., P.O. Box 104, Road Town, Tortola, British Virgin Islands. Call 809-494-3311 or 1-800-356-8937.

Children: Y Pets: N Smoking: Y Handicap Access: N Payment: C, T, A, V, M

SUGAR MILL HOTEL *Rates: deluxe*
Open: October-July *Minimum Stay: three nights*

You'll find the Sugar Mill Hotel on the north shore of Tortola an area where birds outnumber people among the banana and mango groves. Pearl-colored beaches edge crystal-clear water where guests will find many satisfying days of snorkeling, sailing and surfing. Deluxe room accommodations include special beach picnics for two, the use of snorkeling equipment and lessons for scuba diving or guided underwater safaris. At night, enjoy a romantic candlelit dinner for two in the old stone sugar mill, where island specialties tempt you to indulge your taste for splendid local fare. Contact: Catherine Dickens, Sugar Mill Hotel, P.O. Box 425, Road Town, Tortola. Call 1-800-462-8834.

Children: Y Pets: N Smoking: Y Handicap Access: N Payment: C, T, A, V, M

Smuggler's Cove

PINEAPPLE PLACE   *Rates: deluxe*

Open: February-August   *Minimum Stay: one week*

You'll find Pineapple Place on the Belmont Estate, located at the western end of Tortola in a natural environment graced with splendor. Snorkelers will revel in the blue-green waters here, and there's a coral reef for exploring. Spacious and airy, the house is decorated with cool cottons and glass, with plenty of Caribbean flair. Four bedrooms provide plenty of room for up to eight people, and have good views of the woodland garden or entrance courtyard and swimming pool. Large families will enjoy the dining table, roomy enough for 10, and the comfortable drawing room, with armchairs, two large sofas and a color TV and VCR. Contact: Rent A Home International, Inc., 7200 34th Ave., N.W., Seattle, WA 98117. Call 206-545-6963.

Children: Y Pets: N Smoking: Y Handicap Access: N Payment: C, P, T, V, M

West End

FRENCHMAN CAY RESORT HOTEL   *Rates: moderate*

Open: year-round   *Minimum Stay: none*

While snorkeling along the coral reef in the warm Caribbean, you look toward the beach to see your family playing in the beautiful white sand. Maybe tomorrow you'll charter a yacht from the nearby marina for a day together fishing in the sea. Then you'll retire to Frenchman Cay Resort Hotel where an individual one- or two-bedroom villa awaits you with its shady terrace, fully equipped kitchen, dining/sitting room complete with a queen-size sofa bed. Swimming in the freshwater pool, playing tennis or horseback riding provide other diversions for the whole family. Contact: Philippe Leroy, Frenchman Cay Resort Hotel, P.O. Box 1054, West End, Tortola, British Virgin Islands. Call 809-495-4844.

Children: Y   Pets: N   Smoking: Y   Handicap Access: N   Payment: All

VIRGIN GORDA

Leverick Bay

BATHS HOUSE   *Rates: expensive-deluxe*

Open: year-round   *Minimum Stay: one week*

Retreat from the hassles of modern life in this spacious and modern two-bedroom home, located on the northeastern tip of the sunny island of Virgin Gorda. With spectacular views of the blue waters of the sound and tranquil Mosquito Island, the villa lies only steps from two private beaches. Prepare a sumptuous meal in the modern kitchen, which features a dishwasher, washer and dryer. Or spend the day on the owner's dinghy, fishing for your dinner in the sound. Maid service is available, or you can rough it on your own. Contact: Rent A Home International, Inc., 7200 34th Ave., N.W., Seattle, WA 98117. Call 206-545-6963. Ref. RAHI/CH.

Children: Y Pets: N Smoking: Y Handicap Access: N Payment: C, P, T, V, M

CARROW HOUSE   *Rates: deluxe*
Open: year-round   *Minimum Stay: one week*
Commanding a spectacular view of Virgin Gorda Sound, Mosquito Island and the Atlantic Ocean from its own hillside terraces, Carrow House's lush retreat is only a short walk from two private beaches. The private dinghy moored below provides easy access to the five excellent restaurants in the area. Furnished in a comfortable, contemporary style, this modern two-bedroom, two-bath house sleeps four. The modern kitchen is equipped with a dishwasher and washer/dryer. Linens are included and maid service is available. Contact: Villas International, 71 West 23rd St., New York, NY 10010. Call 212-929-7585.

Children: Y   Pets: N   Smoking: Y   Handicap Access: N   Payment: C, P, T

Mahoe Bay

MANGO BEACH RESORT   *Rates: inexpensive*
Open: year-round   *Minimum Stay: three nights*
You'll find Mango Beach Resort right on the edge of a crystal-clear lagoon in the heart of Mahoe Bay. Minutes from the airport, the resort features private villas separated by rolling hills filled with palm and mahogany trees, offering guests an intimate vacation, and access to restaurants, shops and a marina. Smartly decorated in contemporary Italian design, the villas feature one, two or three bedrooms for up to six people. The fully equipped kitchen features a dishwasher, but let the housekeeper take care of the cleaning after you cook up a meal of your choice. A patio deck with a dining table and chairs combines the best of the natural outdoor beauty with the comforts of fine living. Contact: Mango Bay Resort, P.O. Box 1062, The Valley, Virgin Gorda, British Virgin Islands. Call 809-49-55672.

Children: Y   Pets: N   Smoking: Y   Handicap Access: N   Payment: C, P, T

Spring Bay

ROCKMERE   *Rates: budget-moderate*
Open: year-round   *Minimum Stay: one week*
Rockmere presents an enchanting vacation environment for large families or groups of friends in the unspoiled landscape of Virgin Gorda. You'll find a one-bedroom apartment with a bath, a combination living/dining room and a fully equipped kitchen in the main building perfect for first or second honeymoons. If you're vacationing with friends, a second couple can stay in the "guest house," featuring one bedroom and bath, accessible by a short path from the main building. Spectacular beaches are close by, and the mild climate and unspoiled landscape make Virgin Gorda attractive year-round. Contact: Rent A

Home International, Inc., 7200 34th Ave., N.W., Seattle, WA 98117.
Call 206-545-6963. Ref. J.

Children: Y   Pets: N   Smoking: Y   Handicap: N   Payment: C, P, T, V, M

The Valley

FISCHERS COVE BEACH HOTEL   *Rates: budget-moderate*
Open: year-round   *Minimum Stay: two nights*

The natural beauty of this island, with its legendary sunsets and clear,
sheltered waters, forms an ideal backdrop for healthful recreation. A
quarter mile of white sandy beach is spectacular for swimming and
sunbathing. These unique triangular-shaped cottages are positioned
for privacy and tastefully decorated in Caribbean colors. Studio, one-
and two-bedroom units include kitchenettes and daily maid service.
The islanders serve West Indian and continental cuisine that contin-
ually earns the Golden Award of World Famous Restaurants International. Contact: Norma or Dawn Max, Fischers Cove Beach Hotel,
P.O. Box 60, The Valley, Virgin Gorda, British Virgin Islands. Call
809-495-5252.

Children: Y   Pets: N   Smoking: Y   Handicap: N   Payment: C, P, T, A, V, M

Yacht Harbour

BAYVIEW VACATION APARTMENTS   *Rates: inexpensive-moderate*
Open: year-round   *Minimum Stay: none*

Set amid fragrant bougainvillea, hibiscus and frangipani, these three
modern apartments offer visitors sea views and modern comfort on an
island of nearly unspoiled beauty. Balconies and patios are accessible
through sliding glass doors, overlooking a garden that is a perfect place
to get some sun. One spectacular feature is a spiral staircase from the
master bedroom to the roof, the best place around for sunbathing and
relaxing in complete privacy. Free transportation to and from your port
of entry allows you to keep your mind on relaxing and having fun.
Contact: Nora Potter, Bayview Vacation Apartments, P.O. Box 1018,
Virgin Gorda, British Virgin Islands. Call 809-495-5329.

Children: Y   Pets: N   Smoking: Y   Handicap: N   Payment: C, P, T, A, V, M

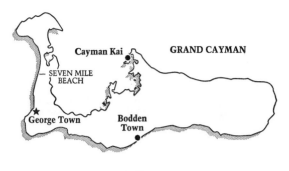

Caribbean Sea

Cayman Islands

BODDEN TOWN

BEACH BAY CONDOMINIUMS
Open: year-round

Rates: inexpensive-expensive
Minimum Stay: three nights

Located on the secluded south side of the Midland District, Beach Bay nonetheless offers visitors access to sports, recreation and nightlife within a short drive. A modern three-story building houses the condominiums here, which range from studios to one- and two-bedroom units. Each apartment has its own central air-conditioning and ceiling fans. The kitchens are extremely modern and feature electric appliances, ice makers and microwave ovens. A cable TV keeps you in touch with the outside world, though with the beach at your doorstep you're sure to spend a lot of time outside. Just 100 feet offshore is a living reef to be explored by snorkelers; shore fishing, shelling and even deep-sea fishing can all be found here. Contact: Debra Tibbetts, Beach Bay Condominiums, P.O. Box 35, Bodden Town, Grand Cayman, British West Indies. Call 809-947-2166.

Children: **Y** Pets: **N** Smoking: **Y** Handicap Access: **N** Payment: **C, T, V, M**

CAYMAN BRAC

BRAC HAVEN VILLAS
Open: year-round

Rates: moderate-expensive
Minimum Stay: none

The little island of Cayman Brac is an unspoiled paradise 85 miles from Grand Cayman. Named (in Gaelic) for the high bluffs at the eastern tip of the island, the island boasts a shoreline and caves where pirates once hid their booty. There are several resorts and a population of just a few thousand, so fishing, diving and boating are available and uncrowded. The villas are part of a community of detached homes, each with two bedrooms and two bathrooms. Cooled by air-conditioning and ceiling fans inside, and with an outdoor lanai that has windows admitting breezes off the Caribbean, the villas are perfect for indoor/outdoor living. The kitchens feature washing machines and dryers and there is a swimming pool on the premises. Contact: Rent A Home International, 7200 34th Ave., N.W., Seattle, WA 98117. Call 206-545-6963.

Children: Y Pets: N Smoking: Y Handicap Access: N Payment: C, P, T, V, M

CAYMAN KAI

BALI HAI KAI   *Rates: deluxe*
Open: year-round   *Minimum Stay: none*

The north shore of Grand Cayman houses some of its most exclusive properties (as well as the legendary Rum Point Club), and this is indubitably one of them. Easily accommodating eight guests, the house features three bedrooms with en suite bathrooms (two king and one twin), all with color TV, ceiling fans and air-conditioning. One of the bedrooms has a charming sitting/library area and a second library area can be found near the formal dining area in the living/dining room. A wall of glass along one side of the house looks out over the beach, while a deck around the house makes outdoor dining convenient. A pool house stands by the 60-foot pool. Maid service is provided twice a week. Contact: Rent A Home International, Inc., 7200 34th Ave. N.W., Seattle, WA 98117. Call 206-545-6963.

Children: Y Pets: N Smoking: Y Handicap Access: N Payment: C, T, V, M

ISLAND HOUSES   *Rates: moderate-expensive*
Open: year-round   *Minimum Stay: three nights*

Eighteen two-bedroom private bungalows are available here by The Cove. Located close to facilities for scuba diving, snorkeling, sailing, fishing and tennis, the houses are surrounded by landscaped gardens and white sand. Each house has two master bedroom suites upstairs, each with en suite bathroom and private balcony. Downstairs are a living/dining area, full kitchen and fine furnishings. Several nearby restaurants dish up island specialities; if you choose to dine in, a candlit dinner on your patio makes a perfect end to the day. Contact: Cayman Kai Development Co., P.O. Box 1074, Grand Cayman Island, British West Indies. Call 800-336-6008 or 809-947-4588.

Children: Y Pets: N Smoking: Y Handicap Access: N Payment: C, P, T, V, M

KAI BOOSE   *Rates: deluxe*
Open: year-round   *Minimum Stay: one week*

A large sloping roof covers this single-level, air-conditioned house, whose rooms all open onto the lanai outside, making it a place for truly tropical living. There are two double bedrooms, each with its own bathroom, a kitchen with a charming breakfast bar, a living area and a dining area inside. The outdoor living/dining space includes a wonderful deck with a built-in Jacuzzi—a perfect spot to soak and watch the sun set over the ocean. The gardens are landscaped, and immediately outside the door is a wide beach of white powdery sand. Diving clubs abound nearby, as do fishing charters and rental boats. Nearby hotels offer a choice of restaurants and nightlife, as well as daytime sports and swimming pools. Contact: Villa Holidays, Inc., 13100 Wayzata Blvd., Suite 150, Minneapolis, MN 55343. Call 612-591-0076 or 800-328-6262.

Children: Y Pets: N Smoking: Y Handicap Access: N Payment: C, P, T, V, M

NO BIG TING   *Rates: expensive-deluxe*
Open: year-round   *Minimum Stay: three nights*

Located on the 400 acres of white sandy beaches and tropical gardens known as Cayman Kai, this house has all the privacy and seclusion of a private home yet is close to all recreation and entertainment sites. It looks out on a coral reef just offshore, beckoning snorkelers and scuba divers. Inside, you'll find two master bedroom suites separated by a living/dining area, plus a kitchen and two screened-in patios. A nearby beach bar and restaurant provide tall drinks and good food. If you choose to prepare your own meals in the fully equipped kitchen, stores are within easy reach. For tennis and other facilities, there are several resorts close by. Contact: Cayman Kai Development Co., P.O. Box 1074, Grand Cayman Island, British West Indies. Call 800-336-6008 or 809-947-4588.

Children: Y Pets: N Smoking: Y Handicap Access: N Payment: C, P, T, V, M

TROLL KAI   *Rates: expensive-deluxe*
Open: year-round   *Minimum Stay: one week*

This house is fronted by a full-length terrace with a dining table, lounge chairs and a view that stretches past the beach and over the turquoise water. An ingenious floor plan separates the two bedroom suites, creating privacy for two couples or a family. Both bedrooms have double beds, large closets and en suite bathrooms. Between them is a kitchen with breakfast bar and adjoining dining area, plus a large, comfortable living room. A ship's ladder leads to an open loft—a little hideaway for the kids, perhaps. The beach runs for about 100 feet before tropical greenery intrudes. For tennis, swimming, diving or fishing there are several major hotels in the immediate area; restaurants and nightlife can be found close by. Contact: Villa Holidays, Inc., 13100 Wayzata Blvd., Suite 150, Minneapolis, MN 55343. Call 612-591-0076 or 800-328-6262.

Children: Y Pets: N Smoking: Y Handicap Access: N Payment: C, P, T, V, M

GEORGE TOWN

INDIES SUITES   *Rates: expensive*
Open: year-round   *Minimum Stay: none*

Indies Suites are situated in a complex that features a swimming pool with a poolside bar, a Jacuzzi, a dining room and facilities for business meetings and conferences. The beach is just steps away, and your scuba diving trips will be enhanced by taking a course in the specially designed pool. Each spacious suite overlooks the courtyard and pool and features one or two comfortable beds, as well as an extra fold-out couch. Cable TV, phone and a full kitchen are provided in each suite, along with a dining room/living area decorated with contemporary island-style furnishings. A convenience store right in the resort lobby carries necessities and ready-to-prepare meals for dining in; a washer and dryer are available. There's even a storeroom for diving gear in every suite. Contact: Rent A Home International, 7200 34th Ave., N.W., Seattle, WA 98117. Call 206-545-6963. Ref IS/001.

Children: Y Pets: N Smoking: Y Handicap Access: N Payment: C, T, V, M

SEVEN MILE BEACH

CAY SEA VILLA   *Rates: moderate-deluxe*
Open: year-round   *Minimum Stay: one week*

Guests here can stroll along the white beach for hours without seeing another soul. Sway on a hammock hung between two palm trees or swim in the crystal-clear waters of the Caribbean completely undisturbed. The villa faces a private beach and has a huge 50-foot screened-in porch overlooking the sea. There is room for six guests inside, with two bedrooms and a large living/dining/kitchen space. There is a washing machine, radio, telephone and daily maid service—so there isn't much to do but relax. Live coral reefs just a few hundred feet from shore provide magnificent views for snorkelers and scuba divers. Full recreation facilities are available at the many resorts along Seven Mile Beach. Contact: Rent A Home International, 7200 34th Ave., N.W., Seattle, WA 98117. Call 206-545-6963.

Children: Y Pets: N Smoking: Y Handicap Access: N Payment: C, P, T, V, M

CAYMAN RESORTS CONDO   *Rates: inexpensive-expensive*
Open: year-round   *Minimum Stay: three nights*

Located in a little cul de sac immediately beside the beach, this condomium unit is within easy reach of shops, restaurants and the major resorts and hotels. The unit offers two bedrooms and two bathrooms, as well as a living/dining area. The kitchen has a microwave oven and a washing machine and dryer—weekly maid service is included. Individual air-conditioning units and ceiling fans keep the rooms cool. Diving clubs and water sports facilities are dotted along the beach, and a new 18-hole golf course in the area is proving popular. The main island city of George Town is at one end of the beach, and at the other is the world's only turtle farm, so sightseeing is both accessible and unique. Contact: Desmond Seales, Seales and Company Ltd., P.O. Box 1103, Grand Cayman, British West Indies. Call 809-947-4325.

Children: Y Pets: N Smoking: Y Handicap Access: N Payment: C, T, V, M

CORAL CAYMANIAN HOTEL/APARTMENTS   *Rates: moderate-deluxe*
Open: year-round   *Minimum Stay: none*

With the astonishing white sands of Seven Mile Beach stretching in either direction, plus all the magnificent diving and snorkeling facilities here, you won't spend too much time indoors. But this resort tempts you indoors with inviting studios, efficiency apartments, two- and three-bedroom condominiums and even an oceanfront three-bedroom beach house. Each unit has air-conditioning and a kitchen that includes a dishwasher, a living room with cable TV and barbecue facilities for outdoor cooking. Daily maid service keeps your rooms spotless, and the large glass doors and outdoor patios bring the island right to your doorstep. There are two new tennis courts outside, and the Britannia Golf Course is not far away. Contact: Iris Phillips, Coral Caymanian Hotel/Apartments, P.O. Box 1093, West Bay Road, Grand Cayman, British West Indies. Call 809-947-5170.

Children: Y Pets: N Smoking: Y Handicap Access: Y Payment: C, T, A, V, M,

ESTATE VILLA *Rates: expensive*
Open: year-round *Minimum Stay: none*

A private condominium like this offers seclusion as no hotel or resort can, yet the Holiday Inn and all its restaurants and nightclubs is only a five-minute walk away. Part of a complex located on a private beach, this condo rental includes access to a freshwater swimming pool. Inside, there are two large double bedrooms in addition to the fold-out couch in the living room, which sleeps two people. There is a full kitchen with breakfast bar for casual meals, and a separate dining room. Furnishings are personal, with tasteful, bright island colors in the upholstery and wall prints. Shopping is easily accessible, as are facilities for the diving and snorkeling that bring so many to this island. Contact: Rent A Home International, Inc., 7200 34th Ave. N.W., Seattle, WA 98117. Call 206-545-6963.

Children: Y Pets: N Smoking: Y Handicap Access: N Payment: C, P, T, V, M

GOLFCOURSE VILLAS *Rates: deluxe*
Open: year-round *Minimum Stay: three nights*

Situated immediately beside the Hyatt Regency Hotel and Britannia Golf Course near Seven Mile Beach, these villas are among the most luxurious to be found. Guests are provided with all the amenities of the Hyatt Regency Grand Cayman, as well as access to its many facilities. The air-conditioned villas have from one to three bedrooms, fully equipped kitchens, washing machines and dryers and ceiling fans that keep up a steady cool breeze. The furnishings are in the island style, casual and comfortable. French doors open from the living quarters onto balconies from which you can observe the golf course or the water. Guests are invited to rent a catamaran, go scuba diving by a live coral reef, try a pedal boat or sunfish or windsurf at the hotel's full-service dive and water sports operation. Contact: Rent A Home International, 7200 34th Ave., N.W., Seattle, WA 98117. Call 206-545-6963. Ref GCI/002.

Children: Y Pets: N Smoking: Y Handicap Access: N Payment: C, P, T, V, M

LONDON HOUSE *Rates: expensive*
Open: year-round *Minimum Stay: none*

Red tiled roofs cover this handsome, three-story resort apartment complex, where only a strip of gleaming sand separates the rooms from the waves. George Town is just five minutes away, where guests can shop at the duty-free stores and experience the Caymanian nightlife. London House has clean bright apartments, with modern kitchens that feature such extras as dishwashers and microwave ovens. The living rooms contain color TVs, and of course the rooms are air-conditioned throughout for your comfort. Guests can pass the days swinging on an outdoor hammock, swimming and lounging at the freshwater pool, playing shuffleboard or volleyball or joining one of the resort barbecue or cocktail parties. Contact: Aqua Adventures, Inc., 114 East 32nd St., Suite 501, New York, NY 10016. Call 212-686-6210 or 800-65-ISLES.

Children: Y Pets: N Smoking: Y Handicap Access: N Payment: C, T, A, V, M

PAN-CAYMAN HOUSE   *Rates: moderate-deluxe*
Open: year-round   *Minimum Stay: none*

Palm trees sway in the trade winds around this complex, which has just ten apartments. The powder sand of Seven Mile Beach lies just outside the door and long, shaded patios and balconies provide views out across the crystal-clear water. The apartments are large, featuring two or three bedrooms, with a living/dining area (where sliding glass doors lead out to a patio or balcony), a full kitchen with microwave oven and two bathrooms. The furnishings are elegant and inviting—rattan couches are illuminated by plenty of reading lamps. Maid service is included and there are laundry facilities at the complex, as well as barbecue facilities for casual meals. Scuba diving boats will pick you up at the beach hotel; offshore snorkeling can be enjoyed by the whole family. Contact: Robyn McCarter, Pan-Cayman House, Seven Mile Beach, Grand Cayman, British West Indies. Call 809-947-4002 or 800-248-5115.

Children: Y Pets: N Smoking: Y Handicap Access: N Payment: C, P, T

PLANTATION VILLAGE BEACH RESORT   *Rates: expensive-deluxe*
Open: year-round   *Minimum Stay: none*

A new resort located on the Cayman Islands' best-known beach, Plantation Village covers four acres of landscaped lawns and gardens that make a perfect complement to the white sand and turquoise waters nearby. The condominiums here are privately owned and have individual furnishings and designs, giving them a true home-away-from-home atmosphere. The sizes vary, but each has two bathrooms, a complete kitchen with all appliances (including a blender and ice maker) and a living area with sliding glass doors that lead to a patio or balcony. The tennis courts here are well-lit at night and there are two swimming pools in addition to the whirlpool spa; nearby is an 18-hole golf course. Contact: Jim Fraser, Plantation Village Beach Resort, P.O. Box 1590, West Bay Road, Grand Cayman, British West Indies. Call 809-949-4199 or 800-822-8903.

Children: Y Pets: N Smoking: Y Handicap Access: N Payment: C, T, A, V, M

THE CARIBBEAN CLUB   *Rates: moderate-deluxe*
Open: year-round   *Minimum Stay: none*

Tiled floors and gracious wicker furniture grace these one- and two-bedroom villas, which can be found either directly on the beach or just off it. All the villas have full kitchens, and room service is available.

Patios, cable TV, daily maid service and complimentary beach towels are among the amenities provided by the club. The sand on the beach glistens white; sunbathing and beachcombing can easily fill the days. A tennis court is available for the energetic, and a unique Cayman golf course designed by the Jack Nicklaus team is just a few minutes away. Snorkeling, windsurfing and diving are accessible from the beach, with several shipwrecks visible from shore. Contact: W. Rivers, Caribbean Club, P.O. Box 504, George Town, Grand Cayman, British West Indies. Call 809-947-4099 or 800-327-8777.

Children: Y Pets: N Smoking: Y Handicap Access: N Payment: C, T, A, V, M

THE DISCOVERY POINT CLUB   *Rates: moderate-deluxe*
Open: year-round   *Minimum Stay: three nights*

Forty-five hotel rooms and condominium units can be found at this club, each of them decorated with muted island colors, wicker and rattan furniture and filled with plants to enhance the tropical atmosphere. Units come with either one or two bedrooms and bathrooms, plus a full kitchen with all utensils and dinnerware. Color cable TV with HBO and a private screened patio mean that guests can relax in indoor comfort, and maid service is included. After an exhilarating game of tennis on the club's championship courts or a round of golf on the nearby course, you are welcome to take a soak in the outdoor hot tub or the swimming pool. Just outside, the beach is dotted with cabanas overlooking world-class diving and snorkeling amidst live coral reefs and sunken treasure. Contact: Celita or Diane, Discovery Point Club, P.O. Box 439 West Bay, Grand Cayman, British West Indies. Call 809-947-4792.

Children: Y Pets: N Smoking: Y Handicap Access: N Payment: C, T, A, V, M

TREASURE ISLAND CONDO   *Rates: expensive-deluxe*
Open: year-round   *Minimum Stay: three nights*

Treasure Island Resort is directly on the beachfront and features water sports facilities, tennis courts, swimming pools and several poolside bars, a restaurant and nightclub. This unit faces the ocean, slightly away from the main bustle of the resort, and the master bedroom with bath opens directly onto a tiled patio and the beach. Another twin bedroom, a queen-size fold-out couch in the den and another bathroom complete the accommodations. The kitchen contains a microwave oven and there is a washing machine and dryer, as well as a TV and telephone. Water sports and diving facilities are within walking distance. Contact: Desmond Seales, Seales and Company Ltd., P.O. Box 1103, Grand Cayman, British West Indies. Call 809-947-4325.

Children: Y Pets: N Smoking: Y Handicap Access: N Payment: C, T, V, M

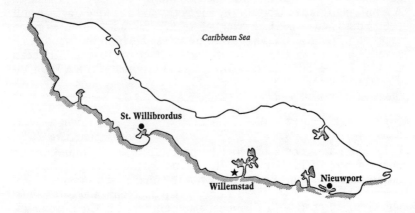

Caribbean Sea

St. Willibrordus

Willemstad

Nieuwport

Curacao

Brakkeput, Arriba Kavel

SPANISH WATERS   *Rates: budget*
Open: year-round   *Minimum Stay: two nights*

Float on your back in the sapphire-blue waters of the Caribbean, explore a coral reef with scuba gear or snorkel up a storm during your days here. Watch fire-eating limbo dancers or gamble away your loose change in any one of the island's famed casinos at night. You'll find four languages spoken on this island and duty-free shops that will dazzle you. Spanish Waters offers several air-conditioned apartments to choose from, each with porch and kitchenette. The units feature TV for those who need it, and you can easily arrange to rent a car to explore the island once you arrive. Contact: Curacao Tourist Board, 400 Madison Ave., Suite 311, New York, NY 10017. Call 212-751-8266.

Children: **Y**   Pets: **N**   Smoking: **Y**   Handicap Access: **N**   Payment: **C, T**

Julianadrop

HOTEL HOLANDA   *Rates: budget*
Open: year-round   *Minimum Stay: two nights*

Just 40 miles off the coast of South America, the island of Curacao is permeated with Dutch charm. Try "rijsttafel"—an Indonesian banquet featuring as many as 24 different dishes—or gamble in the island's casinos when you're not snorkeling, scuba diving or swimming in the gorgeous Caribbean. You'll find both single and double accommodations at Hotel Holanda, complete with private baths, air-conditioning, TV and kitchenettes for whipping up midnight snacks after a day of sightseeing. Rooms can accommodate up to six people when you rent extra beds, so don't hesitate to bring the whole family to enjoy the splendors of the island. Contact: Curacao Tourist Board, 400 Madison Ave., Suite 311, New York, NY 10017. Call 212-751-8266.

Children: **Y**   Pets: **N**   Smoking: **Y**   Handicap Access: **N**   Payment: **C, T**

PALLASSTRAAT

CARVAHOME   *Rates: budget*
Open: year-round   *Minimum Stay: two nights*

Nestled amid the red tile roofs and Dutch architecture of the island of Curacao, this charming bungalow has two bedrooms (one with air-conditioning), a private bath, and a fully equipped kitchen where you can cook up whatever you catch in the waters off the island. Take your coffee on the lovely terrace before setting out to bargain hunt in the island's many duty-free shops, or head straight for any one of the 38 beaches, where you can scuba dive, snorkel or swim when not lazing on the sand. At night, try the famed casinos or dine on international cuisine. Contact: Mr. Brendel, Pallasstraat 6, Curacao, Netherlands Antilles. Call 011-5999-615636.

Children: **Y**   Pets: **N**   Smoking: **Y**   Handicap Access: **N**   Payment: **C, T**

REDAWEG

SUN REEF VILLAGE   *Rates: budget*
Open: year-round   *Minimum Stay: two nights*

Red tile roofs dot this exquisite island paradise, which combines all the pleasures of the Caribbean with an infusion of international culture. You'll hear four languages spoken here and will have your choice of quaint Dutch shops and duty-free bargains on the island, while the nights will sizzle with gambling in the casinos and fire-eating limbo dancers to entertain you. There are 38 beaches on the island, where you can indulge your passion for every imaginable water sport—from scuba diving and snorkeling to deep-sea fishing and waterskiing. At night, come home to the charms of your own air-conditioned villa that sleeps six. Its convenient kitchenette lets you cook dinner for a quiet evening. Studios for two also feature kitchenettes; both accommodations offer maid service. Contact: Mr. R. Mesker, Redaweg 38, Curacao, Netherlands Antilles. Call 407-833-4454 (in Curacao, 011-5999-83594).

Children: **Y**   Pets: **N**   Smoking: **Y**   Handicap Access: **N**   Payment: **C, T**

WILLEMSTAD

LANDHOUSE DANIEL   *Rates: budget*
Open: year-round   *Minimum Stay: two nights*

You'll have two acres of lush tropical Curacao all to yourself when you rent this charming, centuries-old plantation home. The perfect spot for a romantic vacation for two, this recently renovated home features

rooms with a simple, rustic flavor. When you're not indulging your-
selves in the privacy this lovely retreat offers, the island will tempt
you with duty-free shopping, world-famous casinos, and 38 beaches on
the cerulean waters of the Caribbean. Go snorkeling, scuba diving,
windsurfing or boating when you want an active day, and then sample
the delicious cuisine of nearly half a dozen nations when dinner time
rolls around. For sizzling nights, try watching the fire-eating limbo
dancers. Contact: Curacao Tourist Board, 400 Madison Ave., Suite
311, New York, NY 10017. Call 212-751-8266.

Children: **Y**   Pets: **N**   Smoking: **Y**   Handicap Access: **N**   Payment: **C, T**

LAS PALMAS   *Rates: inexpensive-moderate*
Open: year-round   *Minimum Stay: none*

Go reef diving or waterskiing in the Caribbean, play tennis, or just
take a dip in the freshwater pool under sunny skies, eat dinner under
the giant bamboo arches of Palmas Restaurant—on the premises—
while you watch fire-eating limbo dancers, then head for the casinos.
You'll have your choice of air-conditioned one-bedroom suites with
sitting rooms and patios, or spacious two-bedroom villas with fully
equipped kitchens and living rooms with extra sleeping space for
guests. A perfect vacation spot for the entire family, Las Palmas delights children with a kiddie swimming pool and crafts classes, while
volleyball and water sports let mom and dad amuse themselves. Contact: Las Palmas, 343 Neponset St., Canton, MA 02021. Call 800-766-
6016 or 617-821-1012.

Children: **Y**   Pets: **N**   Smoking: **Y**   Handicap Access: **N**   Payment: **C, T**

Portsmouth

Canefield

★ Roseau

Caribbean Sea

Soufriere

Dominica

Roseau

SPRINGFIELD GUEST HOUSE	*Rates: budget-moderate*
Open: year-round	*Minimum Stay: none*

Rent a plantation guest house or a one-, two- or three-bedroom apartment on the lovely island of Dominica and settle in for the perfect vacation. Stretch out on the glorious beach for the day, tee off on the golf course nearby, take a hike around the island or just spend the afternoons fishing. Your accommodations will be cooled by air conditioning if the trade winds ever flag; you can spend quiet evenings in, cooking your dinner in the kitchenette. Order room service when you don't want to cook and have it served on your private deck or balcony. A bar/lounge located on the property makes it easy to mingle with the other guests, as does the on-site restaurant. Full maid service leaves you free from housekeeping worries, and a room telephone makes it easy to keep in touch with the kids if you didn't bring them along. Contact: Robert L. Weisel, Springfield Guest House, Box 41, Roseau, Dominica, West Indies. Call 809-449-1401.

Children: Y Pets: N Smoking: Y Handicap Access: N Payment: C, T, A, V, M

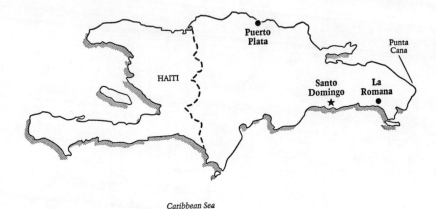

Caribbean Sea

Dominican Republic

LA ROMANA

CASA DE CAMPO   *Rates: inexpensive-moderate*

Open: year-round   *Minimum Stay: none*

Resort living looks fabulous at Casa De Campo, located on the glorious Caribbean and designed to resemble a 16th-century colonial village. Take the kids to the playground before playing tennis or golf, go fishing all afternoon, or take a bicycle ride around the island and come back to dive into the swimming pool. All manner of water sports are here for you to enjoy—from waterskiing to boating—and when the day is done, you'll have your choice of home base, ranging from a modern studio to a four-bedroom suite. Full kitchens allow you to cook any time you like. Your rooms are fully air-conditioned and have room telephones, cable TV, private balconies and full maid service. At night, try the on-site bar/lounge and restaurant for a night on the town just a stone's throw from your door. Contact: Premier Resorts and Hotels, 2600 S.W. Third Ave., 3rd Flr., Miami, FL 33129. Call 305-856-7083 or 800-PREMIER.

Children: Y Pets: N Smoking: Y Handicap Access: N Payment: C, V, A, M, O

CASA OCEANA   *Rates: deluxe*
Open: year-round   *Minimum Stay: one week*
View the seascape from a lounge chair by your private pool when you
choose this exotic four-bedroom, four-bath air-conditioned villa complete with a staff of three. The luxurious rooms here will permit you
to entertain in style, and the maid will keep everything in perfect
order. Give your menu for the day to the cook while you linger over
breakfast by the pool, or go down to the landscaped shoreline to speak
with the gardener about flowers for your table. You'll find an excellent
golf course, plenty of tennis courts, water sports and even a place to
indulge your penchant for polo when you're in the mood for a little
exercise. But then again, you can always lounge away your entire
vacation here being waited on hand and foot. Contact: LaCure Villas,
11661 San Vicente Blvd., Suite 1010, Los Angeles, CA 90049. Call
800-387-2715/2720.
Children: **Y**   Pets: **N**   Smoking: **Y**   Handicap Access: **N**   Payment: **All**

CASA VALDEZ   *Rates: deluxe*
Open: year-round   *Minimum Stay: one week*
Let the maid make your bed, the cook serve your breakfast, and the
butler give your instructions to the gardener while you enjoy the
world-class luxuries of this four-bedroom, four-bath villa on the
grounds of the famous LaCure Resort. Your villa features a private
swimming pool for refreshing dips around the clock, and private terraces off each bedroom. Enjoy your meals outdoors overlooking the
pool, or unwind in the private Jacuzzi. Furnished in exquisite taste,
this home will make entertaining a sheer delight. Sports enthusiasts
will find the resort staff eager to make arrangements for them right on
the premises, and if you're ever tempted to leave this luscious retreat,
there's an entire island to explore. Contact: LaCure Villas, 11661 San
Vicente Blvd., Suite 1010, Los Angeles, CA 90049. Call 800-387-2715/
2720.
Children: **Y**   Pets: **N**   Smoking: **Y**   Handicap Access: **N**   Payment: **All**

PUERTO PLATA

VILLAS MARLENS   *Rates: budget-inexpensive*
Open: year-round   *Minimum Stay: none*
Situated across the bay from Puerto Plata away from all the city hub-
bub, the Costambar resort area boasts nearly three miles of sparkling
beaches. Walk up to any one of the beach bars between swims for a
refreshing drink; tee off on the nine-hole golf course; go horseback
riding or rent a scooter and tour the island. Studios and one-, two- and
three-bedroom apartments and condos all come complete with kitchens, private balconies where you can sun or eat in perfect peace and
there are ceiling fans to keep you cool. Invite friends over for drinks in
the modern living room complete with bar; when it's time to turn in,
cheery bedspreads and lush carpeting will welcome you to your bedroom. Try the pool, pool bar and boutique on the resort property, or
dine in the tropical rooftop garden restaurant. Contact: International

Travel and Resorts, Inc., Four Park Avenue, New York, NY 10016.
Call 800-223-9815 or 212-545-8469.

Children: Y   Pets: N   Smoking: Y   Handicap Access: N   Payment: C, T

PUNTA CANA

PUNTA CANA BEACH RESORT   *Rates: inexpensive-deluxe*
Open: year-round   *Minimum Stay: none*

Located on a 105-acre estate with some of the most beautiful beaches
in the world, Punta Cana offers you a tantalizing combination of activity and seclusion. Pastel villas, contemporary studios and suites all
have terraces or patios where you can hide out with a great book; the
palm trees surrounding you on all sides offer perfect privacy. Inside,
you'll find tiled floors, elegant marble baths and wooden shutters at
the windows—a perfect blend of luxury and simplicity. Take a guided
nature walk and see rare orchids and birds, or arrange to go horeback
riding on the beach. Play tennis day or night on ten clay courts, or
swim in the 3,000-square-foot pool overlooking the sea. Contact:
Punta Cana Beach Resort, Punta Cana, Dominican Republic. Call 212-
545-8469.

Children: Y Pets: N Smoking: Y Handicap Access: N Payment: C, T, A, V, M

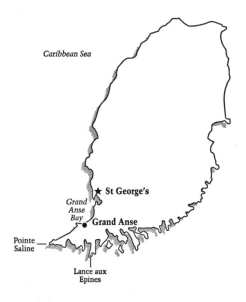

Caribbean Sea

St George's

Grand Anse Bay

Grand Anse

Pointe Saline

Lance aux Epines

Grenada

GRAND ANSE

BLUE HORIZONS COTTAGE HOTEL *Rates: inexpensive-moderate*
Open: year-round *Minimum Stay: none*

These cottages are situated on a terraced hillside amid tropical greenery overlooking a freshwater pool and magnificent miles of gleaming sand. The hotel has a series of comfortable lounges, a poolside bar and a restaurant specializing in Creole and West Indian food. Three styles of cottages—deluxe, superior and standard mini—are completely private and air-conditioned and come with two twin or double beds. The standard is studio-style, but the others have separate bedrooms; each has living/dining areas along with a kitchenette for preparing meals—perhaps with some of the island's famous spices. Guests are also welcome next door, at the beachfront Spice Island Inn. Contact: Mr. Arnold Hopkin, Blue Horizons Cottage Hotel, P.O. Box 4, Grand Anse, St. George's, Grenada, West Indies. Call 800-223-9815 or 212-545-8469.

Children: Y Pets: N Smoking: Y Handicap Access: N Payment: C, T, A, V, M

GRENADA VILLA *Rates: deluxe*
Open: year-round *Minimum Stay: one week*

A private home decorated with care, this villa can accommodate four guests. One bedroom contains a king-sized bed, the other has twin beds; there are two full baths with showers. Opening onto the deck, which runs the full length of the house, is a living/dining room, so guests can eat while enjoying the view down to the sea. A short walk brings you to a beach considered among the finest in the Caribbean. Daily maid service is included, leaving guests free to enjoy the island's pleasures. Visit historic St. George's, with its rows of Georgian colonial houses and botanical gardens, or go bicycle riding around the island. Both fishing and scuba diving are excellent, as the sea abounds with marine life. Contact: At Home Abroad, Inc., 405 E. 56th St., 6-H, New York, NY 10022. Call 212-421-9165.

Children: Y   Pets: N   Smoking: Y   Handicap Access: N   Payment: C, P, T

HIBISCUS HOTEL   *Rates: inexpensive*
Open: year-round   *Minimum Stay: three nights*

Set in a lovely compound surrounded by gardens full of tropical orleander, palm and hibiscus, these five air-conditioned cottages each contain two apartments. Charmingly rustic, with wooden ceilings and tiled floors, the apartments are completely modernized, containing twin bedrooms, a full bath with shower, phone, kitchen or kitchenette. Daily maid service is provided. There are plenty of deck chairs at poolside, or for those who prefer to swim in the ocean, the beach at Grand Anse is a mere three-minute walk away. Children will love to play in the garden, and babysitting can be arranged if the adults want to try out the local golf course or tennis courts. The staff will also be happy to arrange excursions around the island. Contact: Mr. Russell Antoine, P.O. Box 279, St. George's, Grenada, West Indies. Call 809-444-4233/4008.

Children: Y   Pets: N   Smoking: Y   Handicap: N   Payment: C, T, A, V, M, O

SIESTA HOTEL   *Rates: inexpensive-moderate*
Open: year-round   *Minimum Stay: one week*

The Siesta Hotel is a collection of studio, one- and two-bedroom apartments located in an attractive arrangement of three-story buildings around a piano-shaped swimming pool. In all, there are twenty-five air-conditioned apartments with kitchenette, bath, TV, phone, daily maid service and private balcony. Guests have access to a poolside restaurant and store; laundry service and babysitting can be arranged. The capital city of St. George's, boating and fishing waters and golf and tennis facilities are all within easy reach. While on the island, try some snorkeling or scuba diving amid sunken wrecks and coral reefs. Contact: Mr. E. & Mrs. F. Maghami, P.O. Box 27, St. George's, Grenada, West Indies. Call 809-444-4646/4647.

Children: Y   Pets: N   Smoking: Y   Handicap Access: N   Payment: C, T, V, M, A

SOUTH WINDS COTTAGES & APARTMENTS   *Rates: budget-inexpensive*
Open: year-round   *Minimum Stay: five nights*

Set on a flower-strewn hillside, South Winds features 14 one-bedroom apartments and five two-bedroom cottages, as well as a restaurant overlooking St. George's harbor and bay. Each individual accommodation contains a kitchen and bath, and most are air-conditioned.

Babysitting and TV are available if desired. The three-mile stretch of Grand Anse Beach begins just a short walk away; there you can find wonderful facilities for waterskiing, scuba diving, snorkeling, sailing and fishing for the numerous species that populate these clean waters. The capital city of St. George's is minutes away and well worth visiting for its shops, restaurants, botanical gardens and charming, old-world atmosphere. Contact: International Travel & Resorts, Inc., 4 Park Ave., New York, NY 10016. Call 212-840-6636 or 800-223-9815.
Children: Y Pets: N Smoking: Y Handicap: N Payment: C, T, A, V, M, O

SPICE ISLAND INN   *Rates: moderate-deluxe*
Open: year-round   *Minimum Stay: none*
Set amid hills carpeted with tropical forests, on a sparkling stretch of powdered sand, the Spice Island Inn contains a choice of studio and one-bedroom apartments whose names tell you what else awaits: Pool Suites, Whirlpool Beach Suites and more. Just minutes from the three-mile stretch of heaven that is Grand Anse Beach lies the Blue Horizons, whose facilities guests also have access to, including a freshwater pool. The suites have twin or double beds, kitchenette, color TV, phone and covered balcony and are fully air conditioned. Furnishings are modern and tasteful, with splashes of the bright colors so beloved in the islands. A mini-bar is provided in each room. Tennis, golf and bicycling will keep you busy on dry land, or snorkeling, scuba diving, fishing and anything else you can do on the water is waiting for you. Contact: Mr. Arnold Hopkin, Blue Horizons Cottage Hotel, P.O. Box 4, Grand Anse, St. George's, Grenada, West Indies. Call 800-223-9815 or 212-545-8469.
Children: Y Pets: N Smoking: Y Handicap Access: N Payment: C, T, A, V, M

THE FLAMBOYANT HOTEL   *Rates: budget-inexpensive*
Open: year-round   *Minimum Stay: none*
Overlooking Grand Anse Bay and the three-mile beach that surrounds it, the Flamboyant Hotel provides a spectacular view from every room. A selection of one-bedroom apartments and two-bedroom cottages is set on a hillside sloping down to a beach bathed in the spicy island breezes. Recent renovation has added a freshwater pool, restaurant and bar to the facilities, where the units include color TV, radio, air-conditioning and daily maid service. Each unit contains a living/dining room looking out through a sliding glass door over the bay, a kitchen, bath and patios. The decor is modern and bright and the surrounding hillside is covered with lush tropical greenery. Along the beach are numerous facilities for enjoying the water—jet skiing, windsurfing, snorkeling, scuba diving, as well as sailing and fishing. Contact: Lawrence Lambert, P.O. Box 214, St. George's, Grenada, West Indies. Call call 800-223-0888.
Children: Y Pets: N Smoking: Y Handicap Access: N Payment: C, T, V, M

THE VILLAGE HOTEL   *Rates: budget*
Open: year-round   *Minimum Stay: none*

A swimming pool, game room, TV lounge and bar are all included when you stay in one of these studio or one-bedroom apartments. Set on a hillside smothered with exotic plants and tropical flowers, the contemporary hotel is pleasantly small, with only twelve units. After a day lying on Grand Anse Beach, snorkeling or scuba diving around coral reefs and sunken ships or playing tennis or golf at the island clubs, you'll be grateful to return to the air-conditioned comfort of your apartment, where you can relax on the breezy patio. Daily maid service is provided and there are facilities for laundry and babysitting, as well as a barbecue for cooking up some of the day's catch, perhaps seasoned with some of the island's famous spices. Contact: Victoria Williams, Morne Toute Rd., Grand Anse, St. George's, Grenada, West Indies. Call 809-444-4097/4098.

Children: Y Pets: N Smoking: Y Handicap Access: N Payment: C, T, A, V, M, O

WAVE CREST HOLIDAY APARTMENTS   *Rates: budget*
Open: year-round   *Minimum Stay: none*

Three two-story modern buildings perched on a slope house these self-contained apartments. The choice of one or two bedrooms is yours—all twelve apartments are air-conditioned and contain a dining/living room with kitchenette, bath and a balcony where the morning air greets you redolent with the scent of hibiscus and nutmeg. A five-minute walk leads to Grand Anse Beach, a breathtaking three miles of pristine sand and sea, where you can enjoy snorkeling, scuba diving, sailing, fishing, windsurfing and, of course, lying in the tropical sun. Facilities at the complex include color TV, maid and laundry service, babysitting and a dining room for the evenings you choose to let someone else do the cooking. Contact: John R. DaBreo, Grand Anse Post Office, St. George's, Grenada, West Indies. Call 809-444-4847.

Children: Y Pets: N Smoking: Y Handicap: N Payment: C, T, A, V, M O

WINDWARD SANDS INN   *Rates: budget*
Open: year-round   *Minimum Stay: none*

A rum punch welcomes you to this small casual inn, which contains one studio, three one-bedroom and two two-bedroom apartments. Cooled by ceiling fans, the apartments feature such touches as canopy beds and balconies. A cook or barbecue facilities are available on request and maid service is provided. The small dining room at the inn serves up spicy island specialties made with fresh local produce and the catch of the day. Fishing is rewarding in the surrounding waters, and a wide range of water sports are yours to enjoy, including water skiing, snorkeling, scuba diving, or sailing—all on the turquoise waters that ring this Island of Spice. The beaches stretch for miles and the sand is smooth; further inland, visitors are welcome to play tennis and golf. Contact: Mr. Cletus Jordan, P.O. Box 199, St. George's, Grenada, West Indies. Call: 809-444-4238.

Children: Y Pets: N Smoking: Y Handicap Access: N Payment: C, T, A

LANCE AUX EPINES

CORAL COVE

Rates: inexpensive
Open: year-round
Minimum Stay: one week

Tiled floors, tennis courts, daily maid service and sliding glass doors opening onto balconies are features you'll find at this complex of eleven Spanish-style cottages and apartments overlooking the beach and coral reef. An oval swimming pool lies just outside the door of your one- or two-bedroom unit with a living/dining room, kitchen and bath (two-bedroom units have two baths). Laundry, cooking and babysitting service on request make life easier. More than twenty kinds of fish can be caught in these waters and barbecued at home; snorkeling and scuba diving among the coral reefs is a treat. There is a wide range of water sports to choose from, as well as boating or exploring the island on bicycle. Contact: Jill Evans, P.O. Box 187 (Lance aux Epines), St. George's, Grenada, West Indies. Call 809-444-4422/4217 or 800-322-1753.

Children: Y   Pets: N   Smoking: Y   Handicap Access: N   Payment: C, V, M

FAIRDALE HOLIDAY APARTMENTS

Rates: budget-inexpensive
Open: year-round
Minimum Stay: one week

This modern establishment contains six one-bedroom and four two-bedroom apartments, all fully furnished in simple, contemporary style. Either air-conditioned or cooled by a ceiling fan, the apartments are serviced by a maid (the two-bedroom apartments also have a washing machine), and contain a dining/sitting room in which to relax. Sitting on the balcony or patio, you'll absorb the fresh ocean air, delicately tinged with the scent of nutmeg and spices. Nearby is a seemingly endless strip of crystal sand known as Grand Anse Beach where both the fishing and the scuba diving are fabulous. Tennis, golf, windsurfing, jet skiing and sailing are among the other pleasures to be enjoyed on this friendly and vibrant island. Contact: Alice Salhab, Fairdale Holiday Apartments, P.O. Box 180, St. George's, Grenada, West Indies. Call 809-444-4579.

Children: Y Pets: N Smoking: Y Handicap Access: N Payment: C, T, A, V, M, O

HOLIDAY HAVEN SEASIDE VILLAS

Rates: budget-inexpensive
Open: year-round
Minimum Stay: one week

Each of these separate modern villas has either two or three bedrooms, two baths, a living/dining room and a huge kitchen with all appliances. Your wide porch looks down upon a secluded beach, one of the many that line the shores of this temperate island. Air-conditioned for comfort, the apartments come with TV, phone and barbecue facilities and complete maid service including laundry. There's nothing left to do but sample the island's many delights and relax. Try your hand at snorkeling and scuba diving among the coral reefs, sailing or power-boating, windsurfing, jet skiing, deep-sea fishing, tennis or golf. The nightlife of St. George's is only a few moments away. Contact: Dr. John Watts, Church St., St. George's, Grenada, West Indies. Call 809-440-2606 or 809-444-4325 (after 6 P.M.).

Children: Y   Pets: N   Smoking: Y   Handicap Access: N   Payment: C, T

SOLAMENTE UNA VEZ   *Rates: deluxe*
Open: year-round   *Minimum Stay: one week*

A private beach, guest house for two and gazebo greet your eyes each day from this unique Moorish villa designed by the architect owner. Capable of housing up to ten people in five bedrooms (each with en suite bathroom), the villa has its own staff including a cook who can prepare sumptuous meals from this "island of spices" and a gardener to keep the lush grounds looking their best. Gracious furniture and fine art pieces bestow elegance, but you can feel comfortable relaxing here in your bathing suit after a day of sunning or swimming. A wonderful base for exploring Grenada, this island offers some of the finest fishing and scuba diving anywhere as well as boating and a wide choice of water sports. Contact: Rent A Home International, Inc. 7200 34th Ave. NW, Seattle, WA 98117. Call 206-545-6963.

Children: Y Pets: N Smoking: Y Handicap Access: N Payment: C, P, V, M

POINTE SALINE

VILLA TAMARIND   *Rates: expensive*
Open: year-round   *Minimum Stay: one week*

A living room ringed with open arches is the central spot in which to relax and enjoy the spectacular views offered by this hillside villa. Along with three bedrooms, two baths, a Jacuzzi, barbecue and a full staff to make it all work, there is a forty-one-foot yacht with skipper available for guests to charter. All your needs are met by the staff here, including babysitting for the kids, cooking, laundry and all housekeeping. Garden pools reflect the brilliant tropical garden flowers; inside, the cool, breezy rooms are decorated with island art and wicker furniture. The beach is a short walk down the steps; all around the island are opportunities for exploring the waters or playing a set of tennis or a few holes of golf. Contact: C. Kroos or R. Glaser, Villa Holidays, Inc., 13100 Wayzata Blvd., Ste. 150, Minneapolis, MN 55343. Call 612-591-0076 or 800-328-6262.

Children: Y Pets: N Smoking: Y Handicap Access: N Payment: C, P, T, V, M

ST. GEORGE'S

NO PROBLEM APARTMENTS   *Rates: inexpensive*
Open: year-round   *Minimum Stay: one week*

"No problem" is a Caribbean motto, and in this case it points the way to a wealth of amenities in an apartment hotel with white stucco walls and arched balconies. A warm welcome greets you at the end of your complimentary ride from Point Salines Airport, and the attention continues throughout your stay, including daily maid service, babysitting, laundry and free transportation to town. Guests enjoy the famous Grand Anse Beach and free bicycles for touring. The suites have large twin beds in the bedroom, a private bathroom, a kitchenette thoughtfully stocked for your arrival and a TV, radio and phone. The pool is large and has a tropical bar; inside there is a cool, airy reading room. Visit the public beaches that ring the island, pursue a wealth of fish offshore or plunge into water sports galore—scuba diving, sailing, windsurfing, jet-skiing and speedboat trips. Contact: Mr. and Mrs. Godfrey Ventour, True Blue, Box 280, St. George's, Grenada. Call 809-444-4634/4635.

Children: Y Pets: N Smoking: Y Handicap Access: N Payment: C, T, V, M A

TWELVE DEGREES NORTH   *Rates: inexpensive-expensive*
Open: year-round   *Minimum Stay: one week*

Expatriate American Joe Gaylord keeps this resort of eight apartments small in order to preserve the personal touch and exclusive nature of his hospitality. Each apartment comes with a housekeeper who completely pampers you—from keeping your apartment and laundry spotless to preparing delicious meals. Decorated with bright West Indian prints and original island art, the apartments have one or two bedrooms and a private patio that looks down over colorful gardens to the ocean. The resort's tennis court, private beach, freshwater pool and windsurfing equipment are all yours to enjoy; further afield, the island has fabulous reefs and sunken ships where you can scuba dive or snorkel. Contact: Joseph Gaylord, P.O. Box 241, St. George's, Grenada, West Indies. Call 809-444-4580 or 800-322-1753.

Children: N   Pets: N   Smoking: Y   Handicap Access: N   Payment: C, T

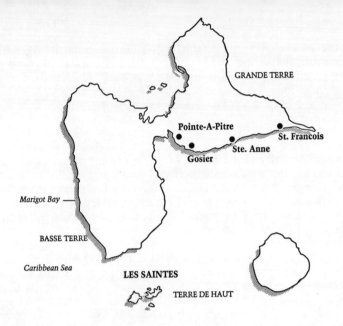

GRANDE TERRE

Pointe-A-Pitre

St. Francois

Ste. Anne

Gosier

Marigot Bay

BASSE TERRE

Caribbean Sea

LES SAINTES

TERRE DE HAUT

Guadeloupe

GOSIER

CARMELITA'S VILLAGE CARAIBE
Open: year-round

Rates: inexpensive
Minimum Stay: none

In addition to the wonderful Creole cooking of owner/manager Jeanne Carmelita, the bungalows here offer air-conditioning and telephones. Each double or single has a private bathroom and a kitchen. Within a few minutes' drive is the bustling resort of Gosier, where the nearly five miles of beach and many hotels and resorts entertain visitors with water sports. Also close by is the beach at the hamlet of St. Felix and the horseback riding school, La Criolo. Contact: International Travel and Resorts, 4 Park Avenue, New York, NY 10016. Call 800-223-9815 or 212-545-8469.

Children: **Y**   Pets: **N**   Smoking: **Y**   Handicap Access: **N**   Payment: **C, T**

LES FLAMBOYANTS
Open: year-round

Rates: budget
Minimum Stay: none

This is a property of great charm and character. An old colonial house has been surrounded by 14 holiday bungalows; the views extend to the lighthouse on Gosier Islet and beyond, over the shimmering sea. Each bungalow has its own bathroom and kitchen, and there is a restaurant on the premises. The nearby beach on Gosier has resorts offering facilities for windsurfing, sailing, waterskiing and tennis. Some of the finest hiking trails in the islands can be found in the Parc Naturel de Guadaloupe, and horseback riding is particularly good at St. Felix. Contact: Mr. Louis Douillard, Perinette Chemin des Phares et Balises, 97190, Gosier, Guadeloupe, French West Indies. Call 011-590-84-14-11.

Children: Y   Pets: N   Smoking: Y   Handicap Access: N   Payment: C, T

PLM AZUR ALLINAGO VILLAGE   *Rates: inexpensive-moderate*
Open: year-round   *Minimum Stay: none*

A choice of studio or duplex apartments are available at this resort in the Gosier area, just 15 minutes east of Pointe-a-Pitre, the port and main city of Guadaloupe. The studios have a living/dining/bedroom area and a complete kitchen with a convenient serving counter, plus a full bathroom. Sliding glass doors open onto a private balcony overlooking Gosier Bay. The duplex apartments have private balconies on both floors and a spiral staircase; these apartments also have a living/dining/bedroom area, bathroom and kitchen on the ground floor and an additional bedroom and bathroom upstairs. Full use of the facilities at next-door Callinago Beach Hotel are included with your visit: beach and water sports activities, a freshwater swimming pool and tennis courts. Contact: Pullman International Hotels, 200 W. 57th St. Suite 1310, New York, NY 10019. Call 212-757-6500 or 800-223-9862.

Children: Y   Pets: N   Smoking: Y   Handicap Access: N   Payment: C, T

LES SAINTES

LOS SANTOS   *Rates: inexpensive-moderate*
Open: year-round   *Minimum Stay: none*

Les Saintes is a collection of eight little islets off the southern coast of Grand Terre. Known for their unspoiled fishing villages, primitive roads and old fortifications, they also offer scuba diving waters favored by Jacques Cousteau. Both air and sea transportation bring you here from the main island. Los Santos is a collection of red-roofed bungalows, some of which are air-conditioned. Many of the single and double bungalows have kitchens, some have balconies that overlook the sea at Marigot Bay. All water sports facilities are provided at the hotel, which has a restaurant on the premises. Hiking on the island can take you to the high peaks that give the island its name—the High Island. Contact: Christian Hamoui, Los Santos, Baie du Marigot, 97137 Terre de Haut, Les Saintes, Guadeloupe, French West Indies. Call 011-590-99-50-40.

Children: Y   Pets: N   Smoking: Y   Handicap Access: N   Payment: C, T

POINTE-A-PITRE

GOSIER RESIDENCE   *Rates: moderate-expensive*
Open: year-round   *Minimum Stay: one week*

Apartments at Gosier Residence are found in several low-rise buildings surrounded by gardens and tropical greenery. Either studio or one-bedroom apartments are available, each with a living/dining area (which serves as a bedroom in the studios), a kitchen and a bathroom. Each apartment features a balcony or terrace providing views of the gardens and the inlet on which the hotel is located. There is a large swimming pool for guests' use when they prefer not to walk down to the beach, and there are courts on the premises for the tennis buff. Fresh produce and seafood can be purchased at the marketplace in nearby Pointe-a-Pitre. The many resorts along the shore have complete water sports facilities, including scuba diving, waterskiing, windsurfing and sailing. Contact: Villas International, 71 West 23rd St., New York, NY 10010. Call 212-929-7585.

Children: Y Pets: N Smoking: N Handicap Access: N Payment: C, P, T

ST. FELIX

ST. FELIX HOUSES   *Rates: expensive-deluxe*
Open: year-round   *Minimum Stay: one week*

On a hillside overlooking the deep blue ocean, this little cluster of three houses and a swimming pool can be found near the hamlet of St. Felix. One of the houses is occupied by the owners and the other two—a one-bedroom and a three-bedroom—are available for holiday rentals. The large house has the bedrooms downstairs and a huge terrace with ocean views upstairs, where the kitchen and dining area are located. The smaller bungalow has a combined living/dining area downstairs and a sleeping mezzanine with a double bed; it makes a perfect choice for a couple. Laundry and maid service are available and a car is put at the disposal of the guests—a sightseeing drive around Grand Terre will take you past rain forests and old sugar plantations to cliffs that are sculpted like those of Brittany. Contact: Villa Holidays, Inc., 13100 Wayzata Blvd., Ste. 150, Minneapolis, MN 55343. Call 612-591-0076 or 800-328-6262.

Children: Y Pets: N Smoking: Y Handicap Access: N Payment: C, P, T, V, M

ST. FRANCOIS

HAMAK VILLAS   *Rates: deluxe*
Open: year-round   *Minimum Stay: none*

This luxury complex can be found on the eastern shore of the Grand Terre. Twenty-eight tropical villas, each with two one-bedroom suites, are available for rental. Twin beds can be found in the bedrooms, which open onto private walled gardens with seating and hammocks for relaxing, as well as an outdoor shower for cooling off while sunbathing. Indoors there is a full bathroom, a kitchenette and a living room. Some villas are ranged along a white sand beach where water sports facilities are available at the beach center; others are nestled amid flowers and foliage in the tropical gardens. Tennis players can enjoy the court, while golfers will flock to the Robert Trent Jones, Sr., Golf Course—one of the island's finest. Contact: Caribbean Inns, P.O. Box 7411, Hilton Head Island, SC 29938. Call 800-633-7411 or 803-785-7411.

Children: Y   Pets: N   Smoking: Y   Handicap Access: N   Payment: C, T

MARINA APARTMENTS AND COTTAGES   *Rates: moderate-expensive*
Open: year-round   *Minimum Stay: one week*

Located on the calm waters of the lagoon at St. Francois, these accommodations occupy a ten-acre resort with all the water sports facilities guests could desire. The apartments are either one-bedrooms or studios, and the cottages have one bedroom; otherwise, each unit contains a living/dining area, kitchen and bathroom. The resort is self-contained and has facilities for tennis, swimming, windsurfing, sailing and deep-sea fishing. The lagoon is surrounded by a coral reef, where snorkelers and scuba divers can enjoy the well-known beauty of Guadeloupe's waters. Nearby is a golf course and the pretty fishing village of St. Francois, which has grown in recent years to include nightclubs, restaurants and other facilities for visitors. Contact: Villas International, 71 West 23rd St., New York, NY 10010. Call 212-929-7585.

Children: Y   Pets: N   Smoking: Y   Handicap Access: N   Payment: C, P, T

RESIDENCE KARUKERA   *Rates: inexpensive-moderate*
Open: year-round   *Minimum Stay: none*

A road leads east from the former fishing village of St. Francois to a castle-like natural rock formation known as Pointe des Chateaux. On this road lies a modern complex of villas in a secluded position, yet within driving distance of the restaurants, casinos and beaches of St. Francois. There are several dozen villas here, with one to four bedrooms, all with kitchenettes that have been fully equipped, and private bathrooms. On the premises is a tennis court and a swimming pool, where guests can find relief from the tropical sun. For those who prefer privacy, two of the villas have their own swimming pools. Contact: Sogestim/Residence Karukera, Pointe des Chateaux, 97118 St. Francois, Guadeloupe, French West Indies.

Children: Y   Pets: N   Smoking: Y   Handicap Access: N   Payment: C, T

TROIS MATS HOTEL   *Rates: inexpensive-moderate*
Open: year-round   *Minimum Stay: none*

Trois Mats consists of several modern buildings located directly on the marina at St. Francois on the southeast coast of Guadaloupe. For those who appreciate boating, scuba diving and fishing, this hotel makes a good choice, but it is also close to resorts that offer tennis, beaches, golf and nightlife. There are 24 studio apartments, which feature kitchen facilities on an open terrace—a perfect way to cook up a fresh catch or a delicacy purchased at the nearby market. The studios also have a bedroom/living room and a bathroom. Twelve duplex apartments have essentially the same layout but include an upstairs bedroom. The hotel features a restaurant on the premises as well as a small grocery store; there is a wider selection of restaurants in St. Francois. Contact: Jean-Francois Rozan, Trois Mats Hotel, St. Francois, 97118 Guadeloupe, French West Indies. Call 011-590-88-59-99.

Children: Y   Pets: N   Smoking: Y   Handicap Access: N   Payment: C, T

STE. ANNE

CORAIL COTTAGES

Rates: inexpensive
Open: year-round
Minimum Stay: four nights

Adjacent to Club Med, which has a wide variety of sports facilities, recreation and restaurants, this collection of simple studio cottages is just steps from the beach. The cottages are popular with "naturists"— meaning that clothes are optional on the beach. The studios have double beds in a sleeping alcove, living/dining rooms and bathrooms— air-conditioning is available for an extra fee. Patios at the front of each cottage provide a place to sit and people-watch; tropical landscaped gardens offer a cool retreat. Contact: Villas International, 71 West 23rd St., New York, NY 10010. Call 212-929-7585.

Children: **Y**   Pets: **N**   Smoking: **Y**   Handicap Access: **N**   Payment: **C, P, T**

LA TOUBANA

Rates: inexpensive-expensive
Open: year-round
Minimum Stay: none

This private little getaway complex is near the sugar town of Ste. Anne, about nine miles from Gosier. There are just over 30 units here, each an air-conditioned bungalow with a kitchenette, private bath and small terraced garden, which makes a perfect spot for sitting in seclusion. Located high on a cliff, the resort boasts fabulous views out to sea; the hotel beach is located below. A swimming pool and tennis court are on the premises, and down at the beach are facilities for water sports; if desired, guests can travel to Gosier for bigger resort facilities. A restaurant on the premises means guests needn't travel far when they don't feel like preparing meals at home, and nightly entertainment is provided. Contact: International Travel Resorts, 4 Park Avenue, New York, NY 10016. Call 800-223-9815 or 212-545-8469.

Children: **Y**   Pets: **N**   Smoking: **Y**   Handicap Access: **N**   Payment: **C, T**

RELAIS DU MOULIN

Rates: budget-inexpensive
Open: year-round
Minimum Stay: none

An old stone windmill once used for grinding sugar cane is the centerpiece of this small, family-run hotel. Set on a hillside surrounded by tropical gardens, this collection of small bungalows with kitchenettes includes one- and two-bedroom units. The bungalows are well shaded by palm trees; their large glass doors open onto private patios, and inside, the furnishings are modern and colorful. The Schooner Bar is where guests mingle, and the Tap-Tap restaurant serves sumptous meals. An inviting swimming pool satisfies the need to cool off, and the sea is just a few minutes' walk. Horseback riding through the gently rolling hills of the surrounding countryside is very popular here, and the hotel also has bicycles to rent. Contact: International Travel and Resorts, Inc., 4 Park Avenue, New York, NY 10016. Call 800-223-9815 or 212-545-8469.

Children: **Y**   Pets: **N**   Smoking: **Y**   Handicap Access: **N**   Payment: **C, T**

Runaway Bay • St. Ann's Bay •
Montego Bay • Discovery Bay • Ocho Rios •
Port Antonio •
Negril •
Bluefield's Bay
ST. ELIZABETH
★ Kingston
Treasure Beach •
Caribbean Sea

Jamaica

BLUEFIELDS' BAY

MILESTONE COTTAGE   *Rates: expensive*
Open: year-round   *Minimum Stay: one week*

Ideal for a romantic honeymoon or for a small family's tropical get-away, this recently renovated villa is tucked away on a very private acre of beachfront property. The two bedrooms and two baths are delightfully furnished, with ceiling fans gently turning above to keep the house cool and inviting. The maid and cook will see to your every need, while the gardener maintains the delightful grounds. Out back you'll find a lovely swimming pool with a spa, or if you prefer the silky waters of the Caribbean, follow the steps down to the sands of the private beach. Contact: C. Kroos or R. Glaser, Villa Holidays, Inc., 13100 Wayzata Blvd., Ste. 150, Minneapolis, MN 55343. Call 1-800-328-6262 (in Minnesota, 612-591-0076).

Children: Y Pets: N Smoking: Y Handicap Access: N Payment: C, P, T, V, M

MULLION COVE   *Rates: deluxe*
Open: year-round   *Minimum Stay: one week*

This gem from Jamaica's past will fulfill all your fantasies of a tropical holiday amid traditional elegance. The six bedrooms and main living areas of the house are graced with fine Irish linens, lace-topped canopy beds, Oriental rugs, mellow mahogany floors and objets d'art. More than just a luxurious villa, though, Mullion Cove offers a plethora of recreational opportunities. Bicycles, snorkeling gear, windsurfers, fishing equipment and a row boat are all included and the competition-size tennis court is illuminated for that friendly nighttime game. Both a private pool and a stretch of beach are available for your swimming pleasure. The courteous staff of six will efficiently see to your every need during your stay. Contact: C. Kroos or R. Glaser, Villa Holidays, Inc., 13100 Wayzata Blvd., Ste. 150, Minneapolis, MN 55343. Call 1-800-328-6262 (in Minnesota, 612-591-0076).

Children: Y Pets: N Smoking: Y Handicap Access: N Payment: C, P, T, V, M

DISCOVERY BAY

HIGH TIDE   *Rates: expensive*
Open: year-round   *Minimum Stay: one week*

This large, welcoming house with its friendly staff is set amid cool tropical gardens near the shore. Here water worshipers can enjoy every one of the sparkling Caribbean varieties: in addition to private beach rights and the swimming pool, there is a sea pool and swimming off the rocky shore. The snorkeling is excellent here, with colorful coral formations and tropical fish. The villa is comfortably furnished and each of its three bedrooms is air-conditioned. A mere four-mile drive will bring you from your secluded retreat to the festive markets and meeting places of Discovery Bay Village. Contact: C. Kroos or R. Glaser, Villa Holidays, Inc., 13100 Wayzata Blvd., Ste. 150, Minneapolis, MN 55343. Call 1-800-328-6262 (in Minnesota, 612-591-0076).

Children: Y Pets: N Smoking: Y Handicap Access: N Payment: C, P, T, V, M

MOUNT CORBETT ESTATE   *Rates: deluxe*
Open: year-round   *Minimum Stay: one week*

This resplendent mansion, which was once the winter retreat of British royalty, was built in the grand style of an 18th-century plantation house. Mount Corbett is opulently furnished with exquisite antiques, Oriental carpets atop polished hardwood floors and brass-trimmed mahogany doors. Off the magnificent drawing room, which extends the full width of the house, you'll find four elegant bedroom suites. Each of these opens through French doors to a wide veranda that surrounds the house and offers splendid views of Discovery Bay. The balustraded swimming pool is quite impressive; badminton and croquet can also be enjoyed on the grounds. Contact: Villas International, 71 W. 23rd St., New York, NY 10010. Call 212-929-7585.

Children: Y Pets: N Smoking: Y Handicap Access: N Payment: C, P, T

SPANISH COURT APARTMENTS   *Rates: budget-inexpensive*
Open: year-round   *Minimum Stay: one week*

Enjoy breathtaking views of the sparkling Caribbean Sea from the breezy balcony outside each of these hillside condominiums. The pleasant bedroom, living room and dining areas are impeccably furnished with a stylish mix of traditional pieces and bright tropical colors. A shared swimming pool is available right in the complex and a short walk will bring you to the warm sands and clay tennis courts of Puerto Seco Beach. Daily maid service will help make your stay carefree and the full kitchen will help make it convenient. Contact: C. Kroos or R. Glaser, Villa Holidays, Inc., 13100 Wayzata Blvd., Ste. 150, Minneapolis, MN 55343. Call 1-800-328-6262 (in Minnesota, 612-591-0076).

Children: Y Pets: N Smoking: Y Handicap Access: N Payment: C, P, T, V, M

THE RIDGE   *Rates: deluxe*
Open: year-round   *Minimum Stay: one week*

The Ridge is the fully restored Great House of a working cattle ranch set in the mountains above Discovery Bay. Spacious rooms with 14-foot-high ceilings, canopied mahogany beds, a handsome old library, and avocado, allspice and coconut harvests add colonial charm. A beautiful swimming pool and courteous staff give you modern convenience. There are wonderful views of the sea from an enormous veranda that wraps itself around the house, and the four large bedrooms are kept marvelously cool by the constant ocean breezes. Contact: C. Kroos or R. Glaser, Villa Holidays, Inc., 13100 Wayzata Blvd., Ste. 150, Minneapolis, MN 55343. Call 1-800-328-6262 (in Minnesota, 612-591-0076).

Children: Y Pets: N Smoking: Y Handicap Access: N Payment: C, P, T, V, M

VILLA SUNDOWN   *Rates: deluxe*
Open: year-round   *Minimum Stay: one week*

This richly appointed villa is found on Discovery Bay's sheltered harbor. Designer chintzes cover the traditional wicker furniture and a handsome arched doorway leads from the enormous living room to the formal dining room. Each of the five spacious bedrooms is air-conditioned. In the best island tradition, there are plenty of outdoor living areas as well. From your comfortable seat on the dining veranda you can see the abundant gardens tempting you to wander their fragrant pathways as well as the beach beyond with its barbecue and fishing pier. There's even a private airfield nearby, in case you decide to whisk your beloved away to this exotic retreat in private luxury. Contact: C. Kroos or R. Glaser, Villa Holidays, Inc., 13100 Wayzata Blvd., Ste. 150, Minneapolis, MN 55343. Call 1-800-328-6262 (in Minnesota, 612-591-0076).

Children: Y Pets: N Smoking: Y Handicap Access: N Payment: C, P, T, V, M

MONTEGO BAY

BELCRAG BEACH COTTAGE   *Rates: moderate-expensive*
Open: year-round   *Minimum Stay: one week*

This pleasant house is found on the incredibly white sands of beautiful Silver Sands Beach. If you can tear yourself away from this splendid beach, take a tour of the owners' 300-year-old sugar farm or check out the tennis at the nearby hotels. The three bedrooms and spacious living and dining room are all comfortably furnished and the balcony boasts marvelous views of the ocean. What better way to end a day of fun in the sun than out on a breezy balcony with a pina colada and a couple of friends, watching the splendor of the setting sun reflected in the friendly Caribbean? Contact: C. Kroos or R. Glaser, Villa Holidays, Inc., 13100 Wayzata Blvd., Ste. 150, Minneapolis, MN 55343. Call 1-800-328-6262 (in Minnesota, 612-591-0076).

Children: Y Pets: N Smoking: Y Handicap Access: N Payment: C, P, T, V, M

CINNAMON HILL   *Rates: deluxe*
Open: year-round   *Minimum Stay: one week*

This elegant 18th-century plantation house has a rich and varied history. Previously owned by the family of Elizabeth Barrett Browning, the villa has also been the vacation home of Johnny Cash. Today it offers exquisite accommodations for discerning guests. The interiors are richly furnished with fine artwork and splendid antiques, including antique four-poster beds in the five bedrooms. The extensive gardens are overflowing with grapefruit, oranges, mangoes, avocados and limes, their luxuriant fragrances of which carrying to the open terraces that surround the house. The beach is only a few minutes away and tennis can be enjoyed at the nearby Rose Hall Hotel. Contact: C. Kroos or R. Glaser, Villa Holidays, Inc., 13100 Wayzata Blvd., Ste. 150, Minneapolis, MN 55343. Call 1-800-328-6262 (in Minnesota, 612-591-0076).

Children: N Pets: N Smoking: Y Handicap Access: N Payment: C, P, T, V, M

HANOVER HOUSE   *Rates: aeluxe*
Open: year-round   *Minimum Stay: one week*

From its ideal situation on Tamarind Hill, the Hanover House commands splendid views of coconut plantations and the ocean beyond. At the center of this sprawling villa you'll find an enormous swimming pool, one of the largest on the island. The pool is surrounded by shaded terraces gracefully ornamented by gentle arches and pale columns; this is a lovely place to relax after a swim or to enjoy the gourmet dinner prepared by your excellent chef. Most of the spacious rooms open onto this central area; upstairs there are large, sunny balconies overlooking the pool. Modern decor is featured in the six comfortable bedrooms and the stylish main rooms of the house. A well-trained staff of five will pamper you during your holiday. Contact: Villas and Apartments Abroad, Ltd., 420 Madison Ave., New York, NY 10017. Call 1-800-433-3020 (in New York, 212-759-1025).

Children: Y Pets: N Smoking: Y Handicap Access: N Payment: C, P, T

HARLEQUIN   *Rates: expensive-deluxe*
Open: year-round   *Minimum Stay: one week, less upon request*

This pleasant hillside villa near Montego Bay is a sheltered spot just perfect for friends or families who want to enjoy the beauty of this tropical isle in languorous seclusion. The cook will fulfill your every culinary fantasy and the maid will look after you during your stay. Comfortably furnished, the four bedrooms and living room are breezy and filled with light. You'll probably want to spend some time out on the veranda with a gin-and-tonic in hand, enjoying the simply marvelous views of the rolling greenery nearby and the ocean beyond. The swimming pool is down an impressive flight of stairs and the sandy beach is only a few minutes away. Contact: Island Hideaways, Inc., 1317 Rhode Island Ave. NW, Ste. 503, Washington, DC 20005. Call 1-800-832-2302 (in the District of Columbia, 202-667-9652).

Children: Y   Pets: N   Smoking: Y   Handicap Access: N   Payment: C, P, T

KINGSWAY VILLA   *Rates: moderate-expensive*
Open: year-round   *Minimum Stay: one week*
As you drive through the gates of this villa you'll immediately be struck by its charming aspect: a tidy white house nestled under palm trees and an endless blue sky. The full staff will welcome you upon your arrival and show you the living and dining room with wet bar and stereo and the three air-conditioned bedrooms. After a refreshing cocktail, perhaps you'd like to stroll around the delightful gardens or take a dip in the refreshing pool. Beach bums will want to check out the Residents' Beach just a few minutes away; tennis fiends can practice their swing at several of the nearby hotels. Contact: C. Kroos or R. Glaser, Villa Holidays, Inc., 13100 Wayzata Blvd., Ste. 150, Minneapolis, MN 55343. Call 1-800-328-6262 (in Minnesota, 612-591-0076).

Children: Y Pets: N Smoking: Y Handicap Access: N Payment: C, P, T, V, M

ROCK HOUSE   *Rates: expensive-deluxe*
Open: year-round   *Minimum Stay: one week*
Set in a picturesque grotto, this lovely home combines privacy and seclusion with breathtaking sea views. Either the small sandy beach or the shady pool by the patio will quench your desire for a refreshing swim. All your favorite aquatic pursuits are readily available in the neighborhood and shopping connoisseurs will want to investigate the colorful crafts at the local markets. The villa contains three comfortable bedrooms with romantic ceiling fans lazily revolving overhead. Friendly staff will see after you during your stay. Contact: C. Kroos or R. Glaser, Villa Holidays, Inc., 13100 Wayzata Blvd., Ste. 150, Minneapolis, MN 55343. Call 1-800-328-6262 (in Minnesota, 612-591-0076).

Children: Y Pets: N Smoking: Y Handicap Access: N Payment: C, P, T, V, M

SUNSHINE VILLAS   *Rates: budget-inexpensive*
Open: year-round   *Minimum Stay: none*
Now you don't have to be a wealthy movie star to live like one. Sunshine Villas boasts a diverse portfolio of richly appointed mansions located all over Jamaica. Whether you choose to sojourn on a mountaintop or down by the soft white sands, your home will delight you with its charming decor, cool chambers (all villas have air-conditioning) and lavish amenities. A cook will prepare you sumptuous feasts featuring exotic fruits, grilled seafood and island-style vegetables from the local market; a housekeeper and houseman will see to it that the villa runs smoothly. Babysitters, chauffeurs, guides and laundresses are also available to cater to your every whim. Contact: Doris Parchment, Sunshine Villas and Apartment Vacations, 257 S. 16th St., 1-D, Philadelphia, PA 19102. Call 1-800-346-5897 (in Pennsylvania, 215-790-1190).

Children: Y   Pets: N   Smoking: Y   Handicap Access: N   Payment: C, P, T

TRANQUILLITY VILLA   *Rates: deluxe*
Open: year-round   *Minimum Stay: four nights*

Tranquillity Villa is nothing less than a Jamaican paradise. Set on two acres of well-manicured grounds, this elegant house is furnished with Dhurrie rugs, English chintzes, refined antiques and marble floors. Each of the three air-conditioned bedroom suites is exquisitely decorated in delicate tones of peach and mauve. The spacious master bedroom features a stylish black-tiled bathroom with two showers and a tub; French doors open onto a private marble terrace. A stairway leads from here down to the pool and private beach. The grounds also include a seaside gazebo—perfect for candlelight dinners—and a tennis court. To complete the fantasy, an efficient staff of six will pamper you during your stay. Contact: Lori Gedon, Vacation Home Rentals Worldwide, 235 Kensington Ave., Norwood, NJ 07648. Call 1-800-633-3284 (in New Jersey, 201-767-9393). Ref. JM119.

Children: N   Pets: N   Smoking: Y   Handicap Access: N   Payment: C, P, T

TYGWYN   *Rates: deluxe*
Open: year-round   *Minimum Stay: one week*

This lovely tile-roofed villa combines the elegance of the Old World with the casual charm of the new. As you pull up to the handsome entryway you'll be greeted by the full staff. After a languorous session of private swimming and basking by the well-landscaped pool in back, enjoy an excellent dinner prepared by your chef out on the breezy dining pavilion. The Jacuzzi may tempt you back into the water before your nightcap, and after a good night's sleep in one of the four spacious bedrooms, you'll be ready to explore some of the island's many alluring beaches, sparkling waterfalls and intimate restaurants. Contact: Villas and Apartments Abroad, Ltd., 420 Madison Ave., New York, NY 10017. Call 1-800-433-3020 (in New York, 212-759-1025).

Children: Y   Pets: N   Smoking: Y   Handicap Access: N   Payment: C, P, T

VILLA OLGA   *Rates: deluxe*
Open: year-round   *Minimum Stay: one week*

This luxurious villa is found on a tranquil hillside surrounded by resplendent tropical gardens. The living room, formal dining room and four bedrooms are graced with fine antiques but also boast such modern amenities as TV and air-conditioning. More casual dining can be enjoyed on the large patio, which enjoys cool ocean breezes and magnificent views of the water. There's even a barbecue outside for that spicy open-air grilling you've been wanting to try. The delightful pool in the front of the house will satisfy loungers and swimmers alike and a staff of three will pamper you with their courteous, efficient service. Once you've savored the pleasures at home, a short drive will bring you to the beaches, restaurants, shops and nightspots of the friendly town. Contact: Olga T. Broeder, 336 86th St., New York, NY 10028. Call 212-628-7144.

Children: Y   Pets: N   Smoking: Y   Handicap Access: Y   Payment: P, T

VILLA PORTOFINO   *Rates: expensive-deluxe*
Open: year-round   *Minimum Stay: one week*

This exquisitely furnished villa has everything in the right place. The large, handsome living room features a wet bar and opens onto a splendid open-air dining terrace; this, in turn, leads down a few steps to a sunny patio. From the terrace you can enter any of the three elegantly appointed bedrooms, each with its own en suite bath. At the center of the floor plan, surrounded by the terrace and patio, is a circular, brick-paved pool. Perhaps best of all, the villa's commanding hilltop location affords fabulous views from every room. Surrounded by beauty and pampered by the full staff, you may choose never to leave; but for those who do, there's tennis and a wonderful sand beach only three miles away. Contact: C. Kroos or R. Glaser, Villa Holidays, Inc., 13100 Wayzata Blvd., Ste. 150, Minneapolis, MN 55343. Call 1-800-328-6262 (in Minnesota, 612-591-0076).

Children: Y Pets: N Smoking: Y Handicap Access: N Payment: C, P, T, V, M

WINDWARD   *Rates: deluxe*
Open: year-round   *Minimum Stay: one week*

This beachside neo-Georgian villa is stylishly formal yet cozy enough to feel like home. The charming four-poster bed in the master bedroom is picturesquely draped with gauze; all three of the bedrooms are air-conditioned. One of the two living rooms opens onto a lovely balcony just right for afternoon tea or evening cocktails. As you enjoy the light breeze and the rustle of palm fronds, you can admire the large swimming pool set like a jewel in its pretty patio or gaze at the marvelous waters of the sea beyond. After a few laps or a lazy afternoon of wading in the Caribbean waters, take a stroll through the delightful floral gardens, which are sure to entice you with their rich fragrance and extraordinary blossoms. Contact: Villas and Apartments Abroad, Ltd., 420 Madison Ave., New York, NY 10017. Call 1-800-433-3020 (in New York, 212-759-1025).

Children: Y Pets: N Smoking: Y Handicap Access: N Payment: C, P, T

NAVY ISLAND

THE ADMIRALTY CLUB   *Rates: budget-deluxe*
Open: year-round   *Minimum Stay: none*

This alluring green jewel in the blue waters off Port Antonio was once the favored haunt of its owner, Errol Flynn. Now you can enjoy the unspoiled natural beauty and tradition of excellent service found on Navy Island. The diverse guest rooms and villas can accommodate parties of varying sizes; all feature large verandas or decks to help you cultivate that breezy outdoor lifestyle so beloved on this island. Three white beaches—one where clothing is optional—tempt you to bronze and bathe your days away. But there's so much more to do: the water-skiing, windsurfing and sailing facilities here are splendid. And you'll never forget the tantalizing dinners enjoyed in the lovely Fountain Room or out on the romantic candle-lit Orchid Terrace. Contact: The

Admiralty Club, 12156 Riverside Dr., No. Hollywood, CA 91607. Call
1-800-634-0765 (in California, 818-985-5757).

Children: Y Pets: N Smoking: Y Handicap Access: N Payment: C, T, A, V, M

NEGRIL

ADDIS KOKEB GUEST HOUSE & COTTAGES   *Rates: budget*
Open: year-round   *Minimum Stay: none*

Addis Kokeb—which means "New Star"—may just be the lucky star
of your vacation. This magnificent guest house is a hand-built edifice
of cedar, mahogany and native blue mahoe; beneath the star-shaped
roof are six bedrooms and shared living quarters. One- and two-
bedroom cottages wrapped in lush vegetation are perfect holiday
houses for families (babysitters are available). As tropical birds flit
from palm to fruit tree, enjoy a peaceful nap swaying in the hammock
on the screened porch. The jagged limestone cliffs afford splendid
swimming as well as magnificent scenery—just walk to the edge and
jump into sparkling waters. Although a tranquil haven, Addis Kokeb is
hardly isolated. Nearby are restaurants, bars and nightspots where you
can dance beneath the friendly stars. Contact: Dennis or Deborah
Luers, P.O. Box 78, Negril, Westmoreland, Jamaica. Call 809-957-4485.

Children: Y Pets: N Smoking: Y Handicap Access: N Payment: C, T, A, V, M

BAR-B-BARN VILLAS   *Rates: budget-inexpensive*
Open: year-round   *Minimum Stay: none*

Renowned for its sumptuous Jamaican barbecue, this resort offers
kitchenette rooms to those who will appreciate the casual ambience
and splendid setting. Tucked between the luxuriant inland greenery
and the dazzling white sands of the shore, the one-bedroom suites are
filled with light and are comfortably furnished. Swimming in the sapphire waters and basking in the warm sun are popular pursuits here;
water sports facilities and other recreational options can be found
nearby. After a magnificent sunset cruise, stop by one of the lively
nightspots nearby where locals and visitors alike spend the evening
swaying to Caribbean rhythms. Contact: Elethia Thompson, Bar-B-
Barn Villas, Norman Manley Blvd., Negril, Westmoreland, Jamaica.
Call 809-957-4267.

Children: Y Pets: N Smoking: Y Handicap Access: N Payment: C, T, A, V, M

CRYSTAL WATERS VILLAS   *Rates: budget-expensive*
Open: year-round   *Minimum Stay: one week*

Located on the gleaming white sands of the Seven Mile Beach, this
collection of holiday houses offer carefree, private accommodations at
a reasonable price. Surrounded by acres of well-kept gardens, the one-,
two- and three-bedroom houses are all beautifully furnished; most
feature sunny decks and breezy screened-in porches. To make your
vacation truly worry-free, a maid and cook will see after you during
your stay. Thatched huts on the beach provide a charming retreat from
the heat of the midday sun; the convenient playground is a great place
for the kids to get their fill of acrobatic fun. A short walk will bring

you to abundant water sports facilities, fine restaurants and energetic nightspots. Contact: C. Kroos or R. Glaser, Villa Holidays, Inc., 13100 Wayzata Blvd., Ste. 150, Minneapolis, MN 55343. Call 1-800-328-6262 (in Minnesota, 612-591-0076).

Children: Y Pets: N Smoking: Y Handicap Access: N Payment: C, P, T, V, M

DREAMSCAPE VILLA   *Rates: budget-expensive*
Open: year-round   *Minimum Stay: none*

This small hotel offers its guests warm hospitality and accommodating service. The rooms are tastefully furnished with flagstone floors, handsome wooden furniture and evocative ceiling fans. Some suites feature private Jacuzzis and oceanview balconies; all offer satellite TV and complimentary breakfast. You'll find your refrigerator stocked with French wines, California champagnes and other goodies and a maid stops by daily to tidy things up. The villa has some secluded coral cliffs for sunbathing and also enjoys private sea access, a convenient way to begin a day of sailing, snorkeling, or scuba diving. Contact: Robert Harris, P.O. Box 51, West End Rd., Negril, Jamaica. Call 1-800-423-4095 or 809-957-4495.

Children: Y Pets: N Smoking: Y Handicap Access: N Payment: C, T, V, M

DRUMVILLE COVE RESORT   *Rates: budget-moderate*
Open: year-round   *Minimum Stay: three nights*

A secluded setting on precipitous cliffs overlooking the sea and generous hospitality in the best island tradition help set this resort apart. Cottages and suites offer guests every self-catering amenity; a meal plan is also available if you wish. After a peaceful nap in the hammock outside your cottage, you can sun and swim at the sparkling pool or by the rocky cliffs; the white sands of Negril are just a few minutes away. More adventurous souls might want to try waterskiing, boating, snorkeling, or the clothing-optional section. The nightlife here is enticing and vibrant: Stop by one of the bars for a rich tropical concoction, or dance the night away to a reggae beat. Contact: Jackie Drummond, 11a Carvalho Dr., Kingston 10, Jamaica. Call 1-800-421-9596 or 809-929-7291.

Children: Y Pets: N Smoking: Y Handicap Access: N Payment: C, T, A, V, M

FOOTE PRINTS ON THE SANDS HOTEL   *Rates: inexpensive-moderate*
Open: year-round   *Minimum Stay: none*

Gently arching palm fronds and a wide sweep of gleaming white sand provide the setting for this romantic getaway. Some of the air-conditioned rooms overlook the gardens, where radiant crotons and brilliant red hibiscus fill the air with their fragrant perfume. Other rooms offer glorious views of the sea. Spend at least one lazy evening on your balcony watching the ocean ablaze with the setting sun's fire. Spicy meals are served either in the elegant dining room or under the thatched roof of the gazebo; your room's kitchenette allows you to try your own hand at island cooking if you're so inclined. Tennis, horseback riding and volleyball on the beach are among the favorite pastimes here; tours of Dunn's River Falls, the Black River and other natural wonders are also available. Contact: Mrs. Audrey Foote or Ms. Ingrid Foote, P.O. Box 100, Negril, Jamaica. Call 809-957-4300.

Children: Y Pets: N Smoking: Y Handicap Access: N Payment: C, T, A, V, M

LLANTRISSANT
Rates: deluxe
Open: year-round
Minimum Stay: one week

This lovely century-old beach house is Negril's oldest property and was once the Caribbean retreat of Queen Victoria's physician. It boasts not one but two private beaches as well as a grass tennis court in the best British tradition. Athletic guests will be further delighted by the regulation squash court, sailboat, windsurfer and snorkeling equipment. Devotees of more sedate pursuits will appreciate the large open verandas and delightful gardens. Llantrissant has been lovingly maintained and is furnished with cane and antique pieces. The main house boasts four bedrooms and the guest house has one more; altogether the property can accommodate 12 people. Contact: C. Kroos or R. Glaser, Villa Holidays, Inc., 13100 Wayzata Blvd., Ste. 150, Minneapolis, MN 55343. Call 1-800-328-6262 (in Minnesota, 612-591-0076).

Children: Y Pets: N Smoking: Y Handicap Access: N Payment: C, P, T, V, M

NEGRIL BEACH CLUB
Rates: budget-expensive
Open: year-round
Minimum Stay: one week

For that breezy Caribbean vacation surrounded by new friends and a welcoming staff, try the Negril Beach Club. The hacienda-style condo complex with studio, one- and two-bedroom units is set around a large courtyard ornamented by swaying palms. The lifestyle here is free and easy, whether you're enjoying the live entertainment in the restaurant and bar or partaking of a festive beach barbecue. The swimming pool, sandy beach and two tennis courts should satisfy active types; intrepid sun worshipers may want to stop by the clothing-optional section of the beach. Every unit has a full kitchen and a balcony and daily maid service is provided. Contact: C. Kroos or R. Glaser, Villa Holidays, Inc., 13100 Wayzata Blvd., Ste. 150, Minneapolis, MN 55343. Call 1-800-328-6262 (in Minnesota, 612-591-0076).

Children: Y Pets: N Smoking: Y Handicap Access: N Payment: C, P, T, V, M

NIRVANA COTTAGES
Rates: inexpensive
Open: year-round
Minimum Stay: one week

Your own private nirvana may be found in one of these beachside cottages on the renowned Seven Mile Beach. The American owners have provided an exceptionally high standard of comfort and service. The two- and three-bedroom cottages are surrounded by an acre of luxuriant tropical gardens that ensure complete privacy. They are kept quite cool by the graceful ceiling fans, and daily maid service is included. Haven't you always dreamed of napping in a hammock suspended between two swaying palms while listening to the calls of exotic birds and gazing at the shimmering waters of the Caribbean? Contact: C. Kroos or R. Glaser, Villa Holidays, Inc., 13100 Wayzata Blvd., Ste. 150, Minneapolis, MN 55343. Call 1-800-328-6262 (in Minnesota, 612-591-0076).

Children: Y Pets: N Smoking: Y Handicap Access: N Payment: C, P, T, V, M

OUR PAST TIME VILLAS *Rates: budget-inexpensive*
Open: year-round *Minimum Stay: three nights*
Surrounded by delightful gardens and only a few steps from the beach, this pleasant resort delights guests with its casual atmosphere and friendly service. The rooms with kitchenettes are kept pleasantly cool with air conditioners or romantic ceiling fans; each suite has a private patio overlooking the sea. The grounds of the villa extend to the lovely white sweep of Negril's famous beaches. Here you can find plenty of snorkeling, scuba diving, waterskiing and windsurfing facilities, as well as sands for relaxing and water for just splashing about. And your evenings will be filled with fun, too; the barbecue on the beach and the calypso and reggae dancing that inevitably follows is a weekly ritual that all look forward to. Contact: Gregg Keesling, Vacation Network, 1501 W. Fullerton, Chicago, IL 60614. Call 1-800-4233-4095 (in Illinois, 809-957-4409 or 809-957-4079).
Children: Y Pets: N Smoking: Y Handicap Access: N Payment: C, T, A, V, M

POINCIANA BEACH VILLAS *Rates: inexpensive-expensive*
Open: year-round *Minimum Stay: one week*
These stylish beachfront condo units are found on one of Jamaica's finest beaches. After a languid swim or a romantic stroll at daybreak along the water's edge, what could be more perfect than stretching out on the fine white sands and soaking up the magic of the Caribbean sun? Those who prefer a vacation of more active pursuits will be pleased by the catamaran sailing, pedal boats and Ping-Pong tables. Each of the units—which range from studios to three-bedroom apartments—features traditional Jamaican cane furnishings and boasts its own private balcony or terrace. Contact: C. Kroos or R. Glaser, Villa Holidays, Inc., 13100 Wayzata Blvd., Ste. 150, Minneapolis, MN 55343. Call 1-800-328-6262 (in Minnesota, 612-591-0076).
Children: Y Pets: N Smoking: Y Handicap Access: N Payment: C, P, T, V, M

ROCK HOUSE *Rates: inexpensive-moderate*
Open: year-round *Minimum Stay: one week*
This perfectly romantic little cluster of thatched cottages is ideal for newlyweds or those enjoying a second honeymoon. Set on the picturesque cliffs of the West End, they offer seclusion, tranquillity and breathtakingly beautiful sunsets. Here you can walk over to the edge of the cliff and make that elegant swan dive into sapphire waters you've always dreamed of; those who prefer security to drama can climb down the rope ladders or splash about in the sparkling cave pool. The rustic one-bedroom cottages are comfortably furnished and include kitchenettes. The ceiling fan gently turning overhead will keep you cool and the daily maid service will ensure you have no worries, only pleasures. Contact: C. Kroos or R. Glaser, Villa Holidays, Inc., 13100 Wayzata Blvd., Ste. 150, Minneapolis, MN 55343. Call 1-800-328-6262 (in Minnesota, 612-591-0076).
Children: Y Pets: N Smoking: Y Handicap Access: N Payment: C, P, T, V, M

SEAGRAPE VILLAS   *Rates: budget-inexpensive*
Open: year-round   *Minimum Stay: three nights*

The Seagrape Villas are luxurious retreats at the east edge of Ocho
Rios. Each of the handsome villas boasts four bedrooms (three are
air-conditioned) and its own swimming pool. The staff will spoil you
with their assiduous care and amazing culinary skills. This is the place
to sample some of the Jamaican delicacies you've heard so much about:
the pumpkin soup, fried bananas, lobster and parrot fish are all excellent. Beautiful tennis and beach facilities are found at the nearby Shaw
Park Beach Hotel; the White River Feast, with its live entertainment
and spicy local food, is hosted here twice weekly. Contact: Gregg
Keesling, Vacation Network, 1501 W. Fullerton, Chicago, IL 60614.
Call 1-800-4233-4095 (in Illinois, 809-957-4409 or 809-957-4079).

Children: Y Pets: N Smoking: Y Handicap Access: N Payment: C, T, A, V, M

VILLAS NEGRIL   *Rates: inexpensive-moderate*
Open: year-round   *Minimum Stay: one week*

These comfortable apartments are located right in the heart of Negril.
This is the place to come for rollicking nightclubs, excellent seafood,
marketplaces bursting with local crafts and reggae dancing far into the
night. Surrounded by acres of lush tropical gardens, the Villas Negril
enjoy splendid views of the ocean. The beach is just a short walk away
and the complex has its own large swimming pool. The one- and
two-bedroom apartments sport casual modern furnishings; daily maid
service is provided. Contact: C. Kroos or R. Glaser, Villa Holidays,
Inc., 13100 Wayzata Blvd., Ste. 150, Minneapolis, MN 55343. Call
1-800-328-6262 (in Minnesota, 612-591-0076).

Children: Y Pets: N Smoking: Y Handicap Access: N Payment: C, P, T, V, M

NEGRIL BEACH

BANANA SHOUT   *Rates: budget-inexpensive*
Open: April 16-December 15   *Minimum Stay: four nights*

For a secluded vacation, get away to one of these six elegant houses.
Three of the accommodations have lush garden views, while the other
three face the tranquil waters of the Caribbean. Kitchenettes, ceiling
fans and maid service keep you cool and relaxed. Waterfront land gives
you direct access to the unparalleled diving and water sports that are
available on Negril Beach. After a day spent doing everything under
the sun, or doing nothing under the sun, stop in at nearby Rick's Cafe
for some tropical refreshments. Contact: Vacation Network, 1501 W.
Fullerton, Chicago, IL 60614. Call 1-800-423-4095 (in Illinois, 312-
883-1020).

Children: Y Pets: N Smoking: Y Handicap Access: N Payment: P, V, M

GOLD NUGGET   *Rates: budget*
Open: April 16-December 15   *Minimum Stay: four nights*

Relax in cool comfort in this two-story motel across from Negril
Beach. All rooms with kitchenettes feature air conditioning or ceiling
fans, with their own balconies or patios. With the motel's pool, bar and

restaurant, you've got everything you need for a relaxing stay. Enjoy a day of snorkeling, swimming or diving in the crystal-clear ocean waters, then explore the local scene with its crafts market and island nightlife. Contact: Vacation Network, 1501 W. Fullerton, Chicago, IL 60614. Call 1-800-423-4095 (in Illinois, 312-883-1020).

Children: Y Pets: N Smoking: Y Handicap Access: N Payment: C, P, T, V, M

RONDEL VILLAGE   *Rates: budget-moderate*
Open: April 16-December 15   *Minimum Stay: four nights*
Rondel Village's one- or two-bedroom villas feature deluxe amenities such as private Jacuzzis, satellite color TVs and maid service amid well-tended tropical greenery. Garden and ocean views abound, and one look around will tell you why Negril Beach continues to grow in popularity. The once anonymous fishing village is now famous among divers, sailors, fishermen, and those who just love to lie on white sand while soaking up the tropical sun. Cook in your private kitchen, or sample the island delicacies at a local restaurant. Contact: Vacation Network, 1501 W. Fullerton, Chicago, IL 60614. Call 1-800-423-4095 (in Illinois, 312-883-1020).

Children: Y Pets: N Smoking: Y Handicap Access: N Payment: P, V, M

SECRET PARADISE   *Rates: budget-inexpensive*
Open: April 16-December 15   *Minimum Stay: four nights*
Off the beaten track, you'll find these one- and two-bedroom oceanfront cottages the perfect place for a secluded getaway. All cottages come with kitchenettes, maid service and modern amenities. Your own transportation is recommended, and there are plenty of activities within driving distance. Visit nearby Lucea, a scenic 18th-century port, or take a trip to famous Montego Bay, where you can sample all the pleasures of a Jamaican holiday. Contact: Vacation Network, 1501 W. Fullerton, Chicago, IL 60614. Call 1-800-423-4095 (in Illinois, 312-883-1020).

Children: Y Pets: N Smoking: Y Handicap Access: N Payment: P, V, M

TREE HOUSE   *Rates: inexpensive*
Open: April 16-December 15   *Minimum Stay: four nights*
This breezy resort offers two-bedroom suites with air conditioning or ceiling fans and marvelous views of the ocean. Rooms with kitchenettes also feature maid service. The resort's own restaurant and bar keep you refreshed and ready to explore the wonders of Negil Beach, which is famous for its coral reefs and clear aqua waters. The scuba diving, snorkeling and windsurfing here can't be beat, and local ordinances protect the natural beauty of the environment from being over-commercialized. Contact: Vacation Network, 1501 W. Fullerton, Chicago, IL 60614. Call 1-800-423-4095 (in Illinois, 312-883-1020).

Children: Y Pets: N Smoking: Y Handicap Access: N Payment: P, V, M

XTABI
Rates: inexpensive

Open: April 16-December 15
Minimum Stay: four nights

These lovely cottages with sea or garden views are situated amid Negril's lush greenery. Units with kitchenettes also offer maid service. Each features ceiling fans to take advantage of cool island breezes. Water sports are a natural here, with a variety of fishing, diving and swimming options available. After a busy day, cool off in the resort's pool or refresh yourself at the bar and restaurant. Contact: Vacation Network, 1501 W. Fullerton, Chicago, IL 60614. Call 1-800-423-4095 (in Illinois, 312-883-1020).

Children: Y   Pets: N   Smoking: Y   Handicap Access: N   Payment: P, V, M

OCHO RIOS

ALMOND TREE
Rates: deluxe

Open: year-round
Minimum Stay: one week

This elegant oceanfront home is surrounded by groves of papaya, lime, mango and ackee trees and features a unique indoor garden. Constructed of cool native stone, this abode is a haven of luxury and style. You'll sleep in a canopied four-poster bed; you'll be served excellent meals on fine china; and you'll be pampered by the impeccably trained staff. The three bedrooms are lavishly furnished and comfortably air-conditioned. The patio around the swimming pool is partially shaded by the arching fronds of palm trees and it's just a short walk to the warm sands of Mammee Bay. Contact: C. Kroos or R. Glaser, Villa Holidays, Inc., 13100 Wayzata Blvd., Ste. 150, Minneapolis, MN 55343. Call 1-800-328-6262 (in Minnesota, 612-591-0076).

Children: Y Pets: N Smoking: Y Handicap Access: N Payment: C, P, T, V, M

BLUE SHADOW
Rates: deluxe

Open: year-round
Minimum Stay: one week

Stately luxury is the keynote of this handsome four-bedroom villa set above the sea. The elegantly appointed living room features magnificent wooden paneling; fine island wood has also been used for the polished floors. Outside, the large sunny terrace overlooks luxuriant tropical gardens sloping down to the green-blue sea. The villa has its own private swimming pool and also enjoys full use of the resort facilities at the nearby Plantation Inn. After a day of exhilarating aquatic activities, you'll return to a wonderful meal prepared by your cook followed by an evening cocktail sipped while watching the last glimmer of sunlight play across the waters. Contact: Villas and Apartments Abroad, Ltd., 420 Madison Ave., New York, NY 10017. Call 1-800-433-3020 (in New York, 212-759-1025).

Children: Y   Pets: N   Smoking: Y   Handicap Access: N   Payment: C, P, T

CAREY ISLAND
Rates: deluxe

Open: year-round
Minimum Stay: one week

This impressive six-acre estate was once the home of a British aristocrat. The magnificent dining hall within the Tudor-style stone house features large, exposed-beam ceilings and handsome old wooden fur-

niture. There are seven elegantly furnished bedrooms in addition to the main function rooms of the house and a courteous staff of six will look after you during your stay. The well-kept grounds include rolling green lawns, a separate guest house, a sparkling swimming pool and a private beach with excellent swimming. There is also a small private island that's perfect for lazy picnics or energetic evening parties. Contact: Villas and Apartments Abroad, Ltd., 420 Madison Ave., New York, NY 10017. Call 1-800-433-3020 (in New York, 212-759-1025).
Children: Y   Pets: N   Smoking: Y   Handicap Access: N   Payment: C, P, T

CARIB OCHO RIOS   *Rates: inexpensive-moderate*
Open: year-round   *Minimum Stay: one week*
These waterfront condos are at once delightfully quiet yet conveniently close to the attractions of Ocho Rios. Each of the one- and two-bedroom suites features a large balcony overlooking the Caribbean and includes a fully equipped kitchenette. For those who want to leave the routine of cooking back in the real world, there is an excellent restaurant on the grounds. The lovely resort includes a refreshing swimming pool, tennis courts and a private stretch of sandy beach. Maid service is included and the rooms are kept cool with ceiling fans and air conditioners. Contact: C. Kroos or R. Glaser, Villa Holidays, Inc., 13100 Wayzata Blvd., Ste. 150, Minneapolis, MN 55343. Call 1-800-328-6262 (in Minnesota, 612-591-0076).
Children: Y Pets: N Smoking: Y Handicap Access: N Payment: C, P, T, V, M

CIRRHOSIS ON THE SEA   *Rates: deluxe*
Open: year-round   *Minimum Stay: one week*
Traditional Jamaican architecture is featured in this pleasant villa with its incredibly high ceilings, open spaces, large windows and plentiful outside living areas. Each of the four bedrooms is comfortably furnished and air-conditioned. The large living room opens onto a sunny patio where you can admire the magnificent ocean views and watch the palm trees around you sway in the breeze; this is also where you'll find the elegant oval swimming pool. The fully staffed villa is located in the prestigious Mammee Bay area and just a short stroll will bring you to the private Mammee Bay Beach Club. Contact: C. Kroos or R. Glaser, Villa Holidays, Inc., 13100 Wayzata Blvd., Ste. 150, Minneapolis, MN 55343. Call 1-800-328-6262 (in Minnesota, 612-591-0076).
Children: Y Pets: N Smoking: Y Handicap Access: N Payment: C, P, T, V, M

COCO PALMS   *Rates: deluxe*
Open: year-round   *Minimum Stay: one week*
Set among rolling green lawns and tall palm trees, this two-bedroom villa outside Ocho Rios is a haven of comfort and tranquillity. The many French doors fill the rooms with light, while the terrazzo floors and wicker furniture create a casual ambience within. The tempting swimming pool with its balustraded patio is right off the living room. For those who prefer the aquamarine waters of the Caribbean, the lovely warm sands of the beach are just a few minutes away. Golf

enthusiasts will be pleased by the nearby courses and everyone will appreciate the full staff of a cook, maid and gardener. Contact: Villas and Apartments Abroad, Ltd., 420 Madison Ave., New York, NY 10017. Call 1-800-433-3020 (in New York, 212-759-1025).

Children: Y Pets: N Smoking: Y Handicap Access: N Payment: C, P, T

COLUMBUS HEIGHTS

Rates: budget-expensive

Open: year-round   Minimum Stay: one week

Three clusters of apartments—the Hummingbird, Alamander and Bauhinia—comprise this group of pleasant seaside condominiums. Some feature TVs and stereos; most have balconies and all enjoy splendid ocean views. There are three shared pools and the beach is just across the street. The studio, one- and two-bedroom suites are light and airy with comfortable modern furnishings. Maid service is provided and shuttles leave twice daily for shopping and sightseeing. Contact: C. Kroos or R. Glaser, Villa Holidays, Inc., 13100 Wayzata Blvd., Ste. 150, Minneapolis, MN 55343. Call 1-800-328-6262 (in Minnesota, 612-591-0076).

Children: Y Pets: N Smoking: Y Handicap Access: N Payment: C, P, T, V, M

CULU CULU

Rates: moderate-expensive

Open: year-round   Minimum Stay: one week

Trade winds gently cool this hilltop villa in the exclusive Ridge Estates area. Inside, the beautiful furnishings feature original artwork, fresh white wicker and colorful island prints. Flanking the large living room are two bedroom suites; this central area also opens onto the spacious covered veranda, the perfect spot for enjoying the island delicacies prepared by your cook. A few paces will take you out on the sunny patio, which surrounds the generous pool. For those who prefer salt water to fresh, the beach is about five minutes away and the nearby hotels also offer tennis. Contact: C. Kroos or R. Glaser, Villa Holidays, Inc., 13100 Wayzata Blvd., Ste. 150, Minneapolis, MN 55343. Call 1-800-328-6262 (in Minnesota, 612-591-0076).

Children: N Pets: N Smoking: Y Handicap Access: N Payment: C, P, T, V, M

GOLDENEYE

Rates: deluxe

Open: year-round   Minimum Stay: one week

Fans of James Bond will want to consider this luxurious villa, previously the home of Ian Fleming. Mr. Fleming's cook will eagerly share many colorful stories with you and perhaps you'll see in Goldeneye some of the inspiration for Goldfinger. The sprawling three-bedroom house is casually furnished, and the full staff will help you enjoy a carefree holiday. Step outside and you'll be impressed by the magnificent Caribbean views in this secluded cove; follow the rock steps down the small cliff and you'll arrive at the estate's splendid private beach. Contact: C. Kroos or R. Glaser, Villa Holidays, Inc., 13100 Wayzata Blvd., Ste. 150, Minneapolis, MN 55343. Call 1-800-328-6262 (in Minnesota, 612-591-0076).

Children: Y Pets: N Smoking: Y Handicap Access: N Payment: C, P, T, V, M

HIGH HOPE ESTATE   *Rates: deluxe*
Open: year-round   *Minimum Stay: one week*

A 15th-century Venetian villa was the inspiration for this extraordinary villa perched above St. Ann's Bay. Swaddled in 40 acres of luxurious grounds—including one of the largest hibiscus collections in the world—this elegantly furnished abode has seven bedrooms, all with air-conditioning. The baby grand piano, extensive library and impressive wine cellar recall the pleasures of yesteryear; the color TV and VCR add the creature comforts of today. Outside you can relax in the cliffside gazebo, nap in the double hammock, enjoy a genteel game of croquet, or frolic in the free-form swimming pool. The full staff will pamper you during your stay. Contact: C. Kroos or R. Glaser, Villa Holidays, Inc., 13100 Wayzata Blvd., Ste. 150, Minneapolis, MN 55343. Call 1-800-328-6262 (in Minnesota, 612-591-0076).

Children: Y Pets: N Smoking: Y Handicap Access: N Payment: C, P, T, V, M

RIO CHICO   *Rates: deluxe*
Open: year-round   *Minimum Stay: one week*

Surely one of the most extravagant vacation retreats in the Caribbean, this 19-room mansion has everything you've fantasized about and more. Six bedrooms and six baths accommodate large groups in sinful comfort. The 3,000 feet of protected shoreline include two separate beaches; there are two swimming pools besides. No fewer than eight rivers flow through the 12-acre grounds, providing a plethora of picturesque waterfalls and ponds to picnic by. Over 300 varieties of palms, flowers and fruit trees are showcased in the exquisite gardens. Tier after tier of patios stretch from the house down to the sea and there is also a tennis court on the grounds. And of course, the ample staff includes a tennis pro and a professional masseuse. Contact: C. Kroos or R. Glaser, Villa Holidays, Inc., 13100 Wayzata Blvd., Ste. 150, Minneapolis, MN 55343. Call 1-800-328-6262 (in Minnesota, 612-591-0076).

Children: Y Pets: N Smoking: Y Handicap Access: N Payment: C, P, T, V, M

SHARWALL VILLA   *Rates: expensive*
Open: year-round   *Minimum Stay: one week*

This lovely home set in a tranquil spot outside Ocho Rios is a crisp new addition to the Jamaican coast. The stylishly modern rooms feature wide-open spaces and contemporary mahogany furniture. The gardens surrounding the house with their lush greenery and fabulous blooms are equally perfect for quietly contemplating Jamaica's unparalleled beauty in solitude or for romantic strolls arm-in-arm at twilight. Beaches and tennis are only a short drive away and the excitement of Ocho Rios is within walking distance. Contact: C. Kroos or R. Glaser, Villa Holidays, Inc., 13100 Wayzata Blvd., Ste. 150, Minneapolis, MN 55343. Call 1-800-328-6262 (in Minnesota, 612-591-0076).

Children: Y Pets: N Smoking: Y Handicap Access: N Payment: C, P, T, V, M

SOMBRA   *Rates: deluxe*
Open: year-round   *Minimum Stay: one week*

The lovely grounds of this large two-story penthouse overlook the blue Caribbean waters; in addition to the shared swimming pool there is a private beach with some of the best snorkeling waters on the North Coast. Inside you'll find three elegant bedrooms, a spacious living and dining area, a well-equipped kitchen and three modern bathrooms. The furnishings throughout are classically elegant and several rooms vaunt large balconies with views of the sea. Perhaps after a refreshing swim you'd like to soak in the Jacuzzi. The penthouse is fully staffed with a maid, cook and gardener, so all you have to do is sit back and enjoy. Contact: Villas and Apartments Abroad, Ltd., 420 Madison Ave., New York, NY 10017. Call 1-800-433-3020 (in New York, 212-759-1025).

Children: Y   Pets: N   Smoking: Y   Handicap Access: N   Payment: C, P, T

SOMEWHERE   *Rates: deluxe*
Open: year-round   *Minimum Stay: one week*

Somewhere can fulfill all your fantasies of the perfect Caribbean holiday. This extensive estate is carpeted by lush tropical flora and shaded by tall trees. Cool and inviting, the spacious rooms feature picture windows overlooking the grounds. Four cheerful bedrooms and a full staff cater to your every need. Perhaps best of all, the magnificent swimming pool and patio behind the house offer splendid views of the sea only a few feet away. After returning from your early morning stroll along the beach, you can swim a few laps before being served breakfast on the dining terrace. Contact: Villas and Apartments Abroad, Ltd., 420 Madison Ave., New York, NY 10017. Call 1-800-433-3020 (in New York, 212-759-1025).

Children: Y   Pets: N   Smoking: Y   Handicap Access: N   Payment: C, P, T

STONEAWAY   *Rates: deluxe*
Open: year-round   *Minimum Stay: one week*

Stoneaway's hillside perch on the ridge above Ocho Rios offers wonderful breezes and splendid panoramic views of the sea. The lavishly decorated rooms are cheerful and inviting, with brightly upholstered sofas, rich carpets and elegant prints hanging on the walls; a party of eight can sleep comfortably in the four sumptuous bedrooms. The large private pool in back is surrounded by a patio partially shaded by luxuriant foliage. Although the fully staffed house is set in a secluded spot, it's only a short drive to the beach, tennis, golf and the festive atmosphere of Ocho Rios. Contact: Villas and Apartments Abroad, Ltd., 420 Madison Ave., New York, NY 10017. Call 1-800-433-3020 (in New York, 212-759-1025).

Children: Y   Pets: N   Smoking: Y   Handicap Access: N   Payment: C, P, T

TURTLE BEACH TOWERS   *Rates: budget-moderate*
Open: year-round   *Minimum Stay: three nights*

The entrancing natural wonders of Jamaica's north shore surround this oceanside hotel, a casual and friendly home away from home. Each of the sun-filled suites is air-conditioned and comfortably furnished; sliding glass doors open onto the private balcony. Tennis is free of charge; parasailing, boating, waterskiing and fishing are some of the other activities available at Turtle Beach Towers. Perhaps you'd be happier gliding through crystalline waters in a glass-bottomed boat or simply relaxing on the powder-soft sands outside your front door. Daily maid service is complimentary; laundry service, a cook and babysitters are available for a truly carefree vacation. Contact: Dennis Latchman, Turtle Beach Towers, P.O. Box 73, Ocho Rios, St. Ann, Jamaica. Call 809-974-2646 or 809-974-2381.

Children: Y Pets: N Smoking: Y Handicap Access: N Payment: C, A, V, M

WOODWINDS VILLA   *Rates: moderate-expensive*
Open: year-round   *Minimum Stay: one week*

Tucked away on a hillside in a wooded nine-acre estate is this villa that can accommodate up to six people. The spacious rooms feature both Jamaican wood and wicker furniture; woodcarvings, paintings and ceramics by local artists enhance the rooms and add a touch of Caribbean charm. Two bedrooms, the living room and the formal dining room open onto a large shaded terrace just right for dining and reclining. The views from this breezy spot encompass the lush rolling hills near the coast and the shimmering waters of the Caribbean beyond. Just a few feet in front of you is a tempting swimming pool and its sunny patio. Other pursuits to be enjoyed in the neighborhood include golf, tennis, fishing, boating and all your favorite water sports. Contact: Joyce Skinner, 5032 Tipperary, St. Croix, U.S. Virgin Islands 00820-4585. Call 809-773-8021.

Children: N   Pets: N   Smoking: Y   Handicap Access: N   Payment: P

PORT ANTONIO

CHATEAU EXOTICA   *Rates: deluxe*
Open: year-round   *Minimum Stay: one week*

Enjoy marvelous, unobstructed views of the Caribbean waters from the deck chairs on the balustraded patio by the pool of Chateau Exotica. Luxuriant tropical flowers and fruit trees wrap the house in greenery; a short stroll will bring you to a private beach. The charming gazebo houses a freshwater spa, and there's a barbecue by the pool. Inside, the three spacious bedrooms are all air-conditioned and each boasts an en suite bathroom. There is a large formal dining room, or you can enjoy your meals out on the terrace. A large video library and color TV are at your disposal and the friendly staff comprises a gourmet chef, a housekeeper and a butler. Contact: Villas International, 71 W. 23rd St., New York, NY 10010. Call 212-929-7585.

Children: Y   Pets: N   Smoking: Y   Handicap Access: N   Payment: C, P, T

CORAL SEAS   *Rates: deluxe*
Open: year-round   *Minimum Stay: one week*

The light, pretty rooms of this three-bedroom villa are cheerfully furnished with softly cushioned wicker furniture, plush carpets, stylish prints and colorful walls. You may not be spending much time indoors, though, once you discover the large, sunny terraces that open off the back of each of the house's three stories. Overlooking the gently rippling waters and secluded by leafy trees, these are wonderful places for sunning, alfresco dining, or just enjoying the tranquil scenery. A small dinghy is provided for lazy jaunts inside the coral reef and a short walk will bring you to some excellent tennis facilities. Contact: Villas and Apartments Abroad, Ltd., 420 Madison Ave., New York, NY 10017. Call 1-800-433-3020 (in New York, 212-759-1025).

Children: Y Pets: N Smoking: Y Handicap Access: N Payment: C, P, T

GOBLIN HILL VILLAS AT SAN SAN   *Rates: budget-inexpensive*
Open: year-round   *Minimum Stay: three nights*

These villas in the exclusive San San district are perfect for family holidays or romantic getaways. The one- and two-bedroom suites all feature air-conditioning, fully equipped kitchens, large living and dining rooms and shaded terraces. A friendly housekeeper will prepare and serve your meals, and babysitters are available. A large swimming pool, two tennis courts and a playground are found on this 12-acre estate, as well as rolling lawns and lush gardens. Nearby San San Beach boasts excellent windsurfing and snorkeling activities, while the Blue Lagoon offers waterskiing and scuba diving. Contact: Andrea Carroll, Goblin Hill Villas at San San, 11 East Ave., Kingston 10, Jamaica. Call 809-925-8108.

Children: Y Pets: N Smoking: Y Handicap Access: N Payment: C, T, A, V, M

PELICAN VILLA   *Rates: deluxe*
Open: year-round   *Minimum Stay: one week*

Set right by the sparkling waters of the Blue Lagoon, this recently renovated home provides luxurious accommodations for up to eight guests. Inside you'll find a spacious living room and a handsome formal dining room, but you'll probably want to do most of your dining and reclining out on the extensive patio areas and decks where you can listen to the gently lapping waters and watch the elegant sailing boats in the distance. Boat moorings and sea swimming are available in your own backyard and the silky sands of exclusive San San Beach are at your disposal. Contact: C. Kroos or R. Glaser, Villa Holidays, Inc., 13100 Wayzata Blvd., Ste. 150, Minneapolis, MN 55343. Call 1-800-328-6262 (in Minnesota, 612-591-0076).

Children: Y Pets: N Smoking: Y Handicap Access: N Payment: C, P, T, V, M

SANDPIPER   *Rates: deluxe*
Open: year-round   *Minimum Stay: one week*

After only a short stay at the Sandpiper, you'll surely understand why this is Peter O'Toole's favorite villa. Flanked by its own private beach and surrounded by swaying palms, the three-story house features magnificent decks that hang over the gently lapping waters below. You can enjoy your chef's creations in the formal dining room with polished floors or dine on the terrace outside while enjoying the unique views of Monkey Island. Many of the large, sunlit rooms feature French doors that tempt you outside with their inviting views; you're sure to

get a good night's rest in one of the three comfortable bedrooms. Contact: Villas and Apartments Abroad, Ltd., 420 Madison Ave., New York, NY 10017. Call 1-800-433-3020 (in New York, 212-759-1025).
Children: Y   Pets: N   Smoking: Y   Handicap Access: N   Payment: C, P, T

SEA STAR *Rates: deluxe*
Open: year-round *Minimum Stay: one week*
This lovely Moorish-style villa is hidden in a grove of trees right on the water's edge. Each of the rooms furnished with original art, antiques and rich native teak overlooks the gentle waters of the lagoon; the sunny terrace even juts out over it, so you'll feel surrounded by the sea as you lie back and sip your rum punch. The ocean is your swimming pool and a variety of water sports can be enjoyed in the neighborhood. In addition, there are three spacious bedrooms and three modern bathrooms inside. The cook, maid and gardener will see after you during your stay. Contact: Villas and Apartments Abroad, Ltd., 420 Madison Ave., New York, NY 10017. Call 1-800-433-3020 (in New York, 212-759-1025).
Children: Y   Pets: N   Smoking: Y   Handicap Access: N   Payment: C, P, T

SEASHELL *Rates: expensive-deluxe*
Open: year-round *Minimum Stay: one week*
Enveloped in a lush acre of fruit trees and flowers, this charming villa in the exclusive San San district sits just ten feet from the crystal-clear Caribbean waters. After snorkeling amid colorful corals and tropical fish, bask for a few minutes on the private beach before strolling up to the terrace for a delicious lunch prepared by your creative cook. The many spacious rooms inside are tastefully decorated in the traditional island style and each of the four bedrooms has its own color-coordinated bathroom. The rooms upstairs have balconies overlooking the luxuriant grounds; those downstairs open directly to the partially shaded patio that surrounds the pool. Contact: B. Saxon, 338 Wesley Drive, Chapel Hill, NC 27516. Call 919-967-5657.
Children: Y Pets: N Smoking: Y Handicap Access: N Payment: C, P, T, V, M

WINDFALL *Rates: expensive-deluxe*
Open: year-round *Minimum Stay: one week*
This dazzling villa high in the hills of San San is an ideal setting for that amorous getaway you've been planning. The wonderful location affords romantic views of the island's rich foliage and brilliant blue waters and at the same time ensures complete privacy. You'll be pampered by the efficient and friendly staff. The villa's stylishly modern interior opens onto a magnificent colonnaded veranda, where you can enjoy an intimate breakfast or sip a pina colada in the moonlight. The generous pool and patio may tempt you to spend every day here lolling in the sun, but don't overlook the friendly beach and the excitement of town, both just a short stroll away. Contact: Villas and Apartments Abroad, Ltd., 420 Madison Ave., New York, NY 10017. Call 1-800-433-3020 (in New York, 212-759-1025).
Children: Y   Pets: N   Smoking: Y   Handicap Access: N   Payment: C, P, T

RUNAWAY BAY

BOONOONOONOOS   *Rates: deluxe*
Open: year-round   *Minimum Stay: one week*

Boonoonoonoos may be a linguist's nightmare, but it's a golfer's dream. Located on the 15th hole of the splendid course at the Runaway Bay Country Club, this handsome villa brings you as close as you could ever want to get to the golfing action. The clubhouse features a lovely restaurant, and guests at the villa are invited to use the club's private beach. The four spacious bedrooms are all air-conditioned and a full staff will attend to your comfort. In addition to the large sunny terrace and a delightful swimming pool outside, there's a wonderful covered dining pavilion where you can enjoy your cook's creations in an atmosphere of casual elegance. Contact: C. Kroos or R. Glaser, Villa Holidays, Inc., 13100 Wayzata Blvd., Ste. 150, Minneapolis, MN 55343. Call 1-800-328-6262 (in Minnesota, 612-591-0076).

Children: Y Pets: N Smoking: Y Handicap Access: N Payment: C, P, T, V, M

CLUB CARIBBEAN   *Rates: budget-inexpensive*
Open: year-round   *Minimum Stay: three nights*

Near where Columbus first landed in Jamaica stands a cluster of holiday cottages known as the Club Caribbean. This charming colony combines the privacy of individual bungalows with all the amenities of a large resort. Tennis, swimming, windsurfing, snorkeling, waterskiing and sailing are offered for the sporting crowd; lessons are available for the uninitiated. The silky, sloping beach is a sunbather's paradise; one section is reserved for naturists. After a day of sun and surf, stop by the bar or head for the disco. Child care, a playground and daily activities for the children make this an ideal spot for families. The daily maid service, complimentary breakfast and buffet dinners ensure that it will be a relaxing trip for the whole family. Contact: Mr. Klaus H. Voss, P.O. Box 65, Runaway Bay, Jamaica. Call 809-973-3507 or 809-973-3508.

Children: Y Pets: N Smoking: Y Handicap Access: Y Payment: C, T, A, V, M

OASIS   *Rates: expensive-deluxe*
Open: year-round   *Minimum Stay: one week*

Surrounded by more than an acre of carefully tended tropical gardens, Oasis is a luxurious villa situated on the unforgettable beaches of Runaway Bay. There are two air-conditioned bedrooms on the ground floor; the master suite (also air-conditioned) enjoys marvelous views from its second-story location. The ground floor is flanked by breezy terraces just right for sipping a planter's punch or enjoying a tasty repast prepared by your cook. A charming little picket fence surrounds the generous swimming pool and from the balustraded balcony upstairs you can look over to the soft white sands of the nearby private beach. Contact: C. Kroos or R. Glaser, Villa Holidays, Inc., 13100 Wayzata Blvd., Ste. 150, Minneapolis, MN 55343. Call 1-800-328-6262 (in Minnesota, 612-591-0076).

Children: Y Pets: N Smoking: Y Handicap Access: N Payment: C, P, T, V, M

SHARPESBURG *Rates: moderate*
Open: year-round *Minimum Stay: one week*
Far from the gimmicky tourist attractions of commercial Jamaica, Sharpesburg allows you to experience the island as few visitors do. The two-bedroom house is tucked away in the foothills behind Runaway Bay, surrounded by untamed greenery and lush gardens. From the long, covered veranda you can enjoy marvelous views of the sea only a few miles away. The swimming pool is delightfully situated in the villa's fruit orchard. Just because you get away from the crowds doesn't mean you have to rough it, though: Sharpesburg comes complete with a full staff, splendid furnishings, TV, stereo and other creature comforts. Contact: C. Kroos or R. Glaser, Villa Holidays, Inc., 13100 Wayzata Blvd., Ste. 150, Minneapolis, MN 55343. Call 1-800-328-6262 (in Minnesota, 612-591-0076).
Children: Y Pets: N Smoking: Y Handicap Access: N Payment: C, P, T, V, M

VILLA CARMEL *Rates: deluxe*
Open: year-round *Minimum Stay: one week*
Serious golfers should not overlook the splendid array of amenities offered by this pleasant villa. Not only is there a wonderful swimming pool and patio on the grounds, but the house fronts on Runaway Beach's championship 18-hole golf course. There's also a wonderfully white sandy beach just a few minutes' walk from your front door. The spacious rooms are tastefully decorated with cheerful island prints and handsome traditional furniture. The magnificently high ceiling in the living and dining area helps keep this part of the house cool; the four bedrooms are all air-conditioned. Contact: C. Kroos or R. Glaser, Villa Holidays, Inc., 13100 Wayzata Blvd., Ste. 150, Minneapolis, MN 55343. Call 1-800-328-6262 (in Minnesota, 612-591-0076).
Children: Y Pets: N Smoking: Y Handicap Access: N Payment: C, P, T, V, M

SOUTH COAST

JAMARA VILLA *Rates: expensive-deluxe*
Open: year-round *Minimum Stay: one week*
This well-appointed villa offers verandas, gardens and patios aplenty for enjoying the breezy indoor-outdoor lifestyle of Jamaica. The roof patio is ideal for sunbathing or star gazing; the covered verandas provide a retreat from the midday sun, where you can sip your punch and watch the exotic greenery around you sway in the gentle breeze. The stylishly decorated interior features four comfortable bedrooms and four bathrooms; the cook and maid will work to make your stay comfortable and carefree. Contact: Island Hideaways, Inc., 1317 Rhode Island Ave. NW, Ste. 503, Washington, DC 20005. Call 1-800-832-2302 (in the District of Columbia, 202-667-9652).
Children: Y Pets: N Smoking: Y Handicap Access: N Payment: C, P, T

ST. ANN

SHAW PARK BEACH HOTEL   *Rates: moderate-deluxe*
Open: year-round   *Minimum Stay: none*

Each of the luxurious suites in this resort hotel has a kitchenette and private balcony overlooking the sea. The private beach, where almond trees and gently arching palms provide cool shade, is ideal for basking in the magic of the Caribbean sun; more active types may want to try the sailing, windsurfing, scuba diving, snorkeling and even deep-sea fishing opportunities on hand. There's also a pool in the garden just a few feet away, with a separate wading pool for the kids to splash in. What makes the Shaw Park really special, though, is the rich social life right on the premises: With an elegant dining room, several convivial bars, a resident band, a nightclub and live floor shows, you'll never have to leave home to enjoy the best of Jamaica. Contact: Janice Campbell, P.O. Box 17, Sutlass Bay, St. Ann, Jamaica. Call 809-974-2552-4 or 809-974-2347.

Children: Y Pets: N Smoking: Y Handicap Access: N Payment: C, T, A, V, M

ST. ANN'S BAY

HIGH HOPE ESTATE   *Rates: deluxe*
Open: year-round   *Minimum Stay: one week*

This captivating estate in lovely St. Ann's Bay is a magnificent setting for family get-togethers or group holidays. Its position on a hillside allows splendid views, and the luxurious swimming pool is sure to please the most discriminating bathers. The large, handsome rooms inside are cool and inviting; up to 14 people will find comfortable accommodations in the seven spacious bedrooms. A full staff will see after you during your stay, preparing and serving gourmet meals, maintaining the lush grounds, tidying the rooms and even handling your laundry if you desire. A private car is provided for touring the countryside and nights on the town, but you may just prefer to stay home and bask in the splendor of High Hope. Contact: June Schoner, Jamaica Villa Vacations, 31-33 Prospect Ave., Park Ridge, IL 60068. Call 1-800-323-5115 (in Illinois, 708-698-9303).

Children: Y Pets: N Smoking: Y Handicap Access: N Payment: C, P, T

ST. ANN'S BAY/RUNAWAY BAY

CHUKKA COVE VILLAS   *Rates: expensive*
Open: year-round   *Minimum Stay: one week*

Whether you're already an accomplished equestrian or have only dreamed of learning to ride horseback, you'll be pleasantly surprised by the extensive facilities at the Chukka Cove Farm. Instruction is offered in dressage, cross-country riding and show jumping as well as the fine points of polo. The recently built villas are elegantly furnished and fully staffed; each of the six independent houses has two bedrooms and two bathrooms. Another unique attraction of this property is the beautiful subterranean cavern, used in the filming of "Papillon." The snorkeling is excellent here and the lush swimming pool is shared by the guests. Contact: C. Kroos or R. Glaser, Villa Holidays, Inc., 13100 Wayzata Blvd., Ste. 150, Minneapolis, MN 55343. Call 1-800-328-6262 (in Minnesota, 612-591-0076).

Children: Y Pets: N Smoking: Y Handicap Access: N Payment: C, P, T, V, M

ST. ELIZABETH

4 MS COTTAGE   *Rates: budget*
Open: year-round   *Minimum Stay: none*

This rustic retreat offers a small number of comfortable rooms that are ideal for guests who truly want to get away from it all. Spare furnishings and kitchenettes keep life simple, as it should be on the island. The friendly service will make you feel right at home; the lavish greenery and gently lapping waters outside will soothe your soul. Although secluded, the 4 Ms is far from isolated. The hotel next door features an excellent restaurant and congenial bar and the excitement of St. Elizabeth is only a few minutes away. There's also plenty to keep you busy during the day: boating, hiking, fishing and waterskiing can all be enjoyed in the area and don't forget to visit the magnificent waterfalls nearby. Contact: Effie Moxam-Campbell, Mountain Side P.O., St. Elizabeth, Jamaica. Call 809-965-2305 or 809-965-2544 (ask for 4 Ms Cottage).

Children: Y   Pets: N   Smoking: Y   Handicap Access: Y   Payment: C, T

TREASURE BEACH

HIKARU VILLA   *Rates: moderate-expensive*
Open: year-round   *Minimum Stay: one week*

Travel an hour from Montego Bay and you'll find yourself transported into Jamaica's past: Quaint little fishing villages dot the coastline, calypso bands play for the pleasure of the local people, the beaches are pristine and uncluttered and life follows the timeless rhythm of the sun and the sea. Hikaru enjoys a splendid setting amid this traditional beauty on a sunny hillside just a few feet from the water. The four bedrooms and main living areas are furnished with native mahoe wood; the shaded terraces overlook the ocean. After sunning and swimming, you can listen to the gentle crooning of the waves while playing tennis on the regulation court. Contact: C. Kroos or R. Glaser, Villa Holidays, Inc., 13100 Wayzata Blvd., Ste. 150, Minneapolis, MN 55343. Call 1-800-328-6262 (in Minnesota, 612-591-0076).

Children: Y Pets: N Smoking: Y Handicap Access: N Payment: C, P, T, V, M

Fort de France

Ste. Anne

Caribbean Sea

Martinique

HARMONIE CREOLE

VILLA OSCAR

Rates: deluxe
Open: year-round
Minimum Stay: one week

The galleries and terraces of this lovely villa run right to the water, offering you wraparound views of the sea on your own semiprivate island. Relax in the shade of the coconut trees, go swimming off the dock or learn as your cook, Philomene, prepares you fabulous creole meals. If a visit to the main island appeals to you, Jacky will take you across in ten minutes on your motorboat *Bailene*. Perfect for a large family or several couples, the villa includes five spacious bedrooms, each with its own bath. There are no phones to disturb you here, so quit worrying and relax! Contact: Villas International, 71 West 23rd St., New York, NY 10011. Call 212-989-4200.

Children: **Y** Pets: **N** Smoking: **Y** Handicap Access: **N** Payment: **C, P, T**

VILLA THIERRY

Rates: deluxe
Open: year-round
Minimum Stay: one week

When only your own island will do, let Jacky pick you up on the mainland in your 28-foot motorboat and drop you at your door. Elevated for a spectacular view of the Atlantic, Villa Thierry is ready to welcome the whole family in six spacious bedrooms and six baths. Wander into the library to find a book to read before bedtime, or take your morning coffee in the sunny solarium. The trade winds will cool you as you laze on the balcony, and when you want excitement on the mainland, Jacky will be there to take you across whenever you're in the mood. When hunger strikes, there's no need for you to fuss: Let your cook, Philomene, prepare a sumptuous creole meal for you. Contact: Villas International, 71 West 23rd St., New York, NY 10010. Call 212-929-7585.

Children: **Y**   Pets: **N**   Smoking: **Y**   Handicap Access: **N**   Payment: **C, P, T**

STE. ANNE

VILLAS STE. ANNE   *Rates: budget-expensive*
Open: year-round   *Minimum Stay: one week*

Situated on a large, sheltered bay on the southwest corner of Martinique, the modern Villas Ste. Anne allow you to relax in ultimate comfort between snorkeling, scuba diving, waterskiing and swimming in the incredibly blue waters of the Caribbean. Studios and one-, two- and three-bedroom villas feature airy rooms cooled by the trade winds. When not dining out on the island's famed French or creole cuisine, you can cook your meals in the fully equipped kitchen that comes with your apartment, and spend a quiet evening at home in your comfortable living room. Sit under the stars on your terrace, or take a late-night swim in the private pool that comes with some of the larger villas. Contact: Villas International, 71 West 23rd Street, New York, NY 10010. Call 212-929-7585

Children: **Y**   Pets: **N**   Smoking: **Y**   Handicap Access: **N**   Payment: **C, P, T**

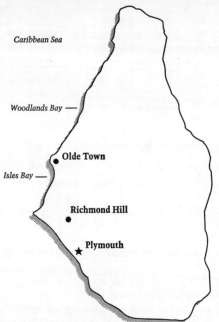

Caribbean Sea

Woodlands Bay —

Olde Town

Isles Bay —

Richmond Hill

★ **Plymouth**

Montserrat

BELHAM VALLEY

VILLAS OF MONTSERRAT   *Rates: expensive-deluxe*
Open: year-round   *Minimum Stay: one week*

Three luxury villas feature private pools and views of paradise. Each one is surrounded by landscaped grounds filled with papaya, mango and banana trees and beautiful flowers. All have three bedrooms, three baths, a gourmet kitchen and living/dining areas with vaulted ceilings, huge windows and tiled floors. The cooling effect of the trade winds is enhanced by ceiling fans; the views from balconies, terraces and poolside are spectacular. Guests are met in Antigua and taken on a private charter flight to Montserrat, where a smiling maid awaits you with a welcome rum punch. On your first morning a tropical breakfast is prepared for you, and a guide takes you around the island to point out the best spots. Contact: Wilson "Pickett" Johnson, Villas of Montserrat, P.O. Box 421, Plymouth, Montserrat, British West Indies. Call 809-491-5513.

Children: **Y**   Pets: **N**   Smoking: **Y**   Handicap Access: **N**   Payment: **C, P, T**

ISLES BAY

VILLA HAMPSTEAD   *Rates: inexpensive-deluxe*
Open: year-round   *Minimum Stay: one week*

West Indian style and modern comfort is what you'll find at this stunning villa overlooking the golf course near Vue Pointe Hotel. Three bedrooms with private baths and maid's quarters make this a generous accommodation for three couples or a family. The upper level is encircled by terraces with private nooks and quiet spots leading from each room; in the garden is a large swimming pool and a Jacuzzi. Downstairs is a little kitchenette and a twin bedroom, plus a bathroom and a laundry room. Temporary membership at the golf course, a rental car and laundry service can all easily be arranged; all linens are provided, and there is a dishwasher and ice maker in the kitchen. Contact: Sharon Margetson, Runaway Travel Real Estate, P.O. Box 54, Marine Drive, Plymouth, Montserrat, British West Indies. Call 809-491-2776/2800.

Children: Y   Pets: N   Smoking: Y   Handicap Access: N   Payment: C, P, T

OLD TOWNE

FIRST CLASS VILLA   *Rates: expensive-deluxe*
Open: year-round   *Minimum Stay: one week*

A private swimming pool, fabulous views and two stories of spacious rooms can be found in this home, which has glass doors that open onto a poolside deck. On the main level is a living/dining area, a double bedroom with a king-sized bed and en suite bathroom and a kitchen. Downstairs is a bedroom/sitting room, a twin bedroom, a bathroom and another kitchen. A maid is on duty from morning until afternoon, five days a week. Laundry facilities are provided, and there are ceiling fans throughout the house. Vue Point Beach is just five minutes away; once there you can sample one of several restaurants, play some golf or tennis, or relax on the sand. Windsurfing, sunfish rentals and water-skiing can be found at the Vue Point Hotel. Contact: At Home Abroad, Inc., 405 East 56th St., #6H, New York, NY 10022. Call 212-421-9165. Ref 9345.

Children: Y   Pets: N   Smoking: Y   Handicap Access: N   Payment: C, P, T

POOLSIDE VILLA   *Rates: expensive*
Open: year-round   *Minimum Stay: one week*

Located on the western side of the island, this luxury villa occupies two levels and is fully furnished with island-style furniture, cheerful prints and hanging plants. Completely screened in, and with ceiling fans that create cool breezes, the house has a large outdoor swimming pool that overlooks the sea. On the main level is a living/dining area, a full kitchen (with a dishwasher, a double refrigerator with an ice maker and all modern appliances), a covered deck for outdoor dining or relaxing and an open terrace around the pool where guests can work on their tans. Two bedrooms open onto this terrace, and completing the floor plan are two bathrooms. On the garden level is a guest bedroom with twin beds and an en suite bathroom. A few minutes away is Vue Point Beach, where you'll find tennis, golf and water sports. Maid service during the week is included, and baby-sitting can be arranged if needed. Contact: Barry

Shepard, At Home Abroad, Inc., 405 East 56th St., #6H, New York, NY 10022. Call 212-421-9165. Ref 5068.

Children: Y   Pets: N   Smoking: Y   Handicap Access: N   Payment: C, P, T

TWO-STORY VILLA   *Rates: expensive-deluxe*
Open: year-round   *Minimum Stay: one week*

Within easy walking distance of tennis, golf, water sports and restaurants, this house is located near Vue Pointe Beach on the western side of the island. An outdoor terrace with dining tables and chaise longues is situated around a beautiful swimming pool—outdoor dining and sunbathing take place amid views out over the sea. On the main level is a living room and dining area that open onto the terrace, as well as a kitchen and two bedrooms, both with twin beds and en suite bathrooms. Downstairs are two more twin bedrooms, also with their own baths. For added convenience, the kitchen is equipped with a dishwasher, and there are laundry facilities as well as weekday maid service. Louvered windows let the ocean air drift through the house; the whole effect is one of relaxed tropical living. Contact: At Home Abroad, Inc., 405 East 56th St., #6H, New York, NY 10022. Call 212-421-9165. Ref 9381.

Children: Y Pets: N Smoking: Y Handicap Access: N Payment: C, P, T, V, M

OLVESTON

OLVESTON HOUSE   *Rates: moderate-expensive*
Open: year-round   *Minimum Stay: one week*

You'll find this family house overlooking the sea near Lime Kiln Bay and surrounded by scenic walking trails and wonderful views. Just five minutes by car brings you to Vue Point Beach and the hotel there, which has tennis, golf and water sports facilities. A living room and dining area are combined, and there is a full kitchen, with maid service included. Both of the twin bedrooms have ceiling fans; there are two bathrooms in the house. A telephone and washing machine complete the amenities, and baby-sitting service can be arranged. Contact: At Home Abroad, Inc., 405 East 56th St., #6H, New York, NY 10022. Call 212-421-9165. Ref 9344.

Children: Y   Pets: N   Smoking: Y   Handicap Access: N   Payment: C, P, T

PLYMOUTH

BELHAM VALLEY RESTAURANT AND HOTEL   *Rates: budget*
Open: year-round   *Minimum Stay: none*

The cottages here are ranged along a hillside overlooking the Belham valley and river. The Frangipani studio cottage is framed by a profusion of tropical shrubs and palm trees and consists of a bedroom, living/dining area, full kitchen and bathroom. The balcony looks out over the golf course and the sea. The Jasmine studio apartment is located beside the restaurant, which is one of the finest on the island. It has a living room/sleeping area, a small dining nook, a bathroom and a kitchen. Its private patio overlooks the sea and the mountains. The

Mignonette is a two-bedroom apartment with a living area, kitchen, bathroom and roomy patio. Guest can hire a cook or daily maid service (weekly service is included). Contact: Mrs. Aileen R. Fenton, Belham Valley Restaurant and Hotel, Old Towne, P.O. Box 409, Plymouth, Montserrat, British West Indies. Call 809-491-5553.

Children: Y Pets: N Smoking: Y Handicap: N Payment: C, P, T, A, V, M

PAULINE'S VILLAS AND APARTMENTS   *Rates: budget-inexpensive*
Open: year-round   *Minimum Stay: none*

Within walking distance of the center of Plymouth, the capital of Montserrat, a selection of villas can be found in the residential area of Richmond Hill. Two- and three-bedroom apartments are also located here, all with mountain and sea views and fully furnished with complete kitchen facilities. The villas also offer laundry facilities and the use of a swimming pool on the premises. Within walking distance you'll find the Montserrat Springs Hotel, where you can hear live music; the beach is only a few minutes away. There are facilities for tennis, golf and water sports on the island, but in general the pace is slow and the atmosphere is quiet and relaxing. Contact: Pauline's Apartments, P.O. Box 180, Plymouth, Montserrat, British West Indies. Call 809-491-2434/2345.

Children: Y Pets: N Smoking: Y Handicap Access: N Payment: C, T, A

WOODLANDS

VILLA ABROGATO   *Rates: expensive*
Open: year-round   *Minimum Stay: one week*

A privately owned home, Villa Abrogato is a large villa done in Italian tile on three levels. On the upper level is a common area with kitchen and a living room/dining room area that leads onto adjoining balconies. The lower levels feature the pool, an outdoor whirlpool, a surrounding patio, two queen-sized bedrooms with private baths, a separate den with a double fold-out couch and another bathroom. A full acre of grounds surrounds the house, carefully tended by a gardener who maintains the flowers and fruit-bearing trees, which are lit at night to make a lovely view from the terrace. Maid service is included. Nearby you'll find a fine golf club, sailing and fishing charters, water sports, tennis and a network of scenic trails that range from gentle to challenging. Contact: Rent A Home International, Inc., 7200 34th Ave. N.W., Seattle, WA 98117. Call 206-545-6963. Ref BWI/R001.

Children: Y Pets: N Smoking: Y Handicap Access: N Payment: C, P, T, V, M

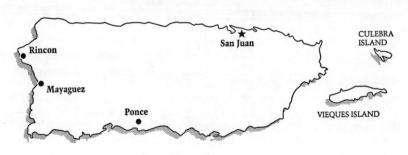

Atlantic Ocean

Rincon

San Juan

CULEBRA
ISLAND

Mayaguez

Ponce

VIEQUES ISLAND

Caribbean Sea

Puerto Rico

CULEBRA

PUNTA ALOE VILLAS
Open: year-round

Rates: inexpensive-expensive
Minimum Stay: one week

A short walk from the town of Dewey, this resort features 15 two-story wood and brick buildings set amid 40 acres of tropical greenery. The buildings house either one or two units, each with two bedrooms and bathrooms, a living room, dining room and kitchen, as well as two fold-out couches in the living room. For a smaller number of guests, studios are also available. Each of the houses has a huge deck that looks out over the crystal-clear waters of this unspoiled paradise. Much of Culebra is protected, and many of its beaches are virtually empty—except for the wild horses that roam the island at will. The trade winds blow gently here, and the windows are jalousied to maximize the cooling effects. Weekly maid service is included. Contact: Rent A Home International, Inc., 7200 34th Ave. N.W., Seattle, WA 98117. Call 206-545-6963.

Children: Y Pets: N Smoking: Y Handicap Access: N Payment: C, P, T, V, M

VILLA FULLADOZA
Open: year-round

Rates: budget
Minimum Stay: two nights

This apartment complex can be found overlooking the Bay at Ensenda Honda, which is dotted with pleasure crafts and sailboats. The mountainous little island of Culebra has a national wildlife refuge and beautiful scenery; the town of Dewey, where visitors can dine or shop, is just a ten-minute walk from the villa. Efficiency apartments at the villa each contain kitchen and bathroom facilities and sleeping accommodations for two or more people. There are washing machines, TVs and phones available for guests' use on the premises, and maid and linen service. At the beach are barbecue grills; fishing trips can be arranged. Try some solitary snorkeling or scuba diving in these warm, unspoiled waters. Contact: Chris C. Hatcher, Villa Fulladoza, Box 162, Culebra, Puerto Rico 00645. Call 809-742-3576.

Children: Y Pets: N Smoking: Y Handicap Access: N Payment: C, P, T, V, M

ISLA VERDE

GREEN ISLE INN   *Rates: budget*
Open: year-round   *Minimum Stay: three nights*

Green Isle Inn has comfortable, American-style rooms and quick access to San Juan and its luxury hotels and casinos. A ten-minute walk brings you from your one-bedroom efficiency apartment to the beach, and there are tennis and water sports facilities nearby. A complimentary "good morning" coffee is provided, and there is a steak and seafood restaurant, La Marina, on the premises. The units are air-conditioned and come with cable TV and daily maid service; laundry facilities are also available. There are two freshwater swimming pools at the hotel, and the nearby nightlife and restaurants keep the evenings full. Contact: Richard Gonzalez, Green Isle Inn, 36 Calle Uno, Isla Verde, Puerto Rico 00913. Call 809-726-4330/8662.

Children: Y Pets: N Smoking: Y Handicap Access: N Payment: C, T, A, V, M

RINCON

HOTEL VILLA COFRESI   *Rates: inexpensive-moderate*
Open: year-round   *Minimum Stay: none*

Both the pool and the outdoor dining terrace here are just steps from the beach, and the owners swear that the sunsets here are the world's best. In addition to single and double rooms at the hotel, you'll find one- and two-bedroom air-conditioned apartments with kitchen facilities and color TV. On weekend nights the air is filled with the sounds of local music; resorts, casinos and restaurants are all close by. A shopping mall proffers supplies and foodstuffs for the self-caterer, while a game room and nearby bowling alley add to your fun. At the beachfront, equipment for scuba diving and fishing can be rented. For those who'd like to explore the island's mountains and Indian and Spanish historic sites, car rental is available. Contact: Sonya Ramos, Hotel Villa Cofresi, Road 115, P.O. Box 1193, Rincon, Puerto Rico 00743. Call 809-823-2450.

Children: Y Pets: N Smoking: Y Handicap Access: N Payment: C, T, A, V, M

PARADOR VILLA ANTONIO   *Rates: budget-inexpensive*
Open: year-round   *Minimum Stay: none*

You'll find beautiful beaches here on the western end of the island, and Parador Villa Antonio has two-bedroom cottages located right on the golden sands. Also available are one- and two-bedroom apartments in the hotel buildings, all with kitchen, living room and full bathroom. Trade winds cool this island, but you'll find air-conditioners and ceiling fans in all the accommodations here, where TV and a game room provide indoor entertainment. Outdoors are tennis courts, a palm-fringed swimming pool and a special playground for children. Each unit has its own private balcony or patio where guests can relax, eat or sip a cool tropical drink. The beaches offer snorkeling, surfing and fishing year-round, and a golf course is located about a half hour away. Contact: Hector R. Ruiz, Parador Villa Antonio, Rd. 115, P.O. Box 68, Rincon, Puerto Rico 00743. Call 809-823-2645/2285.

Children: Y   Pets: N   Smoking: Y   Handicap: N   Payment: C, T, A, V, M, O

SAN JUAN

EL PRADO INN   *Rates: budget-inexpensive*
Open: year-round   *Minimum Stay: none*

The rooms at this inn are clean and comfortable, with louvered windows to let the breeze in and air conditioning to cool down guests after a day at the beach. Centered around a Spanish-style patio and pool, the efficiency units contain either kitchenettes or kitchens and are available as studios or one-bedroom units. Each has a cable TV and telephone and is serviced by a maid daily. Light meals and complimentary morning coffee are served on the flower-filled patio each day. The Condada section of San Juan, where the inn is located, is a short walk from casinos, restaurants, shopping and nightlife. The beach is less than five minutes away, and facilities for boating, fishing, waterskiing and diving can be found locally, as well as golf courses and tennis courts. Contact: Chris Teseo, El Prado Inn and Apartments, 1350 Calle Luchetti, Condado, San Juan, Puerto Rico 00907. Call 809-728-5925 or 800-468-4521.

Children: Y   Pets: N   Smoking: Y   Handicap Access: Y   Payment: All

SAN JUAN CONDOS   *Rates: budget-deluxe*
Open: year-round   *Minimum Stay: none*

These condominiums are offered by a group of private owners and thus vary greatly in size and style, ranging from studios to three-bedroom, three-bathroom units. Individually furnished and equipped, each one has full kitchenware and linens, air-conditioning and bathrooms. Some have cable TV, telephones, dishwashers and laundry facilities. Each condo is located in the San Juan area, most along the beach, and has views of either the ocean or lagoon. Some buildings have swimming pools, around-the-clock security and tennis courts; all are close to shopping areas, nightclubs and casinos, as well as restaurants. Daily maid service and babysitting are available. Contact: San Juan Vacations, 401 E. 86th St., Apt. 6E, New York, NY 10028. Call 212-348-7079.

Children: Y   Pets: N   Smoking: Y   Handicap Access: N   Payment: C, T

VIEQUES

HIGH RIDGE   *Rates: budget*
Open: year-round   *Minimum Stay: one week*

A high ridge runs down the middle of this 21-mile-long island, and perched atop it are many of the most beautiful homes in sparsely populated Vieques. This private villa features large outdoor terraces for dining and relaxing, with views of the Caribbean in the distance and an enclosed dining porch as well. An interior living room has ceiling fans, and there are two bedrooms and two bathrooms, as well as a full kitchen and a laundry room. When you feel like leaving the seclusion of the villa, the fishing villages of Isabel Segunda and Esperanze recall a way of life that has all but disappeared from these islands. The long beaches, phosphorescent waters and coral reefs that ring the island make scuba diving and snorkeling rewarding, and the fishing possibilities are excellent. Contact: Larry Schwartz, 100 Beekman St., New York, NY 10038 Call 212-285-1283.

Children: Y   Pets: N   Smoking: Y   Handicap Access: N   Payment: C, P, T

OCEANFRONT VILLA   *Rates: moderate*
Open: year-round   *Minimum Stay: one week*

The sound of waves lapping against the beach reverberate throughout this villa, which is situated on a small rise between the ocean and a freshwater lagoon ringed with coconut trees. The flat-roofed villa is topped by a sunbathing deck, and arched windows line the walls and porch. Inside are two bedrooms and bathrooms and a combined living/dining/kitchen area; the porch provides an additional dining and sitting area. Guests have use of a car—a true convenience, as this small island has many hidden and deserted beaches to discover. There are full laundry facilities at the villa, and maid service can be arranged. Local restaurants serve fresh fish caught from boats that can be hired for a moonlight cruise in the phosphorescent waters of the bay. Contact: Jeffrey Milham, Design Decisions Inc., 77 Bleecker Street, Suite 327, New York, NY 10012. Call 212-420-0377.

Children: Y   Pets: N   Smoking: Y   Handicap Access: N   Payment: C, P, T

SEA GATE   *Rates: budget*
Open: year-round   *Minimum Stay: two nights*

Perched on the cliffs overlooking the pink walls of a Spanish fort in Isabel Segunda, commanding a panoramic vista stretching west to Puerto Rico and east to St. Thomas, the Sea Gate covers two hillside acres. Vieques is about twenty-five minutes by plane from San Juan, and is considered a well-kept secret that nonetheless has good facilities and wonderful scenery. The Sea Gate is small, quiet and charming, run by friendly and attentive hosts. Efficiency apartments here have kitchenettes; a separate two-bedroom house is suitable for a family. Daily maid and linen service is provided, as is free transportation to the airport and beaches. Guests enjoy get-together evenings, snorkel tours, a well-stocked library and the proprietor's boundless store of information about this island's delights. Contact: Penny Miller, Sea Gate, P.O. Box 747, Vieques, Puerto Rico 00765. Call 809-741-4661.

Children: Y   Pets: N   Smoking: Y   Handicap Access: N   Payment: C, T

SOUND VILLA   *Rates: inexpensive*
Open: year-round   *Minimum Stay: one week*

An ideal accommodation for a family or group who need privacy, this villa is actually divided into two units. Upstairs are two bedrooms, a bathroom and a large open room containing the living room, dining area and kitchen. Downstairs is a separate studio with its own bath and kitchen facilities. The villa is located on a hillside overlooking the main harbor and the Vieques Sound, including a clear view of the lighthouse, which is a century old but still works. The facilities are modern and include a washing machine and dryer. After a day touring this tropical island, which is still largely undiscovered by tourists, or lying on one of the beautiful golden beaches, the shady balcony that wraps around three sides of the house makes a wonderful place to sit and look at the twinkling lights of the harbor down below. Contact: Mary Jane Murphy, Design Decisions Inc., 77 Bleecker Street, Suite 327, New York, NY 10012. Call 212-533-1489, 212-420-0377.

Children: Y   Pets: N   Smoking: Y   Handicap Access: N   Payment: C, P, T

VIEQUES SEA VIEW   *Rates: inexpensive*
Open: year-round   *Minimum Stay: one week*

A huge deck wraps around this lovely villa, providing views of the sea and of the harbor at Isabel Segunda, the fishing village below. Newly renovated, the villa has two bedrooms and two bathrooms as well as a living/dining area and a separate kitchen. A large screened porch provides extra living space. All the furniture is new, and for added convenience there is a washing machine and dryer; maid service can be arranged if needed. Restaurants and shops can be found down in the village, where local fishermen bring their catch daily. In the evenings, a boat ride will reveal the ghostly phosphorescent waters of the bay; by day, the beaches are sandy, sunny and practically deserted. Contact: James Stevens, Design Decisions Inc., 77 Bleecker St., Suite 327, New York, NY 10012. Call 212-420-0377.

Children: Y   Pets: N   Smoking: Y   Handicap Access: N   Payment: C, P, T

Wells Bay

Cove Bay

Spring Bay

Ladder Bay

The Bottom
★

Windwardside
●

Caribbean Sea

Saba

HELL'S GATE

HELL'S GATE 1   *Rates: budget*
Open: year-round   *Minimum Stay: four nights*

This comfortable apartment is a terrifically romantic roost for vacationing couples. Containing a bedroom and a living room with a fully equipped kitchen area, this residence offers shared use of a refreshing pool and features a private terrace—the perfect spot to savor intimate meals while looking out over the ocean and surrounding islands. Here in the elevated Hell's Gate area of the tiny island, the sunrises and sunsets are particularly spectacular, while mountain trails meander through exotic banana plantations and down to the unspoiled shore, where a host of water recreational activities can be enjoyed year-round. Contact: Ruth Hassell, Saba Real Estate N.V., P.O. Box 17, Saba, Netherlands Antilles. Call 011-599-4-62299.

Children: Y   Pets: N   Smoking: Y   Handicap Access: N   Payment: C, P, T

HELL'S GATE 3   *Rates: budget*
Open: year-round   *Minimum Stay: four nights*

With room for up to four, this large one-bedroom apartment is located in Hell's Gate, only minutes from the airport. It features a lovely private terrace overlooking the Caribbean and rugged coastline, where Saba, the tip of a vast underwater volcanic mountain range, descends sharply into the sea. The entire island is within easy reach, and it offers a wide variety of points of interest and other attractions celebrating its provocative history, dating back to Columbus's discovery on his second New World voyage in 1493. Saba has a rich cultural heritage, influenced by a unique and tantalizing blend of English, Dutch, Spanish and African traditions. Contact: Ruth Hassell, Saba Real Estate N.V., P.O. Box 17, Saba, Netherlands Antilles. Call 011-599-4-62299.

Children: Y Pets: N Smoking: Y Handicap Access: N Payment: C, P, T

HELL'S GATE VILLA   *Rates: deluxe*
Open: year-round   *Minimum Stay: four nights*

An extravagant holiday residence for a party of up to 12, this stately villa offers a remarkable, far-reaching view and the finest in luxurious Caribbean island living. The main house, with its parlor, dining area, four bedrooms and kitchen elegantly decorated, rests adjacent to a large porch in front and an enticing pool, accompanied by several bright terraces, in the rear. Enveloped by a flourishing garden bursting with dazzling tropical flowers and fruit trees, the property features two additional self-contained residences, a separate apartment and a cozy cottage, both containing a bedroom, living room and kitchen facilities. Contact: Ruth Hassell, Saba Real Estate N.V., P.O. Box 17, Saba, Netherlands Antilles. Call 011-599-4-62299.

Children: Y Pets: N Smoking: Y Handicap Access: N Payment: C, P, T

TERRACE APARTMENT   *Rates: budget*
Open: year-round   *Minimum Stay: four nights*

This spacious apartment, containing a bedroom, living room, dining area, and complete kitchen, and sleeping up to four, offers particularly handsome furnishings and a beautiful terrace area. From here, guests enjoy panoramic views of the Caribbean, shimmering in the sun. But inviting as it is, the gleaming blue sea is hardly the only attraction available. Enjoy fine shopping, dining on the unique local cuisine and playing croquet on the museum grounds, an enchanting island tradition. You can also hike in the hills, which are carpeted with exotic fruit trees and flowering plants, where another friendly Saban custom, hitchhiking, is available to tired trekkers seeking a rest. Contact: Ruth Hassell, Saba Real Estate N.V., P.O. Box 17, Saba, Netherlands Antilles. Call 011-599-4-62299.

Children: Y Pets: N Smoking: Y Handicap Access: N Payment: C, P, T

THE BOTTOM

CARIBE GUEST HOUSE   *Rates: budget-expensive*
Open: year-round   *Minimum Stay: none*

Situated in Saba's lovely capital village, the Caribe Guest House contains five rooms, which can be rented separately or in any combination, plus a fully equipped kitchen. The comfortable residence is centrally situated for enjoying all the enchanting features of this tiny Dutch island. Shoppers will savor the locally made crafts and regional spices available in markets and boutiques only steps away, while outdoor enthusiasts won't tire of enjoying the fine recreational facilities also nearby. The diving and snorkeling opportunities off the rugged coastline are world famous, unsurpassed in the eastern Caribbean, and hikes along the many scenic mountain trails take trekkers up 3,000 feet for a vantage that is nothing short of breathtaking. Contact: Medhurst and Associates, Inc., 271 Main Street, Northport, NY 11768. Call 1-800-344-4606.

Children: **Y** Pets: **N** Smoking: **Y** Handicap Access: **N** Payment: **C, T**

WINDWARDSIDE

GINGERBREAD COTTAGE *Rates: budget-inexpensive*
Open: year-round *Minimum Stay: four nights*

An enchanting traditional island cottage is available in the Windwardside area, poised on a ridge between Mt. Scenery and Booby Hill. Here, as throughout Saba, the atmosphere is casual, the pace leisurely and the days serene, while nighttime offers the opportunity for friendly barbecues and lively forays to the local bars and dance spots, where the sound is a pulsating blend of West Indian and American music. After a taste of the spirited Saban nightlife, guests appreciate the tranquility and privacy of their vacation cottage, featuring a beguiling gazebo next to the porch and a pool surrounded by an airy terrace. The interior includes two homey bedrooms, a comfortable living area and a well-equipped kitchen. Contact: Ruth Hassell, Saba Real Estate N.V., P.O. Box 17, Saba, Netherlands Antilles. Call 011-599-4-62299.

Children: **Y** Pets: **N** Smoking: **Y** Handicap Access: **N** Payment: **C, P, T**

JULIANA'S *Rates: budget-inexpensive*
Open: year-round *Minimum Stay: none*

Perched 1,500 feet above the Caribbean, surrounded by tropical foliage, this charming inn offers two superb housekeeping units in addition to its guest rooms. The two-and-a-half-room apartment includes a kitchenette and a private balcony overlooking the sea, while "Flossie's Cottage," a renovated two-bedroom traditional Saban house set in a lush hibiscus garden, contains a spacious living room, dining room, and complete kitchen, and features two porches, both commanding splendid views. A short walk away, the fetching town of Windwardshire offers fine shopping and dining and an authentic taste of everyday island life. Contact: Juliana and Franklin Johnson, Juliana's, Windwardshire, Saba, Netherlands Antilles. Call 011-599-46-2269 or 1-800-344-4606.

Children: **Y** Pets: **N** Smoking: **Y** Handicap Access: **N** Payment: **C, P, T, V, M**

PROMONTORY ESTATE *Rates: moderate-expensive*
Open: year-round *Minimum Stay: one month*

This sumptuous two-acre estate is positioned on its own private, lofty promontory, offering sublime seclusion accented by a stunning view of the ocean and nearby Antilles islands. The property includes a main house and guest house, both containing a living room, a fully equipped kitchen and an elegant master bedroom with high ceilings. There's also a separate apartment and studio on the grounds, plus a sparkling swimming pool and sunny deck area. The coast, with its exceptional diving and snorkeling opportunities, is within easy reach, as are scenic trails winding along the volcanic island's steep—but easily manageable—slopes. Contact: Rent A Home International, Inc., 7200 34th Avenue, N.W., Seattle, WA 98117. Call 1-206-545-6963.

Children: Y Pets: N Smoking: N Handicap Access: N Payment: C, P, T, V, M

TERRACE APARTMENT   *Rates: inexpensive-expensive*
Open: year-round   *Minimum Stay: four nights*

Located in the picturesque little village of Windwardside, this luxurious two-bedroom villa overlooks the ocean and contains a living room and a large kitchen/dining area, with a private pool and sunny terraces on the grounds. Nearby a thousand-step path leads to the crest of Mt. Scenery, the island's central volcano, soaring 1,800 feet above the sea. That's just one of many trails—from paved lanes that anyone can traverse to steep treks that test the mettle of even the hardiest hiker—taking visitors all over the island, past quaint old hamlets, an inactive sulphur mine, banana plantations, dry bushlands and rain forests dappled with mango trees, orchids, begonias and six-foot-tall golden heliconias. Contact: Ruth Hassell, Saba Real Estate N.V., P.O. Box 17, Saba, Netherlands Antilles. Call 011-599-4-62299.

Children: Y Pets: N Smoking: Y Handicap Access: N Payment: C, P, T

Caribbean Sea

Anse des Flamands

Colombier

Anse des Cayes

Baie de
St. Jean

Marigot Bay

Grand
Cul de Sac

Lorient

St. Jean

Vitet

Toiny

Gustavia

Lurin

Anse du Governeur

St. Barthelemy

ANSE DE CAYES

THE CAYES   *Rates: deluxe*
Open: year-round   *Minimum Stay: one week*

Set in the hillside overlooking the deep blue waters of the Caribbean, the Cayes boasts magnificent views of the water and the white sandy beach. Lounge around the swimming pool or take shelter from the sun under the covered portico while pondering the day's activities, which might include waterskiing, or perhaps scuba diving or snorkeling around the island's many coral reefs. The well-appointed living room is set apart from the two bedrooms, which are located in a separate bungalow for complete privacy. Contact: West Indies Management Company, 28 Pelham St., Newport, RI 02840. Call 1-800-932-3222 (in Rhode Island, 401-849-8012). Ref. MAT.

Children: Y   Pets: N   Smoking: Y   Handicap Access: N   Payment: P, T, A

ANSE DU GOUVERNEUR BAY

VILLA ESPANA   *Rates: deluxe*
Open: year-round   *Minimum Stay: one week*

Panoramic views of Gouverneur Bay lie below the marvelous covered terraces at this Spanish-style villa, which features a charming tiled courtyard filled with potted palms and island plants. You can dine under the stars, or inside the dining room, which is connected to a fully equipped kitchen with the gourmet chef in mind. Airy and spacious, three bedrooms and two baths provide sleeping accommodations for up to six people. At Gouverneur Bay, you'll find terrific swimming and some local legends of long-ago pirates. Contact: West Indies Management Company, 28 Pelham St., Newport, RI 02840. Call 1-800-932-3222 (in Rhode Island, 401-849-8012). Ref. GLN.

Children: Y   Pets: N   Smoking: Y   Handicap Access: N   Payment: P, T, A

BAIE DE ST. JEAN

VILLAGE ST. JEAN   *Rates: inexpensive-deluxe*
Open: year-round   *Minimum Stay: none*

Relax in shaded seclusion in one of Village St. Jean's cottages, studios or Jacuzzi suites. All units give you lovely terrace views of the ocean and are just a short walk from the beach. Kitchens, private bathrooms, air conditioning and private phones make you feel at home, and access to the village is easy from the nearby airport. There's plenty to do in the area, including visits to Gustavia, which is home to a music festival the first week of February. Water sports enthusiasts will find excellent scuba diving, snorkeling and swimming. Contact: Village Saint Jean, P.O. Box 23, St. Barthelemy, French West Indies. Call 590-276139.

Children: Y Pets: N Smoking: Y Handicap Access: N Payment: C, T, A, V, M

COLOMBIER

THE CLIFFS   *Rates: deluxe*
Open: year-round   *Minimum Stay: one week*

Flowering bougainvillea, fragrant hibiscus and other exotic tropical flowers surround this deluxe house set in the cliffs of Colombier. To the left you'll find magnificent views of Gustavia Harbor, to the right is a wide-open expanse of deep blue sea. A kidney-shaped swimming pool, surrounded by a wooden sun deck, offers an alternative to the beach. Three bedrooms and two baths and a large living room, complete with a piano, make for a relaxing and peaceful vacation. For a special treat in spring and summer, take a walk to the cove below where female sea turtles lay their eggs. Contact: West Indies Management Company, 28 Pelham St., Newport, RI 02840. Call 1-800-932-3222 (in Rhode Island, 401-849-8012). Ref. DAN.

Children: Y   Pets: N   Smoking: Y   Handicap Access: N   Payment: P, T, A

VILLA COLOMBIER   *Rates: deluxe*
Open: year-round   *Minimum Stay: one week*

Luxurious living with magnificent views and all modern amenities await you at Villa Colombier, set in the Colombier hillside overlooking scenic Gustavia Harbor. Two stylish bedrooms, including a master bedroom with an antique four-poster bed, sleep four. A lovely wooden sun deck overlooks the water, and offers a relaxing Jacuzzi. Dine under the sun or stars on the terrace dining table. Contact: West Indies Management Company, 28 Pelham St., Newport, RI 02840. Call 1-800-932-3222 (in Rhode Island, 401-849-8012). Ref. JOL.

Children: Y   Pets: N   Smoking: Y   Handicap Access: N   Payment: P, T, A

VILLA HILLS *Rates: deluxe*
Open: year-round *Minimum Stay: one week*
This peaceful hillside villa boasts dramatic views of the deep blue waters below, accessible by a long stairway set in the rocks. Handsomely furnished throughout with English antiques, the villa features three bedrooms and three baths. Located in a separate section of the villa, the master suite offers complete privacy. Relax on the sun deck between dips in the pool, venture to the secluded Colombier Beach or explore the tropical gardens in town. Contact: West Indies Management Company, 28 Pelham St., Newport, RI 02840. Call 1-800-932-3222 (in Rhode Island, 401-849-8012). Ref. VID.
Children: Y   Pets: N   Smoking: Y   Handicap Access: N   Payment: P, T, A

VILLA ISLAMORADA *Rates: expensive-deluxe*
Open: year-round *Minimum Stay: one week*
Colombier is famous for its breathtaking sunsets, and Villa Islamorada fits in well amid the splendor. This two-bedroom, two-bath property offers seclusion, yet keeps you within a mile of the beach, where the swimming's good, and as an added attraction, you can view the female sea turtles who nest here each spring and summer. A huge redwood deck surrounds the villa's swimming pool, and its interior is packed with amenities such as a wet bar, a stereo, oversized beds and air conditioning. One bedroom is set in a separate wing, ensuring privacy for all. Contact: C. Roos Villa Holidays, Inc., 13100 Wayzata Blvd., Suite 150, Minneapolis, MN 55343. Call 1-800-328-6262 (in Minnesota, 612-591-0076).
Children: Y Pets: N Smoking: Y Handicap Access: N Payment: C, P, T, V, M

CUL DE SAC

ANTILLES *Rates: deluxe*
Open: year-round *Minimum Stay: one week*
Located amid vibrant gardens lush with mangroves and palms, this charming house, designed in an Antillean style, offers magnificent ocean views in appealing surroundings. Both queen-size bedrooms feature private baths, and the cool cottons and rattan furnishings provide comfort and style. Dine or relax outside on the expansive covered terraces while gazing at the tranquil sea. The shallow, calm waters of the bay are an ideal place to learn windsurfing, or to go snorkeling and exploring underwater life. Contact: West Indies Management Company, 28 Pelham St., Newport, RI 02840. Call 1-800-932-3222 (in Rhode Island, 401-849-8012). Ref. NAT.
Children: Y   Pets: N   Smoking: Y   Handicap Access: N   Payment: P, T, A

VILLA LES FLEURS 1 *Rates: budget-moderate*
Open: year-round *Minimum Stay: one week*
This old-fashioned studio apartment is located on the hillside above Grand Cul de Sac, and offers comfortable accommodations at a modest price. Get some fresh air or dine on the covered terrace, or spend some time in a lovely garden area next to the apartment. A ceiling fan

circulates cool island breezes, and a second bedroom is available. At Grand Cul de Sac, you'll find snorkeling, scuba diving and waterskiing, as well as many fine restaurants and shops. Contact: Peg Walsh, St. Barth Properties, 22 Park Road, Franklin, MA 02038. Call 1-800-421-3396 (in Massachusetts, 508-528-7727).

Children: Y Pets: N Smoking: Y Handicap Access: N Payment: C, P, T, V, M

FLAMANDS

VILLA RAYON DE SOLEIL   *Rates: moderate-expensive*
Open: year-round   *Minimum Stay: one week*

The utmost privacy makes this a perfect honeymoon cottage. Its airconditioned loft with a queen-sized bed keeps you cool and comfortable, and the covered terrace and deck directly off the bedroom give the cottage a casual, airy ambiance. Area attractions include Anse des Flamands, a picturesque little cove, and two small offshore islands, from which you can spy migrating sperm whales each May. Contact: Peg Walsh, St. Barth Properties, 22 Park Road, Franklin, MA 02038. Call 1-800-421-3396 (in Massachusetts, 508-528-7727).

Children: Y Pets: N Smoking: Y Handicap Access: N Payment: C, P, T, V, M

GRAND CUL DE SAC

TERRACE HOUSE   *Rates: expensive-deluxe*
Open: year-round   *Minimum Stay: one week*

At Grand Cul de Sac you'll find a fabulous reef-protected bay perfect for all water sports, and at Petite Cul de Sac you'll find unique limestone rock formations. Terrace House, named for its many terraces, provides good views and easy access to both areas. Overstuffed furnishings in island rattan, large scenic windows and three bedrooms offer plenty of room and comfort. Gourmet dining is essential with the magnificent kitchen, which is well equipped for preparing sumptuous meals. Contact: West Indies Management Company, 28 Pelham St., Newport, RI 02840. Call 1-800-932-3222 (in Rhode Island, 401-849-8012). Ref. FIN.

Children: Y Pets: N Smoking: Y Handicap Access: N Payment: P, T, A

VILLA SYLPHES   *Rates: moderate-expensive*
Open: year-round   *Minimum Stay: one week*

This one-bedroom villa lies right on the beach at Grand Cul de Sac, where warm, shallow waters provide a perfect setting for windsurfing and snorkeling. From here you can set out on foot and traverse the volcanic rock hillside to Grand Fond, where the jagged coastlines evoke images of Normandy. The villa's kitchenette makes meal preparation quick and easy, and air conditioning keeps you cool no matter the weather outside. Contact: Peg Walsh, St. Barth Properties, 22 Park Road, Franklin, MA 02038. Call 1-800-421-3396 (in Massachusetts, 508-528-7727).

Children: Y Pets: N Smoking: Y Handicap Access: N Payment: C, P, T, V, M

VITET   *Rates: deluxe*
Open: year-round   *Minimum Stay: one week*

You'll have a bird's-eye view of the ocean waters rolling onto the
shores at Grand Cul de Sac in this hillside villa. The fragrance of
bougainvillea and palms waft up from the lush tropical gardens around
this villa. Haitian artwork adds an authentic touch, and two bedrooms
and baths provide accommodations for up to four. A TV with a VCR
and a stereo fill your entertainment needs, while a deluxe gourmet
kitchen allows for sumptuous meals made up of local delicacies. Contact: West Indies Management Company, 28 Pelham St., Newport, RI
02840. Call 1-800-932-3222 (in Rhode Island, 401-849-8012). Ref. POC.
Children: Y   Pets: N   Smoking: Y   Handicap Access: N   Payment: P, T, A

Lorient

HILLVIEW   *Rates: moderate-expensive*
Open: year-round   *Minimum Stay: one week*

This private and well-maintained villa is located only minutes from
Lorient Beach, one of the most attractive beaches on St. Barthelemy,
yet not as popular with tourists. Enjoy the secluded beaches and tranquil bay, where you'll find fine snorkeling among the many spectacular coral reefs. The air-conditioned villa's sliding glass doors open
from the living/dining room onto an attractive wooden sun deck with
fine views of the sea below. A comfortable sleeping loft for two is
located right above the living room, allowing for quiet, cozy nights.
Contact: West Indies Management Company, 28 Pelham St., Newport, RI 02840. Call 1-800-932- 3222 (in Rhode Island, 401-849-8012).
Ref. LUB.
Children: Y   Pets: N   Smoking: Y   Handicap Access: N   Payment: P, T, A

SEASIDE VILLA   *Rates: expensive-deluxe*
Open: year-round   *Minimum Stay: one week*

Set right on the magnificent beach at Lorient, this beautiful two-
bedroom villa boasts fine views of a beach nearly unknown to tourists.
Enjoy all your meals on the enchanting dining pavilion, set amid bougainvillea and palms and facing the water, or take a relaxing dip in the
private Jacuzzi. Tastefully furnished with comfort in mind, the villa
allows as much privacy as you want, yet is close to shopping and
restaurants, where you can sample exotic local fare or refresh yourself
as you sip tropical delights. Contact: West Indies Management Company, 28 Pelham St., Newport, RI 02840. Call 1-800-932-3222 (in
Rhode Island, 401-849-8012). Ref. GTL.
Children: Y   Pets: N   Smoking: Y   Handicap Access: N   Payment: P, T, A

Lurin

SEAVIEWS   *Rates: deluxe*
Open: year-round   *Minimum Stay: one week*

This large deluxe villa boasts breathtaking views of the rocky coastline rising from the water's edge near the picturesque town of Lurin,
just a short drive from Gouverneur Beach. Two bedrooms are located

in the main villa, and two more are set apart in small bungalows, a perfect arrangement for complete privacy. Relax on the wooden sun deck that surrounds the inviting swimming pool, while taking in the panoramic views. Dine indoors or out, covered or not, on the terrace deck. Contact: West Indies Management Company, 28 Pelham St., Newport, RI 02840. Call 1-800-932-3222 (in Rhode Island, 401-849-8012). Ref. WCH.

Children: Y Pets: N Smoking: Y Handicap Access: N Payment: P, T, A

MARIGOT

VILLA BOUGAINVILLEA   *Rates: expensive*
Open: year-round   *Minimum Stay: one week*

Vacationers come to St. Barthelemy for its tranquility and beauty, and this one-bedroom villa is a perfect base from which to enjoy it all. Set amid gentle palms, its terrace overlooks scenic Marigot Bay. Inside, air conditioning keeps the climate perfect. With this villa as your home, set out to explore St. Bart's eight miles of blossoming shrubs, mahogany trees and rolling volcanic hills. The buildings here have been kept low and unobtrusive, so as not to clash with nature, and the restaurants are among the Caribbean's finest. Contact: Peg Walsh, St. Barth Properties, 22 Park Road, Franklin, MA 02038. Call 1-800-421-3396 (in Massachusetts, 508-528-7727).

Children: Y Pets: N Smoking: Y Handicap Access: N Payment: C, P, T, V, M

MONT JEAN

VILLA LE CHANT DE LA MER   *Rates: deluxe*
Open: year-round   *Minimum Stay: one week*

Cool marble floors in this superluxurious villa create a magnificent ambiance echoed throughout in design and furnishings. With expansive views over Marigot Bay and Grand Cul de Sac, and easy access to both, you won't wonder what to do with your days or nights here. Should you decide to stay home for a meal, the gourmet-equipped kitchen allows for easy preparation of sumptuous island delicacies, and clean-up is a breeze. Four bedrooms and four baths comfortably accommodate eight people. Sunbathe around the large swimming pool, or take a refreshing dip in the private Jacuzzi, or explore the interesting sights below. Contact: Peg Walsh, St. Barth Properties, 22 Park Road, Franklin, MA 02038. Call 1-800-421-3396 (in Massachusetts, 508-528-7727).

Children: Y Pets: N Smoking: Y Handicap Access: N Payment: C, P, T, V, M

POINT MILOU

CLIFFSIDE VILLA   *Rates: expensive-deluxe*
Open: year-round   *Minimum Stay: one week*

This luxurious villa is perched on the cliffs overlooking Pointe Milou, offering breathtaking views of the water as it crashes against the rocky shores of St. Barthelemy. The villa is surrounded by beautiful gardens, and guests can use the poolside gazebo for lazy afternoon picnics or romantic moonlight dinners. A separate bedroom cottage is perfect for extended families, and the large swimming pool is beautifully appointed with mosaic borders and a garden backdrop. Contact: West Indies Management Company, 28 Pelham St., Newport, RI 02840. Call 1-800-932-3222 (in Rhode Island, 401-849-8012). Ref. PMU.

Children: **Y**   Pets: **N**   Smoking: **Y**   Handicap Access: **N**   Payment: **P, T, A**

GARDEN VILLA   *Rates: deluxe*
Open: year-round   *Minimum Stay: one week*

The view is reason enough to stay in this garden villa, from which you can gaze across the water to neighboring islands. With one bedroom and one bath, it's the perfect place for an intimate getaway, but its modern kitchen, dining and room living rooms give you plenty of space to stretch out. Maid service is also provided, and your private swimming pool and gazebo provide an ideal setting for lazy afternoons in the sun. When you're ready for adventure, explore some of St. Barthelemy's 22 beaches. Contact: Villas International, 71 West 23rd St., New York, NY 10010. Call 212-929-7585. Ref. PMU SI.

Children: **Y**   Pets: **N**   Smoking: **Y**   Handicap Access: **N**   Payment: **C, P, T**

GOURMET VILLA   *Rates: deluxe*
Open: year-round   *Minimum Stay: one week*

The unsurpassed cliffside location of this deluxe villa boasts panoramic views of the azure waters of the Caribbean. Decorated with stylish furnishings and fabulous artwork, the villa features two master bedrooms and one guest bedroom, all with lovely pastel-colored patchwork quilts. A covered patio provides shade from the sun after a day of sunbathing around the private swimming pool. Sip cocktails on the lovely terrace while making dinner plans, or enjoy your own concoctions prepared in the gourmet kitchen. Contact: West Indies Management Company, 28 Pelham St., Newport, RI 02840. Call 1-800-932-3222 (in Rhode Island, 401-849-8012). Ref. MOZ.

Children: **Y**   Pets: **N**   Smoking: **Y**   Handicap Access: **N**   Payment: **P, T, A**

PELICAN HOUSE   *Rates: budget-deluxe*
Open: year-round   *Minimum Stay: one week*

Set on a hillside, Pelican House enjoys the cool breezes brought by tropical trade winds, and is located in the exclusive section of Pointe Milou, a quiet residential neighborhood. Named for the numerous pelicans who make this area their home, visitors can enjoy watching the sea birds as they go about their business. Four to five guests will find comfort in two twin bedrooms and a sleeping alcove above the living room. A partially covered patio off the living room features a built-in Jacuzzi, and stretches to the rear deck, which overlooks the Caribbean. In the morning, enjoy fresh croissants and baguettes from a local bakery, just a short walk away. Contact: Hilde Freeman, Rent A Home International, Inc., 7200 34th Ave., N.W., Seattle, WA 98117. Call 206-545-6963.

Children: **Y** Pets: **N** Smoking: **Y** Handicap Access: **N** Payment: **C, P, T, V, M**

THE DECK *Rates: deluxe*
Open: year-round *Minimum Stay: one week*
Several levels of decks and terraces with inspiring sea views complement this extraordinary villa. The furnishing's warm wood tones set
off the white and pastel cotton cushions, creating a cozy ambience
that's relaxing and delightful. Four tastefully decorated bedrooms, each
with a bath, lie in two separate bungalows, ensuring privacy. Landscaped paths wander between the bungalows, allowing you to visit
your friends, or seclude yourself in privacy. Sip cocktails on the furnished terraces, or enjoy a sumptuous island meal while the sun dips
seaward in the distance. Contact: West Indies Management Company,
28 Pelham St., Newport, RI 02840. Call 1-800-932-3222 (in Rhode
Island, 401-849-8012). Ref. VOI.
Children: Y Pets: N Smoking: Y Handicap Access: N Payment: P, T, A

THE HILLS *Rates: expensive*
Open: year-round *Minimum Stay: one week*
This lovely house designed with clean lines in the local style boasts
two terraces—one with a Jacuzzi, the other with a sheltering cover—
offering guests a choice of pleasures. The sunny deck overlooks the
dark blue waters of Pointe Milou, where the sound of Atlantic waves
crashing onto the rocks heightens the island atmosphere. Nearly constant tropical breezes keep the entire house cool, but not so cool that
you wouldn't enjoy a dip in the sea. Contact: West Indies Management
Company, 28 Pelham St., Newport, RI 02840. Call 1-800-932-3222 (in
Rhode Island, 401-849-8012). Ref. VER. 1.
Children: Y Pets: N Smoking: Y Handicap Access: N Payment: C, P, T, A

VILLA EAGLES NEST *Rates: deluxe*
Open: year-round *Minimum Stay: one week*
Set high on a hillside, aptly named Villa Eagles Nest, this vacation
spot boasts breathtaking views. Its three bedrooms, two baths and a
covered balcony give you plenty of private space in which to unwind,
and the villa's swimming pool will make it hard to leave. The snorkeling and scuba diving are spectacular in nearby St. Jean Bay. Divers
will find lobsters, barracuda and other fish, as well as sea turtles and
dolphins just offshore. A day's deep-sea fishing will likely yield tuna,
marlin and even moray eel. Contact: Peg Walsh, St. Barth Properties,
22 Park Road, Franklin, MA 02038. Call 1-800-421-3396 (in Massachusetts, 508-528-7727).
Children: Y Pets: N Smoking: Y Handicap Access: N Payment: C, P, T, V, M

VILLA PELICAN *Rates: deluxe*
Open: year-round *Minimum Stay: one week*
Magnificent views of Pointe Milou, where the rough waters of the
Atlantic meet up with the craggy cliffs of St. Bart, are offered from this
villa's patio and open deck. A swimming pool, a Jacuzzi and the ocean
below offer a variety of water sports during your stay at this modern
two-bedroom villa. The calm waters of St. Jean Bay provide spectacu-

lar snorkeling, and you can easily find a local fisherman to take you to the best diving spots off the island, where you can occasionally spot sea turtles and dolphins. Contact: Peg Walsh, St. Barth Properties, 22 Park Road, Franklin, MA 02038. Call 1-800-421-3396 (in Massachusetts, 508-528-7727).

Children: Y Pets: N Smoking: Y Handicap Access: N Payment: C, P, T, V, M

ST. JEAN

BEACH COTTAGE *Rates: moderate-expensive*
Open: year-round *Minimum Stay: one week*

You'll find carefree beachfront living easy to accomplish at this two-bedroom cottage, which is charming in its simplicity. Twin bedrooms are located on either side of the central living room, affording welcome privacy for all. Each bedroom features sliding glass doors, to let the sunlight in and the guests out onto a private covered terrace. The white sandy beach at St. Jean Bay is a favorite among swimmers, sunbathers and beachcombers. Contact: West Indies Management Company, 28 Pelham St., Newport, RI 02840. Call 1-800-932-3222 (in Rhode Island, 401-849-8012). Ref. EGR 2.

Children: Y Pets: N Smoking: Y Handicap Access: N Payment: C, P, T, A

FONTAINBLEAU *Rates: deluxe*
Open: year-round *Minimum Stay: one week*

The central garden courtyard of this deluxe villa boasts a fountain, a large dining table, a furnished sitting area and a gallery-style kitchen, and overlooks the pool deck and magnificent St. Jean Bay. Off the courtyard you'll find two cozy air-conditioned bedrooms and a sitting room with a TV and a VCR and a stereo. Above the main house, tucked into the hillside, are two more bedrooms with a private bath, a terrace, a kitchenette and a dining and sitting area. With plenty of space and privacy, this is the perfect villa for large families or groups of friends. Contact: West Indies Management Company, 28 Pelham St., Newport, RI 02840. Call 1-800-932-3222 (in Rhode Island, 401-849-8012). Ref. KAR.

Children: Y Pets: N Smoking: Y Handicap Access: N Payment: P, T, A

ST. JEAN BEACHFRONT *Rates: moderate-expensive*
Open: year-round *Minimum Stay: one week*

You'll find this island getaway nestled in a sandy grove of palm trees, offering shade from the hot sun and a cooling place to catch the trade winds. Two air-conditioned studio bungalows are perfect for two couples who wish to share a vacation and still have some privacy. Twin beds, a bath and a kitchenette provide all you need for a relaxing vacation, while the pretty, pristine beach at St. Jean Bay allows for snorkeling, sunbathing and swimming. Contact: West Indies Management Company, 28 Pelham St., Newport, RI 02840. Call 1-800-932-3222 (in Rhode Island, 401-849-8012). Ref. COT A & B.

Children: Y Pets: N Smoking: Y Handicap Access: N Payment: C, P, T, A

VILLAS LA VUE *Rates: inexpensive-moderate*
Open: year-round *Minimum Stay: one week*

You'll feel like you own a spectacular corner of the world while staying in this luxurious hillside villa, which gazes down from a lovely covered balcony to the beautiful bay below. One bedroom provides an intimate setting for two; air conditioning keeps you cool day and night. The bay offers some of St. Jean's finest water sports, and the snorkeling in reef-protected waters is spectacular. The white sandy beaches are equally lovely, and perhaps you'll be tempted to join those who prefer bathing topless. Contact: Peg Walsh, St. Barth Properties, 22 Park Road, Franklin, MA 02038. Call 1-800-421-3396 (in Massachusetts, 508-528-7727).

Children: Y Pets: N Smoking: Y Handicap Access: N Payment: C, P, T, V, M

TOINY

VILLA PAS DE DANSE *Rates: deluxe*
Open: year-round *Minimum Stay: one week*

Nestled in the hillside at Grand Fond, this villa boasts dramatic views over jagged cliffs into the crystal-clear, sparkling Caribbean waters. Relax on the large covered terrace without worrying about getting a sunburn. Ceiling fans circulate the cool island breezes, while you try your hand at the villa's piano. Two bedrooms and two baths and a small additional bedroom accommodate up to five people. Toiny and Grand Fond are an appealing change from the more timid areas of the Caribbean, offering a rugged, more interesting setting. Contact: Peg Walsh, St. Barth Properties, 22 Park Road, Franklin, MA 02038. Call 1-800-421-3396 (in Massachusetts, 508-528-7727).

Children: Y Pets: N Smoking: Y Handicap Access: N Payment: C, P, T, V, M

VenusBay

JenkinsBay

Great Bay

Tumble Down
Dick Bay

★ Oranjestad

Caribbean Sea

BuccaneersBay

St. Eustatius

CHERRY TREE

CHERRY TREE VILLA *Rates: inexpensive-moderate*
Open: year-round *Minimum Stay: none*

The Cherry Tree Villa, on a magnificent 17-acre estate on the intimate
island locals call "Statia," offers a selection of splendid two-bedroom
apartments that each feature a fully equipped gourmet kitchen and an
open-air hot tub. Mediterranean fanlight windows open onto the sea,
while landward, a patio commands a majestic view of the long dormant (but widely discussed) Mazinga volcano. Stroll along the deserted black volcanic sand beaches or climb up to the tropical rain
forest of the Quill, the ancient volcano's crater, where archeological
ruins date back more than 200 years. Tour the nearby islands of St.
Maarten, St. Barts, Saba, Antigua and St. Kitts—but not before you
scuba dive through a sunken city surrounded by rich and colorful
marine life. Contact: Cherry Tree Villa, c/o P.O. Box 12485, St. Louis,
MO 63132. Call: 314-569-2501 or 1-800-325-2222.

Children: **Y** Pets: **N** Smoking: **Y** Handicap Access: **N** Payment: **C, T**

JURIA VILLA OR COTTAGE *Rates: budget*
Open: year-round *Minimum Stay: none*

Located in a private and tranquil setting, this handsomely furnished
two-bedroom private home comfortably accommodates four or more
guests. Here you will be torn between the beauty of the glorious
beaches and the pull of island history, which lures you toward

tumbled-down sugar mills and 200-year-old warehouses; an old Dutch Reform Church and the ruins of the second oldest Jewish synagogue; and the pre-Columbian artifacts now on display at the St. Eustatius Historical Foundation Museum. For further adventure, climb the Quill, a perfectly formed 2,000-foot dormant volcano whose crater contains a lush tropical rain forest rich with bananas, limes and exotic vegetation. Contact: John Thompson, Bifsheuvel Weglin, Concordia, St. Eustatius, Netherlands Antilles. Call 011-599-3-82291.

Children: **Y**   Pets: **N**   Smoking: **N**   Handicap Access: **N**   Payment: **C, T**

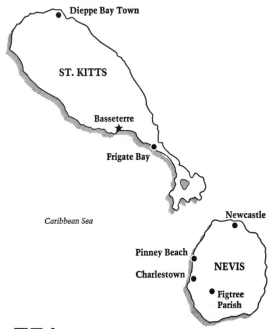

Dieppe Bay Town

ST. KITTS

Basseterre

Frigate Bay

Caribbean Sea

Newcastle

Pinney Beach

Charlestown

NEVIS

Figtree
Parish

St. Kitts and Nevis

NEVIS
Figtree Parish

CITRUS GROVE *Rates: expensive*
Open: January-April *Minimum Stay: two weeks*

Five acres of luscious citrus groves, tropical fruit trees and ornamental plants surround this two-story stone house. The age of this island is reflected in antique furnishings like the four-poster beds, yet modern amenities, such as a radio, stereo and a car, are at your disposal. There are one and a half bathrooms, a living/dining area and a kitchen; linens, utilities and the services of two maids are included, as is laundry service. A short drive from the house brings you to a public beach with a reserved cabana, or you can stay home and enjoy the private swimming pool. Guests can enjoy hiking along the trails that cover the island, or just relaxing on the veranda at home. Contact: Rent A Home International, Inc., 7200 34th Ave. N.W., Seattle, WA 98117. Call 206-545-6963.

Children: Y Pets: N Smoking: Y Handicap Access: N Payment: C, P, T, V, M

HERMITAGE PLANTATION *Rates: moderate-deluxe*
Open: year-round *Minimum Stay: none*

At one time this little island supported many prosperous sugar cane estates; now some have been converted into unique vacation proper ties. This estate features a 250-year-old great house and a few colonial guest cottages—all of which have a charming ambiance and are furnished with canopy beds and antiques. Most of the cottages have kitchenettes and all have balconies, porches and gardens where you can sit in a rocker or swing in a hammock enjoying the pleasure of an endlessly sunny day. The pace here is extrememly relaxed, giving you plenty of time to discover the secluded beaches and unspoiled countryside. The plantation has a freshwater pool, and the staff will be happy to arrange for golf, tennis, scuba diving, sailing, horeseback riding or excursions. Contact: Hermitage Plantation, Nevis, West Indies. Call 809-469-5477.

Children: Y Pets: N Smoking: Y Handicap Access: N Payment: C, T, A, V, M

Newcastle

CABINDISH VILLA   *Rates: expensive-deluxe*
Open: year-round   *Minimum Stay: one week*

Near the northern tip of this little island, this three-bedroom house has views of both the ocean and the mountains. Screened doors and shutters allow the sea breezes to flow through the house, and a large wraparound veranda is furnished for outdoor living. The kitchen is modern, with a gas stove and deep freeze; the cook will prepare breakfast and lunch most days and, by arrangement, dinner. During the week, a maid cleans and does the household laundry. A huge entrance hallway, a living room, a dining area with seating for eight and three bathrooms complete the room plan. A beach lies directly in front of the house, and there are coral formations in the water that will delight the snorkeler and swimmer. Contact: Barry Shepard, At Home Abroad, Inc., 405 East 56th St., 6H, New York, NY 10022. Call 212-421-9165. Ref. 9212.

Children: Y Pets: N Smoking: Y Handicap Access: N Payment: C, P, T

LEEWARD HOUSE   *Rates: budget-inexpensive*
Open: year-round   *Minimum Stay: one week*

This no-frills house reflects the simplicity of the little island upon which it stands, yet it has amenities guaranteed to ensure a comfortable visit. Suitable for four or five guests, it includes three bedrooms (one double and two twins) and two bathrooms. The living room and dining room are combined, and there is a kitchen and a little gallery. Steps lead from the double glass doors down to a garden, from which it is a short walk to both a private and public beach. The house is cooled by ceiling fans; linen and maid service are included. You may have lunch or dinner at one of the local hotels, whose swimming pools and tennis courts are at your disposal. Golf lovers will have to cross the two-mile-wide channel to St. Kitts. Deep-sea fish boats and bicycles and horses for exploring the island can all be rented. Contact: Rent A Home International, Inc., 7200 34th Ave. NW, Seattle, WA 98117. Call 206-545-6963.

Children: Y Pets: N Smoking: Y Handicap Access: Y Payment: C, P, V, M

Oualie Beach

OUALIE BEACH CLUB *Rates: inexpensive-moderate*
Open: year-round *Minimum Stay: none*

Nevis's sister island of St. Kitts is visible across the strait from the garden and porch of this club, and a short boat trip will take you to its lively shores and clubs. The setting is more tranquil back on Nevis, where this beach club, consisting of duplex cottages, a beach bar and restaurant, offers you a chance to enjoy the relaxed pace. A golden, uncrowded beach is just outside your door, and a qualified instructor can take you on a scuba dive at the island's best sites. On solid ground, the staff will be happy to arrange tours of the island's rain forests, a yacht charter, water sports or horseback riding. All the rooms are screened and have ceiling fans; one- or two-bedroom styles are offered. Diving packages and meal plans are available. Contact: Oualie Beach Club, Nevis, West Indies. Call 809-469-9735/5329.

Children: Y Pets: N Smoking: Y Handicap Access: N Payment: C, T, A, V, M

St. Charles

ST. CHARLES HOUSE *Rates: deluxe*
Open: year-round *Minimum Stay: one week*

The volcanic beach just outside this villa stretches all the way into Charleston, a small town that is the largest on the island and offers shops, pubs and restaurants. The villa is completely equipped; it has three twin bedrooms and two full bathrooms as well as a guest powder room. A dramatic cathedral ceiling rises above the living room; there is a separate dining room, and the kitchen is equipped with both gas and electric stoves. A separate suite is divided from the main house by a porch that runs around three sides of the house; it has a twin bedroom and en suite bathroom. A covered tower above the gallery offers a fine view and makes a good place for cocktails before or after dinner. For parties of less than five, there is one cook/maid; for larger parties extra staff can be arranged. Tennis and golf are within reasonable distance. Contact: At Home Abroad, Inc., 405 East 56th St., 6H, New York, NY 10022. Call 212-421-9165. Ref. 8049.

Children: Y Pets: N Smoking: Y Handicap Access: N Payment: C, P, T

ST. KITTS

Basseterre

OCEAN TERRACE INN *Rates: inexpensive-deluxe*
Open: year-round *Minimum Stay: three nights*

Self-contained apartments are available here in a variety of styles, some with views of the ocean, others overlooking the volcanic mountains. All apartments have kitchens and an extensive range of services and amenities—color TV, extra fold-out couches, air conditioning, access to the hotel swimming pool and Jacuzzi, special events, babysitting services and full maid and linen service. Golf, tennis, scuba diving, snorkeling, deep-sea fishing: The list of activities is endless, and for a unique experience, try a rain forest hike or a plantation tour. A pool-side bar and restaurant provide excellent cuisine and entertainment, and casinos and other dining options can be found within easy distance. Contact: Sandra MacLeod, Ocean Terrace Inn, Fortlands, Basseterre, St. Kitts, West Indies. Call 809-465-2754 or 800-223-5695.

Children: Y Pets: N Smoking: Y Handicap Access: N Payment: C, T, A, V, M

OTTLEY'S PLANTATION INN   *Rates: deluxe*
Open: year-round   *Minimum Stay: three nights*

The Gatekeeper's Cottage on this old sugar plantation is available as a rental accommodation, providing guests with full access to the inn's superior amenities as well as a measure of privacy. Over 35 acres of grounds surround the inn and include a rain forest and landscaped lawns; a 60-foot swimming pool is fed by a spring and bordered by the ruins of the sugar factory. The cottage has a living and dining area, a kitchen and two queen-sized bedrooms and is decorated with charming white wicker and florals, with British touches. A charming private patio and garden make a perfect place to sit and take tea, breakfast or cocktails. A beach, a championship golf course, tennis courts, horseback riding stables and more are close by. Contact: Ottley's Plantation Inn, Suite 105, 301 N. Harrison St., Princeton, NJ 08540. Call 609-921-1259/8769.

Children: Y Pets: N Smoking: Y Handicap: N Payment: C, T, A, V, M, O

Dieppe Bay Town

THE GOLDEN LEMON INN AND VILLAS   *Rates: deluxe*
Open: year-round   *Minimum Stay: one week*

When you arrive for a stay at this inn, you'll be escorted from the airport a half hour away. The former 17th-century manor house has been transformed by host Arthur Leaman, one-time decorating editor of *House & Garden* magazine. The main two-story building with a long, covered terrace sits in a coconut grove before magnificent mountains; self-contained villas can be found by the ocean and tucked away in a garden. Each one- or two-bedroom villa features rare and unique furnishings and decor. Tennis courts and an astounding fifteen swimming and plunge pools (your private pool lies at the door of your villa) are available on the premises, and the beach sand is volcanic black in contrast with the deep blue of the sea. Contact: Arthur Leaman, the Golden Lemon Inn and Villas, Dieppe Bay, St. Kitts, West Indies. Call 1-800-633-7411.

Children: N Pets: N Smoking: N Handicap: N Payment: C, P, T, A, V, M

Frigate Bay

FRIGATE BAY BEACH HOTEL   *Rates: inexpensive-deluxe*
Open: year-round   *Minimum Stay: none*

Mountains carpeted with lush rain forest rise up to one side of this hotel, the aquamarine Caribbean lies to another and the vast expanse of the Atlantic stretches out on a third. These small, white buildings with their archways and balconies provide privacy and the advantage of a great location for visitors. The apartments have tile floors, spacious ceilings, tasteful prints and patterns set off by the white walls and modern kitchens with breakfast bars for convenience. Studio, one- and two-bedroom apartments are all available, and daily maid and linen services are included. A bar and restaurant provide hospitality next to the Olympic-sized pool, and each apartment has a private balcony or terrace for private dining or sunbathing. Contact: David Baker or Lynne Archibald, Frigate Bay Beach Hotel, Frigate Bay, St. Kitts, West Indies. Call 809-465-8935.

Children: Y Pets: N Smoking: N Handicap Access: N Payment: C, T, A, V, M

ISLAND PARADISE BEACH VILLAGE   *Rates: moderate-deluxe*
Open: year-round   *Minimum Stay: one week*

The privately owned condominiums here are rented out to vacationers, each one a true family home with individual furnishings. One- to three-bedroom units are available, all with kitchens, living/dining areas and full bathrooms. Daily maid service can be arranged, and there are laundry facilities on the premises. Each unit has a shady balcony or patio; the swimming pool with comfortable poolside furniture is an ideal spot in which to relax. Guests are welcome to use the barbecue or try one of the restaurants in the area, including P.J.'s Pizza Bar on the premises. Active days are filled with scuba diving, golf, sailboat charters or fishing trips; for quieter times include explorations of the island's rain forests, ancient volcanic mountains and old sugar plantations. Contact: Pat Rogers, Island Paradise Beach Village Homeowner's Assoc., P.O. Box 444, Frigate Bay, St. Kitts, West Indies. Call 809-465-8035.

Children: Y   Pets: N   Smoking: Y   Handicap Access: N   Payment: C, T

LEEWARD COVE CONDOMINIUM HOTEL   *Rates: inexpensive-expensive*
Open: year-round   *Minimum Stay: three nights*

At the tip of of this teardrop-shaped island lies a narrow strip of land connecting the Atlantic and Caribbean sides of the island. Here, surrounded by extinct volcanoes and lush rain forests, lies the popular Frigate Bay area, where you'll find this five-acre condominium complex. The one- and two-bedroom suites have bathrooms, kitchens, living/dining areas and patios on both sides so you can catch the sun— or the shade—all day long. The bedrooms are air-conditioned and the living areas cooled by ocean breezes and ceiling fans; a maid looks after your cleaning and linens daily, so there's nothing left to do but relax. Casinos, restaurants and live music can be enjoyed in the evenings on this lively island. Contact: Mrs. D. N. Perta, Leeward Cove Condominium Hotel, P. O. Box 123, Frigate Bay, St. Kitts, West Indies. Call 809-465-8030.

Children: Y Pets: N Smoking: Y Handicap Access: N Payment: C, T, A, V, M

ST. CHRISTOPHER CLUB   *Rates: inexpensive-deluxe*
Open: year-round   *Minimum Stay: none*

The St. Christopher Club is located on a strip of land, just one mile wide, that lies between the Atlantic and Caribbean beaches. The modern, bright condominium suites are available with one or two bedrooms, the largest of which can sleep up to ten guests. A living room with tiled floor leads to a dining room for six and a complete kitchen. Each unit is air-conditioned and has a TV and 110-volt electricity for American convenience. If you choose not to prepare your meals, there is a restaurant-bar that serves croissants in the morning and continental cuisine throughout the day. Guests are welcome to take a rain forest hike or explore a volcanic mountain, visit an old fort or a batik factory. Of course, water sports, deep-sea fishing, scuba diving and snorkeling are all readily available, as are horseback riding and tennis. Contact: Basha Zaidan, St. Christopher Club Hotel, P.O. Box 570, Frigate Bay, St. Kitts, West Indies. Call 809-465-4854.

Children: Y Pets: N Smoking: Y Handicap Access: Y Payment: C, T, A, V, M

SUN N' SAND BEACH VILLAGE   *Rates: inexpensive-expensive*
Open: year-round   *Minimum Stay: none*

The name of this resort says it all—a golden beach with sparkling water lies just a few minutes away from your two-bedroom cottage, and five acres of grounds provide sunbathing and strolling territory. The mountains make a unique backdrop for the tennis courts; a freshwater pool is surrounded by comfortable deck chairs and chaise longues. Each cottage is air conditioned and has a fully equipped kitchenette, cable TV and a phone. Within the village complex is a duty-free shopping arcade, a bar and a restaurant. Golfers will appreciate the links across the road and the staff here will be happy to arrange a scuba diving or horseback riding tour, depending on your taste. When you're feeling lucky, stroll down the road to the Royal St. Kitts Casino. Contact: Robert Reid-Utell, Reservations Center, 10606 Burt Circle, Omaha, NE 68114. Call 1-800-223-6510 or 809-465-8037.

Children: Y   Pets: N   Smoking: Y   Handicap Access: N   Payment: All

TIMOTHY BEACH RESORTS   *Rates: inexpensive-expensive*
Open: year-round   *Minimum Stay: none*

A newly built resort on the Caribbean side of the island, this resort overlooks Frigate Bay and a beautiful curve of white sandy beach. It features one- and two-bedroom apartments, all air conditioned and with maid and laundry service. The living/dining rooms lead to a breeze-cooled deck, and the kitchen is equipped for preparing and serving full meals. The beach club has sailing and water sports facilities; both the beach and a freshwater pool offer sunbathing and swimming. A championship golf course is a few minutes away, and the island is worth exploring for its lush rain forest scenery and the old sugar plantations. A restaurant, Coconut Cafe, is on the premises. Contact. Timothy Beach Resorts, P.O. Box 81, Basseterre, St. Kitts, West Indies. Call 1-800-621-1270.

Children: Y Pets: N Smoking: Y Handicap Access: N Payment: C, T, A, V, M

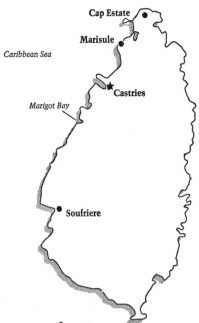

Cap Estate

Marisule

Caribbean Sea

Castries

Marigot Bay

Soufriere

St. Lucia

CAP ESTATE

BANANA HOUSE   *Rates: expensive-deluxe*
Open: year-round   *Minimum Stay: one week*

Banana House is a contemporary two-bedroom, two-bath home that sits on a quiet hillside at Cap Estate, providing glorious views of the Caribbean and Pigeon Point. The villa is in the shape of a graceful half moon, with a wide veranda in front and an attractive swimming pool. A dining area in the living room makes for cozy gatherings; conveniently, there is a kitchen adjacent and a maid on the staff. Contact: Villas International, 71 West 23rd Street, New York, NY 10010. Call 212-929-7585.

Children: Y   Pets: N   Smoking: Y   Handicap Access: N   Payment: C, P, T

CALYPSO COURT   *Rates: expensive-deluxe*
Open: year-round   *Minimum Stay: one week*

There's nothing quite like a coast-to-coast view of both the Atlantic and Caribbean, especially in a setting that's great for families—and that's why there's nothing quite like Calypso Court. This villa offers three bedrooms, each with its own private patio, built around a courtyard. You'll delight in the sitting/dining room, kitchen and pool and the knowledge that you're only a mile and a half from the beach. Six days a week you can enjoy cooking and maid service, a real treat if you do happen to be traveling with your family. Contact: Island Hideaways, Inc., 1317 Rhode Island Avenue N.W., Suite 503, Washington, D.C. 20005. Call 800-832-2302 or 202-667-9652.

Children: Y   Pets: N   Smoking: Y   Handicap Access: N   Payment: C, P, T, A

CASA FINA
Rates: moderate-expensive
Open: year-round
Minimum Stay: one week

Set in two acres of hillside gardens and offering views of both the ocean and the distant mountains, Casa Fina is a spendidly attractive villa. The living and dining rooms are furnished with a sense of island spirit; from here, four archways open to the sun deck beside the private pool. A short walk takes you to the splendid beach. A gardener and a cook/maid do their best to keep you well fed and make sure your grounds are immaculate. Contact: LaCure Villas, 11661 San Vicente Blvd., Suite 1010, Los Angeles, CA 90049. Call 800-387-2715/2720/2726.

Children: Y   Pets: N   Smoking: Y   Handicap Access: N   Payment: All

FINES FOLLY
Rates: moderate-expensive
Open: year-round
Minimum Stay: one week

Surrounded by beautifully landscaped grounds, this comfortable two-bedroom, two-bathroom villa offers views of both the Atlantic and Caribbean. The interior is furnished in tropical style, and outside there's a dining patio and full-sized swimming pool. A cook/maid and a gardener are on the staff to make your stay trouble free. If you can tear yourself away from all this domestic bliss, explore the dramatic mountains and pristine beaches of this still-unspoiled island. Contact: LaCure Villas, 11661 San Vicente Blvd., Suite 1010, Los Angeles, CA 90049. Call 800-387-2715/2720/2726.

Children: Y   Pets: N   Smoking: Y   Handicap Access: N   Payment: All

HIBISCUS COTTAGE
Rates: deluxe
Open: year-round
Minimum Stay: one week

Hibiscus Cottage, set on three acres of fully landscaped gardens, features a kidney-shaped pool spanned by a lovely bridge. Pathways lead to the beach, where all water sports are available. The cottage includes two air-conditioned bedrooms with double beds and bathrooms, a sitting/dining room, patio and the service of a cook/maid six days per week. Contact: Island Hideaways, Inc., 1317 Rhode Island Avenue N.W., Suite 503, Washington, D.C. 20005. Call 800-832-2302 or 202-667-9652.

Children: Y Pets: N Smoking: Y Handicap Access: N Payment: C, P, T, A

JONSON
Rates: expensive-deluxe
Open: year-round
Minimum Stay: one week

This thoroughly modern villa offers sheer comfort in thick, plush contemporary furnishings, and total privacy in a secluded setting. An incredible picture window invites the view in like a friendly neighbor. An adjoining terrace overlooks the sea; a delicious swimming pool is set in the lawn leading to the shore. It's but a short walk to the beach, where you can savor all the island pleasures you came for. Your staff includes a cook/maid and a gardener. Contact: LaCure Villas, 11661 San Vicente Blvd., Suite 1010, Los Angeles, CA 90049. Call 800-387-2715/2720/2726.

Children: Y   Pets: N   Smoking: Y   Handicap Access: N   Payment: All

LA COLLINE   *Rates: deluxe*
Open: year-round   *Minimum Stay: one week*

This stunning villa consists of a main house and a cottage, with bedrooms in both. Set in an acre of landscaped gardens, there are two bedrooms and bathrooms in the main house and one bedroom and bathroom in the cottage. The main house has a view most people only dream of; you'll also be pleased with the comfortable sitting/dining room opening onto the patio and pool. In the cottage, there's a sitting room complete with double and single sofa beds. Cook and maid service is included six days per week. Contact: Island Hideaways, Inc., 1317 Rhode Island Avenue N.W., Suite 503, Washington, D.C. 20005. Call 800-832-2302 or 202-667-9652.

Children: **Y** Pets: **N** Smoking: **Y** Handicap Access: **N** Payment: **C, P, T, A**

LA FALAISE   *Rates: expensive-deluxe*
Open: year-round   *Minimum Stay: one week*

If you've ever wondered whether it would be a thrill to stroll through an interior courtyard on your way to your morning coffee, La Falaise is the place for you. This luxury hillside villa is set on a promontory of land one mile from the beach. There are three air-conditioned bedrooms with twin beds, plus three bathrooms; you'll enjoy lounging about the sitting/dining room, cooking in the full kitchen and viewing the gardens from the large patio. With a pool, terrace and maid's quarters, as well as cook and maid service six days per week, you may finally learn how to relax. Contact: Island Hideaways, Inc., 1317 Rhode Island Avenue N.W., Suite 503, Washington, D.C. 20005. Call 800-832-2302 or 202-667-9652.

Children: **Y** Pets: **N** Smoking: **Y** Handicap Access: **N** Payment: **C, P, T, A**

LES CYCLADES   *Rates: deluxe*
Open: year-round   *Minimum Stay: one week*

Located on a breezy cliffside site overlooking the ocean and the Martinique Channel, Les Cyclades offers among other delights a swimming pool in a Mediterranean setting. There are two bedrooms, two bathrooms, a sitting/dining room, kitchen and an interesting series of multileveled patios. Cook and maid service is included six days per week. Lounge in the sun and take in the spectacular views while savoring the trade winds, or head to the beach for some snorkeling or windsurfing. Contact: Island Hideaways, Inc., 1317 Rhode Island Avenue N.W., Suite 503, Washington, D.C. 20005. Call 800-832-2302 or 202-667-9652.

Children: **Y** Pets: **N** Smoking: **Y** Handicap Access: **N** Payment: **C, P, T, A**

LUXURY VILLA   *Rates: expensive-deluxe*
Open: year-round   *Minimum Stay: one week*

Here are a couple of extras that make life a little gentler: the creme fraiche beside your fruit tart, the tailor who presses your good suit at no charge. You can feel that sort of luxury at this Cap Estate villa, in the shower by the pool, in the raised dining area, in the tropical courtyard. Offering exceptional views to six, this villa includes three bed-rooms, three baths, a pool with terrace, a kitchen, laundry room and maid service. Contact: At Home Abroad, Inc., 405 East 56th Street, #6H, New York, NY 10022. Call 212-421-9165. Ref. 9651.

Children: **Y**   Pets: **N**   Smoking: **Y**   Handicap Access: **N**   Payment: **C, P, T**

MANDERLEY   *Rates: deluxe*
Open: year-round   *Minimum Stay: one week*

The detailing on this spectacular example of West Indian architecture could bring tears to your eyes or a grin a mile wide to your face. Balcony follows balcony and lovely bits of gingerbread trim abound. The very large living room is furnished with antiques, and the sun terrace is complete with private pool and Jacuzzi. On the staff you'll find a cook, a maid and a gardener. There's plenty of room to relax in three bedrooms and three bathrooms, all with a nice homey feeling. Contact: LaCure Villas, 11661 San Vicente Blvd., Suite 1010, Los Angeles, CA 90049. Call 800-387-2715/2720/2726.

Children: **Y**   Pets: **N**   Smoking: **Y**   Handicap Access: **N**   Payment: **All**

PANORAMA   *Rates: deluxe*
Open: year-round   *Minimum Stay: one week*

Tired of villas that provide you with only one extraordinary view? The luxury hillside villa Panorama generously offers astounding views both southward into St. Lucia and westward out to sea toward Martinique. There are three bedrooms with twin beds, three bathrooms, air-conditioning and a private patio; you'll revel in the large pool with a terrace for sunning. Six days per week you can enjoy cooking and maid service; maybe on the seventh you'll take that one-and-a-half-mile drive to the beach. Contact: Island Hideaways, Inc., 1317 Rhode Island Avenue N.W., Suite 503, Washington, D.C. 20005. Call 800-832-2302 or 202-667-9652.

Children: **Y** Pets: **N** Smoking: **Y** Handicap Access: **N** Payment: **C, P, T, A**

SALINE REEF   *Rates: expensive-deluxe*
Open: year-round   *Minimum Stay: one week*

Surrounded by an acre of painstakingly landscaped gardens atop this hill and awash in an unabashedly beautiful view of the ocean, it's hard to imagine you'd feel anything other than very, very happy here at Saline Reef. There are three bedrooms and four bathrooms, in which tropical decor creates a sense of peace. The private pool is encircled by a terrace on which you can sun and snooze to your heart's content. A cook/maid and gardener will care for you while you recuperate from life's stresses. Contact: LaCure Villas, 11661 San Vicente Blvd., Suite 1010, Los Angeles, CA 90049. Call 800-387-2715/2720/2726.

Children: **Y**   Pets: **N**   Smoking: **Y**   Handicap Access: **N**   Payment: **All**

ST. REMY   *Rates: deluxe*
Open: year-round   *Minimum Stay: one week*

Charming St. Remy is a restored estate house high in the hills a 10-minute drive from the beach. There are three bedrooms, one with twin beds and two with four-poster beds, plus two bathrooms, a sitting/

dining room, a kitchen, a patio and a pool. The services of a resident staff of a cook/maid and a gardener are included, leaving you free to enjoy your vacation hideaway in absolute ease. Contact: Island Hideaways, Inc., 1317 Rhode Island Avenue N.W., Suite 503, Washington, DC 20005. Call 800-832-2302 or 202-667-9652.

Children: Y Pets: N Smoking: Y Handicap Access: N Payment: C, P, T, A

THE CEDARS   *Rates: inexpensive-moderate*
Open: year-round   *Minimum Stay: one week*
Cap Estate is a 1,500-acre residential estate on the northernmost tip of St. Lucia, where the Atlantic Ocean washes against the eastern shore and the Caribbean Sea meets the western beaches. The Cedars accommodates six people in three bedrooms, two baths, a living/dining room, a deck and a well-equipped kitchen with service for eight. There is a washing machine, too, and for your water sports needs, you're just a short walk from snorkeling, fishing and swimming at Smuggler's Cove. A quick drive away you'll find entertainment, restaurants, tennis and golf. Maid and linen service are provided; an excellent cook is available at additional cost. Contact: Vacation Home Rentals Worldwide, 235 Kensington Ave., Norwood, NJ 07648. Call 800-NEED-A-VILLA or 800-633-3284. Ref. SL100.

Children: N Pets: N Smoking: Y Handicap Access: N Payment: C, P, T

CASTRIES

EAST WINDS INN   *Rates: budget-inexpensive*
Open: year-round   *Minimum Stay: one week*
This inn offers a unique arrangement of 10 spacious and airy hexagonal cottages, each with modern kitchenette and tile bath. A real treat, the lodgings are surrounded by a lush tropical park spanning more than six acres, with a thatched beachside bar and a top-quality restaurant. Excellent swimming and beaches extend for miles. Cottages are single- and double-occupancy, with skin-diving, shuffleboard, golf, tennis and sailing available. Contact: Rent A Home International, Inc., 7200 34th Ave. N.W., Seattle, WA, 98117. Call 206-545-6963.

Children: Y Pets: N Smoking: Y Handicap Access: N Payment: C, P, T, V, M

SHINGLE COVE   *Rates: deluxe*
Open: year-round   *Minimum Stay: one week*
Three separate houses sleep a total of up to eight vacationers here at Shingle Cove. Rent them separately or together, depending on your needs. The main house is equipped with a master bedroom, family room, bathroom, kitchen and large veranda/dining room overlooking the ocean and cliffs. It features a TV, VCR, stereo cassette system and movie/music library. The second house is nestled among the coconut trees on a hill and offers one bedroom, a kitchen, a bathroom and a veranda with a view of the passing ships. The third house sits by the pool and has a bath, kitchen and living room downstairs, plus two suites—each with double bed, private bath, small kitchen and veranda—upstairs. A maid and caretaker are on staff, and three kayaks,

two windsurfers and several rafts wait for you. Contact: Rent A Home International, Inc., 7200 34th Ave. N.W., Seattle, WA, 98117. Call 206-545-6963.

Children: Y Pets: N Smoking: Y Handicap Access: N Payment: C, P, T, V, M

CASTRIES/RODNEY BAY

HARMONY APARTEL   *Rates: budget-moderate*
Open: year-round   *Minimum Stay: six nights*

Indulge yourself in a view of hills and yachts here at Rodney Bay Marina. Harmony Apartel has studios and two-bedroom apartments, each with a fully equipped electric kitchenette; the two-bedroom units have separate living rooms. Not only do you have access to the beach, tennis, boating, hiking, scuba diving and snorkeling, but there's also sailing, deep-sea fishing, a swimming pool, waterskiing and guided tours in the area. Windsurfing and canoes are available at no extra charge. Maid service is provided daily and linen service twice weekly. You'll come for the view of the coconut palms; you'll stay for the convenient minimart and restaurant as well as laundry and baby-sitting services. Contact: Bob Betts, Julie Betts or Marie Joseph, Harmony Apartel, P.O. Box 155, Castries, St. Lucia, West Indies. Call 809-452-8756/0336.

Children: Y Pets: N Smoking: Y Handicap Access: N Payment: C, T, A, V, M

COUBARIL ESTATES

VILLA SEA VIEW   *Rates: deluxe*
Open: year-round   *Minimum Stay: one week*

Tropical breezes and wonderful views of the sea are the order of the day here at Coubaril Estates. This villa with private pool accommodates eight in style, in its four bedrooms, four baths, a living room opening onto a deck and a modern kitchen with all appliances including a toaster and a blender. There's a TV, VCR, radio and telephone as well. You'll be pampered with luxurious maid service that includes laundry, plus preparation of breakfast and lunch (the maid will cook dinner at extra charge). Contact: At Home Abroad, Inc., 405 East 56th Street, #6H, New York, NY 10022. Call 212-421-9165. Ref. 9652.

Children: Y Pets: N Smoking: Y Handicap Access: N Payment: C, P, T

MARIGOT BAY

MARIGOT HILLSIDE VILLAS AND INN   *Rates: budget-deluxe*
Open: year-round   *Minimum Stay: one week*

This gorgeous part of the island is ideal for the fish in you—there's yachting, sailing, canoeing, snorkeling, scuba diving and of course swimming. Apartment and cottage accommodations are available here, designed for privacy and access to the friendly village, with views that inspire song, poetry and laughter. The villas boast one, two or three bedrooms and have beautifully landscaped gardens and magnificent terrace views of the bay and the sunset. At the inn you'll find studios with kitchenettes and balconies for up to two people. No matter where you stay, you'll have access to the free 24-hour water taxi around the lagoon. Contact: Rent A Home International, Inc., 7200 34th Ave. N.W., Seattle, WA, 98117. Call 206-545-6963.

Children: Y Pets: N Smoking: Y Handicap Access: N Payment: C, P, T, V, M

SMUGGLER'S COVE

BEACH COTTAGE *Rates: moderate-expensive*
Open: year-round *Minimum Stay: one week*

This beach-style cottage is furnished with charming, locally made furniture and offers excellent views of the Caribbean, plus nicely landscaped grounds around a kidney-shaped pool. Take a short walk to the beach to sink your toes into powder-soft sand, then plunge your body into the gentle, warm surf. When you return home, the cook/maid will have tidied your rooms and prepared a meal of island specialties, while the gardener will have adorned the dining room table with fresh-cut flowers. Two bedrooms and two baths accommodate four in casual comfort. Contact: LaCure Villas, 11661 San Vicente Blvd., Suite 1010, Los Angeles, CA 90049. Call 800-387-2715/2720/2726.

Children: Y Pets: N Smoking: Y Handicap Access: N Payment: All

VILLA ANTHONY *Rates: expensive-deluxe*
Open: year-round *Minimum Stay: one week*

An acre of landscaped gardens is the backdrop for this secluded seaside villa made up of a main house and a cottage. There is a swimming pool, though you're within walking distance of Smuggler's Cove and Becune Beach. Cook/maid service is included six nights per week. The main house consists of three bedrooms with bathrooms and double beds, plus a sitting-dining room, patio and kitchen. The cottage (an optional extra) has a bunk bed suitable for small children, a room with two single beds, a bathroom and a patio. Contact: Island Hideaways, Inc., 1317 Rhode Island Ave. NW, Suite 503, Washington, D.C. 20005. Call 800-832-2302 or 202-667-9652.

Children: Y Pets: N Smoking: Y Handicap Access: N Payment: C, P, T, A

SOUFRIERE

DASHEENE VILLA *Rates: moderate-expensive*
Open: year-round *Minimum Stay: one week*

Dasheene is a community of West Indian-inspired houses looking out onto banana and coconut plantations and Anse Jalousie beach. The villa for rent here is made of stone and native wood and is open to the west, where the sun sets behind the mountains and the Caribbean Sea. Three bedrooms and two baths accommodate five people; the master bedroom has a four-poster French colonial bed overlooking the swimming pool. The living room and separate dining room have teak floors and numerous plants and modern art pieces; the kitchen is contemporary and equipped with a stove, refrigerator, freezer and service for eight. The Jacuzzi is fed by a unique stone waterfall. French antiques and wicker make the interior soothing, while sweetly scented trumpet trees outside are dotted with hummingbirds. Contact: Vacation Home Rentals Worldwide, 235 Kensington Ave., Norwood, NJ 07648. Call 800-NEED-A-VILLA or 800-633-3284. Ref. SL104.

Children: Y   Pets: N   Smoking: Y   Handicap Access: N   Payment: C, P, T

LA BATTERIE

Rates: expensive
Open: year-round
Minimum Stay: one week

A spectacular union of stone and mahogany, this plantation-style house features a tiled indoor courtyard and tropical gardens. It stands a 10-minute walk from Anse Chastenet beach, where tennis, scuba-diving and snorkeling are available. Two bedrooms, a sleeping loft and two baths make for spacious lodging; daily maid service provides care-free comfort. The color-splashed living and dining rooms explode with views of the sea and St. Lucia's twin Piton peaks. Contact: Villa Holidays, Inc., 13100 Wayzata Blvd., Suite 150, Minneapolis, MN 55343. Call 800-328-6262 or 612-591-0076.

Children: Y Pets: N Smoking: Y Handicap Access: N Payment: C, P, T, V, M

MANGO POINT VILLA

Rates: expensive
Open: year-round
Minimum Stay: one week

Mango Point offers views of both the Piton mountains and the Caribbean from an interesting perch: It's a recently built replica of an 18th-century French villa on a hill. There are separate wings at Mango Point for sleeping, eating, cooking and leisure. You'll find a living/dining room, a modern kitchen, three bedrooms with twin beds, two baths, a terrace and garden. Maid service is included; linen/laundry service and a cook can be requested. The villa is roughly a mile from the beach and not far from tennis facilities, but if you don't feel like moving, Mango Point's architecture is enough to keep you busy. Contact: Villas International, 71 West 23rd Street, New York, NY 10010. Call 212-929-7585.

Children: Y   Pets: N   Smoking: Y   Handicap Access: N   Payment: C, P, T

Caribbean Sea

Grand Case
Cul de Sac
La Savanne

Baie Rouge Beach
Plum Beach
Baie Rouge

ST. MARTIN

Plum Bay

Marigot

Simpson Bay Lagoon

Long Beach
Baie Longue

Oyster Pond

Dawn Beach

Juliana

ST. MAARTEN

Cupecoy Beach
Mullet Bay
Maho Bay
Burgeaux Bay

Simpson Bay

Guana Bay

Philipsburg

Simpson Bay

Pelican Cay

St. Maarten

BURGEAUX BAY

BURGEAUX CASE

Open: year-round

Rates: moderate
Minimum Stay: one week

This comfortable cottage—a traditional West Indian casa—provides the perfect base for exploring the luxurious resorts at Caravanserai and Mullet Bay, with their superb golf courses, tennis courts and fine restaurants. Simply charming for one couple, the cottage features a living/dining area, bedroom, full kitchen and an extra bedroom large enough for a young child. During the day, step right onto the fine white sands of Burgeaux Bay Beach. At night, a delightful screened-in porch off the living room lets in the cool breezes. Contact: West Indies Management Company, 28 Pelham Street, Newport, RI 02840. Call 1-800-932-3222 (in Rhode Island, 401-849-8012). Ref. JPS-56mh.

Children: **Y** Pets: **N** Smoking: **Y** Handicap Access: **N** Payment: **P, T, A**

CASA BOCO

Open: year-round

Rates: inexpensive-deluxe
Minimum Stay: one week

Located right on the ocean, this villa may be divided into three separate units or rented in its entirety as a four-bedroom house. Lush tropical gardens surround the private walkways, while a huge pool deck and covered dining atrium call for outdoor living. Maid service six days a week takes the sting out of cleaning; high-speed fans throughout cool off the nights. Tennis and golf can be found a short drive away at the major hotels. Contact: Villa Holidays, Inc., 13100

Wayzata Blvd., Suite 150, Minneapolis, MN 55343. Call 1-800-328-6262 (in Minnesota, 612-591-0076).

Children: Y Pets: N Smoking: Y Handicap Access: N Payment: C, P, T, V, M

KASPER COTTAGE *Rates: inexpensive-moderate*
Open: year-round *Minimum Stay: one week*

There's no better way to get away from it all than to relax in a hammock strung between two coconut palms right on Burgeaux Bay's powdery white sand beach. This one-room cottage offers low prices and direct access to the beach while delivering good, basic accommodations. Twin beds, a kitchenette and a private deck are all you'll need for a simply inviting vacation. You can also take time to explore the beautiful resorts at Mullet Bay on the western end of the island. Contact: West Indies Management Company, 28 Pelham Street, Newport, RI 02840. Call 1-800-932-3222 (in Rhode Island, 401-849-8012). Ref. JPS-56s.

Children: Y Pets: N Smoking: Y Handicap Access: N Payment: P, T, A

LA CASITA *Rates: deluxe*
Open: year-round *Minimum Stay: one week*

This superior three-bedroom villa will make you feel like a special pampered guest, with maid service six days a week and comfortable, deluxe furnishings. Dine in the cool night air in the magnificent covered atrium and take in fine views of the lovely gardens. An ample supply of towels and beach chairs help you take advantage of the private sun deck and large sparkling swimming pool. Burgeaux Bay Beach is a short walk away and Maho and Simpson Bays are also close. At night, the nearby hotels offer casinos, discos and fine dining, or you can curl up on the convertible sofa and simply watch TV. Contact: Villa Holidays, Inc., 13100 Wayzata Blvd., Suite 150, Minneapolis, MN 55343. Call 1-800-328-6262 (in Minnesota, 612-591-0076).

Children: Y Pets: N Smoking: Y Handicap Access: N Payment: C, P, T, V, M

ST. MAARTEN VILLA *Rates: deluxe*
Open: year-round *Minimum Stay: one week*

Cooling trade winds keep St. Maarten an average of 80 degrees year-round—which is why air conditioning isn't needed at this posh Caribbean hideaway. Instead, there are atmospheric ceiling fans and a breezy gallery giving way directly onto the beach. There are five bedrooms in all (sleeping eight to ten), three with their own luxurious baths and two sharing another. A housekeeper is on duty to keep the villa tidy and to pick renters up at the airport; she'll also cook by special arrangement. Contact: Rent A Home International, Inc., 7200 34th Street N.W., Seattle, WA 98117. Call 206-545-6963.

Children: Y Pets: N Smoking: Y Handicap Access: N Payment: C, P, T, V, M

VIP HOUSE *Rates: deluxe*
Open: year-round *Minimum Stay: one week*

Perched atop a coral reef right on Burgeaux Bay, VIP House sighs with the rhythm of the waves breaking just a few feet beyond the property's edge. Its patio is graced by tall, shady palms, enclosed by a picket fence and adjacent to a large, freshwater swimming pool. Nearby is a romantically secluded cove, excellent for snorkeling and swimming. Water sports, golf and tennis are all close, too. Five bedrooms and four baths make VIP House a good choice for groups of friends and large families, whose vacation will be made pleasanter still by the attentions of the villa's housekeeping staff. Contact: Vacation Home Rentals Worldwide, 235 Kensington Ave., Norwood, NJ 07648. Call 1-800-633-3284 (in New Jersey, 201-767-9393). Ref. SM106.

Children: Y Pets: N Smoking: Y Handicap Access: N Payment: C, P, T

WAGNER'S WONDER   *Rates: expensive-deluxe*
Open: year-round   *Minimum Stay: one week*

Chic modern furnishings add something special to this two-bedroom villa decorated with an artistic flare seldom seen in rentals. The airy, well-lighted living room features sliding glass doors on three sides, framing astonishing views of brilliant sunsets. A fabulous pool deck overlooks lovely Burgeaux Bay, where you can walk barefoot in the powdery white sand. Spend the day playing a few sets of tennis or 18 holes of golf, recoup over a long leisurely dinner, then try your luck at the casinos or dance the night away in one of the lively discotheques at the major hotels nearby. Contact: West Indies Management Company, 28 Pelham Street, Newport, RI 02840. Call 1-800-932-3222 (in Rhode Island, 401-849-8012). Ref. JPS-60D.

Children: Y Pets: N Smoking: Y Handicap Access: N Payment: P, T, A

WINDWARD II   *Rates: expensive-deluxe*
Open: year-round   *Minimum Stay: one week*

This deluxe modern villa in one of the finest residential areas of Dutch St. Maarten offers spectacular views of Burgeaux Bay. Ceiling fans throughout cool the two bedrooms, making your nights comfortable and pleasant. The kitchen is a gourmet's dream, with a dishwasher for easy cleanup. If you'd like, the maid will also prepare your meals on request. Tennis, golf, fishing, boating and fine restaurants are a short drive away at the major hotels. Contact: Villa Holidays, Inc., 13100 Wayzata Blvd., Suite 150, Minneapolis, MN 55343. Call 1-800-328-6262 (in Minnesota, 612-591-0076).

Children: Y Pets: N Smoking: Y Handicap Access: N Payment: C, P, T, V, M

CAY HILL

CASTLE HILL   *Rates: deluxe*
Open: year-round   *Minimum Stay: one week*

You couldn't imagine a spot more perfect than this for viewing the wide expanse of Simpson Bay on the south shore of the isle of St. Maarten. The modern villa stands at the summit of Cay Hill and provides vistas of surrounding Windward islands like St. Kitts, Saba and St. Eustatius. The interior is furnished in a unique Oriental style, and a huge sliding glass door opens onto a private terrace, patio and pool. Castle Hill has four spacious and beautifully appointed bedrooms, as well as three and a half baths and a staff in residence. Contact: LaCure Villas, 11661 San Vicente Blvd., Suite 1010, Los Angeles, CA 90049. Call 1-800-387-2715.

Children: Y   Pets: N   Smoking: Y   Handicap Access: N   Payment: All

Guana Bay

BARR'S BEAUTY   *Rates: deluxe*
Open: year-round   *Minimum Stay: one week*

The famed tradewinds of the Caribbean cool this new three-bedroom home high in the hills over Oyster Pond Yacht Club. Beautifully furnished with overstuffed rattan chairs and sofas, this contemporary home offers comfort and style. Quick meals are easy at the kitchen's breakfast bar, while a dining room allows for formal dinners. But for elegant gourmet dining, you'll want to experience the restaurant at the yacht club or venture to some of the island's resorts. Contact: West Indies Management Company, 28 Pelham Street, Newport, RI 02840. Call 1-800-932-3222 (in Rhode Island, 401-849-8012). Ref. JPS-79D.

Children: Y   Pets: N   Smoking: Y   Handicap Access: N   Payment: P, T, A

CASA DEL MAR   *Rates: deluxe*
Open: year-round   *Minimum Stay: one week*

Tropical gardens lush with palm trees and exotic flowers surround this St. Maarten villa located just north of Philipsburg and within walking distance of a great beach. Six Caribbean vacationers can fit in its roomy three bedrooms, sharing three baths. One facade is broken by four huge arched windows providing splendid ocean views, and beyond them is a luxurious patio furnished with lounge chairs and a table. Its top-of-the-line amenities include daily maid service, linens, a dishwasher, laundry facilities and a private swimming pool. Contact: Rent A Home International, Inc., 7200 34th Street N.W., Seattle, WA 98117. Call 206-545-6963.

Children: Y Pets: N Smoking: Y Handicap Access: N Payment: C, P, T, V, M

COOPER VILLA   *Rates: expensive-deluxe*
Open: year-round   *Minimum Stay: one week*

Surfers can hang ten on the magnificent Atlantic waves that roll into Guana Bay, while nature lovers will love the natural areas around Guana Point. This home overlooking the bay stands a ten-minute walk to the beach and just five minutes from charming Philipsburg. Ceiling fans in both bedrooms catch the refreshing trade winds and bright cottons and rattan furnishings impart a cool comfort. A new swimming pool lies just off the living room, perfect for morning dips or late-night swims. Contact: West Indies Management Company, 28 Pelham Street, Newport, RI 02840. Call 1-800-932-3222 (in Rhode Island, 401-849-8012). Ref. JPS-54.

Children: Y   Pets: N   Smoking: Y   Handicap Access: N   Payment: P, T, A

GUANA BAY VILLA *Rates: deluxe*
Open: year-round *Minimum Stay: one week*
Legend has it that the boundary line between the French and Dutch parts of this Caribbean paradise was established when a Frenchman and a Dutchman set out walking from opposite ends of the island. Guana Bay is in the Dutch half, near the charming colonial capital of Philipsburg and the Great Salt Pond. This villa provides knockout views of both the mountains and sea and features a lovely tiled patio encircling a private pool and outdoor hot tub. There are three bedrooms, sleeping a total of six in king-sized beds, three baths with showers, a modern kitchen and laundry facilities. Contact: Rent A Home International, Inc., 7200 34th Street N.W., Seattle, WA 98117. Call 206-545-6963.
Children: Y Pets: N Smoking: Y Handicap Access: N Payment: C, P, T, V, M

JOSEPH ESTATE *Rates: deluxe*
Open: year-round *Minimum Stay: one week*
The Caribbean was meant to be enjoyed outdoors, and this four-bedroom house lets you spend most of your time just that way. Relax, lounge and dine outside on the large brick pool deck featuring a wet bar, an ice maker and even a jacuzzi. When you simply must go indoors, you'll find a large kitchen, living/dining room, den, three bedrooms and two baths, all furnished in bright tropical decor on the main floor. Parents will love the privacy of a large master bedroom with bath and terrace on a separate floor. A short walk takes you to the fine white sandy beaches at Guana Bay, which are perfect for soaking up the sun. Contact: West Indies Management Company, 28 Pelham Street, Newport, RI 02840. Call 1-800-932-3222 (in Rhode Island, 401-849-8012). Ref. JPS-74D.
Children: Y Pets: N Smoking: Y Handicap Access: N Payment: P, T, A

PANACEA *Rates: deluxe*
Open: year-round *Minimum Stay: one week*
The sea and a private tennis court may be all you need for a fantastic, healing vacation in this cool beachfront villa. Swaying palm trees and cool breezes complement the property's tropical landscaping, while a covered patio lets you dine comfortably amid the splendor. Three bedrooms and baths, with a fourth bedroom in a separate apartment downstairs, accommodate eight comfortably. Naturalists will want to walk to Guana Point, where pathways allow you to observe wildlife that's nearly undisturbed by human intrusion. Contact: West Indies Management Company, 28 Pelham Street, Newport, RI 02840. Call 1-800-932-3222 (in Rhode Island, 401-849-8012). Ref. AS-181d.
Children: Y Pets: N Smoking: Y Handicap Access: N Payment: P, T, A

JULIANA

MARY'S BOON *Rates: inexpensive-moderate*
Open: year-round *Minimum Stay: one week*
Twelve very large studio apartments for two occupy a sprawling motel-style villa right on the beach. Featuring a kitchenette, bath and private

patio, the studios provide simple comforts at affordable prices. If you choose, take your meals at the seaside dining gallery, where you'll find imaginative fare at breakfast, lunch and dinner. A standing bar allows you to mix your own drinks on the honor system. Catch a flight to neighboring Saba, St. Barts and St. Eustatius from the nearby Juliana Airport. Contact: Rushton H. Little, Mary's Boon, P.O. Box 2078, St. Maarten, Netherlands Antilles. Call 1-800-223-9815.

Children: Y   Pets: N   Smoking: Y   Handicap Access: N   Payment: C, T

Oyster Pond

BURLEIGH HOUSE   *Rates: expensive-deluxe*
Open: year-round   *Minimum Stay: one week*

Graceful arches frame broad views of Oyster Pond and the Atlantic from this new three-bedroom home. Colorful country French decor enlivens the large living room, which opens onto a covered gallery perfect for outdoor dining. Relax on the deck around the large swimming pool before calling it a day, then enjoy a sunset walk on the beach before curling up in front of cable TV in the comfortable library. At Oyster Pond, you're never far from water sports, tennis and golf. Contact: West Indies Management Company, 28 Pelham Street, Newport, RI 02840. Call 1-800-932-3222 (in Rhode Island, 401-849-8012). Ref. JPS-97D.

Children: Y   Pets: N   Smoking: Y   Handicap Access: N   Payment: P, T, A

HOPE MOUNTAIN   *Rates: deluxe*
Open: year-round   *Minimum Stay: one week*

Experience the intimacy of a private home with the conveniences of a large resort at Hope Mountain, a deluxe home overlooking the white sands of Dawn Beach and the sparkling waters of the Atlantic. Privacy is ensured on a secluded beach, at the private swimming pool and in the jacuzzi. Lavishly appointed, the main house, porch and terrace offer 9,000 square feet of living space for ten people, with private bathrooms in each of five bedrooms. Two additional guests may stay in the small adjoining guest house. The modern and well-equipped kitchen allows for quick breakfasts or lavish dinners. Bask in the sun on the private beach, or sail, windsurf or waterski at the Oyster Pond Yacht Club. Contact: Rent A Home International, Inc., 7200 34th Avenue N.W., Seattle, WA 98117. Call 205-545-6963. Ref. C/R004.

Children: Y   Pets: N   Smoking: Y   Handicap Access: N   Payment: C, P, V, M

PARSONT PANORAMA   *Rates: expensive-deluxe*
Open: year-round   *Minimum Stay: one week*

Every room in this delightful three-bedroom home boasts an inspiring ocean view with St. Barts on the horizon. Glass sliders in the bedrooms and living room open directly onto an enticing pool deck, perfect for sunbathing and casual outdoor dining. Take a short walk to a long, white sand beach, where you can enjoy a quick lunch at the beach bar. Oyster Pond Yacht Club offers elegant dining at night only a few steps away. Nearby tennis courts, snorkeling, waterskiing and scuba diving will delight sports enthusiasts. Contact: West Indies Management Company, 28 Pelham Street, Newport, RI 02840. Call 1-800-932-3222 (in Rhode Island, 401-849-8012). Ref. JPS-57D.

Children: Y   Pets: N   Smoking: Y   Handicap Access: N   Payment: P, T, A

VILLA ALBERTI   *Rates: expensive-deluxe*
Open: year-round   *Minimum Stay: one week*

This smartly designed three-bedroom home boasts a living room with glass sliding doors all four sides, offering breathtaking views of the Atlantic with St. Barts in the distance. Tasteful rattan furnishings set on cool Mexican tile floors maintain the island atmosphere, as does a West Indian arched gallery. Days on St. Maarten are meant for sunbathing and ocean swimming, and you'll find the fine white sandy beaches at Oyster Pond most inviting. A "plunge" pool off the living room refreshes before dinner, which you can enjoy inside or out. Contact: West Indies Management Company, 28 Pelham Street, Newport, RI 02840. Call 1-800-932-3222 (in Rhode Island, 401-849-8012). Ref. JPS-53D.

Children: Y   Pets: N   Smoking: Y   Handicap Access: N   Payment: P, T, A

Pelican Key Estates

CORAL SHORES VILLAS   *Rates: inexpensive-moderate*
Open: year-round   *Minimum Stay: one week*

Each unit at Coral Shores Villas offers festive accommodations for up to six people in a colorful mountainside setting. Ceiling fans and designer interiors of wicker and rattan make your stay a pleasure; you won't want to miss dining beneath the stars in your private garden courtyard. The fully equipped kitchens have everything you'll need to cook up a tropical delight. Stroll through the manicured grounds or lounge by the ocean-side pool. Nearby, sports enthusiasts can enjoy tennis, golf and all kinds of water activities. Contact: Vacation Home Rentals Worldwide, 235 Kensington Ave., Norwood, NJ 07648. Call 1-800-633-3284 (in New Jersey, 201-767-9393). Ref. SM100.

Children: Y   Pets: N   Smoking: Y   Handicap Access: N   Payment: C, P, T

LITTLE LESKO   *Rates: expensive-deluxe*
Open: year-round   *Minimum Stay: one week*

Great care has been taken in furnishing this small, immaculate villa highlighted by a graceful swimming pool surrounded by lush green trees and blooming flowers. Tastefully decorated with cheerful contemporary and rattan furniture, ceiling fans and hardwood floors, the house will delight vacationers. Two bedrooms and two baths are located on pool-deck level. The spacious upstairs features a living room, a large kitchen and a dining room with sliding glass doors that open onto a large covered gallery, where you can relax and dine overlooking the pool. Contact: West Indies Management Company, 28 Pelham Street, Newport, RI 02840. Call 1-800-932-3222 (in Rhode Island, 401-849-8012). Ref. JPS-72D.

Children: Y   Pets: N   Smoking: Y   Handicap Access: N   Payment: P, T, A

SHARP VILLA   *Rates: expensive-deluxe*
Open: year-round   *Minimum Stay: one week*

This three-bedroom house faces west, offering breathtaking views of fiery red sunsets. Comfortably decorated with modern furnishings, the house features a large living room and dining area and private baths in each bedroom. Ceiling fans circulate the air to cool off the nights. Sip cocktails and enjoy hors d'oeuvres at the wet bar on the pool deck. Fine dining and sports activities are close by at Pelican Resort. Contact: West Indies Management Company, 28 Pelham Street, Newport, RI 02840. Call 1-800-932-3222 (in Rhode Island, 401-849-8012). Ref. JPS-63D.

Children: **Y**   Pets: **N**   Smoking: **Y**   Handicap Access: **N**   Payment: **P, T, A**

PHILIPSBURG

BOLEN RETREAT   *Rates: expensive-deluxe*
Open: year-round   *Minimum Stay: one week*

Set above Great Bay and the charming village of Philipsburg, this hillside home offers visitors spacious rooms and a convenient location. Dine outside on a long balcony off the kitchen and living room while the cool bay breezes waft by. Three bedrooms, including a large master suite, will accommodate six travelers. Sunbathe on the pool deck, then take a few laps to perk up for the invigorating nightlife at nearby hotel resorts. Contact: West Indies Management Company, 28 Pelham Street, Newport, RI 02840. Call 1-800-932-3222 (in Rhode Island, 401-849-8012). Ref. JPS-76D.

Children: **Y**   Pets: **N**   Smoking: **Y**   Handicap Access: **N**   Payment: **P, T, A**

CASA COSTELLO   *Rates: expensive-deluxe*
Open: year-round   *Minimum Stay: one week*

Families or groups of friends will delight in this four-bedroom villa, with its generous accommodations and extraordinary views of the beaches and neighboring Saba and St. Eustatius. A wide-open terrace borders the large lap pool and a secluded beach is just a few steps away. Meals are easily prepared in the newly decorated kitchen; both formal and informal dining rooms are available to fit your mood. Equestrians can follow trails to Cole Bay, which also offers some of the best beaches on the Dutch side of the island. Contact: West Indies Management Company, 28 Pelham Street, Newport, RI 02840. Call 1-800-932-3222 (in Rhode Island, 401-849-8012). Ref. AS-180D.

Children: **Y**   Pets: **N**   Smoking: **Y**   Handicap Access: **N**   Payment: **P, T, A**

HOLLAND HOUSE BEACH HOTEL   *Rates: inexpensive-expensive*
Open: year-round   *Minimum Stay: no minimum*

Set on Great Bay Beach in Philipsburg, the Holland House Beach Hotel offers 54 rooms, some with sea views, others overlooking the city's bustling center. Spend day the soaking up the sun on white sandy beaches and crystal clear waters, then live up the nights in nearby nightclubs, discos and casinos. All rooms have air-conditioning for comfort and color TV for relaxation. Most have their own kitchenettes, but if you dine at the hotel's own Beach Terrace Restaurant, you can watch cruise ships and yachts slip through the bay. Sailboat tours to nearby islands can be arranged. Contact: Mr. P. Verheyen, Holland House Beach Hotel, Frontstreet, P.O. Box 393, Philipsburg, St. Maarten, Netherlands Antilles. Call 1-800-223-9815.

Children: Y Pets: N Smoking: Y Handicap: N Payment: C, T, A, V, M, O

LA VISTA HOTEL
Rates: inexpensive-deluxe
Open: year-round
Minimum Stay: one week

An enchanting small resort, La Vista offers simple suites, elegant penthouses and deluxe cottages, plus all the amenities of a luxurious hotel and a good central location. You'll find the best ocean views in the large penthouse suites, which feature bedrooms on the first floor and a spiral staircase to the living area. The one-bedroom cottages charmingly replicate the traditional Antillian homes, with open-door-style bedrooms, large porches and ocean views. Cable TV, telephones and kitchenettes make your stay comfortable. You'll find a plethora of activities from watersports to horseback riding here; fine restaurants and the Pelican Resort Casino and Health Spa are nearby. To get you in the mood, the first bottle of chilled champagne is on the house. Contact: Andrea Schertinger, La Vista Hotel, P.O. Box 40, Philipsburg, St. Maarten, Netherlands Antilles. Call 1-800-223-9815 (in New York, 212-545-8469).

Children: Y Pets: N Smoking: Y Handicap: N Payment: C, P, T, A, V, M

MUKAMEL VILLA
Rates: deluxe
Open: year-round
Minimum Stay: one week

Mukamel Villa is set amid palm trees and cacti with tremendous views of Little Bay and the lush greenery of the surrounding hills. Stylishly appointed in Moroccan beach decor, the villa features four large bedrooms with three baths, a spacious living room, modern kitchen and laundry room for convenience. Lounge around the large swimming pool and don't worry about a thing, because the maid and gardener will take care of the details. Contact: Villas International, 71 West 23rd Street, New York, NY 10010. Call 212-929-7585.

Children: Y Pets: N Smoking: Y Handicap Access: N Payment: C, P, T

ST. MAARTEN CONDOMINIUMS
Rates: moderate-deluxe
Open: year-round
Minimum Stay: one week

These posh, paradisiacal pieds-a-terre are convenient to the St. Maarten airport and capital, to the French side of the island with its haute couture and cuisine, to Treasure Island Casino and to Cupecoy's Piazza, where visitors will find a wide array of duty-free shops. One-bedroom units feature two double beds and a living room with a sleep sofa (meaning there's room for a total of six), plus two baths, a well-equipped kitchen and patio facing the water. In the larger condos there are two bedrooms (one with a king-sized bed, the other with two doubles), a living room with a sleep sofa, kitchen and two patios. The condo complex boasts its own freshwater pool, "swim-up bar" and restaurant. Standard amenities include air conditioning, cable TV and imported marble floors. Contact: Rent A Home International, Inc., 7200 34th Street N.W., Seattle, WA 98117. Call 206-545-6963. Ref. RAH1/CBC.

Children: Y Pets: N Smoking: Y Handicap Access: N Payment: C, P, T, V, M

THE HORNY TOAD GUESTHOUSE *Rates: inexpensive-moderate*
Open: year-round *Minimum Stay: one week*

The Horny Toad Guesthouse, a former governor's house tastefully renovated into spacious housekeeping apartments, offers close proximity to the water, tennis courts, golf courses, boating and fishing. Each apartment overlooks the secluded beach of Simpson Bay and includes one bedroom with bath, fully equipped kitchen with living area and private gallery. Stroll down the beach to fabulous restaurants, or venture into the nearby town of Philipsburg for excellent dining. Contact: Betty and Earl Vaughan, Box 397, Philipsburg, St. Maarten, Netherlands Antilles. Call 011-599-5-44323.

Children: N Pets: N Smoking: Y Handicap Access: N Payment: C, P, T

SIMPSON BAY

PELICAN VILLA *Rates: deluxe*
Open: year-round *Minimum Stay: one week*

This Simpson Bay villa features a dreamy, curving pool overlooking the ocean, and with its formal living and dining rooms, it's suitable for high-toned Caribbean vacationing. A sliding door separates this area from the more casual part of the house, which contains three bedrooms and four and a half baths. Other amenities include handsome ceramic tile floors, comfy cane furniture, a "swim-up bar," air conditioning, a wide terrace and a cook and maid on the premises. Contact: LaCure Villas, 11661 San Vicente Blvd., Suite 1010, Los Angeles, CA 90049. Call 1-800-387-2715.

Children: Y Pets: N Smoking: Y Handicap Access: N Payment: All

SIMPSON BEACH CONDO *Rates: expensive-deluxe*
Open: year-round *Minimum Stay: one week*

You'll find this two-bedroom condominium directly on the fine white sandy beach at Simpson Bay. Delightfully furnished in white wicker and rattan, the condo maintains a pleasant airy ambience conducive to relaxation. Air-conditioning and ceiling fans keep you cool day and night and a large jacuzzi tub in the master bath soothes after a day's sightseeing. Swimmers have a choice of the gentle waters in the bay or a community pool; children will enjoy the kiddy pool designed just for them. Contact: West Indies Management Company, 28 Pelham Street, Newport, RI 02840. Call 1-800-932-3222 (in Rhode Island, 401-849-8012). Ref. JPS-93D.

Children: Y Pets: N Smoking: Y Handicap Access: N Payment: P, T, A

SIMPSON BAY LAGOON

SERENDIPITY   *Rates: expensive-deluxe*
Open: year-round   *Minimum Stay: one week*

Your privacy is ensured in this villa set in an enclosed community complete with a gate keeper. The view is tranquil, with Simpson Lagoon and the islands of St. Maarten's mountains on the horizon. Enjoy sunbathing and swimming in your private pool, then play a few sets on the tennis court. Recently redecorated, the villa's interior sleeps six; its two bedrooms each have a private bath. Stretch out in the spacious living room and entertain yourself with the villa's TV, VCR and cassette player. Maid service is provided six days per week. Contact: Riviera Holidays, 31 Georgian Lane, Great Neck, NY 11024. Call 516-487-8094. Ref. 742.

Children: Y   Pets: N   Smoking: Y   Handicap Access: N   Payment: P

SIMINOFF ON THE LAGOON   *Rates: deluxe*
Open: year-round   *Minimum Stay: one week*

This fully air-conditioned home serves as a comfortable base for long leisurely hikes through the delightful western peninsula of St. Maarten with its gorgeous coastline and magnificent beaches. Wake to a light breakfast on the sunny pool deck, swim a few laps, then take in a round of golf or tennis at the beautiful resorts at Maho and Mullet Bay. Families will find the two bedrooms—one king and one twin—ideal. The clear waters of Simpson Bay Lagoon might just inspire you to don snorkeling gear and explore the colorful corals just below the surface. Contact: West Indies Management Company, 28 Pelham Street, Newport, RI 02840. Call 1-800-932-3222 (in Rhode Island, 401-849-8012). Ref. AS-178F.

Children: Y   Pets: N   Smoking: Y   Handicap Access: N   Payment: P, T, A

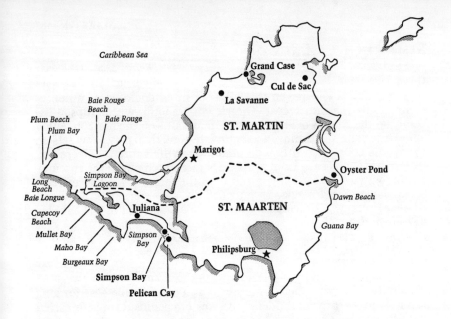

Caribbean Sea

Grand Case

Cul de Sac

Baie Rouge
Beach
Baie Rouge

La Savanne

Plum Beach
Plum Bay

ST. MARTIN

Marigot

Oyster Pond

Long
Beach
Baie Longue

Simpson Bay
Lagoon

Juliana

ST. MAARTEN

Dawn Beach

Cupecoy
Beach

Mullet Bay

Maho Bay

Simpson
Bay

Guana Bay

Philipsburg

Burgeaux Bay

Simpson Bay

Pelican Cay

St. Martin

BAIE LONGUE

DREYFUS   *Rates: expensive-deluxe*

Open: year-round   *Minimum Stay: one week*

A freshwater swimming pool provides a refreshing alternative to the ocean's salty waters in this typical West Indian beach cottage on Baie Longue. Relax in the hammock on the covered terrace or in the large screen-enclosed living room, where you can experience the cool breezes without exposure to the sun's rays. At night, fall asleep in one of three bedrooms while listening to the waves only a few feet away. Contact: West Indies Management Company, 28 Pelham Street, Newport, RI 02840. Call 1-800-932-3222 (in Rhode Island, 401-849-8012). Ref. JPS-35.

Children: Y   Pets: N   Smoking: Y   Handicap Access: N   Payment: P, T, A

FROLIC   *Rates: deluxe*

Open: year-round   *Minimum Stay: one week*

Frolic, situated beside the glowing sands of Long Beach in St. Martin, is really more an estate than a simple vacation home. Its interior, decorated with Indonesian artifacts, is unique and truly exotic. A wide sliding glass door separates its interior living space from a columned patio, from which it's an easy leap into the pool. The villa has four bedrooms and four baths, maid service and a private tennis court, and is close to island delights like the golf course at Mullet Bay and the marketplace in Marigot. Contact: LaCure Villas, 11661 San Vicente Blvd., Suite 1010, Los Angeles, CA 80049. Call 1-800-387-2715.

Children: Y   Pets: N   Smoking: Y   Handicap Access: N   Payment: All

PLUMBAGO *Rates: deluxe*
Open: year-round *Minimum Stay: one week*
This exquisite beachfront villa offers many amenities for vacationing in solitude and luxury. Entertain new friends in the formal living and dining rooms or invite them to dine alfresco on the open yet secluded terrace. Three luxuriously furnished bedrooms (one boasts a sumptuous four-poster bed complete with curtains) make for comfortable nights. A lovely new greenhouse provides an added touch of class. Contact: West Indies Management Company, 28 Pelham Street, Newport, RI 02840. Call 1-800-932-3222 (in Rhode Island, 401-849-8012). Ref. AS-068.
Children: Y   Pets: N   Smoking: Y   Handicap Access: N   Payment: P, T, A

SANDY WAY *Rates: deluxe*
Open: year-round *Minimum Stay: one week*
St. Martin is known throughout the world for its beaches; indeed, there are at least three dozen of them on this tiny French island. One of the most breathtaking by far is Long Beach, and Sandy Way sits right there in the sun. The single-level villa is decorated in classic St. Martin rattan, and its large living room has a peaked ceiling, which tends to invite in those cooling ocean breezes. Its roomy quarters include three bedrooms, each with its own bath. Outside is a quiet, shaded terrace surrounding the swimming pool, beyond that a garden and beyond that the wide Caribbean. Contact: LaCure Villas, 11661 San Vicente Blvd., Suite 1010, Los Angeles, CA 90049. Call 1-800-387-2715.
Children: Y   Pets: N   Smoking: Y   Handicap Access: N   Payment: All

TIMMERMAN-EGRET VILLA *Rates: deluxe*
Open: year-round *Minimum Stay: one week*
This deluxe villa blends in seamlessly with the outstanding natural beauty of the western end of the island. Long open terraces, ideal for basking in the warm sun and inhaling the fresh sea air, surround the swimming pool and front the bougainvillea-covered hillside down to the beach. The delicately landscaped patio features a built-in barbecue pit and table and chairs, perfect for casual outdoor cooking and dining. A covered terrace, punctuated by graceful archways, provides shelter from the sun. Inside, an airy living room and dining room and four bedrooms allow for comfortable living. Contact: West Indies Management Company, 28 Pelham Street, Newport, RI 02840. Call 1-800-932-3222 (in Rhode Island, 401-849-8012). Ref. C-TIM.
Children: Y   Pets: N   Smoking: Y   Handicap Access: N   Payment: P, T, A

VILLA DE LA MER *Rates: deluxe*
Open: year-round *Minimum Stay: one week*
Graceful almond trees and towering palms surround Villa de la Mer, built on the historic site of a plantation house dating from the colonial period. Apart from the stunning grounds, the house's details are worthy of a palace, including mahogany carpentry, marble floors, stylish

wicker furniture and elegant French antiques. One long side of the parlor is composed of a many-paned window looking out on the swimming pool and private tennis court. On the far side of the pool lies a cool curve of Caribbean beach. The villa contains four bedrooms and four baths and comes complete with maid service. Contact: LaCure Villas, 11661 San Vicente Blvd., Suite 1010, Los Angeles, CA 90049. Call 1-800-387-2715.

Children: Y   Pets: N   Smoking: Y   Handicap Access: N   Payment: All

---

VILLA LA CROIX   *Rates: deluxe*
Open: year-round   *Minimum Stay: one week*

Baie Longue, on the eastern end of St. Martin, is considered by many to be the most beautiful beach in the whole Caribbean; this luxurious vacation hideaway overlooks it. Villa La Croix enjoys an enviable hillside location providing unparalleled views of the azure ocean. Its large living room and three bedrooms, furnished in contemporary rattan, give access to a roofed gallery and from there a neatly manicured terrace and private pool. For alfresco dining surrounded by wildly blooming tropical plants, there's a gazebo. Maid service and myriad other amenities are included. Contact: LaCure Villas, 11661 San Vicente Blvd., Suite 1010, Los Agneles, CA 90049. Call 1-800-387-2715.

Children: Y   Pets: N   Smoking: Y   Handicap Access: N   Payment: All

BAIE LONGUE/BAIE ROUGE

LE COLIBRI   *Rates: deluxe*
Open: year-round   *Minimum Stay: one week*

A live-in gardener and maid maintain this immaculate villa, and it shows. Wake to breakfast in lounge chairs on the covered terrace and then take a refreshing morning dip in the pool accented by attractive archways. Rattan furnishings and cheerful island touches throughout create an airy, cool ambience. Three bedrooms sleep six, with private showers for added comfort. Contact: West Indies Management Company, 28 Pelham Street, Newport, RI 02840. Call 1-800-932-3222 (in Rhode Island, 401-849-8012). Ref. C-GOL.

Children: Y   Pets: N   Smoking: Y   Handicap Access: N   Payment: P, T, A

BAIE ROUGE

BEAULIEU   *Rates: deluxe*
Open: year-round   *Minimum Stay: one week*

Designed to take advantage of long sunny days in the mild Caribbean climate, Beaulieu sports a huge sun deck with chairs and lounges around a large swimming pool, offering spectacular views over Baie Rouge and beyond to the island of Anguilla. An attractive mix of brightly colored fabrics and traditional cane decorate the interior, and the dining room opens onto a cool, leafy courtyard. Six can sleep in three bedrooms in the main house, all with king or queen beds and private bathrooms. For added privacy, a separate guest cottage houses a fourth bedroom, perfect for extended families. A resident caretaker and maid service six days a week add to your comfort. Contact: Villas International, 71 West 23rd Street, New York, NY 10010. Call 212-929-7585.

Children: N   Pets: N   Smoking: Y   Handicap Access: N   Payment: C, P, T

BENNETT HOUSE   *Rates: expensive-deluxe*
Open: year-round   *Minimum Stay: one week*
Delicate flowers and brightly colored leaves on tropical bougainvillea vines fill the lush gardens around the Bennett House, yet it's only a minute's walk from the beach. Sliding glass doors in the living/dining room open to a covered terrace, perfect for outdoor dining while enjoying cool ocean breezes. Three sunny bedrooms open onto a spacious pool deck, making early morning dips a temptation hard to resist. To make things easier, a housekeeper lives on the property. Contact: West Indies Management Company, 28 Pelham Street, Newport, RI 02840. Call 1-800-932-3222 (in Rhode Island, 401-849-8012). Ref. JPS-17.

Children: Y   Pets: N   Smoking: Y   Handicap Access: N   Payment: P, T, A

BLUE HERRON   *Rates: deluxe*
Open: year-round   *Minimum Stay: one week*
Stunning Italian designer rattan and brilliantly colored paintings done by Haitian artists make Blue Herron an extremely elegant Caribbean retreat. It overlooks Baie Rouge just south of Marigot, though lush gardens separate its terraced pool and gazebo from the sand and surf. Four bedrooms and four and a half baths provide privacy and a sense of space, and the villa's tennis court offers opportunities for exercise between sessions in the sun. The villa's permanent staff is made up of a maid and gardener. Contact: LaCure Villas, 11661 San Vicente Blvd., Suite 1010, Los Angeles, CA 90049. Call 1-800-387-2615.

Children: Y   Pets: N   Smoking: Y   Handicap Access: N   Payment: All

BORDES-BEAULIEU   *Rates: deluxe*
Open: year-round   *Minimum Stay: one week*
The creation of architect Robeilson Ward, this villa looks out over Baie Rouge Beach and Anguilla from every room. The main house features three bedrooms and three baths, while another bed and bath occupy the adjacent guest house. Rattan furnishings and a covered porch with open archways add casual elegance. Outside, take the sun on the tiled deck between refreshing dips in the pool. Contact: West Indies Management Company, 28 Pelham Street, Newport, RI 02840. Call 1-800-932-3222 (in Rhode Island, 401-849-8012). Ref. C-BOR.

Children: N   Pets: N   Smoking: Y   Handicap Access: N   Payment: P, T, A

BORDIER   *Rates: deluxe*
Open: year-round   *Minimum Stay: one week*
Elegant and spacious, this magnificent home has an air of sophistication and beauty, with precious antiques adorning each room. The ballroom-sized living room includes two separate sitting areas, fine for quiet conversation and private get-togethers. Sliding glass doors lead to the covered terrace overlooking brilliant tropical blossoms and fruit trees. Here, you can take in the night air and gaze up at the stars, then

step into one of the bedrooms, both of which also open onto the terrace. A large pool and deck add to your privacy and comfort. Contact: West Indies Management Company, 28 Pelham Street, Newport, RI 02840. Call 1-800-932-3222 (in Rhode Island, 401-849-8012). Ref. JPS-82.

Children: Y   Pets: N   Smoking: Y   Handicap Access: N   Payment: P, T, A

CASA MARE   *Rates: deluxe*
Open: year-round   *Minimum Stay: one week*

From the elevated deck at Casa Mare you can see the mountains of St. Martin to one side, and to the other, gemlike Anguilla miles away in the Caribbean Sea. The villa is built on two levels surrounded by wraparound porches, rich green plants and exotic blooms. It holds four bedrooms, a well-equipped kitchen and a sweeping living/dining/bar area furnished in glass and wicker. The ceiling is lofty, facilitating the circulation of tropical breezes. After a horseback ride across the island or day spent on some perfect, sandy shore, a dip in Casa Mare's pool will seem like just the thing. Contact: Island Hideaways, 1317 Rhode Island Avenue, N.W., Suite 503, Washington, DC 20005. Call 1-800-832-2302 (in Washington, 202-667-3392).

Children: Y   Pets: N   Smoking: N   Handicap Access: N   Payment: C, P, T

COONEY HOUSE   *Rates: expensive-deluxe*
Open: year-round   *Minimum Stay: one week*

Restrained elegance is the keynote at Cooney House, a comfortable two-bedroom, two-bath villa in the southwestern corner of St. Martin. Its large living room area is separated from the kitchen by a convenient counter. Sliding glass doors open onto a covered gallery, whose West Indian archways lead directly to the deck and swimming pool beyond. The views here are delightful and varied; in one direction the shimmering blue expanse of Simpson Bay opens before you, and in another the colorful rooftops of Marigot. The villa is within easy reach of Baie Rouge Beach and both the Dutch and French capital cities, where shopping, dining, and sightseeing opportunities abound. Contact: Island Hideaways, 1317 Rhode Island Ave. N.W., Washington, DC 20005. Call 1-800-832-2302 (in Washington, 202-667-9652).

Children: Y   Pets: N   Smoking: Y   Handicap Access: N   Payment: C, P, T

COWLES VILLA   *Rates: deluxe*
Open: year-round   *Minimum Stay: one week*

Nestled in the hills above Baie Rouge, this large, three-level villa offers paradise in the tropics for four couples or two families. Creatively designed, the main (second) floor features a den and living room for entertaining and a large kitchen and dining room for meals. Four people can retreat to the third floor at night, and four others will find comfort and privacy on the first floor—it's almost like renting two separate houses. The second floor also sports a covered gallery that overlooks the large pool, deck and the bay. Contact: West Indies Management Company, 28 Pelham Street, Newport, RI 02840. Call 1-800-932-3222 (in Rhode Island, 401-849-8012). Ref. JPS-85.

Children: Y   Pets: N   Smoking: Y   Handicap Access: N   Payment: P, T, A

DRAKE'S HIDEAWAY *Rates: expensive-deluxe*
Open: year-round *Minimum Stay: one week*
Nestled on a gentle hillside smothered with beautiful gardens and trees, this lovely home offers inspiring views of the ocean and Anguilla on the horizon. Cathedral ceilings with fans complement the lively island decor of the rattan-furnished living/dining room, and enhance the cool, airy ambience. Step right onto a covered terrace, which borders the deck and private swimming pool, and enjoy a morning swim or an evening cocktail. Further afield, explore exclusive Baie Rouge and the surrounding cliffs. Contact: West Indies Management Company, 28 Pelham Street, Newport, RI 02840. Call 1-800-932-3222 (in Rhode Island, 401-849-8012). Ref. JPS-31.
Children: Y   Pets: N   Smoking: Y   Handicap Access: N   Payment: P, T, A

IVERSON CLIFF HOUSE *Rates: deluxe*
Open: year-round *Minimum Stay: one week*
The fragrance of beautiful gardens filled with colorful tropical blooms and swaying palm trees permeates the air at this deluxe villa set on a hill overlooking Baie Rouge. A paved cliff walk leads down to the fine sandy beach, perfect for secluded sunbathing or catching the cool night breeze. Breakfast on the covered terrace as you watch the sun come up on Baie Rouge or sip cocktails at dusk in between dips in the pool. Four bedrooms, two with king-sized beds and all with private showers, make for comfortable nights. With the resident staff tending to the property, you can spend your time exploring every nook and cranny of the many inlets and cays. Contact: West Indies Management Company, 28 Pelham Street, Newport, RI 02840. Call 1-800-932-3222 (in Rhode Island, 401-849-8012). Ref. C-IVE.
Children: Y   Pets: N   Smoking: Y   Handicap Access: N   Payment: P, T, A

LAS SIESTA-BAUDIN *Rates: deluxe*
Open: year-round *Minimum Stay: one week*
The living's easy in this large villa, which offers expansive views across the pool deck to the French capital of Marigot. Five air-conditioned bedrooms with baths provide privacy, while the open-plan living areas allow for relaxing meals and entertainment during the day. Distinctive touches throughout, such as a pool table under the pavilion, charming terra cotta pottery on the stone deck and a custom L-shaped swimming pool, enhance your vacation. A resident caretaker deals with the details, leaving you free to sunbathe, explore and shop. Contact: West Indies Management Company, 28 Pelham Street, Newport, RI 02840. Call 1-800-932-3222 (in Rhode Island, 401-849-8012). Ref. C-BAU.
Children: Y   Pets: N   Smoking: Y   Handicap Access: N   Payment: P, T, A

LITTLE JAZZ BIRD *Rates: deluxe*
Open: year-round *Minimum Stay: one week*
Recreation options abound at this Baie Rouge-area vacation villa, beginning with panorama-gazing from its tiled deck. Then there's swimming in the large swimming pool, dining—or perhaps high tea—in the

poolside gazebo, a set of tennis played on your own private court and entertaining in the graceful setting of Little Jazz Bird's airy living room. The villa features a high peaked roof, tiled floor covered in places by colorful woven rugs, glass and rattan furniture and cooling ceiling fan. Little Jazz Bird has three sizable bedrooms, all of which open right onto the terrace and pool deck. Contact: Island Hideaways, 1317 Rhode Island Ave. N.W., Suite 503, Washington, DC 20005. Call 1-800-832-2302 (in Washington, 202-667-9652).

Children: **Y**   Pets: **N**   Smoking: **Y**   Handicap Access: **N**   Payment: **C, P, T**

MCCULLOUGH RANCH   *Rates: expensive-deluxe*
Open: year-round   *Minimum Stay: one week*

Extended families or groups of friends will find this lovely ranch-style home with separate guest cottage perfect for relaxing vacations. A large, tiled pool deck, surrounded by tropical plants and trees, offers superb views of Baie Rouge and Anguilla. For alfresco dining, retreat under the gazebo just off the deck. Two bedrooms are in the main house, and a third, with bath and terrace, is in a separate cottage. Contact: West Indies Management Company, 28 Pelham Street, Newport, RI 02840. Call 1-800-932-3222 (in Rhode Island, 401-849-8012). Ref. JPS-14.

Children: **Y**   Pets: **N**   Smoking: **Y**   Handicap Access: **N**   Payment: **P, T, A**

POINTE DES FLEURS   *Rates: deluxe*
Open: year-round   *Minimum Stay: one week*

Baie Rouge is a secluded curve of sand most easily reached by boat. But for guests at Pointe des Fleurs it lies just outside the window, for this villa is perched atop a cliff. Pointe des Fleurs has four big bedrooms and a tiled swimming pool, around which are scattered comfortable lounge chairs. Adjacent to the pool is an arched loggia leading into the central salon. Living is easy and peaceful in this corner of St. Martin, making it a fine place to come home to after a day of duty-free shopping in Philipsburg or Marigot, scuba diving, tennis, golf, or simply touring the little island that is one of the Caribbean's most scenic. Contact: Island Hideaways, 1317 Rhode Island Ave. N.W., Washington, DC 20005. Call 1-800-832-2302 (in Washington, 202-667-9652).

Children: **Y**   Pets: **N**   Smoking: **Y**   Handicap Access: **N**   Payment: **C, P, T**

RED BAY VILLA   *Rates: deluxe*
Open: year-round   *Minimum Stay: one week*

Beautiful Baie Rouge lies just south of La Belle Creole, the legendary resort created by Claude Philippe of Waldorf-Astoria fame. This villa overlooking the bay is really a luxurious vacation compound, with a main house holding two large bedrooms and a living/dining/sitting room area whose French doors open onto the terrace, deck and pool. Tucked nearby is the Lily Pad, with a cozy twin-bedded room and bath. Another 50 feet away lies a charming cottage with its own bedroom, bath and terrace providing spectacular views of the ocean. Nearby are numerous beaches—included one for nudists near the village of Cul de Sac—golf, tennis, duty-free shops, restaurants and casinos. Contact: Vacation Home Rentals Worldwide, 235 Kensington Avenue, Norwood, NJ 07648. Call 1-800-NEED-A-VILLA or 1-800-633-3284 (in New Jersey, 201-767-5510). Ref. SM105.

Children: N   Pets: N   Smoking: Y   Handicap Access: N   Payment: C, P, T

SAND DOONS   *Rates: deluxe*
Open: year-round   *Minimum Stay: one week*

On the southwestern arm of St. Martin, a way up from Long Beach and with its back to big Simpson Bay Lagoon (premier windsurfing waters, especially for novices), stands Sand Doons. Its front door opens right onto the beach, though it has a large swimming pool as well. From the gazebo on the poolside deck, the views of Baie Rouge and the wide-open Caribbean beyond are stunning. Three bedrooms and three and a half baths decorated in stylish rattan, with air conditioning, maid service and many more amenities, make Sand Doons an immensely comfortable place to get away from it all. Contact: LaCure Villas, 11661 San Vicente Blvd., Suite 1010, Los Angeles, CA 90049. Call 1-800-387-2715.

Children: Y   Pets: N   Smoking: Y   Handicap Access: N   Payment: All

---

SMITH VILLA   *Rates: expensive-deluxe*
Open: year-round   *Minimum Stay: one week*

Tropical plants adorn the landscape at this two-bedroom villa; stone walls and walkways and a superb view across to Anguilla making it a charming vacation spot. A gazebo offers shelter from the hot Caribbean sun after you take a dip in the swimming pool surrounded by a deck. Privacy is assured for those who like to retire early, as both bedrooms and baths are semi-detached from the living room. An abundance of sliding glass doors make the most of the superb sea view. Rouge Beach offers nude sunbathing for true sun worshippers. Contact: West Indies Management Company, 28 Pelham Street, Newport, RI 02840. Call 1-800-932-3222 (in Rhode Island, 401-849-8012). Ref. JPS-39.

Children: Y   Pets: N   Smoking: Y   Handicap Access: N   Payment: P, T, A

ST. MORITZ   *Rates: deluxe*
Open: year-round   *Minimum Stay: one week*

Sailors glancing up at the heights around Terre Basse in St. Martin might catch a glimpse of the glistening tile roofs and arched loggias of St. Moritz. Its marvelous hilltop locale ensures that guests at the villas will see all the passing yachts as well as picture postcard views of the island's green peaks. St. Moritz is an elegant and romantic Caribbean vacation home with four bedrooms and four and a half baths. Almost all of its stylishly decorated chambers adjoin a tiled terrace, which provides easy access to the swimming pool and Jacuzzi. Maid service and air conditioning are featured, too. Contact: LaCure Villas, 11661 San Vicente Blvd., Suite 1010, Los Angeles, CA 90049. Call 1-800-387-2715.

Children: Y   Pets: N   Smoking: Y   Handicap Access: N   Payment: All

TAMARIND

Rates: deluxe

Open: year-round

Minimum Stay: one week

Catch the cooling trade winds in this hillside home while viewing the calm seas and white sandy beaches of Baie Rouge below. An attractive kidney-shaped swimming pool and surrounding tiled terrace make for long, lazy days in the sun and a barbecue allows for outdoor dining as well. Graceful arches adorn the open living area, furnished in wicker, while the luxurious master bedroom features a king bed and balcony. Two twin bedrooms offer private baths. For added comfort, a caretaker will tend to problems, while maid service six days a week makes cleaning a snap. Contact: Villas International, 71 West 23rd Street, New York, NY 10010. Call 212-929-7585.

Children: N   Pets: N   Smoking: Y   Handicap Access: N   Payment: C, P, T

VENDEL-MAEVA

Rates: deluxe

Open: year-round

Minimum Stay: one week

This unique villa stands across the street from a small sandy beach in a sheltered lagoon on the forested northern end of the island. Refreshing dips are closer than that, however, in the large saltwater swimming pool right at your doorstep, which has the added attractions of a sliding pond and diving board. A big deck and covered terrace offer outdoor shelter. Four couples or a group of friends will delight in the four twin bedrooms. Contact: West Indies Management Company, 28 Pelham Street, Newport, RI 02840. Call 1-800-932-3222 (in Rhode Island, 401-849-8012). Ref. C-VEN.

Children: Y   Pets: N   Smoking: Y   Handicap Access: N   Payment: P, T, A

VICTORIO

Rates: deluxe

Open: year-round

Minimum Stay: one week

Use this large new home as a base for exploring the untamed parts of St. Martin, including the fabulous Simpson Bay Lagoon, an excellent spot for water sports. At Victorio, you can sunbathe around a graceful swimming pool and dine while viewing the bay and the town of Marigot. After an invigorating day in the sun, relax in front of your television with satellite dish reception, then sleep comfortably in three bedrooms with private baths. Conditions are ideal at the lagoon for snorkeling, where the calm waters allow for beautiful views of coral reefs. For scuba diving, hire a boat to take you about a mile offshore, where you'll find lobsters, nurse sharks, and even the wreckage of a British man-of-war. Contact: West Indies Management Company, 28 Pelham Street, Newport, RI 02840. Call 1-800-932-3222 (in Rhode Island, 401-849-8012). Ref. JPS-87.

Children: Y   Pets: N   Smoking: Y   Handicap Access: N   Payment: P, T, A

VILLA DALMING

Rates: deluxe

Open: year-round

Minimum Stay: one week

A long lane leads up to this posh vacation home in the southwestern corner of St. Martin. Its seven-gabled roofline imitates the contours of the surrounding mountains. From it, panoramas of Anguilla and Baie

Rouge spread majestically before you. Dalming has four bedrooms and a pool and makes an excellent base of operations for exploring the island's many beaches, recreation hubs like the resort at Mullet Bay, and charming French villages where streetside cafes offer wayfarers crusty pastries and cafe au lait. Contact: Island Hideaways, 1317 Rhode Island Ave. N.W., Washington, DC 20005. Call 1-800-832-2302 (in Washington, 202-667-9652).

Children: **Y** Pets: **N** Smoking: **Y** Handicap Access: **N** Payment: **C, P, T**

BAIE ROUGE BEACH

GOLDEN BRIDGE   *Rates: deluxe*
Open: year-round   *Minimum Stay: one week*

The swimming pool is the main eye-catcher at this St. Martin villa. It's crossed by a bridge leading to a Jacuzzi. Between the house and the pool there's a lavishly furnished covered terrace with a sliding glass door leading directly into the house. There, guests find four bedrooms and five baths, as well as a living area highlighted by handsome tropical rattan tables and chairs. As if all this isn't enough, Golden Bridge sits immediately on Baie Rouge Beach, where the aquamarine Caribbean laps gently at your feet. Contact: LaCure Villas, 11661 San Vicente Blvd., Suite 1010, Los Angeles, Ca 90049. Call 1-800-387-2715.

Children: **Y** Pets: **N** Smoking: **Y** Handicap Access: **N** Payment: **All**

LA FALAISE   *Rates: deluxe*
Open: year-round   *Minimum Stay: one week*

This airy island villa offers plenty of room in which to stretch out and gaze at magnificent views of the ocean. Swimming at Baie Rouge Beach is just a short walk away, or take a dip in the pool surrounded by a large patio of inlaid stone. Inside, high ceilings with fans keep things cool. A spacious dining/living area makes for fine relaxation and entertainment, and four bedrooms with private baths complete the accommodations. Contact: West Indies Management Company, 28 Pelham Street, Newport, RI 02840. Call 1-800-932-3222 (in Rhode Island, 401-849-8012). Ref. C-RUS.

Children: **Y** Pets: **N** Smoking: **Y** Handicap Access: **N** Payment: **P, T, A**

LIL' JAZZ BIRD   *Rates: deluxe*
Open: year-round   *Minimum Stay: one week*

Colorful and free-spirited Haitian paintings and sculpture enliven this deluxe villa set right on Baie Rouge Beach. Quality rattan furnishings, cheerful floral chintzes and cool tile floors create a carefree island ambience. For added comfort and privacy, all three bedrooms feature separate bathrooms. After soaking up the sun in the morning, spend the afternoon cooling off in the private swimming pool or playing an impromptu game of tennis on the villa's court. Contact: West Indies Management Company, 28 Pelham Street, Newport, RI 02840. Call 1-800-932-3222 (in Rhode Island, 401-849-8012). Ref. C-PAL.

Children: **N** Pets: **N** Smoking: **Y** Handicap Access: **N** Payment: **P, T, A**

PETIT POINT   *Rates: deluxe*
Open: year-round   *Minimum Stay: one week*

An unusual bridge crosses over the swimming pool to the Jacuzzi at this newly built villa, and also provides direct access to beautiful Baie Rouge Beach. Sip cocktails on the large pool deck after a refreshing swim, as the palm trees sway in the ocean breeze. A well-equipped kitchen including an ice maker gives you a place in which to whip up your most exotic blender drinks. Four bedrooms, three with king-sized beds, all have private baths and allow for complete privacy at night. Contact: West Indies Management Company, 28 Pelham Street, Newport, RI 02840. Call 1-800-932-3222 (in Rhode Island, 401-849-8012). Ref. C-LEO.

Children: N   Pets: N   Smoking: Y   Handicap Access: N   Payment: P, T, A

THOMPSON TERRACE   *Rates: expensive-deluxe*
Open: year-round   *Minimum Stay: one week*

Distinctive West Indian arches front the outdoor gallery on this villa, which is separated from the living room by sliding glass doors offering terrific sunny views of the pool and sea. The terraced pool juts out over Baie Rouge, one of the island's most secluded beaches, where you'll have your choice of sites for sunbathing. Brightly colored fabrics in the four bedrooms and rattan furnishings in the living/dining room maintain a tropical flavor throughout. Contact: West Indies Management Company, 28 Pelham Street, Newport, RI 02840. Call 1-800-932-3222 (in Rhode Island, 401-849-8012). Ref. JPS-12.

Children: Y   Pets: N   Smoking: Y   Handicap Access: N   Payment: P, T, A

BAIE ROUGE HILLS

JOHNSON COMPLEX   *Rates: deluxe*
Open: year-round   *Minimum Stay: one week*

Extended families or a group of friends will find a perfect vacation haunt in the main house, annex and separate cottage here. The main house features two bedrooms and two baths, a large well-furnished living room, a dining room and a sitting room that opens onto the terrace and pool deck. Lily Pad, the quaint annex adjacent to the main house, and a separate cottage each feature a bedroom with bath. Explore the fabulous caves and rocks on the west end of Rouge Beach, or the beautiful coral formations on the east end. Contact: West Indies Management Company, 28 Pelham Street, Newport, RI 02840. Call 1-800-932-3222 (in Rhode Island, 401-849-8012). Ref. JPS-18.

Children: Y   Pets: N   Smoking: Y   Handicap Access: N   Payment: P, T, A

CUPECOY BEACH

FIELDS OF AMBROSIA   *Rates: deluxe*
Open: year-round   *Minimum Stay: one week*

Lovely views of Simpson Bay and Marigot from every room in this villa will waft your cares away like a sweet Caribbean breeze. Relax near the gently swaying palm trees on the sun deck, then take a refreshing dip in the pool or Jacuzzi. For a change of pace, walk two minutes to lovely Cupecoy Beach. Meals are easy in the well-equipped kitchen, and tiled floors with bright rattan furnishings create a tropical feeling throughout. Six can find comfort and privacy in three large bedrooms. Contact: West Indies Management Company, 28 Pelham Street, Newport, RI 02840. Call 1-800-932-3222 (in Rhode Island, 401-849-8012). Ref. C-TRG.

Children: Y Pets: N Smoking: Y Handicap Access: N Payment: P, T, A

DAWN BEACH

SEAWATCH   *Rates: deluxe*
Open: year-round   *Minimum Stay: one week*

Dawn Beach, in the less trammeled northeast corner of St. Martin, is a favorite with surf lovers, since the waves there wash in off the Atlantic with thunder and froth. Seawatch sits on this beach's southern flank, so there are great water views from its tile patios. The villa's style is Spanish hacienda revisited, with tile roofs and many archways. There are three bedrooms and a modern kitchen inside. Nearby is a resort hotel providing recreational facilities; Orient Bay, a beach for swimming and sunbathing in the buff; and tiny, secluded Ilet Pinet, accessible by charter boat. Contact: Island Hideaways, 1317 Rhode Island Ave. N.W., Suite 503, Washington, DC 20005. Call 1-800-832-2302 (in Washington, 202-667-9654).

Childen: Y Pets: N Smoking: Y Handicap Access: N Payment: C, P, T

GRAND CASE

CUL DE SAC   *Rates: moderate-inexpensive*
Open: year-round   *Minimum Stay: one week*

Just outside the village of Grand Case, you'll find this one-bedroom house affording simplicity and privacy with easy access to the many beaches and restaurants in the area. An outdoor Jacuzzi offers relaxing views of rolling fields down to the sea, or of a canopy of stars at night. Water sports enthusiasts need not look far for recreation, whether it's waterskiing, snorkeling or scuba diving. For added comfort, contact one of the many provisioning firms, who will deliver all your food and drinks right to your doorstep. Contact: West Indies Management Company, 28 Pelham Street, Newport, RI 02840. Call 1-800-932-3222 (in Rhode Island, 401-849-8012). Ref. JPS-4.

Children: Y Pets: N Smoking: Y Handicap Access: N Payment: P, T, A

LA SAMANNA BEACH

PARADISE   *Rates: deluxe*
Open: year-round   *Minimum Stay: one week*

As the name implies, the living's easy at Paradise, whose splendid wrap-around terrace commands spectacular views of the bay and ocean. A three-person staff and spacious accommodations for nine offer the ultimate in comfort. Ceiling fans in each room take full advantage of the tropical breezes, or you can simply turn on the air-conditioning. For privacy and comfort, four large bedrooms feature a bath and access to the terrace, while a fifth is located on the lower level. Enjoy fresh vegetables from the garden prepared in the kitchen, which has a freezer, dishwasher and two ovens. A caretaker, gardener and housekeeper will tend to the house while you explore the resorts at nearby Mullet Bay. Contact: Villas International, 71 West 23rd Street, New York, NY 10010. Call 212-929-7585.

Children: Y   Pets: N   Smoking: Y   Handicap Access: N   Payment: C, P, T

La Savanne

VILLA SAVANNE-MARY   *Rates: expensive-deluxe*
Open: year-round   *Minimum Stay: one week*

You'll find plenty of peace and solitude in this simple but attractive home 15 minutes from the beach. Sun on a deck surrounding the sparkling pool or retreat from the rays under the gazebo. The lovely garden provides a cool alternative to the pool. Your comfort is assured inside, where two king-size master bedrooms boast air-conditioning; a third is on a separate floor and all have private baths. Twenty of the island's most tempting and famous restaurants are within a 15-minute walk. Contact: West Indies Management Company, 28 Pelham Street, Newport, RI 02840. Call 1-800-932-3222 (in Rhode Island, 401-849-8012). Ref. AS-22.

Children: Y   Pets: N   Smoking: Y   Handicap Access: N   Payment: P, T, A

Marigot

BEAU RIVAGE   *Rates: deluxe*
Open: year-round   *Minimum Stay: one week*

About 150 miles east of Puerto Rico in the midst of the Windward Islands lies a little bit of France—tiny, 21-square-mile St. Martin. Beau Rivage, near its quaint capital of Marigot, is a St. Martin classic, clinging to the dramatic heights of Falaise des Oseax, with show-stopping views of the smaller Windward island, Anguilla. Its interior is a symphony in white rattan and pastel fabrics, and from its graceful living room an arched terrace leads to a deck and pool. Beau Rivage has four bedrooms, each with its own private bath, as well as daily maid service. Contact: LaCure Villas, 11661 San Vicente Blvd., Suite 1010, Los Angeles, CA 90049. Call 1-800-387-2715.

Children: Y   Pets: N   Smoking: Y   Handicap Access: N   Payment: All

DRAKE HOUSE   *Rates: expensive-deluxe*
Open: year-round   *Minimum Stay: one week*

The neighboring island of Anguilla is visible from both the pool and deck of this elegant villa clinging to a hillside in French St. Martin. It has two bedrooms and two baths, cathedral ceilings and ceiling fans, sliding glass doors leading to a comfortable covered terrace and handsome rattan furnishings painted in bright colors. All of this is surrounded by two acres of tropical paradise. Drake is nicely located for

Saturday-morning excursions to the French market at Marigot or gourmet dinners in Grand Case. Contact: Island Hideaways, 1317 Rhode Island Ave. N.W., Suite 503, Washington, DC 20005. Call 1-800-832-2302 (in Washington, 202-667-9654).
Children: Y   Pets: N   Smoking: Y   Handicap Access: N   Payment: C, P, T

HARMON VILLA   *Rates: expensive-deluxe*
Open: year-round   *Minimum Stay: one week*
Halfway between the shopping mecca of Marigot and Grand Case's myriad gourmet restaurants is about halfway to heaven. This is the location of Harmon Villa, prettily encamped atop a terraced hillside overlooking Friar's Bay and the island of Anguilla. Its two bedrooms—featuring wicker and brass beds—two baths, kitchen with microwave, and spacious living and dining room make for exceedingly comfortable vacationing. Little extras like TV, radio, stereo and tape deck, washer, ceiling fans, private pool, linen and maid service abound. Guests are met at the airport and can arrange for a rental car to await them at the villa. Contact: Rent A Home International, Inc., 7200 34th Street N.W., Seattle, WA 98117. Call 206-545-6963.
Children: Y Pets: N Smoking: Y Handicap Access: N Payment: C, P, T, V, M

LA SCALA   *Rates: deluxe*
Open: year-round   *Minimum Stay: one week*
Among St. Martin villas, La Scala is truly a flagship. Perched upon a hilltop in the southwestern part of the island, it commands views of the ocean, surrounding islets and the French capital of Marigot. Rattan accented by leather are the design keynotes of the stylish interior, making La Scala a splendid setting for upscale entertaining. Just outside is a covered terrace for snoozes in the shade and alfresco dining. The spacious pool lies beyond, forming a semicircle around the whirlpool. La Scala is air conditioned and staffed with a maid. Contact: LaCure Villas, 11661 San Vicente Blvd., Suite 1010, Los Angeles, CA 90049. Call 1-800-387-2715.
Children: Y   Pets: N   Smoking: Y   Handicap Access: N   Payment: All

MONGOOSE RUN   *Rates: deluxe*
Open: year-round   *Minimum Stay: one week*
You'll find this lovely two-bedroom villa on the Falaise des Oiseaux (cliff of the birds) with breathtaking views of the island of Anguilla and the mountains of St. Martin. Hidden by hibiscus, bougainvillea and banana trees, the villa offers sunny rooms with simple but charming furnishings. Spend long lazy days soaking up the sun on the large stone-and-brick patio around a small swimming pool, then retreat to an enclosed area for outdoor dining. Ceiling fans and screens in both bedrooms help circulate the air, and a dishwasher, washer/dryer, TV, stereo and telephone add to your comfort. Explore the French capital at Marigot, only a five-mile drive away. Contact: Villas International, 71 West 23rd Street, New York, NY 10010. Call 212-929-7585.
Children: Y   Pets: N   Smoking: Y   Handicap Access: N   Payment: C, P, T

OCEAN VILLA   *Rates: deluxe*
Open: year-round   *Minimum stay: one week*

This St. Martin villa sits just above the beach close to the sophisticated little city of Marigot. Its spacious living room and dining area are
floored with attractive tile and separated from the open-air gallery
beyond by large sliding glass doors. A stroll through the gallery takes
guests poolside, where smashing views are to be had in all directions
from the comfortable lounge chairs. Ocean Villa features four bedrooms and five baths, handsomely landscaped grounds and an on-
premises staff. Contact: LaCure Villas, 11661 San Vicente Blvd., Suite
1010, Los Angeles, CA 90049. Call 1-800-387-2715.

Children: Y   Pets: N   Smoking: Y   Handicap Access: N   Payment: All

SMITH HOUSE   *Rates: expensive-deluxe*
Open: year-round   *Minimum Stay: one week*

The central living/dining/kitchen area in this Spanish-style St. Martin
villa is surrounded by sliding glass doors, providing views of the hills
and the Caribbean. Semiattached to the living room are the two well-
appointed bedrooms, each with its own bath. A series of wide West
Indian arches frame the lush tropical garden beyond. Quaint stone
walkways meander about the grounds, leading to romantic hideaways
and eventually terminating at the pool, beside which is a gazebo and
deck. At nearby resorts, tennis, golf, sailing, windsurfing, jet skiing
and other diversions can be found; and for those who like to gamble,
St. Martin's many casinos open at one P.M. Contact: Island Hideaways,
1317 Rhode Island Ave. N.W., Washington, DC 20005. Call 1-800-832-
2302 (in Washington, 202-667-9652).

Children: Y   Pets: N   Smoking: Y   Handicap Access: N   Payment: C, P, T

MARIGOT/GRAND CASE

JAPEC   *Rates: expensive-deluxe*
Open: year-round   *Minimum Stay: one week*

The French capital town of Marigot and the beach town of Grand Case
are both just five minutes from this villa, which offers intimate privacy and proximity to the beaches and nightlife. Rattan, wicker and
brass furnishings create an airy ambience throughout this two-
bedroom villa, and ceiling fans in the master bedroom make the sleeping accommodations comfortable. Enjoy the popular Sunday beach
parties on Grand Case Beach, a great place to meet people, or rent
equipment to waterski, scuba dive or snorkel. Contact: West Indies
Management Company, 28 Pelham Street, Newport, RI 02840. Call
1-800-932-3222 (in Rhode Island, 401-849-8012). Ref. AS-070.

Children: Y   Pets: N   Smoking: Y   Handicap Access: N   Payment: P, T, A

MARIGOT/SIMPSON BAY

VILLA AMBROSE   *Rates: deluxe*
Open: year-round   *Minimum Stay: one week*

Chic St. Martin shares a small Caribbean island with Dutch St.
Maarten, and from the capital of one nation to the capital of the other,

it's just an eight-mile trip. Villa Ambrose is located on a hilltop on the French side near scads of sophisticated shops and gourmet restaurants. From its huge windows there are breathtaking views of Simpson Bay and the town of Marigot. Designer rattan prevails in its three bedrooms, and in its living room there's an audio/visual entertainment center. Other attractions include air conditioning, a deck and pool, maid service and a breezy covered terrace. Contact: LaCure Villas, 11661 San Vicente Blvd., Suite 1010, Los Angeles, CA 90049. Call 1-800-387-2715.

Children: Y   Pets: N   Smoking: Y   Handicap Access: N   Payment: All

MONTE ROUGE

PAPE-BABILU   *Rates: deluxe*
Open: year-round   *Minimum Stay: one week*

Two levels of furnished terraces help this villa take full advantage of panoramic views of the sea. A swimming pool keeps you cool while rattan furnishings throughout keep the mood casual. Three bedrooms, one with a king-sized bed, sleep six in comfort, and separate bathrooms in each allow for complete privacy. An added touch of luxury is the private outdoor spa. Contact: West Indies Management Company, 28 Pelham Street, Newport, RI 02840. Call 1-800-932-3222 (in Rhode Island, 401-849-8012). Ref. C-PAP.

Children: Y   Pets: N   Smoking: Y   Handicap Access: N   Payment: P, T, A

OYSTER POND

VILLA BUDWILLER   *Rates: expensive-deluxe*
Open: year-round   *Minimum Stay: one week*

Honeymooners, two couples, or small families might well gravitate toward this three-bedroom split-level vacation house overlooking Simpson Bay Lagoon—the largest inland body of water in the Caribbean. It has a well-equipped kitchen with microwave, stereo and TV, not to mention a deck, swimming pool and spacious terrace. Guests can see the wide Caribbean, the lagoon and St. Barts; a beach can be reached by an easy walk. Maid service and airport transportation are included. Contact: Riviera Holidays, 31 Georgian Lane, Great Neck, NY 11024. Call 516-487-8094. Ref. 744.

Children: Y   Pets: N   Smoking: Y   Handicap Access: N   Payment: C, P, T

PHILIPSBURG

CASTELLO   *Rates: expensive-deluxe*
Open: year-round   *Minimum Stay: one week*

Panoramic views of surrounding countryside, islands and sea are to be had from this lovely property. Enjoy the sights from the large terrace and the swimming pool. Cook up some spicy island cuisine in the smartly appointed kitchen, then enjoy the meal in one of two dining rooms—one casual, the other formal. Four bedrooms and as many baths make the villa a perfect spot for large families or small groups. Contact: West Indies Management Company, 28 Pelham Street, New-

port, RI 02840. Call 1-800-932-3222 (in Rhode Island, 401-849-8012).
Ref. AS-180.

Children: Y   Pets: N   Smoking: Y   Handicap Access: N   Payment: P, T, A

PLUM BAY

HARMONY   *Rates: deluxe*
Open: year-round   *Minimum Stay: one week*

This superior villa is set about 10 minutes from exclusive Plum Bay,
but a private swimming pool makes visits to the beach unnecessary.
Take in the sun or retreat to a shady area on the large pool deck.
Choose to dine inside or out—even around the pool. All three bedrooms offer separate baths for complete privacy, and there's an extra
loft bed in the spacious living room. For the adventuresome, Plum Bay
Beach allows topless bathing. Contact: West Indies Management Company, 28 Pelham Street, Newport, RI 02840. Call 1-800-932-3222 (in
Rhode Island, 401-849-8012). Ref. C-HAR.

Children: Y   Pets: N   Smoking: Y   Handicap Access: N   Payment: P, T, A

PLUM BAY HILL   *Rates: deluxe*
Open: year-round   *Minimum Stay: one week*

This group of four bungalows can be rented individually or together for
groups of friends or business associates. Each offers separate bedrooms,
with terraces overlooking exclusive Plum Bay in all rooms. Modern
furnishings of rattan and lively prints highlight the airy, spacious
rooms, which feature high ceilings and fans to make the most of gently
flowing breezes from the sea. A private pool makes swimming easy for
those too shy for the topless bathing at Plum Bay. Contact: West
Indies Management Company, 28 Pelham Street, Newport, RI 02840.
Call 1-800-932-3222 (in Rhode Island, 401-849-8012).

Children: Y   Pets: N   Smoking: Y   Handicap Access: N   Payment: P, T, A

PLUM TREE VILLA   *Rates: deluxe*
Open: year-round   *Minimum Stay: one week*

Plum Bay lies just around St. Martin's southwestern peninsula from
Long Beach, the St. Maarten border and Juliana Airport. Steps away
from its glistening, golden sands is where Plum Tree Villa lies, vacation quarters spacious enough to accommodate two to three couples or
one large family. It has three bedrooms and two baths, and roomy
living and dining areas. Beachside, there are terraces on two levels and
a pretty swimming pool surrounded by palm trees. Your rental includes maid service. Contact: LaCure Villas, 11661 San Vicente Blvd.,
Suite 1010, Los Angeles, CA 90049. Call 1-800-387-2715.

Children: Y   Pets: N   Smoking: Y   Handicap Access: N   Payment: All

VILLA CLAIR DE LUNE   *Rates: deluxe*
Open: year-round   *Miminum Stay: one week*

There's a live-in gardener on duty at the Villa Clair de Lune, which
explains its lovely landscaping. It's set above Plum Bay and close to
one of the Caribbean's best sandy spots, Long Beach. Built in 1988, the

villa is decorated with rattan furniture and has three bedrooms, each with its own private bath. Air conditioning, stereo, video, a modern kitchen, maid service and airport transportation are all standard amenities. In the rear there's a sweeping terrace next to a private swimming pool. Contact: Riviera Holidays, 31 Georgian Lane, Great Neck, NY 11024. Call 516-487-8094. Ref. 750.

Children: Y   Pets: N   Smoking: Y   Handicap Access: N   Payment: C, P, T

PLUM BAY/BAIE LONGUE

MOGADOR *Rates: deluxe*
Open: year-round *Minimum Stay: one week*

Only three minutes from the beach, this deluxe wooden villa in the local style offers views of beautiful Plum Bay and Baie Longue. The dramatic pool deck doubles as a pavilion for elegant dining and entertaining in the cool evening breezes. Comfortable furnishings and luxurious features fill three spacious bedrooms (two king and a queen) with private baths, making this villa a perfectly delightful getaway for three couples or a large family. Seclusion is ensured on the white sandy beaches at Plum Bay. Contact: West Indies Management Company, 28 Pelham Street, Newport, RI 02840. Call 1-800-932-3222 (in Rhode Island, 401-849-8012). Ref. C-SEV.

Children: Y   Pets: N   Smoking: Y   Handicap Access: N   Payment: P, T, A

PLUM BEACH

BALABAN *Rates: moderate-expensive*
Open: year-round *Minimum Stay: one week*

Two couples will find this newly furnished villa a perfect base for exploring the natural beauty of the western end of the island, whose dramatic sandstone cliffs are dotted with small caves and many fine sandy beaches. Closer to home, relax on the porch and sun deck as you watch the sun go down in the blazing hues of a tropical sunset. Both bedrooms have private baths and king-sized beds; one features a ceiling fan to catch the night breeze, the other offers air-conditioning. Picturesque Plum Beach, which offers topless bathing, is only a five-minute walk from the house. Contact: West Indies Management Company, 28 Pelham Street, Newport, RI 02840. Call 1-800-932-3222 (in Rhode Island, 401-849-8012). Ref. AS-033.

Children: Y   Pets: N   Smoking: Y   Handicap Access: N   Payment: P, T, A

BEACHFRONT WONDER *Rates: deluxe*
Open: year-round *Minimum Stay: one week*

Listen to the rolling waves of the sea lapping at the clean white sand of Plum Beach while sipping cocktails at the in-pool table or relaxing on the patio of this beachfront villa. Oriental rugs and antique furnishings create a rich atmosphere for lounging or small get-togethers. Families will like the sleeping arrangements, with the master bedroom and large sitting room with bar upstairs, and two smaller bedrooms downstairs. Privacy is ensured on secluded Plum Beach.

Contact: West Indies Management Company, 28 Pelham Street, Newport, RI 02840. Call 1-800-932-3222 (in Rhode Island, 401-849-8012). Ref. AS-062.

Children: Y   Pets: N   Smoking: Y   Handicap Access: N   Payment: P, T, A

VILLA LENER   *Rates: deluxe*
Open: year-round   *Minimum Stay: one week*

Isolated from the bustle of the island towns, this beachfront villa offers access to the miles of fine white sand that make up secluded Plum Beach. Tastefully furnished in the light and airy style of the Caribbean, with rattan, chintz and decorative touches throughout, the villa features three bedrooms, a well-equipped kitchen, dining area, large living room and den that opens to a covered terrace. You may neglect the private swimming pool, as Plum Beach is one of the finest beaches in the Caribbean. Contact: West Indies Management Company, 28 Pelham Street, Newport, RI 02840. Call 1-800-932-3222 (in Rhode Island, 401-849-8012). Ref. JPS-28.

Children: N   Pets: N   Smoking: Y   Handicap Access: N   Payment: P, T, A

PLUM BEACH/MT. ROUGE

PERCUDANI   *Rates: deluxe*
Open: year-round   *Minimum Stay: one week*

Set on a hillside on delightful Mont Rouge, this home offers wide-open views of the sea, with St. Kitts and Nevis on the horizon. The cool pastel decor of the living room sets the tone for a relaxing vacation, and the lovely rattan furniture adds an island touch. During the day, sip cocktails in the gazebo next to the pool deck, and at night, retire to a luxurious master bedroom or two smaller guest rooms, all with private baths. Explore the rugged side of the island on the many walking trails near Percudani. Contact: West Indies Management Company, 28 Pelham Street, Newport, RI 02840. Call 1-800-932-3222 (in Rhode Island, 401-849-8012). Ref. JPS-86.

Children: Y   Pets: N   Smoking: Y   Handicap Access: N   Payment: P, T, A

SIMPSON BAY

BAYVIEW VILLA   *Rates: expensive-deluxe*
Open: year-round   *Minimum Stay: one week*

This two-bedroom villa provides a convenient base for exploring the many delights of Simpson Bay Beach, which offers some of the best snorkeling in the Caribbean and many outdoor recreational opportunities. Attractively furnished and nearly maintenance-free, the villa features a living room and kitchen decorated with island accents. A covered terrace provides welcome shelter from the strong rays of the sun, but for those who want to soak it up, sandy beaches are nearby. Contact: Villas International, 71 West 23rd Street, New York, NY 10010. Call 212-929-7585.

Children: Y   Pets: N   Smoking: Y   Handicap Access: N   Payment: C, P, T

GRANDVIEW *Rates: deluxe*
Open: year-round *Minimum Stay: one week*
The setting for this lovely vacation villa is a secluded hilltop overlooking the largest lagoon in the Caribbean—Simpson Bay, whose warm waters beckon windsurfers and sailors. Six beautifully landscaped acres surround the house, and on its flank lies a handsome scallop-shaped swimming pool. Four bedrooms are located in the villa itself and a separate guest cottage. The interior is a stunning blend of glass, wicker and cool potted plants. Ceiling fans keep Grandview cool, and the floors are finished in smooth tile. Contact: Island Hideaways, 1317 Rhode Island Ave. N.W., Washington, DC 20005. Call 1-800-832-2302 (in Washington, 202-667-9652).
Children: Y Pets: N Smoking: Y Handicap Access: N Payment: C, P, T

VILLA LA SIESTA *Rates: deluxe*
Open: year-round *Minimum Stay: one week*
Cupecoy Beach and the charming village of Terre Basse on Simpson Bay are both close to this luxurious three-bedroom villa with views from every window of the water and the island's French capital, Marigot. Its big, airy living room is furnished in delightful island rattan and opens directly onto a large deck and swimming pool. Two bedrooms feature king-sized beds and the other has twins; for every chamber, there's an individual bath with shower. State-of-the-art best describes its amenities, including a microwave, washer and dryer, ice machine, air conditioning, barbecue, stereo, CD, TV and video. Contact: Riviera Holidays, 31 Georgian Lane, Great Neck, NY 11024. Call 516-487-8094. Ref. 769.
Children: Y Pets: Y Smoking: Y Handicap Access: N Payment: C, P, T

VILLA MAEVA *Rates: deluxe*
Open: year-round *Minimum Stay: one week*
Sweeping Simpson Bay Lagoon in central St. Martin is fringed by tall palm trees and the blue-green outlines of the jagged mountains rising in the interior of the island. Villa Maeva occupies a front-row seat on all this, with its own private beach and pier providing water lovers immediate access to the lagoon. In addition, the home has a large saltwater swimming pool with a diving board and slide, four bedrooms, and one vast central living area with soaring vaulted ceilings. Wicker sofas and chairs, glass-topped tables, potted plants and cool tile floors are the main elements of its stylish decor. Contact: Island Hideaways, 1317 Rhode Island Ave. N.W., Washington, DC 20005. Call 1-800-832-2302 (in Washington, 202-667-9652).
Children: Y Pets: N Smoking: Y Handicap Access: N Payment: C, P, T

SIMPSON BAY LAGOON

MARVERA *Rates: expensive-deluxe*
Open: year-round *Minimum Stay: one week*
Families will appreciate this secluded French villa surrounded by more than an acre of hillside overlooking Simpson Bay Lagoon. Nearby Pelican Key provides opportunities for some of the best snorkeling on St.

Martin. At Mavera, four sleep comfortably in two bedrooms, a swimming pool and deck make for great sunning, and a patio allows for al fresco meals cooled by the tropical breezes. Contact: West Indies Management Company, 28 Pelham Street, Newport, RI 02840. Call 1-800-932-3222 (in Rhode Island, 401-849-8012). Ref. AS-208.

Children: Y Pets: N Smoking: Y Handicap Access: N Payment: P, T, A

SODERBURG   *Rates: expensive-deluxe*
Open: year-round   *Minimum Stay: one week*

La Belle Creole resort lies just below this two-bedroom villa on the beautiful white sandy beaches of Simpson Bay Lagoon. You can enjoy this idyllic setting from a tiled terrace a step above the swimming pool and patio, or dine outdoors while viewing the lagoon's peaceful waters. Glass sliding doors lead to the warmly furnished living room. Cross the vine-covered walkway to reach the two bedrooms, a perfect layout for complete privacy and sleeping late. Drive ten minutes to the French capital town of Marigot, where you can find specialty shops, fine foods and island treats. Contact: West Indies Management Company, 28 Pelham Street, Newport, RI 02840. Call 1-800-932-3222 (in Rhode Island, 401-849-8012). Ref. JPS-83.

Children: Y Pets: N Smoking: Y Handicap Access: N Payment: P, T, A

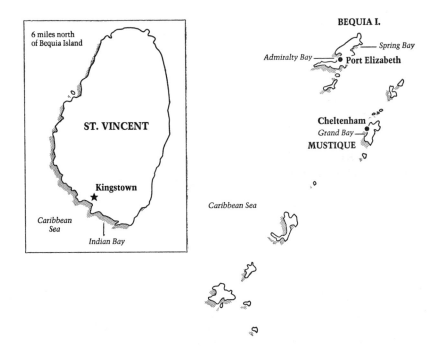

6 miles north
of Bequia Island

ST. VINCENT

Kingstown

Caribbean
Sea

Indian Bay

BEQUIA I.

Spring Bay

Admiralty Bay

Port Elizabeth

Cheltenham

Grand Bay

MUSTIQUE

Caribbean Sea

St. Vincent and the Grenadines

St. Vincent

Indian Bay Beach

BREEZEVILLE APARTMENTS

Rates: inexpensive

Open: year-round

Minimum Stay: none

Conveniently located just three miles from the airport, these studio apartments offer accommodations for two to four and feature full kitchens and private balconies. Each air-conditioned unit includes a TV and telephone service. Outside, you can enjoy the freshwater swimming pool located on a hillside overlooking a beautiful sandy beach and boasting a panoramic mountain view. Those who are determined to stay fit while on vacation will find tennis and squash courts nearby. Whether you've come to swim, snorkel and sail or to read, sleep and daydream, you'll find this mountainous Caribbean island unspoiled and the people especially friendly. Contact: Robert Brisbane, Breezeville Apartments, P.O. Box 222, St. Vincent, West Indies. Call 809-458-4004.

Children: Y Pets: N Smoking: Y Handicap Access: N Payment: C, T, A, V, M

Indian Bay Beach

TRANQUILLITY BEACH APARTMENT HOTEL   *Rates: budget*
Open: year-round   *Minimum Stay: none*

Located right on the beach away from the hustle and bustle of city life, these one-, two- and three-bedroom apartments promise you a place in the sun. Each apartment features a handy kitchenette as well as a private balcony overlooking the pristine waters below and a clear view of the beautiful neighboring Grenadine Islands. Wake to the sound of the sea lapping the shore and make your way through the day in as unhurried a fashion as you choose. The nearby coral reef offers a rich look at aquatic life; a walk along the sleepy roads shows a sky bigger than any you've ever seen. For a closer look at the islands visible from your balcony—Bequia, Mustique, Canouan—you can take the regular boat service. Contact: Joel or Ceford Providence, P.O. Box 71, St. Vincent, West Indies. Call 809-458-4021.

Children: Y Pets: N Smoking: Y Handicap Access: N Payment: C, T, A, V, M

Kingstown

RICK'S APARTMENTS   *Rates: budget*
Open: year-round   *Minimum Stay: none*

This charming house offers six simply appointed two-bedroom apartments with full kitchens and outdoor barbecues. Located in the lively and colorful city of Kingstown, these accommodations put many of the attractions of this special island just outside your door. Here, you'll find St. Vincent's Craftsmen's Center, a crafts market where you can acquaint yourself with the heritage of the island. By mini-van, taxi or rented car you can explore the pre-Columbian petroglyphs and rock carvings near the pretty fishing village of Layou. To get to the top of La Soufriere, a 4,000-foot volcano which last erupted in 1979, you must be an ambitious hiker, but it's well worth the climb. On this island you will also find the oldest botanical garden in the Caribbean, with trees and shrubs grown from the original plants brought to the island in 1793. Contact: Rick's Apartments, P.O. Box 63, St. Vincent, West Indies. Call 809-456-1242 or 457-1181.

Children: Y   Pets: N   Smoking: Y   Handicap Access: N   Payment: C, T

Kingstown

UMBRELLA BEACH HOTEL   *Rates: budget*
Open: year-round   *Minimum Stay: none*

Conveniently located in the capital city of Kingstown, this hotel offers one-bedroom suites with full kitchens and balconies offering a scenic view of Young Island. With all the charm of Kingstown just outside your door, you can explore the many historic sights in and near the town as well as the cluster of shops and markets filled with local crafts and wares and fine imported jewelry and luxury items from Europe. You might try chartering a yacht for the afternoon for a special look at some of the exclusive harbors on the smaller islands of the Grenadines. If a little fishing sounds like the most relaxing way to pass your days, you'll find the tiny village of Barrouallie on the leeward coast especially appealing. Contact: Jacques Thevenot, Umbrella Beach Hotel, P.O. Box 530 Kingstown, St. Vincent, West Indies. Call 809-458-4651.

Children: Y Pets: N Smoking: Y Handicap Access: N Payment: C, T, A, V, M

Ratho Mill

RIDGEVIEW TERRACE APARTMENTS *Rates: budget*
Open: year-round *Minimum Stay: two nights*

Here in St. Vincent, thought to be one of the few islands in the Caribbean that still retains its Old World charm, you'll find these newly built one- and two-bedroom apartments. Spacious and airy, each apartment features a living/dining room, a full kitchen, a sun terrace and private balconies. Maid service can be arranged, including cooking for a small extra charge; groceries are available nearby or you can stock up in the lively capital city of Kingstown, just a short drive away. To relax watch the dawn illuminate spectacular mountain scenery or view the beautiful water aboard a yacht chartered for the day. Contact: Clifford Frank, Ridgeview Terrace Apartments, P.O. Box 176, St. Vincent, West Indies. Call 809-456-1615 or 458-4212.

Children: Y   Pets: N   Smoking: Y   Handicap Access: N   Payment: C, T

The Grenadines

Bequia

FRIENDSHIP HOUSE *Rates: moderate*
Open: year-round *Minimum Stay: one week*

The people of this seven-square-mile island just nine miles south of St. Vincent enjoy a fine reputation as seafaring people, boat builders and sailors. It's no wonder, with such calm, clear, deep waters surrounding the island and the surrounding hills that protect the bay from high winds and rough seas. Here in this lovely beach house surrounded by lush tropical trees and bushes above Friendship Bay, you'll enjoy panoramic views of the sparkling water as well as of neighboring islands including Mustique. Attractively furnished in tropical island decor, the house boasts two twin bedrooms, two and a half baths, a living/dining room, a modern kitchen and several terraces. For the ultimate in luxury, a housekeeper and cook is provided Monday through Saturday. The beach lies just 800 feet away, a perfect spot for watching the Bequian sunset. Contact: Villas International, 71 West 23rd Street, New York, NY 10010. Call 212-929-7585.

Children: Y   Pets: N   Smoking: Y   Handicap Access: N   Payment: C, P, T

Mustique

CALLALOO *Rates: deluxe*
Open: year-round *Minimum Stay: one week*

From the handsome and comfortably furnished main covered terrace of this newly renovated villa, the green, lush countryside and blue sea spread out before you like a panoramic wonder. Three bedrooms, which open onto a pool and deck, plus a master suite on the upper level which has its own private terrace, accommodates eight exceedingly fortunate guests. The attentive and highly regarded staff attends to the care of the home and prepares meals as you require. If you're looking for a little distraction, you'll find Basil's Bar on the jetty, just a short drive from the villa, the perfect spot for a light lunch or a tropical drink. Here you can watch the sailing and yachting traffic, though traffic is hardly the word for the motion of the stately and graceful white vessels that dot these waters. Contact: Island Hideaways, 1317 Rhode Island Ave., N.W., Suite 503, Washington, D.C. 20005. Call 1-800-832-2303 (in Washington, call 202-667-9652).

Children: **Y** Pets: **N** Smoking: **Y** Handicap Access: **N** Payment: **C, P, T**

Mustique

CIBONEY   *Rates: deluxe*
Open: year-round   *Minimum Stay: one week*

A dramatic and spacious living area and three bedroom suites surround the center courtyard and swimming pool of this striking villa, creating a decidedly Japanese air with an unmistakably open and luminous tropical feeling. The island's own natural stone and timber shape these handsome rooms as well as the deck that surrounds the pool. Sliding louvered walls in each of the villa's units can be adjusted to admit the trade winds or the vista of neighboring islands and the sea. You can have no worries here—the house includes full maid service as well as a cook—so you are obligated to relax and enjoy the serene atmosphere of the island. For a romantic diversion you can ride horseback on the beach or in the hills or walk to the Cotton House Hotel for an alfresco lunch overlooking the water. Contact: Island Hideaways, 1317 Rhode Island Ave., N.W., Suite 503, Washington, D.C. 20005. Call 1-800-832-2303 (in Washington, call 202-667-9652).

Children: **Y** Pets: **N** Smoking: **Y** Handicap Access: **N** Payment: **C, P, T**

Mustique

FORT SHANDY   *Rates: deluxe*
Open: year-round   *Minimum Stay: one week*

A more dramatic and evocative vacation home than Fort Shandy cannot be imagined. Here atop Mustique's graceful hills you'll find a rambling four-bedroom villa built on the ruins of an 18th-century English fort. The sprawling rooms feature rich woods, gray stone and colorful tiles, making this exciting fortress an unusual and altogether comfortable holiday home. A swimming pool and a broad gallery suggest endless possibilities for entertaining and socializing—with the welcome assistance of the maid and cook—and the exciting westerly views of beautiful Brittania Bay will be the center of attention every day at sunset. If you hanker for a closer look at the water, you can rent a sailfish or sunfish at the one bar in town or charter a yacht for a day. Contact: Island Hideaways, 1317 Rhode Island Ave., N.W., Suite 503, Washington, D.C. 20005. Call 1-800-832-2303 (in Washington, call 202-667-9652).

Children: **Y** Pets: **N** Smoking: **Y** Handicap Access: **N** Payment: **C, P, T**

Mustique

GINGERBREAD *Rates: deluxe*
Open: year-round *Minimum Stay: one week*

Remarkable attention to detail marks both the design and appointments of this custom-designed four-bedroom villa. Much in demand, especially since it was featured in *Architectural Digest*, this home boasts exteriors of chalk white and pink contrasted with rich woods. Built on several levels, including one dedicated to the free-form swimming pool surrounded by lush tropical greenery, the layout separates the master bedroom with private terrace from the gracious open living area and is cared for by a maid and a cook. A lovely path winds downhill through jungle to a guest beach cottage, a romantic bamboo hut as simple as the main house is lavish. Contact: Island Hideaways, 1317 Rhode Island Ave., N.W., Suite 503, Washington, D.C. 20005. Call 1-800-832-2303 (in Washington, call 202-667-9652).

Children: **Y** Pets: **N** Smoking: **Y** Handicap Access: **N** Payment: **C, P, T**

Mustique

JACARANDA *Rates: deluxe*
Open: year-round *Minimum Stay: one week*

Situated on L'Ansecoy Bay, the quietest corner of this remarkably quiet island, this elegant two-bedroom villa marries distinctly European appointments with an utterly tropical setting. Exquisite and unusual furnishings, such as Old World stencilled pieces, evoke images of Colonial times and lend an especially romantic feeling to this beach house. The centerpiece, a freshwater pool, further enhances your sense of well-being and the ease of outdoor living under the palms. Deep-sea fishermen will find the waters here ideal for grouper, snapper and butter fish. The less ambitious can bring home the catch local Bequian fishermen sell at the beach near the Cotton House, the island's one hotel. Contact: Island Hideaways, 1317 Rhode Island Ave., N.W., Suite 503, Washington, D.C. 20005. Call 1-800-832-2303 (in Washington, call 202-667-9652).

Children: **Y** Pets: **N** Smoking: **Y** Handicap Access: **N** Payment: **C, P, T**

Mustique

LES JOLIES EAUX *Rates: deluxe*
Open: year-round *Minimum Stay: one week*

Take a deep breath: This is the private retreat of Princess Margaret, available for rent when Her Royal Highness is not in residence. How do the aristocracy live? In a palatial house set high on a secluded promontory with extraordinary views over both the Caribbean and the Atlantic as well as the outlying Grenadines. The garden locations of the swimming pool and the gazebo suggest an almost fairytale setting. Appointed with a flair for the theatrical and cared for by a maid and cook, the elegant rooms open onto extensive terracing, a sun deck and a balcony. Four bedrooms accommodate eight in utter romance and luxury; separate staff quarters are provided for the resident maid and cook. During your stay in this fabulous home, you'll discover that the old time feeling of plantation living is alive and thriving on this gorgeous tropical island. Contact: At Home Abroad, Sutton Town House, 405 East 56th Street, 6-H, New York, NY 10022. Call 212-421-9165.

Children: Y   Pets: N   Smoking: Y   Handicap Access: N   Payment: C, P, T

Mustique

NIRVANA   *Rates: deluxe*
Open: year-round   *Minimum Stay: one week*

This may be as close to heaven as you can imagine: a four-bedroom villa with breathtaking, panoramic views of both the Caribbean Sea and the Atlantic Ocean. Surrounded by gloriously landscaped grounds lush with gardenias, jasmine, oleander, bougainvillaea, hibiscus and fruit trees, the house features dramatic stone, cool tile and rich island woods. The 60-foot freshwater swimming pool, the air-conditioned squash court and a number of large verandas make this a great place for alternating ambitious exercise with utter relaxation. You can explore this 1,400-acre island by jeep or horseback and learn its waters by wading along its peaceful shores or snorkeling the lush reefs. Contact: Island Hideaways, 1317 Rhode Island Ave., N.W., Suite 503, Washington, D.C. 20005. Call 1-800-832-2303 (in Washington, call 202-667-9652).

Children: Y   Pets: N   Smoking: Y   Handicap Access: N   Payment: C, P, T

Mustique

PELICAN BEACH HOUSE   *Rates: deluxe*
Open: year-round   *Minimum Stay: one week*

Known for its promise of utter relaxation, Mustique can still muster up some lively recreation for "les sportifs," and this two-bedroom villa offers the perfect location for such vacationers. Here in a lovely custom-designed house attended by a maid and a cook, you'll find the beach at L'Ansecoy Bay only inches away, the perfect spot for swimming, sunning and windsurfing. The second-floor bedrooms offer wonderful views of this yachting and sailing center; the first-floor living area boasts simple but elegant furnishings and a covered veranda with a hammock is just right for an afternoon snooze. You'll also find this waterside address conveniently close the Cotton House swimming pool and tennis courts. Contact: Island Hideaways, 1317 Rhode Island Ave., N.W., Suite 503, Washington, D.C. 20005. Call 1-800-832-2303 (in Washington, call 202-667-9652).

Children: Y   Pets: N   Smoking: Y   Handicap Access: N   Payment: C, P, T

Mustique

PHIBBLESTOWN   *Rates: deluxe*
Open: year-round   *Minimum Stay: one week*

Imagine the perfect marriage of comfort and elegance, and an image of this gracious home will begin to form. Enter the classical, custom-designed house through a serene courtyard with a lily pond. The three-sided living room and dining room loggia open onto terraces for sunning and outdoor dining. Three large bedroom suites and a kitchen complete this elegantly appointed home where fine fabrics, dramatic window and door treatments and the best of furnishings afford guests a feeling of utter luxury. Sitting on a rocky bluff, the house connects to the beach below via a picturesque garden path. On this tiny island, you'll find a bar here and there, a general store and a bakery, but Mustique is for those who seek the bare minimum in diversion and the maximum in elegance. Contact: Villas and Apartments Abroad, 420 Madison Avenue, New York, NY 10017. Call 1-800-433-3020 (in New York, call 212-759-1025).

Children: Y   Pets: N   Smoking: Y   Handicap Access: N   Payment: C, P, T

Mustique

POINT LOOKOUT   *Rates: deluxe*
Open: year-round   *Minimum Stay: one week*

A formal, stone-walled exterior encloses this elegant, comfortable seaside custom-designed villa. Situated on a mere slip of land and bounded on the east and west by pristine beaches, this secluded home boasts extensive private grounds for strolling. Meditative hours pass in perfect repose inside this four-bedroom home, which features the very finest in wood, rattan and bamboo furnishings and includes a maid and a cook. Formerly a sugar plantation and more recently a cotton estate, Mustique was bought in 1958 by a devotee of island life. Everyone who has had a hand in the gradual development of the island has seen to it that the old charm is preserved. You will no doubt find that your stay at the Point embodies the timeless values of peace, tranquillity and beauty. Contact: Island Hideaways, 1317 Rhode Island Ave., N.W., Suite 503, Washington, D.C. 20005. Call 1-800-832-2303 (in Washington, call 202-667-9652).

Children: Y   Pets: N   Smoking: Y   Handicap Access: N   Payment: C, P, T

Mustique

RUTLAND HILL   *Rates: deluxe*
Open: year-round   *Minimum Stay: one week*

The open architecture of this truly Caribbean villa offers framed vistas from each of its rooms and a network of wooden walkways. Its magnificent pool and elaborate gazebo, built 250 feet above the sea, overlook the entire eastern coastline of Mustique. Highly polished wood floors accentuate the white interiors and harmonize nicely with the bamboo and rattan furnishings of this four-bedroom villa which includes a maid and a cook. With this exquisitely light and airy home as your point of departure and full service staff to cater to your every need, your stay on Mustique will be filled with both romance and calm; a horseback ride on the beach, days of swimming, sun and beachcombing and peaceful nights. Contact: Island Hideaways, 1317 Rhode Island Ave., N.W., Suite 503, Washington, D.C. 20005. Call 1-800-832-2303 (in Washington, call 202-667-9652).

Children: Y   Pets: N   Smoking: Y   Handicap Access: N   Payment: C, P, T

Mustique

SEA STAR

Rates: deluxe

Open: year-round

Minimum Stay: one week

Three separate and exquisite buildings comprise this beach cottage complex. A pavilion for entertaining includes a dramatic entrance portico to one side, a huge semi-circular covered terrace for outdoor living, and in between, a bright and elegant living/dining room with furnishings made by local craftsmen, plus a kitchen fit for an accomplished chef. A main cottage with a master bedroom suite and a lovely terrace facing the sea along with a guest cottage with two large bedroom suites flank the pavilion cottage; all offer 24-hour-a-day splendor with views of the gentle waters that kiss the beach only a few feet away. Those seeking complete privacy in an environment of unspoiled and unparalleled beauty will find this island and villa ideal. Contact: Villas and Apartments Abroad, 420 Madison Avenue, New York, NY 10017. Call 1-800-433-3020 (in New York, call 212-759-1025).

Children: Y   Pets: N   Smoking: Y   Handicap Access: N   Payment: C, P, T

Mustique

SUNRISE

Rates: deluxe

Open: year-round

Minimum Stay: one week

Overlooking Simplicity Bay, this lavish, contemporary beachfront villa features a main house surrounded by gardens. On the upper level you'll find a spacious, glass-walled living and dining room opening onto a large terrace, plus a study, a sun deck and a fabulously appointed kitchen. On the lower deck two sprawling bedrooms and two exquisite, modern baths face the 60-foot swimming pool and sun decks. Nearby are the fully equipped exercise room and an all-weather Laykold tennis court. Nestled between the island greenery and a private white sand beach sits an intimate beachhouse with a third bedroom, plus two gazebos for entertaining—making this one of exclusive Mustique's most sumptuous villas. Contact: Villas and Apartments Abroad, 420 Madison Avenue, New York, NY 10017. Call 1-800-433-3020 (in New York, call 212-759-1025).

Children: Y   Pets: N   Smoking: Y   Handicap Access: N   Payment: C, P, T

Mustique

TETTO ROSSO

Rates: deluxe

Open: year-round

Minimum Stay: one week

Subtly dramatic yet quietly moody, this three-bedroom villa offers an oasis of tranquillity with the finest appointments. Recently redesigned and refurnished, cared for by a maid and a cook, the villa features red Barbados tile roofing, rich rustic woods and many windows and doors louvered a la Casablanca. The verandas, patio, outdoor dining terrace and lovely swimming pool all serve to enhance the beauty and serenity of this gorgeous home. Here you'll be surrounded by the island's spectacular natural beauty, the perfect spot for slowing down, shedding the worries of your day-to-day life and allowing yourself to fully appreciate the unhurried, low-key atmosphere of Mustique. If you must stir, you'll find excellent snorkeling, swimming and shelling in the glorious waters. Contact: Island Hideaways, 1317 Rhode Island Ave., N.W., Suite 503, Washington, D.C. 20005. Call 1-800-832-2303 (in Washington, call 202-667-9652).

Children: Y   Pets: N   Smoking: Y   Handicap Access: N   Payment: C, P, T

Mustique

THE FISHER HOUSE   *Rates: deluxe*
Open: year-round   *Minimum Stay: one week*

A deep, cool veranda runs the length of this exquisite house in the Endeavour Hills. Stunning views from the covered wrap-around deck display the green countryside and the beautiful blue sea beyond. Three suites of double bedrooms as well as a sitting room, all connected by the veranda, circle the superb kitchen. The layout and decoration of this mansion with its own swimming pool surrounded by thick lush gardens make this a breathtakingly luxurious and also comfortable vacation home. You'll find the snorkeling, swimming and shelling in the calm waters off the shores of this tiny island, only three by one and a half miles in size, unparalleled and inspiring. Contact: Villas and Apartments Abroad, 420 Madison Avenue, New York, NY 10017. Call 1-800-433-3020 (in New York, call 212-759-1025).

Children: Y   Pets: N   Smoking: Y   Handicap Access: N   Payment: C, P, T

Mustique

TORTUGA   *Rates: deluxe*
Open: year-round   *Minimum Stay: one week*

From it verandas and windowed walls, Italianate Tortuga displays alternately dramatic and tranquil vistas of Brittania Bay and several neighboring islands. Exquisite fabrics and furnishings made in Italy provide this four-bedroom villa suspended high above the sea a luscious Roman flair. The two-level cascading swimming pool is the centerpiece of the multi-unit estate, which offers precipice views at every turn. Lavish tropical gardens surround the property and link the various buildings with vines of jasmine and bougainvillaea. You may need a first week here just to take in the remarkable beauty of the place while the maid and cook do the fussing, and then at least one more week for lolling around this three-mile by mile-and-a-half tropical paradise. Contact: Island Hideaways, 1317 Rhode Island Ave., N.W., Suite 503, Washington, D.C. 20005. Call 1-800-832-2303 (in Washington, call 202-667-9652).

Children: Y   Pets: N   Smoking: Y   Handicap Access: N   Payment: C, P, T

Mustique

WHITE CEDARS   *Rates: deluxe*
Open: year-round   *Minimum Stay: one week*

Ascend a broad stairway flanked by native stone walls draped with yellow allamande to reach this cliff-top three-bedroom villa overlooking Macaroni and Simplicity Bays. On the main level with spectacular sea views, the entertaining and dining areas connect to the separate teak- and pine-panelled master bedroom suite by a series of interjoining deck and patio areas. Here you can enjoy the Edenesque delight of fresh tropical fruits and flowers from your own gardens. Choose between a freshwater pool with breathtaking sea views or one of the two white sand beaches only a few feet from the villa for swimming. Mustique has a native population of about 80 and usually houses less than 100 residents and visitors at the height of the winter season. Contact: Island Hideaways, 1317 Rhode Island Ave., N.W., Suite 503, Washington, D.C. 20005. Call 1-800-832-2303 (in Washington, call 202-667-9652).

Children: Y   Pets: N   Smoking: Y   Handicap Access: N   Payment: C, P, T

Mustique

WINDSONG   *Rates: deluxe*
Open: year-round   *Minimum Stay: one week*

This newest of Mustique's sprawling tropical island estates features a memorable view from the swimming pool—you'll see horses grazing on the hillside far below and the gentle blue sea beyond. Open, light and airy, the rooms boast elegant but utterly comfortably Vincentian white and yellow furnishings. Outdoor accents include thick tropical gardens filled with rare flowers and an all-weather tennis court for perfecting your serve or your backhand. When you tire of racquet sports you can retire to a chartered yacht, a sunfish or the nearest beach for peaceful communing with the gorgeous Caribbean Sea. Contact: Island Hideaways, 1317 Rhode Island Ave., N.W., Suite 503, Washington, D.C. 20005. Call 1-800-832-2303 (in Washington, call 202-667-9652).

Children: Y   Pets: N   Smoking: Y   Handicap Access: N   Payment: C, P, T

Trinidad and Tobago

TOBAGO

Charlotteville

MAN-O'-WAR BAY COTTAGES

Rates: budget-inexpensive

Open: year-round

Minimum Stay: two nights

Part of Charlotteville Estate, a 1,000-acre cocoa plantation, these cottages stand amid colorful landscaped grounds, a tropical garden, flowers shimmering with all the colors of the rainbow and trees heavy with papaya, breadfruit and limes. The airy and spacious cottages range from one to four bedrooms and feature a comfortably furnished living room with a dining area, a full kitchen and one bath. Each cottage features a veranda with lounge chairs, where you can relax and enjoy the incredible beauty surrounding you. Two living coral reefs start right at the beach and extend offshore for about 100 feet, a welcome sight to those who enjoy snorkeling. Home to about 420 species of birds, Tobago and its neighbor island Trinidad offer fabulous sightings for bird-watchers, and inspire many people to begin this satisfying hobby. Contact: Charles and Pat Turpin, Charlotteville Estate, Charlotteville, Tobago, West Indies. Call 809-660-4327.

Children: **Y**   Pets: **N**   Smoking: **Y**   Handicap Access: **N**   Payment: **C, P, T**

Crown Point

CORAL REEF GUEST HOUSE AND APARTMENTS   *Rates: budget*
Open: year-round   *Minimum Stay: three weeks*

It's just a five-minute walk from these studio apartments to the nearest beaches, where the beauty of the sunswept, candy-colored sands by day is matched only by the moonlight on the shimmering fronds of the coconut trees by night. Apartments for two to six people include wall-to-wall carpeting, air conditioning, kitchenettes and TV. Nearby, you can enjoy a round of golf or deep-sea fishing, but the real attraction is the remarkable natural beauty. Here in this island paradise, where hundreds of different species of birds make their winter homes, you can explore tropical forest trails, hidden rivers, waterfalls and virgin forests. Contact: Cora Murray, Coral Reef Guest House and Apartments, Milford Road, P.O. Box 316, Tobago, West Indies. Call 809-639-0770.
Children: Y Pets: N Smoking: Y Handicap Access: N Payment: C, T, A, V, M

Crown Point

JIMMY'S HOLIDAY RESORT   *Rates: budget*
Open: year-round   *Minimum Stay: none*

Ideally suited for the vacationing family or a group of friends, this resort offers 18 air-conditioned two-bedroom apartments for up to six, each featuring either a full kitchen or a kitchenette. Located in the hub of Tobago's resort area, Jimmy's puts you just five minutes from the airport and two minutes from the lovely Store Bay Beach. You'll find taxis and public transportation readily available, but you may prefer to explore this beautiful and friendly island in a rented car or on a motor scooter. The adventurous among you can set out to sea with a local fisherman and catch all you can eat. Nature lovers will find Tobago a true paradise, where clear waters, coral reefs and marine life abound; even the huge, shy and harmless sea turtles have been seen just a few yards from shore. Contact: Mr. Hollison McMillan, Jimmy's Holiday Resort, P.O. Box 109, Scarborough, Tobago, West Indies. Call 809-639-8929.
Children: Y Pets: N Smoking: Y Handicap Access: N Payment: C, T, A

Speyside

BLUE WATERS INN   *Rates: inexpensive-expensive*
Open: year-round   *Minimum Stay: none*

Tucked away in its own private bay on 46 acres of lush grounds on Tobago's northeast coast, this inn is the perfect spot for guests seeking seclusion and tranquility. A number of housekeeping units offer accommodations for four and include full kitchens and spacious, open-air porches. Golfers will enjoy a magnificent 18-hole championship course under the palms and scuba divers can discover some of the finest and least-explored waters in the world. Those with a bent for history will find this island rich in colonial sites, such as Richmond House and a number of old cocoa plantations. Contact: Mr. and Mrs.

R. Maclean, Blue Waters Inn, Batteaux Bay, Speyside, Tobago, West Indies. Call 809-660-4341.

Children: **Y** Pets: **N** Smoking: **Y** Handicap Access: **N** Payment: C, T, A, M

TRINIDAD
Maraval
CHACONIA INN   *Rates: budget-inexpensive*
Open: year-round   *Minimum Stay: none*

Nestled in a cool mountain valley just north of Port of Spain, this resort offers guests an ideal location for exploring this rich and colorful island, famous for its February carnival celebration. Studios with kitchenettes and two-bedroom apartments with full kitchens include daily maid service. You'll be glad for the many extra services available here, including laundry, fax service and child care. The inn features dancing nightly as well as live entertainment on weekends spotlighting performers of the spirited music and dance native to the island. During the day you can enjoy the refreshing swimming pool or slip into the lively capital city of Port of Spain for shopping and sightseeing. Contact: Chaconia Inn, P.O. Box 3340, Maraval, Trinidad, West Indies. Call 809-628-8603/5 or 628-3214.

Children: **Y** Pets: **N** Smoking: **Y** Handicap: **N** Payment: C, T, A, V, M, O

St. Clair
KAPOK HOTEL   *Rates: budget-moderate*
Open: year-round   *Minimum Stay: none*

Conveniently located at the tip of the Queen's Park Savannah, this handsomely appointed hotel offers the amenities traditionally associated with a larger resort, while still maintaining the warm and personal touch that vacationers appreciate. The several studio apartments, which sleep two, include kitchenettes with charming sitting areas furnished in bamboo furniture. A large swimming pool in the center courtyard awaits guests, but more energetic visitors will head for the 2.5-mile jogging track and numerous sports activities. Very close to Port of Spain's landmarks, such as Stollmeyer's Castle and the lush botanical gardens, this hotel also boasts two fine restaurants, a beauty salon and a gift shop. Contact: Jane Chan, Kapok Hotel, 16-18 Cotton Hill, St. Clair, Trinidad, West Indies. Call 809-622-6441.

Children: **Y** Pets: **N** Smoking: **Y** Handicap Access: **N** Payment: C, T, A, V, M

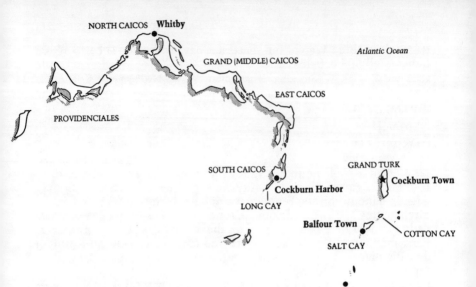

NORTH CAICOS **Whitby**

Atlantic Ocean

GRAND (MIDDLE) CAICOS

EAST CAICOS

PROVIDENCIALES

GRAND TURK

SOUTH CAICOS

Cockburn Town

Cockburn Harbor

LONG CAY

Balfour Town

COTTON CAY

SALT CAY

Turks and Caicos

Grand Caicos

FALCON EAST AND WEST

Open: year-round

Rates: budget-moderate
Minimum Stay: one week

With exceptional swimming, snorkeling and beachcombing practically right outside the door, this brand-new duplex lies 200 feet from a pristine two-mile-long beach blanketed with sugar-white sand. Both units are terrifically well equipped, with accommodations for up to six; a living area featuring a stereo, TV and VCR, and a fully equipped modern kitchen, where seafood caught on a dive or bought from local fishermen can be prepared into delicious meals. Isolated coves, ideal for picnics, very private swims, and sea hunts for the next fish dinner, are within easy reach by land or sea, and the island's celebrated caves, also close by, make for unforgettable adventures as well. Contact: Rent A Home International, Inc., 7200 34th Avenue, N.W., Seattle, WA 98117. Call 1-206-545-6963.

Children: Y Pets: N Smoking: N Handicap Access: N Payment: C, P, T, V, M

Grand Turk

EAGLES REST VILLA

Open: year-round

Rates: budget-expensive
Minimum Stay: one week

Positioned on a lofty ridge, commanding breathtaking views and 200 feet of private beachfront, Eagles Rest Villa is a captivating holiday residence for a party of up to eight. The three-bedroom house, which receives its crystal-clear water from a 17,000-gallon cistern, contains a lovely living room and bright kitchen with an adjoining dinette, while outside there's a large covered terrace, with a hammock and other inviting patio furniture, and a sun deck, cooled by the gentle and fragrant trade winds, overlooking the ocean and a nearby bay. Before a languid afternoon, guests can enjoy a swim in the warm turquoise ocean waters or some of the Caribbean's best diving and snorkeling opportunities, as well as a number of other recreational pursuits on land. Contact: Rent A Home International, Inc., 7200 34th Avenue, N.W., Seattle, WA 98117. Call 1-206-545-6963.

Children: Y Pets: N Smoking: N Handicap Access: N Payment: C, P, T, V, M

HARBOUR SANDS CONDOMINIUMS

Rates: inexpensive-moderate
Open: year-round
Minimum Stay: three nights

Located six miles from Cockburntown on the southern beach of Grand Turk, Harbour Sands features eight large, fully equipped condominium apartments. Each unit includes two bedrooms containing king-sized beds, two baths, a living area and complete kitchen, with ceiling fans wafting cool Atlantic breezes throughout the rooms, and a private balcony facing the ocean. The peaceful and well-maintained grounds feature lush tropical landscaping, an enticing swimming pool and an abundance of sunny patio space. To make their guests' stay on the island a memorable one, the staff will help arrange diving expeditions, sightseeing tours and dinner cruises that take full advantage of the sensational West Indian sunsets. Contact: Kim Douglas Lund, Harbour Sands Condominiums, South Beach, Grand Turk, Turks and Caicos, B.W.I. Call 1-809-946-4700 or 1-800-637-7686.

Children: Y Pets: N Smoking: Y Handicap Access: N Payment: C, T, A, V, M

HOTEL KITTINA

Rates: inexpensive-moderate
Open: year-round
Minimum Stay: none

A delightful low-rise hotel on the beach, the Kittina offers 20 outstanding housekeeping seaside suites, each containing a comfortable bedroom and living area, complete kitchen facilities and other handy amenities. The grounds feature a freshwater swimming pool, if guests ever tire of the shimmering warm ocean waters, and barbecues are located on the sand for captivating beach cookouts. Bikes and motor scooters are also available for rent—a delightful and refreshing way to explore the unspoiled and picturesque island, where striking limestone caves and intriguing Indian and plantation ruins make fascinating destinations. Contact: Janet Williams, Hotel Kittina, Duke St., P.O. Box 42, Grand Turk, Turks and Caicos, B.W.I. Call 1-809-946-2232/592 or 1-800-548-8462.

Children: Y Pets: N Smoking: Y Handicap Access: N Payment: All

ISLAND REEF RESORT

Rates: budget-moderate
Open: year-round
Minimum Stay: none

Twenty-one studio, one- and two-bedroom suites, each containing a fully equipped kitchenette, are available at Island Reef, an exquisite and very modern little resort on the coast, two miles from Grand

Turk's main shopping district in Cockburntown. The complex's secluded private beach is protected by an offshore coral reef—a fascinating spot for snorkelers and divers—making the waters perfect for totally safe swimming. The grounds also feature a freshwater swimming pool and a tennis court, plus a friendly restaurant and bar. Contact: Island Reef Resort, P.M.B. 10, Grand Turk, Turks and Caicos, B.W.I. Call 1-800-223-6510.

Children: Y   Pets: N   Smoking: Y   Handicap Access: N   Payment: C, T

NORTH CAICOS

OCEAN BEACH HOTEL CONDOMINIUMS   *Rates: inexpensive-deluxe*
Open: year-round   *Minimum Stay: none*

Attractively constructed from a blend of cedar and colorful native stone, these self-contained condominiums are situated right on the beach, where pink flamingos and pelicans join guests on the sand to enjoy the gentle West Indies sun. Single-story one-bedroom units, opening onto a spacious common courtyard, and two- and three-bedroom apartments, with balconies and sun decks or patios, are available, each tastefully furnished and offering complete kitchen facilities and large picture windows that give a sweeping ocean view. The recreational opportunities in the immediate area are unsurpassed; a coral reef just offshore means safe swimming and the bounteous marine life, including dolphin, tuna, sailfish, mackerel and lobster, will delight fishers, scuba divers and foragers for fresh seafood. Contact: Karen L. Preikschat, P.O. Box 1152, Station B, Burlington, Ontario, Canada, L7P 359. Call 1-416-336-2876 or 1-809-946-7113.

Children: Y Pets: N Smoking: Y Handicap Access: N Payment: C, P, T, O

PROVIDENCIALES

CHALK SOUND VILLAS   *Rates: expensive-deluxe*
Open: year-round   *Minimum Stay: one week*

Built in a distinctive wooden island house style, each luxury waterfront villa at the Chalk Sound complex on Providenciales consists of two separate buildings, one containing two or three bedrooms and a bath and the other a kitchen and living and dining areas. The homes all are graced with generous private decks and far-reaching views of beautiful Chalk Sound and the bright turquoise waters of the Atlantic. A full assortment of water recreational opportunities are available nearby, and the entire island, featuring cosmopolitan tourist centers and lush green countryside alike, is well worth exploring by car, bike, motorscooter or on foot. Contact: Chalk Sound Villas, Providenciales, Turks and Caicos, B.W.I. Call 1-809-946-4253 or 1-404-351-2200.

Children: Y   Pets: N   Smoking: Y   Handicap Access: N   Payment: C, T

OCEAN CLUB   *Rates: moderate-deluxe*
Open: year-round   *Minimum Stay: none*

Decorated to convey a casual elegance, studio, one-, two- and three-bedroom condominium units are available at the Ocean Club, a luxurious beachside complex sitting right on the gleaming white sands of

Providenciales. Each unit contains an open living area, a fully equipped kitchen, and a private balcony offering panoramic views of Grace Bay, spectacular any time of day, but imbued with particular loveliness at sunset. The impeccably maintained grounds feature a swimming pool and Jacuzzi area, while an enticing array of other recreational opportunities in or on the translucent sea waters—diving and snorkeling, fishing and sailing, to name a few—are available nearby. Contact: Kay Stubbs, P.O. Box 240, Providenciales, Turks and Caicos, B.W.I. Call 1-809-946-4880 or 1-800-327-5039.

Children: Y   Pets: N   Smoking: Y   Handicap Access: N   Payment: All

THE ADMIRALS CLUB   *Rates: inexpensive-expensive*
Open: year-round   *Minimum Stay: none*

Decorated in an appealing nautical style, the Admiral Club is located on the scenic Turtle Cove marina of Providenciales, the colony's major vacation destination, called "Provo" by those in the know. Eight handsomely furnished one- and two-bedroom units are offered, featuring fully equipped kitchens and private balconies. The beach, glistening with white sand, is 350 feet away, and boat docking slips and fine diving facilities are also available, while the bar next door, overlooking the water, is one of the island's liveliest gathering spots. Contact: Paulette Daley, Manager, The Admirals Club, Turtle Cove, Providenciales, Turks and Caicos, B.W.I. Call 1-809-946-4375.

Children: Y Pets: N Smoking: Y Handicap Access: N Payment: C, T, A, V, M

TREASURE BEACH VILLAS   *Rates: inexpensive-moderate*
Open: year-round   *Minimum Stay: none*

The 20 alluring beachfront one- and two-bedroom homes of Treasure Beach each contain a complete kitchen and living/dining area, and offer a sunny terrace. Enjoying a tranquil tropical setting, the complex sits on a long, sandy beach, minutes from the airport. Its facilities feature a swimming pool and tennis courts, and all kinds of water sports, from diving and deep-sea fishing to swimming and windsurfing, can be enjoyed nearby on the Atlantic. There are also a variety of recreational opportunities available inland, including hiking, cycling and bird- and butterfly-watching. Contact: Treasure Beach Villas Reservations, Box 8409, Hialeah, FL 33012. Call 1-809-946-4108 or 1-303-8787-8854.

Children: Y Pets: N Smoking: Y Handicap Access: N Payment: C, T, A, V, M

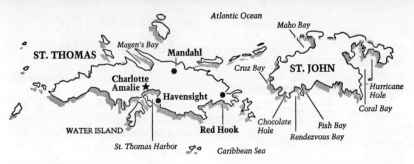

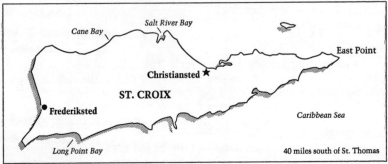

U.S.
Virgin Islands

St. Croix
Buccaneer Bay

SUNDANCE

Open: year-round

Rates: deluxe

Minimum Stay: one week

A parrot who resides in the garden welcomes you to this cheerful beachfront villa, which features a private garden, Jacuzzi and pool. Its interior is just as colorful, furnished with tropical prints and rattan, with a living room that opens onto a pool deck and more gardens. Each of the four air-conditioned bedrooms has its own bathroom opening onto a romantic courtyard garden. Across the lawn you'll find a secluded beach, where you can sunbathe on the fine white sands and swim in the crystal-clear waters. Explore the irregular coastline, once the playground of pirates. Contact: West Indies Management Company, 28 Pelham Street, Newport, RI 02840. Call 1-800-932-3222 (in Rhode Island, 401-849-8012). Ref. TC-SUD.

Children: **Y** Pets: **N** Smoking: **Y** Handicap Access: **N** Payment: **C, P, T, A**

Cane Bay

CANE BAY REEF CLUB

Open: year-round

Rates: budget-moderate

Minimum Stay: one week

The Cane Bay Reef Club is a comfortable home away from home on the north shore of St. Croix; in its cozy little poolside bar guests congregate to tell tall tales of their island adventures. It features nine two-room suites (composed of a bedroom and living area with pull-out sofa) that all have fully equipped kitchens and balconies overlooking the sea. Ceramic tile floors and airy cathedral ceilings round out the picture of relaxed stylishness. Nearby are the 18-hole Robert Trent Jones Carambola Golf Course, Cane Bay Wall (named one of the ten best diving sites in the world by *Skin Diver* magazine), historic plantation homes and the lovely Danish twin cities, Christiansted and Frederiksted. Contact: Cane Bay Reef Club, Box 1407 Kingshill, St. Croix, U.S. Virgin Islands 00851. Call 809-778-2966.

Children: N Pets: N Smoking: Y Handicap Access: N Payment: C, P, T, V, M

Cane Bay

THE WAVES AT CANE BAY　　　　　　　　　*Rates: budget-moderate*
Open: year-round　　　　　　　　　　　　*Minimum Stay: three nights*

The Waves at Cane Bay is a diminutive private resort on the north shore of St. Croix, possessing just 12 units in all, shaded by leafy coconut palms and drowsing at the water's edge. Its tidy efficiency apartments have kitchenettes, two twin beds or a king-sized bed, ceiling fans to keep the cooling trade winds blowing and screened-in balconies. Below them lie a lovely grotto-style saltwater pool and a patio bar. Groceries and other necessities are available just six miles away, and directly offshore is one of St. Croix's best snorkeling spots, the coral reef and exotic underwater world of Cane Bay Wall. Contact: The Waves at Cane Bay, P.O. Box 1749, Kingshill, St. Croix, U.S. Virgin Islands 00851. Call 1-800-545-0603 (in St. Croix, 809-778-1805).

Children: Y Pets: N Smoking: Y Handicap Access: N Payment: C, T, A, V, M

Carambola

BETTER THAN PAR　　　　　　　　　　　　*Rates: deluxe*
Open: year-round　　　　　　　　　　　　*Minimum Stay: one week*

This is, quite simply, a golfer's paradise. The master bedroom of this luxurious villa sits beside the 18th green at the Carambola Golf Course. Mahogany and glass doors that open onto a wraparound deck make the most of the lush scenery. Inside, tastefully casual furnishings and ceiling fans add to the sporting atmosphere. When you've had enough golf, cool off in the community pool. Three bedrooms and three baths provide plenty of room for vacationing groups or families. Contact: West Indies Management Company, 28 Pelham Street, Newport, RI 02840. Call 1-800-932-3222 (in Rhode Island, 401-849-8012). Ref. TC-PAR.

Children: Y Pets: N Smoking: Y Handicap Access: N Payment: C, P, T, A

Christiansted

CHENAY BAY BEACH RESORT　　　　　　*Rates: inexpensive-moderate*
Open: year-round　　　　　　　　　　　　*Minimum Stay: none*

Chenay Bay Beach Resort is a modest but extremely comfortable little enclave of cottages on the north shore of St. Croix, just 10 minutes from charming Christiansted. Honeymooners favor its neat one-room apartments with kitchenettes, ceiling fans, air conditioning and easy access to the compound's swimming pool, tennis courts, barbecue pits and casual beachside restaurant. Snorkelers and scuba divers gravitate here likewise, due to the resort's proximity to Buck Island National Monument, a 300-acre volcanic rock surrounded by 550 acres of underwater coral gardens—all just three and a half miles offshore. What's more, there's a windsurfing school on the premises. Contact: Chenay Bay Beach Resort, P.O. Box 24606, Christiansted, St. Croix, U.S. Virgin Islands 00824. Call 1-800-548-4457 (in St. Croix, 809-773-2918).

Children: Y   Pets: N   Smoking: Y   Handicap Access: N   Payment: All

Christiansted

CLUB COMANCHE   *Rates: budget-moderate*
Open: year-round   *Minimum Stay: none*

Veteran Caribbean travelers know Christiansted on the north shore of St. Croix as one of the prettiest ports in the archipelago. With yacht sails dotting the harbor, colonial-era homes and shops painted in cheerful pastels and a vintage Danish fort—built in 1749 and recently renovated by the U.S. Park Service—it's small wonder why. The Club Comanche Hotel, which features four kitchenette units, offers Christiansted explorers a comfortable and economical way to get to know both the town and the 85-square-mile island of St. Croix. The kitchenette suites have views of the water, air conditioning, cable TV and antique furnishings—and they all come with use of the biggest swimming pool in town. Contact: Club Comanche Hotel, 1 Strand Street, Christiansted, St. Croix, U.S. Virgin Islands 00820. Call 1-800-524-2066 (in St. Croix, 809-773-0210).

Children: Y   Pets: N   Smoking: Y   Handicap: N   Payment: C, T, A, V, M, O

Christiansted

CLUB ST. CROIX   *Rates: moderate-deluxe*
Open: year-round   *Minimum Stay: none*

Club St. Croix occupies a 13-acre parcel of land on the north shore of the island. Its private, 1,000-foot sandy beach fringed by palm trees looks out toward Buck Island National Monument. The Club offers a wide range of lodging options, including studios, one- to three-bedroom suites and posh penthouses, all decorated in soothing West Indian pastels. Kitchens, telephones, cable TV and maid service are all included with rental. The complex is a self-contained vacation hub, with its own tennis courts, gourmet restaurants, convenience store, two swimming pools and a marina ready to equip windsurfers, snorkelers, scuba divers and sailors for adventures in the warm blue Caribbean.Contact: Club St. Croix, Estate Golden Rock, Christiansted, St. Croix, U.S. Virgin Islands 00820. Call 1-800-635-l533 (in St. Croix, 809-773-4800).

Children: Y   Pets: N   Smoking: Y   Handicap Access: N   Payment: C, T, A, V, M

Christiansted

CORMORANT COVE   *Rates: expensive-deluxe*
Open: year-round   *Minimum Stay: none*

This luxurious beachfront complex is one of the newest in St. Croix, built in singular Danish colonial style. It features spacious one- to three-bedroom apartments overlooking the water, complete with kitchens, air conditioning, designer decor, marble baths and daily maid service. Activities at Cormorant Cove include swimming in the over-sized freshwater pool, sunbathing on the third-of-a-mile-long sandy beach, dining in the renowned Cormorant Beach Club Restaurant, playing a few sets of tennis or taking a snorkeling trip through the live reef that lies just 100 feet offshore. The resort is just three miles from delightful Christiansted, with its restored Danish fort, picturesque harbor and dozens of shops. Contact: Cormorant Cove, 4127 La Grande Princess, St. Croix, U.S. Virgin Islands 00820. Call 1-800-344-5770 (in St. Croix, 809-778-8920).

Children: Y   Pets: N   Smoking: Y   Handicap Access: N   Payment: All

Christiansted

HIGH HOPES   *Rates: deluxe*
Open: year-round   *Minimum Stay: one week*

These three bungalows join each other via covered breezeways to form a giant compound. All together, four bedroom suites make the villa perfect for large families or groups of friends traveling together. Enjoy a dip in the pool, play a round of golf at the adjacent course, or just enjoy the peaceful view of the Caribbean itself. Tasteful furnishings and five bathrooms make you feel at home, while beaches are just minutes away. Contact: West Indies Management Company, 28 Pelham Street, Newport, RI 02840. Call 1-800-932-3222 (in Rhode Island, 401-849-8012). Ref. IV-HIG.

Children: Y   Pets: N   Smoking: Y   Handicap Access: N   Payment: C, P, T, A

Christiansted

HONEYMOON COVE   *Rates: expensive-deluxe*
Open: year-round   *Minimum Stay: one week*

Honeymoon Cove is part of an exclusive residential area called Judith's Fancy after one of the island's many historic sugar plantations. It's a split-level home with a private pool and several patios perched on a small cliff overlooking the Caribbean. Inside are four bedrooms (one with a king-sized bed and three with twins, accommodating eight in all), living and dining rooms and a kitchen complete with myriad appliances, including a microwave, washer/dryer and dishwasher. The beach is a half mile away. Also nearby is the spot where Columbus landed in 1493, a championship golf course, supermarkets and all the sights and sounds of the charming Danish colonial village Christiansted. Contact: Vacation Home Rentals Worldwide, 235 Kensington Avenue, Norwood, NJ 07648. Call 1-800-NEED-A-VILLA or 1-800-633-3284 (in New Jersey, 201-767-9393). Ref. SX102.

Children: Y   Pets: N   Smoking: Y   Handicap Access: N   Payment: C, P, T

Christiansted

LADY MAGIC
Open: year-round

Rates: expensive-deluxe
Minimum Stay: one week

The evocative ruins of an old sugar mill, the rooftops of Christiansted and the wide, blue Caribbean Sea are the views from Lady Magic, a two-story villa nestled on a hillside near the exclusive Buccaneer Resort. With four bedrooms and four baths, it's roomy enough to accommodate eight. Appropriately, a tropical theme dominates the decor in the big living room, and there are ceiling fans to keep the trade winds circulating. Other amenities include linens and maid service, a fully equipped kitchen, big swimming pool surrounded by chaises, wet bar, TV, washer/dryer and telephone. Contact: Vacation Home Rentals Worldwide, 235 Kensington Avenue, Norwood, NJ 07648. Call 1-800-NEED-A-VILLA or 1-800-633-3284 (in New Jersey, 201-767-9393).

Children: Y   Pets: N   Smoking: Y   Handicap Access: N   Payment: C, P, T

Christiansted

LITTLE PRINCESS HILL
Open: year-round

Rates: expensive-deluxe
Minimum Stay: one week

A Danish colonial-era gem, Christiansted, with its fort, historic wharf and Steeple Building, is considered one of the most picturesque towns in the whole Caribbean. Little Princess Hill overlooks its rooftops as well as a 40-mile panorama of the Caribbean, which takes in St. Thomas to the north. Wicker furniture and Italian tile floors grace its interior, which is composed of a living room, modern kitchen, three bedrooms and two baths. Each bedroom opens directly onto a private patio, and in the master suite there's a sunken tub and rooftop garden. Outside is a pool with a 12-foot European sunbathing seat, a deck, a private beach, a boat mooring and lush tropical gardens. Contact: Rent A Home International, Inc., 7200 34th Street, N.W., Seattle, WA 98117. Call 206-545-6963.

Children: Y Pets: N Smoking: Y Handicap Access: N Payment: C, P, T, V, M

Christiansted

LOBSTER DOC
Open: year-round

Rates: inexpensive-moderate
Minimum Stay: one week

Near Christiansted and overlooking Grapetree Bay, this villa is a fine rental value, offering guests room to spread out in three comfortably decorated bedrooms sharing three baths. It sits on a hilltop, from which a winding path leads down to the beach. Nearby is the Grapetree Bay Hotel, where water sports enthusiasts can rent sailing, windsurfing, snorkeling and scuba equipment, play tennis or dine in elegant surroundings. Back at the villa, there's a well-equipped kitchen, TV, telephone, and sun deck for quiet snoozes or private suntanning stints. Contact: Vacation Home Rentals Worldwide, 235 Kensington Avenue, Norwood, NJ 07648. Call 1-800-NEED-A-VILLA or 1-800-633-3284 (in New Jersey, 201-767-9393).

Children: Y   Pets: N   Smoking: Y   Handicap Access: N   Payment: C, P, T

Christiansted

MARCH HOUSE   *Rates: expensive-deluxe*
Open: year-round   *Minimum Stay: one week*

The tropical decor and island art in this delightful house set the stage for an adventurous vacation in unique St. Croix. The breezy, furnished courtyard surrounded by native greenery gazes out over Christiansted. A bedroom in the main house and another in the separate pavilion make the villa perfect for families or two couples. Cool off in the pool, then explore the many wonders of the island, including refuges for birds and leatherback turtles, botanical gardens and even an undersea park. Contact: West Indies Management Company, 28 Pelham Street, Newport, RI 02840. Call 1-800-932-3222 (in Rhode Island, 401-849-8012). Ref. IV-MAR.

Children: Y   Pets: N   Smoking: Y   Handicap Access: N   Payment: C, P, T, A

Christiansted

QUEEN'S QUARTER   *Rates: moderate-deluxe*
Open: year-round   *Minimum Stay: one week*

Hills tumbling down to the sea create stunning views from this picturesque mountainside villa. Each bedroom opens onto the pool and its furnished patio, perfect for late night or early morning dips. Skylights let the sun and stars shine in on the cool stone walls of each bedroom's private bath. The sunken living room offers relaxation after a day of discovery at the wildlife refuges, working harbors and botanical gardens throughout St. Croix. Contact: West Indies Management Company, 28 Pelham Street, Newport, RI 02840. Call 1-800-932-3222 (in Rhode Island, 401-849-8012). Ref. IV-VAL.

Children: Y   Pets: N   Smoking: Y   Handicap Access: N   Payment: C, P, T, A

Christiansted

SEAVIEW VILLA   *Rates: deluxe*
Open: year-round   *Minimum Stay: one week*

This luxurious modern villa boasts breathtaking ocean views and a charming courtyard with a relaxing fountain, pool and covered patio, perfect for outdoor dining morning and night. Comfortable rattan furnishings decorated in cool tropical colors create an airy, homey ambiance. Air conditioning keeps the master bedroom cool, but you probably won't need it on St. Croix, which is constantly bathed in cooling trade winds. Nearby Buccaneer Resort provides the beaches, sailing, snorkeling, horseback riding, golf and tennis you seek on a vacation. Contact: West Indies Management Company, 28 Pelham Street, Newport, RI 02840. Call 1-800-932-3222 (in Rhode Island, 401-849-8012). Ref. FR-VIL.

Children: Y   Pets: N   Smoking: Y   Handicap Access: N   Payment: C, P, T, A

Christiansted

SPYGLASS HILL VILLA
Open: year-round

Rates: expensive-deluxe
Minimum Stay: one week

A Jacuzzi and swimming pool relax the body while tranquil decor soothes the soul in this walled garden villa. From the porch just off the dining/living room, gaze out over Christiansted Harbor—there's even a telescope to give you a better view. All three bedrooms feature fine views, too, along with large baths. The modern kitchen supplies all the tools you need to create sumptuous meals. Sliding glass doors surround you with island scenery. Contact: West Indies Management Company, 28 Pelham Street, Newport, RI 02840. Call 1-800-932-3222 (in Rhode Island, 401-849-8012). Ref. IV-SPY.

Children: Y Pets: N Smoking: Y Handicap Access: N Payment: C, P, T, A

Concordia

SONGBIRD
Open: year-round

Rates: expensive-deluxe
Minimum Stay: one week

Stone-inlaid pathways through tropical woods lead to this breezy villa, which graces a tropical hillside overlooking the sea. Sliding glass doors keep the interior bright and cool, while an outdoor pool keeps you refreshed and relaxed. Three bedrooms and four baths give guests plenty of living space. An indoor/outdoor garden and a large oval tub make the master bedroom something special. Contact: West Indies Management Company, 28 Pelham Street, Newport, RI 02840. Call 1-800-932-3222 (in Rhode Island, 401-849-8012). Ref. IV-SON.

Children: Y Pets: N Smoking: Y Handicap Access: N Payment: C, P, T, A

East End

THE TREEHOUSE
Open: year-round

Rates: deluxe
Minimum Stay: one week

This homey yet romantic tropical enclave is located on St. Croix's prestigious eastern shore. It's a two-story villa surrounded by dense greenery to ensure privacy, with a freshwater pool and deck. The interior features island mahogany and rattan, colorful Oriental rugs, original artwork, ceramics and stained glass. The master bedroom has a king-sized water bed, and in the second sleeping chamber there's a regular king. Other amenities include exercise equipment, a modern kitchen, 45-inch TV/VCR, stereo/tape deck and microwave. Contact: Rent A Home International, Inc., 7200 34th Street, N.W., Seattle, WA 98117. Call 206-545-6963.

Children: Y Pets: N Smoking: Y Handicap Access: N Payment: C, P, T, V, M

Frederiksted

BUTLER BAY PLANTATION
Open: year-round

Rates: deluxe
Minimum Stay: one week

Take a step back in time at this 18th-century Danish West Indian great house, listed in the National Register of Historic Places. A cool, covered courtyard complete with wicker furniture elicits the feel of an old plantation, while a swimming pool and Jacuzzi update the amenities.

Four bedrooms with four-poster canopied beds evoke this villa's charming past. Lush greenery surrounding the property fills the air with the fragrance of tropical foliage. Contact: West Indies Management Company, 28 Pelham Street, Newport, RI 02840. Call 1-800-932-3222 (in Rhode Island, 401-849-8012). Ref. RA-BBP.

Children: **Y** Pets: **N** Smoking: **Y** Handicap Access: **N** Payment: **C, P, T, A**

Frederiksted

COTTAGES BY THE SEA   *Rates: budget-inexpensive*
Open: year-round   *Minimum Stay: two nights*

St. Croix, 1,000 miles southeast of Miami, has the distinction of being the only locale now under the American flag that was visited by Christopher Columbus. Back in 1493 he was driven away by hostile Indians; today the reception for visitors is much warmer, particularly at pretty little Cottages by the Sea, a scant half-mile south of Frederiksted on the island's west coast. Its efficiency units with kitchenettes and maid service lie two to 40 yards from a beach. Many have their own private patios and outdoor grills. Ceiling fans, cable TV and air conditioning are other standard features. Contact: Cottages by the Sea, Box 1697, Frederiksted, St. Croix, U.S. Virgin Islands 00841. Call 1-800-323-7252 (in St. Croix, 809-772-0495).

Children: **Y**   Pets: **N**   Smoking: **Y**   Handicap Access: **N**   Payment: **All**

Frederiksted

ESTATE PROSPECT HILL   *Rates: deluxe*
Open: year-round   *Minimum Stay: one week*

This spacious five-bedroom villa is set on three acres of landscaped grounds lush with blooming tropical plants, swaying palms and a garden fountain. Plenty of lounge chairs around the enormous tiled swimming pool make for long lazy days in the sun; a gazebo provides shelter and a comfortable place for casual outdoor dining. More formal dining is possible inside at a table that seats 12. Families or groups of friends will be delighted with this villa, which even has a tennis court for impromptu games. A white sand beach is within walking distance. Contact: West Indies Management Company, 28 Pelham Street, Newport, RI 02840. Call 1-800-932-3222 (in Rhode Island, 401-849-8012). Ref. RA-PEC.

Children: **Y** Pets: **N** Smoking: **Y** Handicap Access: **N** Payment: **C, P, T, A**

Frederiksted

FREDERIKSTED VILLA   *Rates: moderate-expensive*
Open: year-round   *Minimum Stay: one week*

Surrounded by one and a half acres of landscaped lawns and a broad stretch of golden sand and turquoise surf, this vacation home is a perfect spot for Caribbean-style relaxation. A 65-foot gallery faces the ocean, adjoining the handsomely decorated, tile-floor living area. Its two bedrooms have private baths; and additional sleeping arrangements can be made. Linens, a laundry room, a full-time caretaker and modern kitchen with dishwasher are all included. The villa makes a fine base for exploring beautiful St. Croix, an island slightly lower keyed than neighboring St. Thomas and dotted with historic sugar plantations, beaches and bays that beckon water sports enthusiasts. Contact: Rent A Home International, Inc., 7200 34th St., N.W., Seattle, WA 98117. Call 206-545-6963.

Children: Y Pets: N Smoking: Y Handicap Access: N Payment: C, P, T, V, M

Frederiksted

WILLIAM'S WHIM   *Rates: deluxe*
Open: year-round   *Minimum Stay: one week*

William's Whim sits right on the beach at the historic Whim estate, two miles southeast of Frederiksted, a deep-water port where cruise ships dock. Its 60-foot gallery spans the length of the house, allowing tropical trade winds to filter in. There are three big bedrooms in the main house, each with its own bath, and two more located in a second wing, reached by a breezeway. William's Whim is close to golf, tennis and shopping. By special arrangement, the rental can include a cook, membership at the La Grange Beach and Tennis Club and a boat charter. Contact: Rent A Home International, Inc., 7200 34th St., N.W., Seattle, WA 98117. Call 206-545-6963.

Children: Y Pets: N Smoking: Y Handicap Access: N Payment: C, P, T, V, M

Long Point Bay

HIBISCUS HOUSE   *Rates: deluxe*
Open: year-round   *Minimum Stay: one week*

This villa's rich decor, stunning architecture and lush surroundings will tempt you to stay forever. Arched verandas, French doors and Danish shutters provide a graceful elegance that extends to the two master bedrooms in the main house. An adjacent cottage holds two more bedrooms, plus a second living room and kitchenette. All together, five bathrooms provide for everyone's privacy and comfort. Outside, a swimming pool awaits, shaded by tranquil palm trees; just 100 feet away, Long Point Bay Beach offers fine bathing. Contact: West Indies Management Company, 28 Pelham Street, Newport, RI 02840. Call 1-800-932-3222 (in Rhode Island, 401-849-8012). Ref. IV-HIB.

Children: Y Pets: N Smoking: Y Handicap Access: N Payment: C, P, T, A

Oakley Bay

OAKLEY BAY CONDOMINIUMS   *Rates: moderate-expensive*
Open: year-round   *Minimum Stay: five nights*

Oakley Bay Condominiums face St. Croix's magnificent Buck Island National Monument, a scuba and snorkeling paradise, rookery for frigate birds and pelicans and hatchery for the endangered green turtle. The three-story complex is luxurious by any measure, with its own freshwater swimming pool, in-season restaurant and nearby beach. Two-bedroom suites feature 1,500 square feet of living space, two baths, telephones, fully equipped kitchens, balconies with grills and cable TV. Fifteen minutes away lies lovely Christiansted, a fine spot to explore historic sites and a picture-perfect harbor. Contact: Rent A

Home International, Inc., 7200 34th Steet, N.W., Seattle, WA 98117.
Call 206-545-6963.
Children: Y Pets: N Smoking: Y Handicap Access: N Payment: C, P, T, V, M

Salt River Bay

COLUMBUS LANDING   *Rates: deluxe*
Open: year-round   *Minimum stay: one week*

This north shore St. Croix villa overlooks a landmark—the landing
site of Christopher Columbus, a place he named Cabo de la Fleches (or
Cape of the Arrows) due to the reception the fierce Carib Indians gave
him and his crew. A 2,100-square-foot living room provides views of
the infamous cape through a spacious gallery. Right outside is a deck
and pool lined with cushioned lounge chairs. Three bedrooms and two
baths make Columbus Landing Villa suitable for groups or families of
up to seven. Nearby is the world-class Carambola Golf Course, Buck
Island National Monument and the duty-free shops and restaurants of
pretty Christiansted. Contact: Rent A Home International, Inc., 7200
34th Street, N.W., Seattle, WA 98117. Call 206-545-6963.
Children: Y Pets: N Smoking: Y Handicap Access: N Payment: C, P, T, V, M

Salt River Bay

LANDMARK VILLA   *Rates: deluxe*
Open: year-round   *Minimum Stay: one week*

The style of this stunning St. Croix hideaway is singular: It's Japanese, with interior decorations to match. Surrounded by one and a half
acres and set on a hill overlooking Columbus Landing, it has three
bedrooms and three baths equipped with hair dryers and scales. The
lavish master bedroom is located on the main floor and has a water bed
and sea views; two more bedrooms are reached by a fanciful spiral
staircase from the living room. A fully stocked bar, stereo system, CD
player and TV/VCR complete with an excellent collection of movies
makes the sitting area a true home away from home. Lining its walls
are shelves of books, including guides to local flora and fauna. There's
a 40-foot pool outside, as well as a deck with a sunny southern exposure, and at the foot of the hill a broad sandy shore. Contact: Rent A
Home International, Inc., 7200 34th Street, N.W., Seattle, WA 98117.
Call 206-545-6963.
Children: Y Pets: N Smoking: Y Handicap Access: N Payment: C, P, T, V, M

ST. JOHN

Boatman's Point

VILLA CAPRI   *Rates: deluxe*
Open: year-round   *Minimum Stay: one week*

This luxurious five-bedroom villa is a fabulous holiday home for large
groups, family reunions, or those who expect to do some entertaining.
The elegantly appointed interior features marble floors and wide-open
spaces. French doors open off the living room to the generous balcony.
Around the large swimming pool there are more decks and terraces,

many with comfortable furniture and all with spectacular views. Indeed, from its hilltop position, this villa offers unobstructed panoramas in every direction. Contact: LaCure Villas, 11661 San Vicente Blvd., Suite 1010, Los Angeles, CA 90049. Call 1-800-387-2715.

Children: Y   Pets: N   Smoking: Y   Handicap Access: N   Payment: C, T

Calabash Boom

PELICAN PEEK   *Rates: expensive*
Open: year-round   *Minimum Stay: one week*

Built as the owner's dream home in 1981, this gracious hillside home for six overlooks the protected lands of the Virgin Islands National Park. Views from the sprawling covered porch and sun deck encompass many offshore reefs and cays, the gentle movement of sailboats in the bay and pelicans diving for their lunch. Beautifully appointed with lovely wicker furniture, the house offers three bedrooms and is cooled throughout by softly whirring ceiling fans. A vacation in this beautiful home on the smallest of the Virgin Islands offers a wealth diversions, from the shops, restaurants and calypso clubs of Cruz Bay to the twisting trails, mysterious petroglyphs and ruined sugar plantations in the national park. Contact: C. Kroos, Villa Holidays, Inc., 13100 Wayzata Blvd., Suite 150, Minneapolis, MN 55343. Call 1-800-328-6262.

Children: Y Pets: N Smoking: Y Handicap Access: N Payment: C, P, T, V, M

Calabash Boom

THE WELLS HOUSE   *Rates: expensive*
Open: year-round   *Minimum Stay: one week*

Activity in this sprawling house usually centers on a huge wraparound deck with an incredible panoramic view of Coral Bay, Tortola and Norman Island (known to many as Treasure Island). An eight-person Jacuzzi sunk in the deck provides the perfect spot for enjoying the view; an outdoor dining area and barbecue complete the picture nicely. Accommodations for eight include the tiled living/dining room with sliding glass doors and a bar area overlooking the kitchen—an ideal post from which to harass the cook. Two double bedrooms in the main house, two additional doubles in a separate bedroom house and a screened-in living area connecting the two houses make for roomy comfort. If you can get yourself to leave this hillside paradise, you are of course only minutes away from the beautiful sandy beaches and natural beauty of the national park. Contact: Abigail Imbrie, Imbrie Design and Management, Inc., P.O. Box 426, St. John, U.S. Virgin Islands 00831. Call 809-776-6680.

Children: Y   Pets: N   Smoking: Y   Handicap Access: N   Payment: C, P, T

Chocolate Hole

ARGONAUTA   *Rates: deluxe*
Open: year-round   *Minimum Stay: one week*

The hilly emerald of St. John awaits you with gorgeous beaches and endless blue skies. The Argonauta sits on the crest of Constant Point, commanding excellent views in every direction—the prospect toward Chocolate Hole across Pillsbury Sound to St. Thomas is particularly nice. Inside you'll find two sumptuous bedrooms in addition to the spacious main rooms of the house, which feature an open floor plan and high, exposed-beam ceilings. The rooms throughout are adorned with French country furnishings and vivid Mexican tiles. This quiet retreat is the perfect place to spend your days in tropical solitude, yet the charm of the town is only five minutes away. Contact: West Indies Management Company, 28 Pelham St., Newport, RI 02840. Call 1-800-932-3222 (in Rhode Island, 401-849-8012). Ref. VV-ARG.

Children: Y Pets: N Smoking: Y Handicap Access: N Payment: C, P, T, A

Chocolate Hole

AURORA   *Rates: deluxe*
Open: year-round   *Minimum Stay: one week*

Slim columns, covered walkways, pale walls and arched doorways give an air of neoclassical elegance to this unusual villa. The main part of the house boasts three spacious bedrooms, two of which open to the large deck overlooking the pool, providing lovely views of Pillsbury Sound. The splendidly appointed master suite is downstairs; it has its own sitting area and private bathroom and opens directly to the pool area—you can roll right out of bed and into the refreshing water, if you choose. The sunny patio is festively planted with several local varieties, including a shady palm. Contact: West Indies Management Company, 28 Pelham St., Newport, RI 02840. Call 1-800-932-3222 (in Rhode Island, 401-849-8012). Ref. CT-AUR.

Children: Y Pets: N Smoking: Y Handicap Access: N Payment: C, P, T, A

Chocolate Hole

DELUXE VILLA   *Rates: deluxe*
Open: year-round   *Minimum Stay: one week*

This is what dreams are made of! Located only minutes from some of the world's most beautiful beaches and coral reefs, this magnificent home provides the ideal setting for your vacation. From the large veranda and the beautifully furnished deck—chaise lounges, umbrella table, chairs and a gas grill—surrounding the luxurious swimming pool, you and your family and friends can take in the stunning views of the sea, the lush green mountains and the endless sky of St. John. Inside, the living/dining room and open kitchen promise hours of comfortable relaxation, and each of the four bedrooms opens onto either the pool terrace or a large furnished patio. Try horseback riding across the hills and along the beaches, or enjoy a fine meal at the famed Caneel Bay Resort or the Grand Virgin Beach Hotel. Contact: Barry Shepard, At Home Abroad, Inc., 405 East 56th St., 6H, New York, NY 10022. Call 212-421-9165.

Children: Y Pets: N Smoking: Y Handicap Access: N Payment: C, P, T

Chocolate Hole

FRENCH CAP
Open: year-round

Rates: expensive-deluxe
Minimum Stay: one week

The magnificent great room at the center of this home boasts incredibly high ceilings and massive stone archways. Sliding glass doors open to a wraparound deck, a partially covered outdoor living area that enjoys splendid unobstructed views of Deever's Bay. The two spacious bedrooms, located on either side of the great room, also open onto this deck, an arrangement designed to help you perfect the indoor-outdoor lifestyle of the tropics. You'll want to spend at least one lazy afternoon on the deck, lulled by the blues and greens of the scenery and perhaps sipping some of St. John's famous bay rum. Contact: West Indies Management Company, 28 Pelham St., Newport, RI 02840. Call 1-800-932-3222 (in Rhode Island, 401-849-8012). Ref. HH-CAP.

Children: Y Pets: N Smoking: Y Handicap Access: N Payment: C, P, T, A

Chocolate Hole

LIMETREE
Open: year-round

Rates: moderate-deluxe
Minimum Stay: one week

This unusual home in the exclusive Chocolate Hole Estate is shaped like a V, which gives every room delightful views of either the tropical gardens that surround it or the exquisite bays below. Modern conveniences include a microwave, a color TV and a VCR. Concealed in the master bathroom is a special treat: the sunken tiled tub is bordered by a lush indoor garden. There are three comfy bedrooms in all. Although it's placed high on a hill and away from the bustle, Limetree is actually only a few minutes away from the local beaches, shops, sports facilities and restaurants. Contact: Katherine DeMar, Vacation Homes, P.O. Box 272, Cruz Bay, St. John, U.S.V.I. 00831. Call 809-776-6094.

Children: Y Pets: N Smoking: Y Handicap Access: N Payment: C, P, T

Chocolate Hole

SEA VIEW
Open: year-round

Rates: expensive-deluxe
Minimum Stay: one week

From the terrace, decks and splendid swimming pool which make this brand-new four-bedroom villa one of the island's choicest homes, your view of St. John's beautiful south shore is dotted with boats sailing in and out of Chocolate Hole. This elegant house features tropical architecture at its best—creamy stucco with a red tile roof surrounded by always blooming bougainvillaea and other tropical plants. You can retire from the splendor of the outdoors to a cool and comfortable rattan-furnished interior, where a cable TV, VCR and CD player offer the best in entertainment. Ten minutes in your Jeep will take you to the picturesque port of Cruz Bay where marketing, restaurants and shopping are plentiful. Contact: Eileen Sundra, P.O. Box 704, Cruz Bay, St. John, U.S. Virgin Islands 00830. Call 809-776-6641.

Children: Y Pets: N Smoking: Y Handicap Access: N Payment: C, P, T

Chocolate Hole

SOUTHERN COMFORT
Open: year-round

Rates: inexpensive-moderate
Minimum Stay: one week

With a name so evocative you can practically taste the mint juleps, this home for four is situated on a bay at the southwestern corner of the island. Your deck's wonderful 180-degree views of the sea and the island of St. Thomas will spark your imagination. Appointments such as white stucco walls, tile floors and high-beamed ceilings and the lushness of tropical plants and flowers all around make this two-bedroom, two-bathroom retreat the answer to your vacation prayers. Conveniences include a color TV with VCR, a cassette deck and a washer/dryer. For excitement and diversion, a walk in the volcanic mountains may introduce you to a wild burro or a mongoose. And in addition to endless water sports, you may also enjoy hiking to the petroglyphs and exploring the old sugar plantations. Contact: Private Homes for Private Vacations, Mary-Phyllis Nogueira, Mamey Peak, St. John, U.S. Virgin Islands 00830. Call 809-776-6876.

Children: Y   Pets: N   Smoking: Y   Handicap Access: N   Payment: C, P, T

Chocolate Hole

THE TEMPTRESS
Open: year-round

Rates: expensive-deluxe
Minimum Stay: two weeks

This exquisite, contemporary, modular home constructed of glass, masonry and natural stone offers the kind of detail featured in *Architectural Digest*. Accommodations for four include a living room furnished in island rattan, an aviary, a dining room and a kitchen filled with conveniences such as a blender, a juicer, a food processor and a dishwasher. Rambling decks with chairs, chaise lounges and a barbecue offer breathtaking views of four of St. John's prettiest bays, and decorative fountains and well-maintained tropical gardens adorn the grounds. A ten-minute walk leads to an excellent snorkeling beach; tennis and golf devotees can make use of the nearby courts and 18-hole course. Contact: Lori Gedon, Vacation Home Rentals Worldwide, 235 Kensington Avenue, Norwood, NJ 07648. Call 1-800-633-3284. Ref. SJ100.

Children: N   Pets: N   Smoking: Y   Handicap Access: N   Payment: C, P, T

Chocolate Hole

VILLA PRASANTHI
Open: Dec. 15-April 15

Rates: deluxe
Minimum Stay: one week

Interiors with tasteful rattan furniture, spacious rooms of natural wood and local stone, wide verandas with beautiful sea views and all around you the magnificence of pristine Virgin Islands National Park: If you wake here, you may think you are dreaming! Villa Prasanthi offers luxurious accommodations for six people, which include three bedrooms (one with skylights for star-gazing), an indoor tropical garden, a sun-drenched deck furnished for dining and the privacy of estate living. And yet, only five minutes away you'll find Virgin Grand Beach, and a little beyond are the nightspots and shops of Cruz Bay. Contact: Villas International, 71 West 23rd Street, New York, NY 10010. Call 212-929-7585.

Children: Y Pets: N Smoking: Y Handicap Access: N Payment: C, P, T

Chocolate Hole

WINCHESTER   *Rates: inexpensive-moderate*
Open: year-round   *Minimum Stay: one week*

Sparkling tile, warm woods and loving care grace this charming hillside home that enjoys lovely views of the shimmering turquoise sea and neighboring St. Croix. Open to the sea breezes from its roost above the bays of Chocolate Hole North, this home sleeps four in perfect privacy, with each of the two bedrooms with bath on a separate level. With the added comfort of a telephone, a color TV and a VCR, only determination will get you out of the house to the sandy beaches nearby. Go on to explore the miles of tropical wilderness of the national park or schedule a sailing lesson in Cruz Bay. And don't forget to try a refreshing drink made from the local soursop fruit. Contact: Private Homes for Private Vacations, Mary-Phyllis Nogueira, Mamey Peak, St. John, U.S. Virgin Islands 00830. Call 809-776-6876.

Children: Y Pets: N Smoking: Y Handicap Access: N Payment: C, P, T

Cinnamon Bay

AEOLIA   *Rates: expensive-deluxe*
Open: year-round   *Minimum Stay: one week*

Cinnamon Bay boasts some excellent snorkeling—which you may discover if you can tear yourself away from your own private holiday paradise on the hill. The main living area of the house opens on three sides to a spacious, sunny patio with panoramic views of white sands, blue waters and the verdant British Virgin Islands. Lush tropical plants adorn this patio, a perfect spot to soak up a bit of the magical sunshine with a cool rum punch in hand. Two bedrooms (each with its own bathroom) are found off the living room; downstairs is another bedroom with its own bathroom. Contact: West Indies Management Company, 28 Pelham St., Newport, RI 02840. Call 1-800-932-3222 (in Rhode Island, 401-849-8012). Ref. VV-AEO.

Children: Y Pets: N Smoking: Y Handicap Access: N Payment: C, P, T, A

Cinnamon Bay

CINNAMON RIDGE   *Rates: moderate-expensive*
Open: year-round   *Minimum Stay: one week*

One of the island's most spacious and luxurious homes, the five-bedroom Cinnamon Ridge enjoys the elegant appointments of island stone, high ceilings and heavy tiled floors. With accommodations for ten and wrap-around decks, this hillside retreat on the north shore of the island overlooks the shimmering waters of Cinnamon Bay. You'll be sure to enjoy the many conveniences that make a vacation truly restful—a dishwasher and washer/dryer, a color TV with cable and a VCR, an outdoor grill and a telephone. From here you can explore the volcanic beauty of this island's shoreline and forested interior by foot, by Jeep and by boat. A short drive brings you to the shops and restaurants of Cruz Bay and home again to the nighttime wonder of this beautiful hillside retreat. Contact: Private Homes for Private Vacations, Mary-Phyllis Nogueira, Mamey Peak, St. John, U.S. Virgin Islands 00830. Call 809-776-6876.

Children: Y   Pets: N   Smoking: Y   Handicap Access: N   Payment: C, P, T

Cinnamon Bay

PALMELUND   *Rates: moderate-expensive*
Open: year-round   *Minimum Stay: one week*

Warm and glowing Brazilian hardwood accents a 24-foot sliding glass door that opens onto the fabulous deck of this spacious home. Here, spectacular views of the sparkling blue sea, dramatic cliffs and sandy beaches offer uninterrupted amazement and delight. A master bedroom with its own double Jacuzzi and two additional bedrooms with baths accommodate six. A color TV with a VCR and cable, a cassette deck, a washer/dryer and too many other conveniences to list assure you all the comforts of home and then some. Excursions to the nearby sugar plantations, a game of tennis, an afternoon amid the colorful wonders of the island's coral reefs—all will thrill you. At day's end, return to your luxurious holiday home where the colors of yet another exquisite U.S. Virgin Islands' sunset fill the sky. Contact: Private Homes for Private Vacations, Mary-Phyllis Nogueira, Mamey Peak, St. John, U.S. Virgin Islands 00830. Call 809-776-6876.

Children: N   Pets: N   Smoking: Y   Handicap Access: N   Payment: C, P, T

Coral Bay

BAYVIEW   *Rates: moderate*
Open: year-round   *Minimum Stay: one week*

Two buildings connected by huge decks on each of two levels comprise this truly magnificent house for four. The main house features a living room and kitchen with two walls of glass doors opening the entire interior to panoramic views of Coral Bay and neighboring Tortola. Sleeping quarters on the two levels of the adjoining house afford maximum privacy for two couples. On the lower level, you'll also find the swimming pool, ideal for cool dips by day and languorous swims under the stars. Tear yourself away from this paradise, if you can, to charter a sunfish or a windsurfer, or to express your true nature as a beach bum, mountain hiker or shell collector. Contact: Abigail Imbrie, Imbrie Design and Management, Inc., P.O. Box 426, St. John, U.S. Virgin Islands 00831. Call 809-776-6680.

Children: Y   Pets: N   Smoking: Y   Handicap Access: N   Payment: C, P, T

Coral Bay

CORAL RHAPSODY   *Rates: moderate*
Open: year-round   *Minimum Stay: one week*

The name of this gorgeous home is no exaggeration: The magnificent 30-foot paneled living and dining room with cathedral ceiling opens onto a wide, covered wrap-around deck. From here, stunning views of

Bordeaux Mountain and Coral Bay are themselves a rhapsody of tropical beauty. A kitchen superbly equipped with a microwave, grill, blender and dishwasher, a sky-lit master bedroom and two bedrooms on the lower level complete these accommodations for six. The beaches on the north and south shores, with their miles of coral reefs, white sands and sea shells, lay only a short ride away. And on St. John, national park status ensures that nearly every hilltop and tropical forest is protected and preserved. Contact: Abigail Imbrie, Imbrie Design and Management, Inc., P.O. Box 426, St. John, U.S. Virgin Islands 00831. Call 809-776-6680.

Children: Y   Pets: N   Smoking: Y   Handicap Access: N   Payment: C, P, T

Coral Bay

EAST GATE   *Rates: moderate*
Open: year-round   *Minimum Stay: one week*

Decorative details abound in this spacious home for eight, situated in the middle of the island. Outdoor living here is enhanced by a wide covered deck with a dining table and chairs. Beyond that, an open deck gives you the distinct feeling that you are floating above Coral Bay. The two-level, four-bedroom house also features a spectacular living and dining room with a magnificent mahogany bar opening into the kitchen area. Beautiful red glazed Mexican tile covers the floors of the entire main level and unglazed tiles finish the decks. Sail on a trade wind or ride your Jeep down to the nearby beaches or the town of Cruz Bay, where goods, services and calypso make life on St. John lively. Contact: Abigail Imbrie, Imbrie Design and Management, Inc., P.O. Box 426, St. John, U.S. Virgin Islands 00831. Call 809-776-6680.

Children: Y   Pets: N   Smoking: Y   Handicap Access: N   Payment: C, P, T

Coral Bay

FRANGIPANI   *Rates: moderate*
Open: year-round   *Minimum Stay: one week*

Two couples will find this lovely home ideal for a vacation offering both complete privacy and the pleasure of each other's company when desired. The main floor features a large deck, perfect for daytime sunning and nighttime star gazing, a living room, a kitchen, and above, a lovely bedroom with windows on four sides. The lower level provides a complete apartment with a shady deck, a living room, a kitchen, a bedroom and a bath. From this hillside spot surrounded by wild and fragrant frangipani, you can plan all sorts of expeditions to the many island ruins, old sugar plantations, the village of Cruz Bay with its many shops and restaurants and of course to the beaches and the waters that make this island the natural beauty it is. Contact: Abigail Imbrie, Imbrie Design and Management, Inc., P.O. Box 426, St. John, U.S. Virgin Islands 00831. Call 809-776-6680.

Children: Y   Pets: N   Smoking: Y   Handicap Access: N   Payment: C, P, T

Coral Bay

INTERLUDE
Rates: moderate
Open: year-round
Minimum Stay: one week

Two separate structures connected by a very large wooden deck comprise this carefully designed home. The main house features an immense living room with sliding glass doors on three sides, affording a wide angle view of Coral Bay and neighboring Tortola. The kitchen within is equipped with a dishwasher and a microwave, and on the lower level this house has one double bedroom. The house offers two additional bedrooms, and between them, a large bath with a garden shower and a sunken tub. Though you may arrive determined to do nothing more than meditate on the beautiful vistas, the water will call to you, and you will find your way to the beaches, the coral reefs, the windsurfing, snorkeling and scuba diving for which this island is so famous. Contact: Abigail Imbrie, Imbrie Design and Management, Inc., P.O. Box 426, St. John, U.S. Virgin Islands 00831. Call 809-776-6680.

Children: Y   Pets: N   Smoking: Y   Handicap Access: N   Payment: C, P, T

Coral Bay

ISLAND BREEZE
Rates: inexpensive
Open: year-round
Minimum Stay: one week

Take a private road to this charming house set in the midst of a tropical garden. This quiet and secluded villa features a gracious living room opening onto a large screened porch and offering calming views of the many sailboats on lovely Coral Bay. A kitchen, an open-air shower, a master bedroom (which also opens onto the porch), a second bedroom and a study with twin couches complete the substantial accommodations here. Located only a short distance from East Gate and Coral Rhapsody, these houses provide a comfortable holiday setting for two families or groups of friends. In your Jeeps, you can drive caravan-style to the beautiful north shore beaches. Contact: Abigail Imbrie, Imbrie Design and Management, Inc., P.O. Box 426, St. John, U.S. Virgin Islands 00831. Call 809-776-6680.

Children: Y   Pets: N   Smoking: Y   Handicap Access: N   Payment: C, P, T

Coral Bay

MIRAMAR
Rates: inexpensive-moderate
Open: year-round
Minimum Stay: one week

Three sets of French doors reveal the beautiful vistas of Coral Bay and the British Virgin Islands beyond. This breezy retreat, only a few minutes from the north shore beaches, features rich island stonework. Accommodations for six include three bedrooms and a large deck where the glowing sun greets early risers each morning. With this home as your base camp, you can plan your days around activities in the national park: guided snorkeling tours, hikes through the tropical forest, explorations of the sugar plantations and more. And of course, the glorious waters and incomparable reefs and fish of the U.S. Virgin Islands are yours by boat or flipper! Contact: Private Homes for Private

Vacations, Mary-Phyllis Nogueira, Mamey Peak, St. John, U.S. Virgin Islands 00830. Call 809-776-6876.

Children: Y   Pets: N   Smoking: Y   Handicap Access: N   Payment: C, P, T

Coral Bay

PALOMA

Open: year-round

Rates: inexpensive
Minimum Stay: one week

Two entirely self-contained levels make this spacious house for six ideally suited for two vacationing couples or families. The upper level includes a large living room that opens onto a large screened deck, blending indoor and outdoor space into one lovely tropical garden space. You'll also find the kitchen and large master bedroom suite on this floor. On the lower level, two bedrooms, a living room with a kitchenette and a deck surrounded by lush greenery overlooking Coral Bay complete the accommodations. You can hire a crewed sailboat for the day, take the ferry to nearby St. Thomas or trek through the hills of the national park to ancient petroglyphs and old sugar plantations. Contact: Abigail Imbrie, Imbrie Design and Management, Inc., P.O. Box 426, St. John, U.S. Virgin Islands 00831. Call 809-776-6680.

Children: Y   Pets: N   Smoking: Y   Handicap Access: N   Payment: C, P, T

Coral Bay

THE GARDEN

Open: year-round

Rates: moderate
Minimum Stay: one week

Perched on the highest spot on St. John atop 1,250-foot Bordeaux Mountain, this astoundingly private home for six commands a panoramic view of the east end of the island, including Coral Bay and the British Virgin Islands. Sit on the beautiful deck on a starlit night for a sight not easily forgotten. This large home includes a spacious and particularly comfortable living room with a dining area, a kitchen, and three bedrooms, one of which features sliding glass doors onto the deck. When you come down from your mountain you can enjoy a snorkeling lesson or a guided tour through the national park. Nighttime amusements in the village of Cruz Bay—calypso, reggae and dancing—provide island diversion. Contact: Abigail Imbrie, Imbrie Design and Management, Inc., P.O. Box 426, St. John, U.S. Virgin Islands 00831. Call 809-776-6680.

Children: Y   Pets: N   Smoking: Y   Handicap Access: N   Payment: C, P, T

Coral Bay

THE PRINCE HOUSE

Open: year-round

Rates: moderate
Minimum Stay: one week

Located on the southeasterly slope of Bordeaux Mountain about 300 feet above the sea, this generously proportioned home overlooks the settlement of Emmaus with its picturesque Moravian Church, historic Fort Burt and the beautiful sailboats at anchor in Coral Bay. Private, cool and filled with soft tropical breezes, the house features an oversized living room that opens through sliding glass doors onto the covered gallery overlooking the bay. A large dining room, a kitchen, three double bedrooms and two bathrooms, one of which includes a Jacuzzi, complete these white-tiled accommodations for six. For your outdoor pleasure, an open deck with a dining table and chairs invites fantasies of cool drinks under the stars. For livelier nights, there's plenty of calypso and reggae music to be heard in the village of Cruz Bay. Contact: Abigail Imbrie, Imbrie Design and Management, Inc., P.O. Box 426, St. John, U.S. Virgin Islands 00831. Call 809-776-6680.

Children: **Y** Pets: **N** Smoking: **Y** Handicap Access: **N** Payment: C, P, T

Coral Bay

TONRYVILLE   *Rates: inexpensive*
Open: year-round   *Minimum Stay: one week*

Set atop Ajax Peak and located at the end of a private road, this lovely home for six commands a stunning 180-degree view of the whole chain of the British Virgin Islands surrounded by the bluest waters imaginable. Enter the house through a beautifully crafted native stone arch, across a little bridge to a screened breezeway. You'll enjoy the opportunity for privacy in accommodations that feature one bedroom along one side of the breezeway, a second bedroom on the lower level, complete with its own private deck, and a pair of couches in the living room for two extra guests. Sea breezes invite you to explore the island around you, where some of the world's most beautiful beaches await you. Contact: Abigail Imbrie, Imbrie Design and Management, Inc., P.O. Box 426, St. John, U.S. Virgin Islands 00831. Call 809-776-6680.

Children: **Y** Pets: **N** Smoking: **Y** Handicap Access: **N** Payment: C, P, T

Coral Bay

TREE HOUSE   *Rates: inexpensive*
Open: year-round   *Minimum Stay: one week*

Here at this mountainside home for six, a pair of decks put the world at your feet. The long front deck provides a sweeping view of Coral Bay and the back deck, set up for outdoor dining, looks over Sir Francis Drake Channel to Tortola. The spacious living room opens onto both decks through sliding glass doors, filling the house with soft sea breezes and tropical air. A short Jeep ride down the mountainside will deliver you to the beautiful beaches and coral reefs of this U.S. Virgin Islands jewel. And daily activities at the national park—snorkeling lessons, historic bus tours and cultural demonstrations of life as it was lived in the early days of the century on old St. John—promise to enrich your understanding of this spectacular island environment. Contact: Abigail Imbrie, Imbrie Design and Management, Inc., P.O. Box 426, St. John, U.S. Virgin Islands 00831. Call 809-776-6680.

Children: **Y** Pets: **N** Smoking: **Y** Handicap Access: **N** Payment: C, P, T

Coral Bay

TRILOGY   *Rates: moderate*
Open: year-round   *Minimum Stay: one week*

If you're coming to the U.S. Virgin Islands looking for the sun, look no further than the beautiful accommodations at Trilogy, where the living and dining areas open onto a 40-foot covered deck with both eastern and western exposure, affording sunbathing opportunities at any time of day. Three bedrooms sleep eight and share a screened porch which features beautiful views of Coral Bay and the mountains above. Situated only a short walk from the Wells House, Interlude and Pelican Peak, Trilogy offers an ideal setting for a large family reunion or a retreat for a large group of friends. Your group can colonize a favorite spot on the beach, occupy hillsides of the splendid national park and fill the decks of the ferries that make the short trip to St. Thomas. Contact: Abigail Imbrie, Imbrie Design and Management, Inc., P.O. Box 426, St. John, U.S. Virgin Islands 00831. Call 809-776-6680.

Children: Y   Pets: N   Smoking: Y   Handicap Access: N   Payment: C, P, T

Coral Bay

WINDSPREE   *Rates: moderate*
Open: year-round   *Minimum Stay: one week*

Life in the tropics requires that the indoors and outdoors blend, and nowhere is that blend more happily achieved than here at Windspree, a house for eight open to every breeze that wafts its way across the island. On the main level, a 40-foot living room opens onto a shaded deck of equal length where the banana quits fly around your dining table begging for a bit of sugar. A spacious kitchen, the master bedroom and, one level up, a breezy twin bedroom complete the accommodations. On the lower level, you'll find two bedrooms as well as a 30-foot deck ideal for reading and reflecting on Coral Bay below. From this exotic roost you can make your way to any point on the island—the beaches, the national park, the ferry docks and restaurants of Cruz Bay—in only a few minutes. Contact: Abigail Imbrie, Imbrie Design and Management, Inc., P.O. Box 426, St. John, U.S. Virgin Islands 00831. Call 809-776-6680.

Children: Y   Pets: N   Smoking: Y   Handicap Access: N   Payment: C, P, T

Cruz Bay

BATTERY HILL   *Rates: inexpensive-expensive*
Open: year-round   *Minimum Stay: none*

Exquisitely landscaped with perpetually blooming flowers, palm trees and other lush vegetation, Battery Hill offers eight beautifully appointed two-bedroom apartments in three classically designed buildings just up the hill from the lively town of Cruz Bay. Each apartment features Brown Jordan and Ficks Reed furnishings as well as breathtaking views of the surrounding islands, the harbor and the most memorable of U.S. Virgin Islands' sunsets. You may be content to spend your days watching the sailboats crossing the bay from your furnished patio. Or you can laze at the swimming pool or go for a stroll on the white sandy beach only a three-minute walk away. The magnificent hiking trails, beaches and views of the national park are a short ride away by Jeep or island shuttle bus. Contact: Diane Jannelle, U.S. Virgin Islands Villas & Resort Management, P.O. Box 458, Cruz Bay, St. John, U.S. Virgin Islands 00831. Call 1-800-338-8084.

Children: Y Pets: N Smoking: Y Handicap Access: N Payment: C, P, T, V, M

Cruz Bay

CRUZ VIEWS   *Rates: inexpensive-moderate*
Open: year-round   *Minimum Stay: none*

Like a West Indian hillside village, these ten one- and two-double-bedroom condominium apartments offer naturally landscaped, lush vegetation and spectacular views of island sunsets. But like a modern home, they also offer the conveniences that make a vacation relaxing and enjoyable: swimming pool, large covered decks, high ceilings with ceiling fans, cable TV and spacious living and dining areas. There's even an outdoor garden shower for the special delight of a fresh-water rinse. Secluded enough to assure you the peace and quiet you want, Cruz Views is also a short walk from the village where scuba diving, windsurfing and sailing arrangements await you. And for those who like a change of pace when the sun goes down, the night life of Cruz Bay offers lively diversion. Contact: Diane Jannelle, U.S. Virgin Islands Villas & Resort Management, P.O. Box 458, Cruz Bay, St. John 00831. Call 800-338-8084.

Children: Y Pets: N Smoking: Y Handicap Access: N Payment: C, P, T, V, M

Cruz Bay

FRICKE HOUSE   *Rates: inexpensive-moderate*
Open: year-round   *Minimum Stay: one week*

Perched high on a bluff with only the dazzling blue sea below, this gracious one-bedroom house of native stone makes a lovely honeymoon hideaway. Enter through dramatic stone arches from the tiled patio into the generous living/dining area with kitchen. Outdoor space includes a small patio off the kitchen, a garden sitting area and a very large gallery facing southwest toward stunning St. Thomas and sunset views. Closer to home in the turquoise waters and reefs below, you may even see a sea turtle or two. When you stir from this precious roost you'll find the snorkeling and scuba diving among the best in the U.S. Virgin Islands and the historical richness of the island enchanting. Contact: Katherine DeMar, Vacation Homes, P.O. Box 272, Cruz Bay, St. John 00831. Call 809-776-6094.

Children: Y Pets: N Smoking: Y Handicap Access: N Payment: C, P, T

Cruz Bay

GIFFT HILL   *Rates: expensive-deluxe*
Open: year-round   *Minimum Stay: none*

This is what you've always dreamed of: A tropically landscaped hilltop hideaway home of your own. This dream includes a private pool, an open courtyard with interior gardens and a kitchen with professional cooking appliances. From the fully furnished poolside deck, the blue sky and sea lie before you like a meditation on beauty and serenity. Five homes offer accommodations for six or eight, with three or four bedrooms, a roofed walkway, spacious living and dining areas and a seemingly endless list of conveniences, such as laundry, barbecue, cable TV, air-conditioning and maid service. But the sea breezes will lure you away, even from this luxury, and then all of the magnificence

of this naturally breathtaking island awaits you. Contact: Diane Jannelle, U.S. Virgin Islands Villas & Resort Management, P.O. Box 458, Cruz Bay, St. John, U.S. Virgin Islands 00831. Call 1-800-338-8084.
Children: Y Pets: N Smoking: Y Handicap Access: N Payment: C, P, T, V, M

Cruz Bay

GREAT CRUZ BAY STONE HOUSE   *Rates: moderate-expensive*
Open: year-round   *Minimum Stay: one week*

Enter this beautifully detailed home for eight via a broad stairway leading down to a paved central courtyard and a glistening fish pond. Massive wooden arched doors open onto the spacious living/dining room with its own magical indoor tropical garden. An adjoining deck surrounded by lush island vegetation displays gorgeous views of Great Cruz Bay and St. Thomas. A master bedroom with a private deck, a library with a queen-size convertible sofa and a guest bedroom that sleeps four complete the accommodations here. This spot is an ideal point of departure for forays to coral reefs, national park trails and neighboring islands. Contact: Katherine DeMar, Vacation Homes, P.O. Box 272, Cruz Bay, St. John, U.S. Virgin Islands 00831. Call 809-776-6094.
Children: Y Pets: N Smoking: Y Handicap Access: N Payment: C, P, T

Cruz Bay

HART BAY VILLA   *Rates: deluxe*
Open: December 15-April 15   *Minimum Stay: one week*

Every nature lover will revel in the unspoiled beauty of this tiny U.S. Virgin island and the comfort and charm of this retreat. Comfortably furnished and featuring many terraces from which to view the sea and the spectacular sunsets, this home for six includes a living room with a sofa bed, a dining room opening onto a large terrace, a kitchen with a dishwasher and two bedrooms (each with their own bath, one with its own terrace). From this convenient spot to the beaches and the village of Cruz Bay, explore all 32 square miles of this natural paradise. Guided tours of the national park, ferry boats to neighboring islands, duty-free shopping and more will fill your days with pleasure and relaxation. Contact: Villas International, 71 West 23rd Street, New York, NY 10010. Call 212-929-7585.
Children: Y Pets: N Smoking: Y Handicap Access: N Payment: C, P, T

Cruz Bay

LAVENDER HILL ESTATES   *Rates: budget-deluxe*
Open: year-round   *Minimum Stay: three nights*

The smallest of the Virgin Islands, St. John offers stunning national park beauty: 70 percent of the island is a natural seashore and mountain protected and preserved for your pleasure. Located only a five-minute walk from the beach town of Cruz Bay, these one- and two-double-bedroom condominium apartments are situated closer yet to the shimmering blue waters of North Beach. But the proximity of the beach only hints at the splendor of this island retreat. Each bright apartment, decorated with its own special island details, features a private tiled deck off a spacious living/dining room, offering views of Cruz Bay Harbor, neighboring cays and the island of St. Thomas. A freshwater pool and a laundromat on the premises make these airy apartments the vacation home of your dreams. Contact: Ann and Joe Hobbs, Box 8306, Cruz Bay, St. John, U.S. Virgin Islands 00831. Call 809-776-6969.

Children: Y Pets: N Smoking: Y Handicap Access: N Payment: C, P, T, V, M

Cruz Bay

PASTORY ESTATES   *Rates: inexpensive*
Open: year-round   *Minimum Stay: none*

Ten spacious and airy apartments perched on a lush hilltop overlook the aquamarine U.S. Virgin Islands Sea. Each condominium apartment for two or four features fine hardwood and cypress finishings for a warm and comfortable feeling. Brightly colored furnishings set the tropical mood and full private decks and bedrooms with queen-sized beds make these holiday homes a private paradise. Additional conveniences such as cable TV, barbecue, laundry and Fax access ensure the most relaxed holiday lifestyle. And of course, the tropical St. John wilderness and parkland hold something for everyone—hiking, sailing, sea kyacking and star gazing. Contact: Diane Jannelle, U.S. Virgin Islands Villas & Resort Management, P.O. Box 458, Cruz Bay, St. John, U.S. Virgin Islands 00831. Call 1-800-338-8084.

Children: Y Pets: N Smoking: Y Handicap Access: N Payment: C, P, T, V, M

Cruz Bay

PELICAN'S PERCH   *Rates: inexpensive-deluxe*
Open: year-round   *Minimum Stay: one week*

A serene, secluded retreat built in the island style, Pelican's Perch is a delightful place for enjoying the casual, carefree life of St. John. The lush forest behind the house offers tropical splendor and cooling breezes; on the other side you can look out and enjoy spectacular views of the neighboring bays and islands. The handsome stone-and-wood house has at its center a magnificent great room. Off this is one of the two bedrooms; the other is on the lower level. Both the great room and the adjoining bedroom open onto a large deck, which is flooded with golden sunshine every morning. Warm beaches and shady trails await you outside. Contact: Katherine DeMar, Vacation Homes, P.O. Box 272, Cruz Bay, St. John, U.S.V.I. 00831. Call 809-776-6094.

Children: Y   Pets: N   Smoking: Y   Handicap Access: N   Payment: C, P, T

Cruz Bay

POINT OF VIEW   *Rates: expensive*
Open: year-round   *Minimum Stay: three nights*

Built by a sophisticated team experienced in classical island home design, this villa set on a knoll overlooking Great Cruz Bay features high-beamed ceilings, Danish brick- and stonework and the extensive use of specially finished wood and tile. The master bedroom offers four-poster beauty and mahogany antiques and two other bedrooms include their own bathrooms and the utmost privacy. A large open area with living, dining and kitchen space features "Casablanca" type ceiling fans and beautiful rattan furniture. Views from the small deck and pool promise all the delights of this tropical island: the snorkeling and scuba diving, travel to nearby Tortola or St. Croix or the quieter pleasure of a walk along the seemingly endless shore. Contact: John and Fran Wasilchak, 2012 E. Randol Mill Road, Suite 202, Arlington, TX 76011. Call 817-265-4608.

Children: Y Pets: N Smoking: Y Handicap Access: N Payment: C, P, T

Cruz Bay

RAINTREE INN
Open: year-round

Rates: budget-inexpensive
Minimum Stay: three nights

Conveniently located in the center of the village of Cruz Bay, these three cozy studio apartments sleep two to four people. The efficiencies feature high ceilings, decks with a charming view of the town and a small dining area where four can dine comfortably. With its year-round summer weather and the U.S. Virgin Islands National Park, the riches of this island are right outside your door. You can use the nearby tennis court, plan a ferry trip to St. Thomas or Tortola, rent a Jeep and explore the hills or find the best beach for shell collecting. The inn features its own cocktail lounge and restaurant for last-minute meals. Contact: Lonnie Willis, Raintree Inn, Box 566 Cruz Bay, St. John, U.S. Virgin Islands 00830. Call 809-776-7449.

Children: Y Pets: N Smoking: Y Handicap Access: N Payment: C, P, T, V, M

Cruz Bay

ROBIN'S ROOST
Open: year-round

Rates: moderate
Minimum Stay: one week

Constructed of native stone and wood, this warm and spacious house provides private, tranquil and convenient accommodations for six. Each room opens onto a large covered and furnished lounging deck where you can enjoy the cooling trade winds, the hypnotizing sound of the sea and day after day of magnificent sunrises. With two bedrooms and a queen-sized convertible sofa in the living room, plus a well-equipped kitchen with a coffee maker, blender and washer/dryer, this vacation home offers all the comforts of home on an island of incomparable natural beauty. It's only a couple of miles from the house to the shops, restaurants and nightlife of Cruz Bay, and never more than a few miles to the incomparable beaches of the north shore. Contact: Hilde Freeman, Rent A Home International, Inc., 7200 34th Avenue, N.W., Seattle, WA 98117. Call 206-545-6963.

Children: Y Pets: N Smoking: Y Handicap Access: N Payment: C, P, V, M

Cruz Bay

SAMUELS COTTAGES   *Rates: budget*
Open: year-round   *Minimum Stay: none*

Spend your nights in these cottages just a quick jaunt up the hill from the town of Cruz Bay, where you'll find the best of St. John's shops and restaurants. With the conveniences of cable TV and a barbecue and the endless pleasures of a deck overlooking the bay and the harbor, these charming one-bedroom vacation cottages offer a real home away from home. In town, you can take ferryboat excursions to the neighboring islands of St. Thomas and Tortola. Here, too, you can enjoy the water pleasures for which St. John is famous—snorkeling and scuba diving in the gorgeous reefs, sailing and cruising the turquoise waters visible at every turn and swimming and windsurfing to your hearts' content. Contact: Julien Harley, Samuels Cottages, P.O. Box 124, Cruz Bay, St. John, U.S. Virgin Islands 00830. Call 809-776-6643.

Children: Y   Pets: N   Smoking: Y   Handicap Access: N   Payment: C, P, T

Cruz Bay

SEA VIEW   *Rates: budget-inexpensive*
Open: year-round   *Minimum Stay: four nights*

From the large deck of this two-bedroom house, the bays of St. John spread out before you like emerald-rimmed sapphires. Near the restaurants and shops of the village of Cruz Bay, the tennis courts and ferry docks invite you to plunge into the life of the island. You may take your time leaving home because the swimming pool and a good book are sometimes too compelling to resist. But when you're ready, it's nice to know that the only National Park in the West Indies awaits you, filled with natural and historical wonders. Contact: Marlene M. Carney, Star Villa St. John Vacation Homes, P.O. Box 599, Cruz Bay, St. John 00830. Call 809-776-6704.

Children: Y   Pets: N   Smoking: Y   Handicap Access: N   Payment: C, P, T

Cruz Bay

SERENDIP VACATION APARTMENTS   *Rates: budget-inexpensive*
Open: year-round   *Minimum Stay: two nights*

Situated on a hillside on three-and-a-half acres of tropical grounds, these lovely vacation apartments accommodate two to four and feature kitchens with the convenient touches of blenders, toasters and microwaves. Every apartment provides spacious and private deck space with splendid views of Pillsbury Sound and St. Thomas. For a close look at St. Thomas or Tortola, plan a day trip to remember; you can take the ferry from the village dock. While you're in town, you can also make arrangements for Jeep and scuba equipment rentals, and collect information on the best beaches, the greatest hikes and the favored underwater trails to coral gardens. Contact: Ginny Scurlock, Serendip Vacation Apartments, P.O. Box 273, Cruz Bay, St. John, U.S. Virgin Islands 00830. Call 809-776-6646.

Children: Y   Pets: N   Smoking: Y   Handicap Access: N   Payment: C, P, T

Cruz Bay

STAR VIEW

Rates: budget-moderate

Open: year-round

Minimum Stay: four nights

This brand-new, cozy, two-story house offers sublime views of the ocean and the incomparable U.S. Virgin Islands' sunsets from its two balconies. Located at the far side of the swimming pool deck that it shares with Star Villa, this one-bedroom home can be booked together with the larger house, making it ideal for parties of six. Comfort and convenience are ensured with ceiling fans and an air-conditioned bedroom as well as a color TV and a kitchen with a microwave. When you tire of the beauty in your immediate surroundings, you can stroll over to the beach at Frank Bay for a dip in the crystalline water of the sea. From there, it's only a matter of time before you're roaming the rest of the island, acquainting yourself with the coral reefs, the national park trails and the old sugar plantations. Contact: Marlene M. Carney, Star Villa St. John Vacation Homes, P.O. Box 599, Cruz Bay, St. John, U.S. Virgin Islands 00830. Call 809-776-6704.

Children: Y   Pets: N   Smoking: Y   Handicap Access: N   Payment: C, P, T

Cruz Bay

STAR VILLA

Rates: moderate-expensive

Open: year-round

Minimum Stay: four nights

As if the exceedingly exquisite natural surroundings of the island of St. John were not enough, this lovely home also offers the sensual delights of a Jacuzzi and an open-air shower. A large wooden deck affords superb views of St. Thomas, the smaller islands which cluster in the bays and as much blue sea as the eye can take in. Accommodations for four feature ceiling fans and tile floors throughout as well as a gas barbecue for outdoor dining, cable TV and a free-form swimming pool that the villa shares with five other houses. Be a homebody in this tropical paradise or make a date for tennis, beachcombing, coral exploring or island hopping. Contact: Marlene M. Carney, Star Villa St. John Vacation Homes, P.O. Box 599, Cruz Bay, St. John , U.S. Virgin Islands 00830. Call 809-776-6704.

Children: Y   Pets: N   Smoking: Y   Handicap Access: N   Payment: C, P, T

Cruz Bay

SUGARBIRD

Rates: inexpensive-moderate

Open: year-round

Minimum Stay: four nights

From the covered deck of this large one-bedroom home you can enjoy splendid views of two of St. John's bays, where the lush green of the island spills languorously into the blue U.S. Virgin Islands. Twin couches in the living room provide sleeping accommodations for an additional two. White tiled floors are cool on bare feet and lazy turning ceiling fans, a gas barbecue and a color TV in addition to a swimming pool could turn you into an idle dreamer. On the other hand, you may not be able to resist the call of the coral reefs or the mystery of the petroglyphs and ruins in the interior of the island. Those who are hard-hit by wanderlust can island-hop to nearby Tortola and St. Thomas. Contact: Marlene M. Carney, Star Villa St. John Vacation Homes, P.O. Box 599, Cruz Bay, St. John 00830. Call 809-776-6704.

Children: Y   Pets: N   Smoking: Y   Handicap Access: N   Payment: C, P, T

Cruz Bay

SURFSIDE *Rates: budget-inexpensive*
Open: year-round *Minimum Stay: four nights*

Leave your formal duds at home, for life in this wonderful summer cottage is at its most relaxed. On St. John, where it's summer all year round, you can really make the most of the hibachi grill and dining area on the deck overlooking the sea, and the swimming pool and sandy white beach only a few steps from you door. If you're really ambitious, you can tuck in your shirt and walk into town for a look at the shops and restaurants. Reserve a tennis court for the morning or consider the ferry schedule to St. Thomas. Perhaps you'll rent a Jeep to explore the rugged interior and less developed coastline of this gorgeous island. It's not unlikely that you'll turn into a devoted beachcomber. Contact: Marlene M. Carney, Star Villa St. John Vacation Homes, P.O. Box 599, Cruz Bay, St. John, U.S. Virgin Islands 00830. Call 809-776-6704.

Children: Y   Pets: N   Smoking: Y   Handicap Access: N   Payment: C, P, T

Cruz Bay

THALASSA *Rates: inexpensive-moderate*
Open: year-round *Minimum Stay: one week*

This simply designed and utterly secluded modern house may suit you perfectly. Here, five decks display the immense natural beauty of this U.S. Virgin island. Four or more people can sleep comfortably in the two twin bedrooms, with two cushioned couches housing larger families or groups. A spacious yet intimate living room, a kitchen and a bathroom whose shower has an unobstructed panorama of the south coast complete the accommodations. In nearby Cruz Bay, you can stock up on groceries, consult the ferry schedule for excursions to St. Thomas and Tortola or make an appointment for a scuba diving lesson or a sailboat rental. Contact: Hilde Freeman, Rent A Home International, Inc., 7200 34th Avenue, N.W., Seattle, WA 98117. Call 206-545-6963.

Children: Y   Pets: N   Smoking: Y   Handicap Access: N   Payment: C, P, V, M

Cruz Bay

THE CRUZ INN *Rates: budget-inexpensive*
Open: year-round *Minimum Stay: three nights*

This warm and charming island inn offers several housekeeping units for two to four with the additional convenience of a cocktail lounge and nightly entertainment just a few steps from your door. The Papaya Suite features porches and wrap-around decks with lovely views of Enighed Pond and a scattering of small islands. Seagrape welcomes vacationing couples with its cozy rooms and air-conditioning. Situated only a short walk from the ferry docks and the shops and restaurants of the village, the inn provides an ideal center for exploring the national park and seemingly endless coast of this U.S. Virgin Islands jewel. Public shuttles and Jeep rentals ensure visitors easy access to every bit of St. John's beauty. Contact: Gayle Gosselin, The Cruz Inn, 277 Enighed, Cruz Bay, St. John, U.S. Virgin Islands 00831. Call 809-776-7688.

Children: Y Pets: N Smoking: Y Handicap Access: N Payment: C, T, V, M

Cruz Bay

THE LOST CHORD   *Rates: inexpensive*
Open: year-round   *Minimum Stay: one night*

The world of blue sea and lush green hills and coast belong to you at this beautifully designed tropical villa. A covered dining area on the ample deck will inspire many starlit dinners, with the moon and the shimmering water setting your heart aglow. Both double bedrooms and the stone-walled living room with two sofa beds open onto private deck space. Conveniences include a kitchen equipped to turn out anything from a tropical drink to a gourmet meal, as well as a stereo, a cassette deck and a telephone. With days of nonstop glorious weather, you may want to stir no further than the nearest beach. But if you're so moved, the island holds a wealth of natural and historical enticements, from the national park to the old sugar plantations. Contact: Mary F. Blazine, P.O. Box 184, Cruz Bay, St. John, U.S. Virgin Islands 00831. Call 809-776-7105.

Children: Y Pets: N Smoking: Y Handicap Access: N Payment: C, P, T

Cruz Bay

THE SUGARBIRD NEST   *Rates: budget-inexpensive*
Open: year-round   *Minimum Stay: four nights*

Especially secluded and private, this cozy one-bedroom home nestles into a hillside beneath the main house. Twin Murphy beds pull down to sleep two comfortably and a small living/dining room and a kitchen with a microwave complete the accommodations. Large glass sliding doors lead to the outside deck where views through tropical foliage reveal the beauty of two neighboring bays. From this breezy hideaway you can walk the short distance to the highly regarded white beaches of Frank Bay or take the shuttle bus to the beaches of the north shore. The athletic have much to choose from: hiking, tennis, snorkeling, windsurfing and more. Contact: Marlene M. Carney, Star Villa St. John Vacation Homes, P.O. Box 599, Cruz Bay, St. John, U.S. Virgin Islands 00830. Call 809-776-6704.

Children: Y Pets: N Smoking: Y Handicap Access: N Payment: C, P, T

Cruz Bay

TRADE WIND COTTAGES   *Rates: inexpensive-expensive*
Open: year-round   *Minimum Stay: one week*

Cooled by the trade winds that gently caress the hills of St. John, these three cottages are excellent bases for island holidays. Each cottage comprises a comfy bedroom, bathroom, living room, kitchenette and spacious deck; there are two daybeds in the living room, and additional bedrooms may also be let. The cottages are clustered around a friendly inn, which offers guests the use of an open-air Jacuzzi and can even arrange for a soothing massage. Lovely views of either the Caribbean or the Atlantic are yours to savor; the white sands and warm waters of the beach are scarcely 10 minutes away. Contact: Rent A Home International, 7200 34th Ave. N.W., Seattle, WA 98117. Call 206-545-6963.

Children: Y Pets: N Smoking: Y Handicap Access: N Payment: C, P, V, M

Cruz Bay

VILLA BOUGAINVILLAEA *Rates: inexpensive-moderate*
Open: year-round *Minimum Stay: three nights*

Surrounded by a garden filled with the fragrance and beauty of jasmine, hibiscus, euphorbia and bougainvillaea, this hillside house offers two spacious apartments. Formerly the home of a well-known island potter, Villa Bougainvillaea has been lavished with great care, filled with a personal art collection of paintings and sculptures by island artists. Each apartment sleeps four in two bedrooms and includes the conveniences of telephone, color TV, laundry and outdoor barbecue. Located just a few minutes' walk from the shops and restaurants of Cruz Bay, this villa also offers easy access to the excellent snorkeling beach at Frank Bay. Contact: Donald Schnell, Villa Bougainvillaea, c/o Schnell Studio, Mongoose Junction, St. John, U.S. Virgin Islands 00830. Call 809-776-6420.

Children: Y Pets: N Smoking: Y Handicap: N Payment: C, P, T, A, V, M

Cruz Bay

VILLA TAMARIND *Rates: expensive*
Open: year-round *Minimum Stay: one week*

Set on a ledge carved into rock near the summit of a cone-shaped mountain, this white-washed and wood-beamed vacation home commands a 270-degree view of the sparkling turquoise waters and the lush green hills of St. John. High enough to look down on birds in flight, low enough to hear the song of the sea, the house accommodates six in three bedrooms and also includes two and a half baths, a large living/dining room and a kitchen. You'll need a Jeep (available from the owner) to come and go from this remarkable address, where you can almost feel the ocean spray from the furnished deck. You can throw your snorkeling gear in the back seat and look for a special cove or pack a picnic to eat at the far end of one of the national park trails. Contact: Hilde Freeman, Rent A Home International, Inc., 7200 34th Avenue, N.W., Seattle, WA 98117. Call 206-545-6963.

Children: Y Pets: N Smoking: Y Handicap Access: N Payment: C, P, V, M

Cruz Bay

WESSON HOUSE

Open: year-round

Rates: moderate-expensive

Minimum Stay: one week

Covered walkways connect the several modular structures of this hilltop home for six to eight, providing comfort and privacy for a large family or group of friends. Surrounded by tropical plants and flowering trees and kissed by cooling trade winds, the house features a stereo and TV/VCR-equipped great room where living, dining and kitchen areas are combined. A spacious covered deck wraps around this fine living area and offers the outdoor comforts of a dining table and chairs, cocktail tables and lounge chairs. This lovely home can be your break from the winter or a lively summertime retreat, when the early July festivals offer all the warmth and exuberance for which the U.S. Virgin Islands is famous. Contact: Katherine DeMar, Vacation Homes, P.O. Box 272, Cruz Bay, St. John, U.S. Virgin Islands 00831. Call 809-776-6094.

Children: **Y**   Pets: **N**   Smoking: **Y**   Handicap Access: **N**   Payment: **C, P, T**

Enighed

CASA MARIPOSA

Open: year-round

Rates: budget-moderate

Minimum Stay: one week

In this lovely island retreat enhanced by the warmth of island stonework, three one-bedroom apartments offer lovely lodgings for vacationing couples. Each apartment features a large deck with sweeping views of the bluer-than-blue U.S. Virgin Islands Sea and the at-home pleasure of a color TV with a VCR. One apartment even has its own Jacuzzi, just in case the sea breezes and palm trees don't relax you fully. Only a five-minute walk from the conveniences of restaurants and shops, these apartments also assure that all the wonders of this tiny island—the water sports, the acres of national parkland, the history and endless natural wonder—are only a short distance away. Contact: Joanna Jarrett, 14F Enighed, St. John, U.S. Virgin Islands 00830. Call 809-776-6639.

Children: **N**   Pets: **N**   Smoking: **Y**   Handicap Access: **N**   Payment: **C, T**

Fish Bay

ALTAVISTA

Open: year-round

Rates: inexpensive

Minimum Stay: five nights

This secluded three-bedroom home enjoys the great beauty of a site adjacent to the national park. Its decks and walls of windows offer splendid views of lush green hills plunging into the crystalline blue waters of Fish Bay. Delightfully furnished with rattan and bamboo and appointed in cedar, this home provides the perfect point of departure from which to make the island your own. You can rent a Jeep to explore the interior of the island or take a shuttle to the beautiful white beaches of the north shore. Shell collectors and history lovers will find their niches here too, and the village of Cruz Bay offers a fine collection of restaurants and shops. Contact: Mary F. Blazine, P.O. Box 184, Cruz Bay, St. John, U.S. Virgin Islands 00831. Call 809-776-7105.

Children: **Y**   Pets: **N**   Smoking: **Y**   Handicap Access: **N**   Payment: **C, P, T**

Fish Bay

GOODBYE COLUMBUS
Open: year-round

Rates: inexpensive-moderate
Minimum Stay: one week

A ceiling fan turns slowly and a sweet ocean breeze stirs the leaves of palm fronds by the deck. Air and light move like magic through the rooms of this two-bedroom home where the views are of endless ocean and sky. Situated down a rough and unpaved road on the south side of St. John, this house offers a special invitation to vacationers looking for the ultimate in privacy and natural beauty. Accommodations for four include a living room with a gracious dining area and a comfortable kitchen. Features such as sliding glass doors and a spacious deck enhance the days and nights of your holiday with a feeling of openness and freedom. Modern conveniences such as a color TV and VCR, a cassette deck and a washer/dryer make life as easy as it should be. Contact: Private Homes for Private Vacations, Mary-Phyllis Nogueira, Mamey Peak, St. John, U.S. Virgin Islands 00830. Call 809-776-6876.
Children: **Y**   Pets: **N**   Smoking: **Y**   Handicap Access: **N**   Payment: **C, P, T**

Fish Bay

OVER THE RAINBOW
Open: year-round

Rates: inexpensive-moderate
Minimum Stay: one week

Adventurers will take special pleasure in the unpaved, two-mile road that leads to this beautiful house for four. A dining patio is set amid the colorful splendor of a vast array of tropical plants and a wide sunny deck overlooks the blue waters of Reef and Fish bays. Accommodations for two include two bedrooms and two bathrooms filled with a gracious collection of wood, wicker and rattan furniture. The architectural appointments in exotic wood and stone make the interior especially rich. From this secluded spot, you can walk the short distance to Reef Bay National Park Beach, one of the island's most beautiful stretches of sand and sun. Contact: Private Homes for Private Vacations, Mary-Phyllis Nogueira, Mamey Peak, St. John, U.S. Virgin Islands 00830. Call 809-776-6876.
Children: **Y**   Pets: **N**   Smoking: **Y**   Handicap Access: **N**   Payment: **C, P, T**

Fish Bay

SOFT WINDS
Open: year-round

Rates: inexpensive-moderate
Minimum Stay: one week

From the three decks of this hilltop home you can see what seems like all the world—Reef and Fish bays, St. Croix and St. Thomas and all of the beautiful blue U.S. Virgin Islands Sea. With its ideal southern exposure, the house offers unforgettable sunsets. Featuring tile and stonework appointments, this beautifully decorated and lovingly furnished home accommodates six in three bedrooms. In the well-designed kitchen with a dishwasher and microwave you may make some of your best meals. Of course, you may prefer a picnic on the beautiful nearby beach or a drive down the dirt road to the town of Cruz Bay for a gracious restaurant meal. Contact: Private Homes for

Private Vacations, Mary-Phyllis Nogueira, Mamey Peak, St. John, U.S. Virgin Islands 00830. Call 809-776-6876.

Children: Y   Pets: N   Smoking: Y   Handicap Access: N   Payment: C, P, T

Francis Bay

VILLA RIVA *Rates: deluxe*
Open: year-round *Minimum Stay: one week*

Two-thirds of St. John is national parkland, the result of a generous gift from the Rockefeller family. Lovely Villa Riva is located within this leafy domain, poised on a hillside overlooking Sir Francis Drake Channel. The tropical-style living and dining area is a cool retreat with high ceilings, tile floors and comfy furniture—the views of the water and neighboring islands from the many windows are superb. This room opens onto a large, sunny balcony complete with a hot tub and even more impressive views. Four bedrooms with bathrooms are found inside, and the beach is only a five-minute walk through the shady parklands. Contact: West Indies Management Company, 28 Pelham St., Newport, RI 02840. Call 1-800-932-3222 (in Rhode Island, 401-849-8012). Ref. VV-RIV.

Children: Y   Pets: N   Smoking: Y   Handicap Access: N   Payment: C, P, T, A

Great Cruz Bay

EAGLESNEST *Rates: deluxe*
Open: year-round *Minimum Stay: one week*

This handsome aerie is built of native stone and redwood and perches on a hillside overlooking Great Cruz Bay. The two-story home features a spacious living/dining area separated from the open kitchen only by a dining counter. This commodious space opens out onto a large, covered deck with comfy furniture and excellent views of the blue bay and the surrounding green hillsides. All three bedrooms have their own bathrooms; the bedroom on the lower level enjoys its own private deck, a lovely place to enjoy a glass of freshly squeezed juice in the morning and greet the new day. Contact: West Indies Management Company, 28 Pelham St., Newport, RI 02840. Call 1-800-932-3222 (in Rhode Island, 401-849-8012). Ref. HH-EAG.

Children: Y   Pets: N   Smoking: Y   Handicap Access: N   Payment: C, P, T, A

Great Cruz Bay

HAIKU *Rates: expensive-deluxe*
Open: year-round *Minimum Stay: one week*

As befits a home bearing this name, Haiku exemplifies the Japanese aesthetic of simplicity and elegance. The enchanting open-air living and dining pavilion features a smooth tiled floor, spare furnishings, high ceilings and a rugged stone wall. Luxuriant tropical gardens surround you as you sit here to converse with friends, enjoy your meals or just contemplate the splendor of the scenery. There are three bedrooms here: One has its own bath; the master bedroom and remaining bedroom share a dressing room and bathroom and a delightful outside shower. Contact: West Indies Management Company, 28 Pelham St.,

Newport, RI 02840. Call 1-800-932-3222 (in Rhode Island, 401-849-8012). Ref. HH-HAI.
Children: Y   Pets: N   Smoking: Y   Handicap Access: N   Payment: C, P, T, A

Great Cruz Bay

KARIBU   *Rates: deluxe*
Open: year-round   *Minimum Stay: one week*

Stylishly eclectic furnishings, wide-open spaces defined by magnificent arches, handsome stonework and sleek tile floors add grace and charm to this house, but perhaps its greatest attraction is the fabulous view over Great Cruz Bay. Indulge yourself with the master suite's bathroom, which features an over-sized tub and a spacious skylighted shower. Downstairs there are two more bedrooms, both with bathrooms, which open onto another pleasant tile deck. Fine restaurants and abundant water sports are close at hand, and the warmth and generosity of the island will greet you at every turn. Contact: West Indies Management Company, 28 Pelham St., Newport, RI 02840. Call 1-800-932-3222 (in Rhode Island, 401-849-8012). Ref. HH-KAR.
Children: Y   Pets: N   Smoking: Y   Handicap Access: N   Payment: C, P, T, A

Great Cruz Bay

RAINBOW VILLA   *Rates: moderate*
Open: year-round   *Minimum Stay: one week*

Palm trees, flamboyants, and papaya and lime trees adorn the grounds of this gracious two-bedroom home perched in the hills above Cruz Bay. An enormous deck runs along the front of the house and boasts access from either the Italian-tile living room or the spacious master bedroom. From here there are breathtaking views of glittering St. Thomas, St. Croix and the outer islands. Romantic ceiling fans throughout enhance the cooling effects of the trade winds. Modern amenities include a color TV, a barbecue and a VCR. Only a few minutes away you'll find the fun of Cruz Bay and the gentle waters of the beach. Contact: Katherine DeMar, Vacation Homes, P.O. Box 272, Cruz Bay, St. John, U.S.V.I. 00831. Call 809-776-6094.
Children: Y   Pets: N   Smoking: Y   Handicap Access: N   Payment: C, P, T

Great Cruz Bay

TESSERACT   *Rates: moderate-expensive*
Open: year-round   *Minimum Stay: one week*

This older home with mature tropical landscaping and a large in-ground masonry pool offers casual and comfortable island living for six. With its western exposure and a split-level living dining/room, the house and poolside enjoy all-day sunlight and day after day of those uninterrupted, beyond compare, U.S. Virgin Islands' sunsets. At this address you will find yourself only a short distance from the shops and restaurants of Cruz Bay. Here, you can easily make arrangements to enjoy the great water sports of St. John—snorkeling, scuba diving, sailing, fishing and cruising. This end of the island also gives easy access to the rugged roads upon which a rented Jeep can take you into the wild interior of the island. Contact: Private Homes for Private Vacations, Mary-Phyllis Nogueira, Mamey Peak, St. John, U.S. Virgin Islands 00830. Call 809-776-6876.

Children: N   Pets: N   Smoking: Y   Handicap Access: N   Payment: C, P, T

Great Cruz Bay

VILLA DE VIDA
Open: year-round

Rates: moderate-deluxe
Minimum Stay: one week

High ceilings, ceramic tiles, mellow wood paneling and playful arches delight the eye throughout this villa. The full kitchen is well equipped; there's also a wet bar for your convenience. Each of the three bedrooms offers delightful accommodations: the master suite boasts a tropical garden bathroom with a sunken tub; another features a ceramic outdoor shower; the last has its own private bath and kitchenette. One of the many decks sports a Jacuzzi, the perfect way to soothe away the stress of the real world. Every modern convenience has been provided, which, together with the splendid situation and elegant furnishings, makes this a perfectly delightful holiday home. Contact: Katherine DeMar, Vacation Homes, P.O. Box 272, Cruz Bay, St. John, U.S.V.I. 00831. Call 809-776-6094.

Children: Y   Pets: N   Smoking: Y   Handicap Access: N   Payment: C, P, T

Hart Bay

HART BEACH VILLA
Open: year-round

Rates: deluxe
Minimum Stay: one week

A plethora of sliding glass doors in the elegantly furnished living room perform the double function of providing superb views of the bay and opening onto a delightful deck. This villa boasts a private swimming pool; the warm waters of the ocean also beckon nearby. The four bedrooms are cooled by trade winds in the time-honored local fashion. Snorkeling is among the favorite amusements on this tropical island, where novices are in for a real treat. Hiking through the lush countryside on the Reef Bay Trail is also popular, as are the gentler pursuits of sun worshipping and splashing about in the crystal-clear waters. Contact: LaCure Villas, 11661 San Vicente Blvd., Suite 1010, Los Angeles, CA 90049. Call 1-800-387-2715.

Children: Y   Pets: N   Smoking: Y   Handicap Access: N   Payment: C, T

Hart Bay

LAS TREMENTINAS
Open: year-round

Rates: inexpensive-deluxe
Minimum Stay: one week

This contemporary home is an artful blending of native stone, mahogany and cypress, pine and redwood, sea and sky. Las Trementinas is really more of a compound: several independent buildings each set to best advantage on the hillside and connected by lovely walkways. The main part of the house includes a master suite with a deck and patio; an upper bedroom with a its own bathroom and patio; and another bedroom suite complete with a kitchenette, deck and spa. The guest house is a bit higher on the hill. Complete tranquillity and privacy is ensured by the mampoo, papaya, banana, flamboyant and lime trees that cover the hillside; gardens of hibiscus, orchids and bougainvillaea add their ambrosial scents to the clean salt air. Contact: Katherine DeMar, Vacation Homes, P.O. Box 272, Cruz Bay, St. John, U.S.V.I. 00831. Call 809-776-6094.

Children: Y   Pets: N   Smoking: Y   Handicap Access: N   Payment: C, P, T

Hart Bay

SOUNION   *Rates: inexpensive-expensive*
Open: year-round   *Minimum Stay: one week*

Nestled on a hillside overlooking the vivid blues of coral-strewn Hart Bay, this spacious and airy home for six offers both privacy—no other homes are visible from this villa—and convenience—the village of Cruz Bay is only minutes away. With its high ceilings, bamboo furniture, large fans and cedar construction, this beautifully furnished house exemplifies island living. The living/dining area includes a sofa bed for two, and two double bedrooms complete the sleeping quarters. Deck views of St. Croix and St. Thomas and twilights of the most astounding coloration will enchant you. A winding path leads from the house to a little-used white sandy beach with pristine waters and coral reef. Naturalists can also enjoy the national park's guided tours of island flora, fauna and natural history. Contact: Mary F. Blazine, P.O. Box 184, Cruz Bay, St. John, U.S. Virgin Islands 00831. Call 809-776-7105.

Children: Y   Pets: N   Smoking: Y   Handicap Access: N   Payment: C, P, T

Hart Bay

XANADU   *Rates: expensive-deluxe*
Open: year-round   *Minimum Stay: one week*

Follow a winding path from lovely Hart Bay up the shady hillside, and you'll find the gardens of Xanadu overflowing with pomegranates, oranges, bananas, papayas, lemons, limes and other tropical fruits just ripe for the picking. Its perch on the hillside gives this vacation villa gentle cooling breezes and spectacular views of nearby St. Croix and St. Thomas—not to mention the unbearably beautiful sunsets. The crash of the surf below will serenade you as you sit out on either of the spacious decks. Inside is a living room, a full kitchen and three comfy bedrooms. Contact: Katherine DeMar, Vacation Homes, P.O. Box 272, Cruz Bay, St. John, U.S.V.I. 00831. Call 809-776-6094.

Children: Y   Pets: N   Smoking: Y   Handicap Access: N   Payment: C, P, T

Hawksnest Bay

SAGO PALMS   *Rates: inexpensive-expensive*
Open: year-round   *Minimum Stay: one week*

Like the great camps of the northeastern United States, this secluded luxury home features an elegant, high-ceilinged great room which connects with three very private sleeping areas by a spacious deck.

Accommodations for six and a seeming infinity of comforts and features—such as a dishwasher, a washer/dryer, a microwave and an outdoor grill—ensure that you will begin to wind down here as soon as you kick off your shoes. Surrounded by the beauty of the national park and illuminated daily by spectacular sunsets and water views, this spot offers an ideal center for your island holiday. Days and nights of quiet repose on the nearby beaches or exploring the wealth of natural wonders and local history will send you home with wonderful memories and bring you back again and again. Contact: Private Homes for Private Vacations, Mary-Phyllis Nogueira, Mamey Peak, St. John, U.S. Virgin Islands 00830. Call 809-776-6876.

Children: N   Pets: N   Smoking: Y   Handicap Access: N   Payment: C, P, T

Hawksnest Bay

TERRAHAWK *Rates: deluxe*
Open: year-round *Minimum Stay: one week*

Hawksnest Bay is a quiet little cove with lovely white beaches, generally unblemished by tourist swarms. From your roost at Terrahawk you can enjoy excellent views of the open water and green-swathed countryside, yet the soft sands are only a minute away. You have your choice of relaxing in either a cool inside living room or a breezy outside living room. The three bedrooms are found off these central areas; all are comfortably furnished and have their own bathrooms. The modern kitchen is equipped with a full complement of appliances. Contact: West Indies Management Company, 28 Pelham St., Newport, RI 02840. Call 1-800-932-3222 (in Rhode Island, 401-849-8012). Ref. HH-TER.

Children: Y Pets: N Smoking: Y Handicap Access: N Payment: C, P, T, A

Hurricane Hole

ESTATE ZOOTENVAAL *Rates: inexpensive-moderate*
Open: year-round *Minimum Stay: one week*

A week or two on the private beach reserved for the use of guests in the three beach houses of this estate guarantees a calm mind and a sweeter view of the world. With shell collecting, beachcombing, swimming and snorkeling at your doorstep and all of the West Indies' national park forests beyond, you might decide never to return to civilization. Each house sleeps two to four people and features custom-designed fabrics and local shells and plants. On this island where summer never ends, you can come to know the underwater worlds of the coral gardens and the terrestrial marvels of the tropical forests. History lovers will be especially interested in the vine- and brush-covered ruins of the sugar plantations that flourished here 200 years ago. Contact: Robin Clair, Estate Zootenvaal, Hurricane Hole, St. John, U.S. Virgin Islands 00830. Call 809-776-6321.

Children: Y Pets: N Smoking: Y Handicap Access: N Payment: C, P, T

Maho Bay

TREE HOUSE   *Rates: budget-inexpensive*
Open: year-round   *Minimum Stay: one week*

This spacious home for seven appeals to all who enjoy 200-degree views of rolling hills and blue ocean—and who wouldn't? Any large family with young children will especially enjoy the roominess as well as the inside stairwell with a railing. This high, breezy, split-level home offers many of the other conveniences families so love—a color TV with a VCR, a cassette deck, a washer/dryer and an outdoor grill. With the beaches of the north shore only a lazy stroll away and the miles of national park at your back door, you'll spend the beautiful days basking in the beauty of the island. Lovers of history may make trips to the old sugar plantations and the petroglyphs. Contact: Private Homes for Private Vacations, Mary-Phyllis Nogueira, Mamey Peak, St. John, U.S. Virgin Islands 00830. Call 809-776-6876.

Children: Y   Pets: N   Smoking: Y   Handicap Access: N   Payment: C, P, T

Maho Bay/Mamey Peak

MILESAWAY   *Rates: inexpensive-expensive*
Open: year-round   *Minimum Stay: one week*

Located on one of the highest peaks of St. John, this house has decks on both levels offering majestic views of Coral Bay Harbor and Sir Francis Drake Channel. The master bedroom and twin guest room look out onto the patio and an enticing pool where sun chaises invite reading, sunning and relaxing in perfect privacy. A kitchen equipped with a blender, a microwave and a full bar and indoor, outdoor and poolside dining areas ensure mealtimes of elegance and ease. From here, you can make your descent to this small jewel of an island where the pleasures of fishing, cruising, sailing, snorkeling and windsurfing await you. Contact: Private Homes for Private Vacations, Mary-Phyllis Nogueira, Mamey Peak, St. John, U.S. Virgin Islands 00830. Call 809-776-6876.

Children: N   Pets: N   Smoking: Y   Handicap Access: N   Payment: C, P, T

Pillsbury Sound

HUMMINGBIRD HILL   *Rates: expensive-deluxe*
Open: year-round   *Minimum Stay: one week*

Lovely views of the verdant countryside, the sparkling waters of Pillsbury Sound and St. Thomas across the way will reward those who pause to enjoy the prospect from this home's spacious tile deck. In fact, it's rather difficult not to come out here and spend an hour or three, as the cool, shady terrace tempts guests through sliding glass doors from the spacious living room. Your time inside is well spent, too, as festive plants and personal artistic touches grace the rooms. There are two pleasant bedrooms off the living area; an airy sleeping porch can accommodate one more visitor. Contact: West Indies Management Company, 28 Pelham St., Newport, RI 02840. Call 1-800-932-3222 (in Rhode Island, 401-849-8012). Ref. HH-HUM.

Children: Y   Pets: N   Smoking: Y   Handicap Access: N   Payment: C, P, T, A

Rendezvous Bay

BETT HAWA
Open: year-round

Rates: deluxe
Minimum Stay: one week

Perched just above the incredibly blue waters of the Caribbean, this stylish contemporary villa enjoys enchanting views of the bay from its gallery of windows. The handsome tile floors, spare furnishings, pale walls and atmospheric ceiling fans keep you feeling cool and comfortable, even in the heat of midday. Water sports await you outside, and the cheerful bustle of red-roofed Cruz Bay is less than five minutes away; the quaint stores, interesting galleries and delightful eateries here are sure to give your credit cards a bit of a workout. Contact: West Indies Management Company, 28 Pelham St., Newport, RI 02840. Call 1-800-932-3222 (in Rhode Island, 401-849-8012). Ref. CT-HAW.

Children: Y Pets: N Smoking: Y Handicap Access: N Payment: C, P, T, A

Rendezvous Bay

POINCIANA
Open: year-round

Rates: inexpensive-expensive
Minimum Stay: one week

Your vacation at waterfront Poinciana puts the sparkling U.S. Virgin Islands nearly at your feet—your bare feet, that is. This beautifully furnished home features a living/dining area, a tiled kitchen and the master bed- and bathroom on the second floor, plus a spiral staircase leading to the first-floor bedrooms and bath. This deluxe home also includes cable TV and a microwave, as well as a washer/dryer and outdoor barbecue. From this lovely hideaway, you launch athletic hikes in the national park and the interior of the island to see the ancient petroglyphs. But perhaps you will save your nights for the simple pleasures of counting the stars and watching the twinkling lights of the nearby islands. Contact: Private Homes for Private Vacations, Mary-Phyllis Nogueira, Mamey Peak, St. John, U.S. Virgin Islands 00830. Call 809-776-6876.

Children: Y Pets: N Smoking: Y Handicap Access: N Payment: C, P, T

Suzannaburg

LYON'S PRIDE
Open: year-round

Rates: expensive-deluxe
Minimum Stay: one week

You would be proud, too: Native stonework, cool tile floors and elegant modern furnishings make this hillside home a delight both inside and out. From either the comfy living room or the deck you can enjoy lovely views of the water and St. Thomas. Perhaps while savoring this view, you'd like to partake of a dinner prepared in the large, modern kitchen of your holiday home. The master bedroom also opens onto the deck, and the other bedroom—with twin beds—boasts its own sitting area. Contact: West Indies Management Company, 28 Pelham St., Newport, RI 02840. Call 1-800-932-3222 (in Rhode Island, 401-849-8012). Ref. CT-LYO.

Children: Y Pets: N Smoking: Y Handicap Access: N Payment: C, P, T, A

St. Thomas

Bolongo

ELYSIAN BEACH RESORT   *Rates: moderate-deluxe*
Open: year-round   *Minimum Stay: none*

These units range in size from intimate studios to deluxe two-bedrooms with lofts. All boast color cable TV, well-stocked bars, modern kitchens, security safes and large terraces with splendid ocean views. Nightly entertainment is provided in the restaurant or lounge, and in addition to the pool there's an exercise room complete with sauna. Scuba lessons are available for novices and some packages include the use of windsurfers, sunfish and snorkeling equipment. As an added feature, there are frequent complimentary shuttles that will carry you to and from area beaches, pools and restaurants. Contact: Debra Danekas, Elysian Beach Resort, Red Hook Suite 51, St. Thomas, USVI 00802. Call 1-800-343-4079 or 1-800-524-4746 (in St. Thomas, 809-775-1000).

Children: **Y**   Pets: **N**   Smoking: **Y**   Handicap Access: **N**   Payment: **All**

Charlotte Amalie/Magen's Bay

HARBOR VIEW   *Rates: expensive-deluxe*
Open: year-round   *Minimum Stay: one week*

High ceilings, delicate furnishings and air-conditioned splendor combine to create an incomparably light and airy feeling in this contemporary two-bedroom apartment. The many picture windows add to the effect, bringing the golden sunshine inside and letting you walk directly out onto the long sun terrace. From here and from the living and dining area, there are splendid views of the sapphire harbor ringed with white beaches and lush green hills. You can wander down to join the action at Magen's Bay Beach or take a dip in luxurious privacy in the property's own swimming pool. Contact: Villa Holidays, 13100 Wayzata Blvd., Suite 150, Minneapolis, MN 55343. Call 1-800-328-6262 (in Minnesota, 612-591-0076).

Children: **Y** Pets: **N** Smoking: **Y** Handicap Access: **N** Payment: **C, P, T, V, M**

Charlotte Amalie/Magen's Bay

PARROT'S NEST   *Rates: deluxe*
Open: year-round   *Minimum Stay: one week*

From its secluded perch, this lavish resort enjoys fabulous views in almost every direction. The three bedrooms all have atrium baths en suite. The tropical luxury is enhanced by the Jacuzzi and tennis court and many terraces where you can sit out and enjoy the scenery. Graceful stairways lead to the outdoor dining pavilion, cabana with kitchen and bath and a spectacular pool—a splendid arrangement for those who plan to do a bit of entertaining or just want to relax in style. A maid and caretaker will see after you during your stay. Contact: Villa Holidays, 13100 Wayzata Blvd., Suite 150, Minneapolis, MN 55343. Call 1-800-328-6262 (in Minnesota, 612-591-0076).

Children: **Y** Pets: **N** Smoking: **Y** Handicap Access: **N** Payment: **C, P, T, V, M**

Charlotte Amalie

BLACKBEARD'S CASTLE HOTEL   *Rates: inexpensive-moderate*
Open: year-round   *Minimum Stay: three nights*

Yes, Blackbeard's Castle was indeed the fortress of the infamous Edward Teach, who used it as a lookout and a hideaway. During its colorful history, the building has served as a plantation and a private home and it now houses a splendid restaurant and guest accommodations. The hotel suites feature cable TV and air-conditioning and come with complimentary breakfast served every morning; the guest apartments boast full kitchens. Everyone is invited to enjoy the marvelous views and to swim in the delightful pool beneath the shadow of an imposing 17th-century tower. Contact: Bob Harrington, Blackbeard's Castle, 38-39 Dronningens Gade, P.O. Box 6041, Charlotte Amalie, St. Thomas, USVI 00804. Call 1-800-344-5771 (in St. Thomas, 809-776-1234).

Children: Y   Pets: N   Smoking: Y   Handicap Access: N   Payment: All

Charlotte Amalie

MAISON FLAMBOYANT   *Rates: deluxe*
Open: year-round   *Minimum Stay: one week*

Poised high above Charlotte Amalie, this opulent villa commands astounding views of the harbor and the deep blue Caribbean. Rich mahogany, Oriental rugs and fine antiques are delightfully blended with rattan furniture and contemporary amenities to create an inviting aura of casual luxury. The enormous living room, with large windows displaying panoramic views, opens to a covered dining veranda. There are five large bedrooms and the gourmet kitchen features a dishwasher, snack bar and microwave. Other rooms include an art gallery and a well-equipped entertainment area. Outside there is a pool framed by tropical greenery. Maid service is included and a cook and babysitter are also available. Contact: Vacation Home Rentals Worldwide, 235 Kensington Ave., Norwood, NJ 07648. Call 1-800-633-3284 (in New Jersey, 201-767-9393). Ref. ST105.

Children: N   Pets: N   Smoking: Y   Handicap Access: N   Payment: C, P, T

Charlotte Amalie

OVERLOOK   *Rates: deluxe*
Open: year-round   *Minimum Stay: one week*

Set high upon Flag Hill, Overlook features lovely views of the cruise ships elegantly gliding by Frenchman's Reef. Beneath the tiled roof of this sprawling contemporary home you'll find four air-conditioned bedrooms, a soundproof media room with a VCR and movie library, a gourmet kitchen and an enormous tiled living and dining room. In this last room, a wall of sliding glass doors lets in the glorious Caribbean sun and opens out to the lighted pool surrounded by a spacious patio with a grill and dining area; the views here are superb. Contact: Nancy Anderson or Donajen Farrar, McLaughlin Anderson Vacations, 100

Blackbeard's Hill, St. Thomas, USVI 00802. Call 1-800-537-6246 (in St. Thomas, 809-776-0635).

Children: Y   Pets: N   Smoking: Y   Handicap Access: N   Payment: C, P, T

Charlotte Amalie

ROSENBAUM VILLA   *Rates: deluxe*
Open: year-round   *Minimum Stay: one week*
This unique home was designed by its architect-owner to give every room the ultimate in privacy and delightful vistas. Each of the four bedroom suites occupies its own wing, radiating like spokes from the central hub of the living and dining area. The many sun decks offer fabulous views of the mysterious Caribbean waters and the well-landscaped property includes its own stretch of sandy beach. Cool breezes keep the house quite comfortable and frequent maid service will make your stay here carefree. The shops and restaurants of Charlotte Amalie are just five minutes away. Contact: Villa Holidays, 13100 Wayzata Blvd., Suite 150, Minneapolis, MN 55343. Call 1-800-328-6262 (in Minnesota, 612-591-0076).

Children: Y Pets: N Smoking: Y Handicap Access: N Payment: C, P, T, V, M

Charlotte Amalie

SECRET HARBOUR BEACH RESORT   *Rates: moderate-deluxe*
Open: year-round   *Minimum Stay: none*
Despite its name, it's hard to keep this resort a secret, with its luxurious accommodations and festive amenities. The studio, one- and two-bedroom suites feature delightful tropical-inspired furnishings, air conditioning, ceiling fans, daily maid service and large terraces with breathtaking views of the sea. You can relax with a rum punch under the umbrellas and palms of the beach bar outside after a workout in the fitness center or a swim in the large pool. There's also an impressive water sports center right on the premises, offering windsurfing and scuba instruction and snorkel and boat rentals. You can prepare your own meals in your suite's complete kitchen or partake of the exotic fare at the Eden Restaurant. Contact: Evelyn Stetler, Secret Harbour Beach Resort, P.O. Box 7576, St. Thomas, USVI 00801. Call 1-800-524-2250 (in St. Thomas, 809-775-6550).

Children: Y   Pets: N   Smoking: Y   Handicap Access: N   Payment: All

Charlotte Amalie

SNUG HARBOR   *Rates: deluxe*
Open: year-round   *Minimum Stay: one week*
A handsome stone fireplace is the focal point of this home's delightfully open living room decorated with striking dark tiles and traditional furniture. Doors and windows open to the beautiful green foliage of the tropics and reveal fabulous views of both the harbor and the British Virgin Islands. There are four spacious bedrooms, all but one on ground level. Water sports, tennis, golf and shopping are among the favorite pursuits of energetic guests. Others prefer to ride through the

lush, tranquil hillsides, searching for a perfect picnic spot or to bake in the glorious sun and wade in the warm waters of a secluded cove. Contact: Island Hideaways, 1317 Rhode Island Ave. NW, Suite 503, Washington, DC 20005. Call 1-800-832-2302 (in the District of Columbia, 202-667-9652).

Children: Y Pets: N Smoking: Y Handicap Access: N Payment: C, P, T

Charlotte Amalie

SOUTHWIND

Rates: deluxe

Open: year-round

Minimum Stay: one week

Elegant tiles, pale dhurrie carpets, stylish rattan furniture and gracefully arching doorways characterize this elegantly appointed villa above Charlotte Amalie Harbor. Several of the archways open onto a large tiled gallery with delightful views, a perfect place to enjoy your meals. The main part of the house includes two master suites with private baths, while down by the pool there is another bedroom suite with its own living room and kitchenette—a delightful arrangement for friends who want to vacation but not live together. Contact: Wimco, 28 Pelham St., Newport, RI 02840. Call 1-800-932-3222 (in Rhode Island, 401-849-8012). Ref. BB-STH.

Children: Y Pets: N Smoking: Y Handicap Access: N Payment: C, P, T, A

Charlotte Amalie

THE SUGAR APPLE

Rates: deluxe

Open: year-round

Minimum Stay: one week

Poised above the harbor in a quiet residential neighborhood, this home offers both seclusion and convenience. Furnished in typical island fashion, it enchants guests with its cool white tiles, exposed-beam ceilings, tropical houseplants and comfortable furniture. There are three large bedrooms in addition to the spacious living room and dining room inside, and outside you'll find a pool and beautiful gardens. A plethora of charming restaurants and duty-free shops specializing in luxury items await you below. Contact: Island Hideaways, 1317 Rhode Island Ave. NW, Suite 503, Washington, DC 20005. Call 1-800-832-2302 (in the District of Columbia, 202-667-9652).

Children: Y Pets: N Smoking: Y Handicap Access: N Payment: C, P, T

Charlotte Amalie

VILLA BLANCA

Rates: budget-moderate

Open: year-round

Minimum Stay: none

Surrounded by tropical flowers and prolific fruit trees, this small hotel offers splendid views from the balconies in each room. To the east there are the magnificent rolling hills, the turquoise ribbon of Drake's Channel, and the mountainous British Virgin Islands beyond—a panorama that shimmers into brilliance with every sunrise. To the west you'll look out on the energetic harbor where elegant ships glide serenely and where the sun sets in a sultry blaze. Your charming hostess and her efficient staff have created a tropical retreat that is relaxed, tranquil, and intimate. The single and double rooms are beautifully furnished with modern decor; each includes a color TV, a kitchenette, and a ceiling fan for setting the mood. Contact: Blanca Smith, 4 Raphune Hill, P.O. Box 7505, St. Thomas, U.S. Virgin Islands 00801. Call 809-776-0749 or 809-776-9059.

Children: Y Pets: N Smoking: Y Handicap access: N Payment: C, T, A, V, M

Cowpet Bay

ANCHORAGE BEACH VILLAS   *Rates: moderate-deluxe*
Open: year-round   *Minimum Stay: three nights*

Enjoying a fine location in a very prestigious neighborhood, these two- and three-bedroom condos can accommodate up to six vacationers and offer the luxurious amenities generally found only at larger resorts. The tastefully furnished rooms are air-conditioned and boast color TV, and most feature decks with charming views. Both a friendly bar and a charming restaurant are found on the premises, perfect places for refreshment after an invigorating swim in the pool. Frequent maid service is provided and there are laundry facilities available. Perhaps best of all, these condos are conveniently close to a number of popular pursuits, from boating, snorkeling and other water sports, to golf and tennis at nearby facilities. Contact: Barbara Shuett, Property Management Caribbean, Anchorage Rt. 6, No. 8, St. Thomas, USVI 00802. Call 1-800-524-2038 (in St. Thomas, 809-775-6220).

Children: Y   Pets: N   Smoking: Y   Handicap Access: N   Payment: All

Cowpet Bay

COWPET BAY RESIDENCE   *Rates: deluxe*
Open: year-round   *Minimum Stay: one week*

The diamond-studded night sky at quiet Cowpet Bay is beautiful enough, but the sunrises here are simply ravishing. This stylish holiday home is elegantly furnished with tile floors, glass-top tables, comfy rattan furniture and cheerful tropical prints; the four bedrooms can accommodate up to eight guests. Whether your dream vacation includes snorkeling and sailing, tennis and golf, shopping and restaurant hopping or just soaking up the sun on a flower-laden terrace or sugar-white beach, St. Thomas promises to make your fantasies come true. Contact: Rent A Home International, 7200 34th Ave. N.W., Seattle, WA 98117. Call 206-545-6963.

Children: Y Pets: N Smoking: Y Handicap Access: N Payment: C, P, T, V, M

Cowpet Bay

DECK POINT ROAD HOME   *Rates: moderate-deluxe*
Open: year-round   *Minimum Stay: three nights*

Surrounded by luxuriant tropical foliage, this stylish contemporary home in the prestigious Anchorage area offers splendid accommodations for up to eight people. Furnishings in the very large living and dining area highlight rattan, wrought iron and Italian ceramic tile. The festive main bathroom boasts a sunken tub, a long white vanity and tropical pink tile. A sun room, kitchen and two bedrooms round out the accommodations. Swimming, fishing, snorkeling, scuba diving and other water sports can be enjoyed at the nearby beach, as can the time-honored practices of sand-castle construction and soaking up some rays. Contact: Vacation Home Rentals Worldwide, 235 Kensington Ave., Norwood, NJ 07648. Call 1-800-633-3284 (in New Jersey, 201-767-9393). Ref. ST100.

Children: Y   Pets: N   Smoking: Y   Handicap Access: Y   Payment: C, P, T

Denmark Hill

ISLAND STAR   *Rates: deluxe*
Open: year-round   *Minimum Stay: one week*

Located on a mountain above Charlotte Amalie, this gracious three-bedroom, three-and-a-half-bath villa is surrounded by the aquamarine Caribbean on all sides. Traditionally furnished, the spacious interior houses a dining area with a library, living areas that open onto decks overlooking the sea and a beautiful walled-in garden. A private pool with spacious deck lets you sun and swim in perfect peace; at night, you can try star-gazing through the telescope located on the corner of one of the terraces. You're only a few minutes' walk from town here, making this a great spot for a full island holiday. Contact: LaCure Villas, 11661 San Vicente Blvd., Suite 1010, Los Angeles, CA 90049. Call 800-387-2715/2720

Children: Y   Pets: N   Smoking: Y   Handicap Access: N   Payment: All

East End

PAVILIONS AND POOLS HOTEL   *Rates: moderate-deluxe*
Open: year-round   *Minimum Stay: none*

Living up to its name, this unusual hotel offers completely private one-bedroom villas, each with its own pavilion and pool surrounded by lush tropical gardens. The villas themselves feature handsome rattan furniture, complete kitchens, fully tiled bathrooms with sunken garden showers, dressing rooms and spacious living and dining areas; all are air-conditioned. The convivial lounge is a great place to meet both old friends and new, and the creamy white sands of beautiful Sapphire Beach are only a few minutes away. Contact: Tammy Hurst, Pavilions and Pools Hotel, Route 6, St. Thomas, USVI 00802. Call 800-524-2001 (in St. Thomas, 809-775-6110).

Children: Y   Pets: N   Smoking: Y   Handicap Access: N   Payment: All

Frenchman's Bay

EL SOL   *Rates: deluxe*
Open: year-round   *Minimum Stay: one week*

This newly built home on a cool hillside will delight you with its views of the neighboring isles: St. Croix and Vieques stretch out before you like so many emeralds in a sapphire setting. The elegantly furnished living and dining area features incredibly high ceilings with exposed beams and a row of sliding glass doors through which you can enjoy the scenery. The doors open to the very large sun deck, just right for dining or reclining. Both a pool and a Jacuzzi are found on the premises and there are three pleasant bedrooms inside. Contact: Villa

Holidays, 13100 Wayzata Blvd., Suite 150, Minneapolis, MN 55343. Call 1-800-328-6262 (in Minnesota, 612-591-0076).

Children: Y Pets: N Smoking: Y Handicap Access: N Payment: C, P, T, V, M

Frenchman's Bay

HARBORSIDE HOUSE *Rates: expensive-deluxe*
Open: year-round *Minimum Stay: one week*

Perched on a bluff above the picturesque harbor of Charlotte Amalie, this very private home offers splendid holiday lodgings for up to six people. In addition to the three spacious bedrooms and combined living and dining area, there is a wraparound gallery outside with another eating area, where you can dine while enjoying sweeping views of the aquamarine Caribbean. The kitchen is fully modern; conveniences include a dishwasher and a washer and dryer. The maid service will help make your Caribbean holiday even more carefree. It's just a short walk to the beach for some swimming or tennis, and water sports facilities, golf, tennis, shops and dining are all just a few minutes away by car. Contact: Rent A Home International, 7200 34th Ave. N.W., Seattle, WA 98117. Call 206-545-6963. Ref. VS/R003.

Children: Y Pets: N Smoking: Y Handicap Access: N Payment: C, P, T, V, M

Frenchman's Bay

SEA FOREVER *Rates: deluxe*
Open: year-round *Minimum Stay: one week*

You almost feel that you can see forever when you sit out on the covered patio of this home, enjoying the splendid emerald panorama of the island's entire southern side spread out beneath you; the living room's other patio offers equally charming views. Also found on this level are the master suite and a modern kitchen; a quaint spiral staircase leads down to two more bedrooms and another bathroom. The entire home has been recently redecorated to the highest standards. The pool outside is framed by luxuriant gardens, the perfect setting for a morning stroll or afternoon tea. Contact: Villa Holidays, 13100 Wayzata Blvd., Suite 150, Minneapolis, MN 55343. Call 1-800-328-6262 (in Minnesota, 612-591-0076).

Children: Y Pets: N Smoking: Y Handicap Access: N Payment: C, P, T, V, M

Frenchman's Bay

VILLA ODEON *Rates: deluxe*
Open: year-round *Minimum Stay: one week*

Expansive gardens featuring jasmine and oleander, brilliant blossoms of bougainvillaea and hibiscus and delicious fruits such as papayas and mangoes surround this luxurious home. They are easily appreciated on one of the many terraces and walkways that encircle the villa and also lead out to the very large kidney-shaped pool. The four bedrooms and main living areas of this house display a tasteful blend of Asian and Caribbean furnishings, and architectural delights such as slate floors, French doors and ceiling fans are found throughout. Lovely Limetree Beach is just a few minutes away, as is all the duty-free shopping you could desire. Contact: Nancy Anderson or Donajen Farrar, McLaughlin Anderson Vacations, 100 Blackbeard's Hill, St. Thomas, USVI 00802. Call 1-800-537-6246 (in St. Thomas, 809-776-0635).

Children: Y   Pets: N   Smoking: Y   Handicap Access: N   Payment: C, P, T

Havensight

HARBOR STAR
Open: year-round

Rates: moderate-expensive
Minimum Stay: one week

Furnished by one of the island's foremost decorators, this lovely villa poised above the bay offers you comfortable accommodations, modern amenities and exciting views. The living room and terrace overlook the deep blue harbor, the hub of this vibrant island where elegant cruise ships sail in and out. Inside you'll find high ceilings and impeccable decor in the one bedroom and main living areas of the house. Outside are an inviting pool and sumptuous gardens. Dedicated shoppers will be delighted by the duty-free shopping within walking distance and everyone will be charmed by the gentle waters of Morningstar Beach. Contact: Villa Holidays, 13100 Wayzata Blvd., Suite 150, Minneapolis, MN 55343. Call 1-800-328-6262 (in Minnesota, 612-591-0076).

Children: Y Pets: N Smoking: Y Handicap Access: N Payment: C, P, T, V, M

Havensight

LOVEJOIS'
Open: year-round

Rates: moderate
Minimum Stay: one week

A swath of lush foliage, a sparkling blue bay alive with sailing ships, the charming harbor and green hills beyond can be the delightful panorama you enjoy over your morning coffee when you stay at this lovely traditional West Indian-style home. The house offers two bedrooms, stylish living areas and a well-equipped kitchen. The warm waters of renowned Morningstar Beach are just a few minutes away, and Charlotte Amalie awaits you with interesting historical sights, friendly restaurants and pubs and irresistible boutiques. Contact: Villa Holidays, 13100 Wayzata Blvd., Suite 150, Minneapolis, MN 55343. Call 1-800-328-6262 (in Minnesota, 612-591-0076).

Children: Y Pets: N Smoking: Y Handicap Access: N Payment: C, P, T, V, M

Havensight

MY LADY'S MANOR
Open: year-round

Rates: deluxe
Minimum Stay: one week

This graciously appointed villa commands excellent views of the bay and harbor from its hillside position. The living room features a delightful cathedral ceiling and opens onto both the pool and courtyard. Two of the bedrooms are found off this courtyard, while the elegantly balustraded swimming pool and deck are flanked by the master bedroom wing and lovely veranda. There is also a comfortable family room with a well-stocked library for informal relaxing indoors. The picturesque streets, excellent restaurants, intimate cafes and enchanting shops of Charlotte Amalie are only a few minutes away. Contact:

Wimco, 28 Pelham St., Newport, RI 02840. Call 1-800-932-3222 (in Rhode Island, 401-849-8012). Ref. MA-MLM.
Children: Y Pets: N Smoking: Y Handicap Access: N Payment: C, P, T, A

Havensight

SEA WATCH   *Rates: deluxe*
Open: year-round   *Minimum Stay: one week*

Expansive walls of glass open the rooms of this lovely home to the even more exquisite views outside: a glittering harbor town nestled between rolling green hills and the sapphire-blue waters. An ambience of cool splendor is created by the tile used throughout the main living areas and the two large bedrooms (each with a private bath). The location is ideal for avid shoppers and sightseers who want to explore the duty-free bargains and picturesque streets of nearby Charlotte Amalie. After a day of pounding the pavement, you can relax in the hot tub of your tranquil retreat or take a dip in the pool, which also enjoys fabulous views. Contact: Wimco, 28 Pelham St., Newport, RI 02840. Call 1-800-932-3222 (in Rhode Island, 401-849-8012). Ref. MA-WAT.
Children: Y Pets: N Smoking: Y Handicap Access: N Payment: C, P, T, A

Havensight Hills

HARBOR VIEW   *Rates: expensive-deluxe*
Open: year-round   *Minimum Stay: one week*

A charming retreat for two, this one-bedroom, one-bath villa offers exquisite views from the stone terrace, which also features a pool for those who need a change of pace from the Caribbean. The spacious interior is cozily furnished and air-conditioned throughout. Boredom will never strike, for you're just minutes from the island capital of Charlotte Amalie, where you can rent bikes, scooters and boats for your adventures, or find bargains galore in the duty-free shops. You can arrange to have the villa fully staffed if you choose to just lean back and forget the meaning of the word "stress." Contact: LaCure Villas, 11661 San Vicente Blvd., Suite 1010, Los Angeles, CA 90049. Call 800-387-2715/2720.
Children: Y   Pets: N   Smoking: Y   Handicap Access: N   Payment: All

Hull Bay

ESTRELLITA   *Rates: deluxe*
Open: year-round   *Minimum Stay: one week*

Every luxury you've ever dreamt of—plus a few more—is waiting for you at Estrellita. First of all, this luxury resort enjoys a fabulous cliffside perch high above Hull Bay and beach access to the waters below. Added to this are the creature comforts of a Jacuzzi in the sumptuous master suite, another bedroom with its own bath, a gourmet kitchen, a wine fridge and a host of electronic gadgets. A large deck practically hangs over the water. Weekly maid service is included and those dedicated to vacationing in style can easily arrange for a chef and table service. Contact: Villa Holidays, 13100 Wayzata

Blvd., Suite 150, Minneapolis, MN 55343. Call 1-800-328-6262 (in Minnesota, 612-591-0076).

Children: Y Pets: N Smoking: Y Handicap Access: N Payment: C, P, T, V, M

Hull Bay

VILLA SATORI   *Rates: deluxe*
Open: year-round   *Minimum Stay: one week*

Secluded on a lushly planted acre of tropical foliage and profuse blossoms, this lovely villa is just a few minutes from the glorious beaches at either Hull Bay or Magen's Bay. As you walk into the capacious entrance hall, you'll be delighted by the full-sized Genip tree under the skylight. Upstairs is a large living room with cable TV, a VCR, stereo and a fully stocked bar. Two bedrooms are also found on this floor, while another bedroom, the kitchen and a den are located downstairs. Outside you can splash in the pool or soak in the Jacuzzi or just enjoy the spectacular views of the Brass Islands from one of the many decks. There is also a lovely lily pond with a melodic waterfall and exotic orchids, where you can contemplate the beauty of the tropics. Contact: Rent A Home International, 7200 34th Ave. N.W., Seattle, WA 98117. Call 206-545-6963.

Children: Y Pets: N Smoking: Y Handicap Access: N Payment: C, P, T, V, M

Magen's Bay

BEACH BLANKET BUNGALOW   *Rates: expensive-deluxe*
Open: year-round   *Minimum Stay: one week*

Those who seek an active vacation will be delighted with this cozy bungalow. Found just a few steps above the creamy white sands of a quiet pocket beach, the house offers two windsurfers for your recreational pleasure. The mile-long beach of Magen's Bay is just a bit further; here you can rent a sailboat or try some snorkeling. There's tennis less than two miles away and the fabulous Mahogany Run Golf Course is also nearby. After a day of sun and fun, you'll return to this comfortably furnished home with a complete kitchen. Each of the three bedrooms has its own private balcony, where you can listen to the sound of the waves and wish the moon good night. Contact: Island Hideaways, 1317 Rhode Island Ave. NW, Suite 503, Washington, DC 20005. Call 1-800-832-2302 (in the District of Columbia, 202-667-9652).

Children: Y Pets: N Smoking: Y Handicap Access: N Payment: C, P, T

Magen's Bay

EVER-GREEN   *Rates: deluxe*
Open: year-round   *Minimum Stay: one week*

It's no wonder that so much of Ever-Green's wall space has been devoted to sliding glass doors: What artificial decoration could possibly be more alluring than the luscious blue of Magen's Bay and the emerald hues of the neighboring islands, all beneath an endless azure sky? This lovely home in a very exclusive neighborhood offers tropical elegance with its delightfully furnished rooms and unbelievably large sun deck. Palm fronds, cool tiles and pale ceilings adorn the interior, which includes three bedrooms and a TV room. The wonderfully landscaped grounds encompass an L-shaped pool flanked by a charming cabana. Contact: Villa Holidays, 13100 Wayzata Blvd., Suite 150, Minneapolis, MN 55343. Call 1-800-328-6262 (in Minnesota, 612-591-0076).

Children: Y Pets: N Smoking: Y Handicap Access: N Payment: C, P, T, V, M

Magen's Bay

FAIRWINDS *Rates: deluxe*
Open: year-round *Minimum Stay: one week*

The architectural splendor of Fairwinds offers sumptous accommodations for six people distributed among several very private buildings connected by walkways. Each of the three suites includes a sitting area, dressing room, a full bathroom and an outdoor shower with privacy fencing. The main area of the house boasts a kitchen exquisitely equipped right down to the food processor and automatic coffee maker, a sunken living room with a cable TV and a CD player and a charming dining area with a skylight. Outside there is almost endless deck area, a large swimming pool and fabulous views of the azure Caribbean. Contact: Nancy Anderson or Donajen Farrar, McLaughlin Anderson Vacations, 100 Blackbeard's Hill, St. Thomas, USVI 00802. Call 1-800-537-6246 (in St. Thomas, 809-776-0635).

Children: N Pets: N Smoking: Y Handicap Access: N Payment: C, P, T

Magen's Bay

FRANGIPANI *Rates: expensive-deluxe*
Open: year-round *Minimum Stay: one week*

The tile floors, high exposed-beam ceilings and sleek furnishings of this light and airy home combine to create the cool, casual elegance that is the epitome of island living. Situated in a glade of flowering shrubs, it also enjoys delightful views of Magen's Bay, whose beaches are reputed to be some of the most beautiful in the world. Each of the two large bedrooms boasts a private bathroom; a variety of sitting areas provide plenty of living space—the open-air dining room is a particularly nice place to spend an evening with old friends or new. To top it all off, there is a luxurious pool awaiting you outside. Contact: Wimco, 28 Pelham St., Newport, RI 02840. Call 1-800-932-3222 (in Rhode Island, 401-849-8012). Ref. MA-FRA.

Children: Y Pets: N Smoking: Y Handicap Access: N Payment: C, P, T, A

Magen's Bay

GRIMM COTTAGE *Rates: moderate*
Open: year-round *Minimum Stay: one week*

A charming cottage perched on a hillside, featuring comfortable accommodations within and lovely views outside—Grimm Cottage makes a most cheerful vacation home. The casual look of this cabana-style house is complemented by rustic Mexican tile and simple archways. The high ceilings, spare furnishings and pale walls will keep you feeling cool and comfortable; louvered glass windows open to catch just a bit more of the cool trade winds. To really enjoy a sea breeze, though, just throw open the sliding glass doors in the living room and step out onto the marvelously sunny deck, where the views of the open sea go on and on. Contact: Villa Holidays, 13100 Wayzata Blvd., Suite 150, Minneapolis, MN 55343. Call 1-800-328-6262 (in Minnesota, 612-591-0076).

Children: Y Pets: N Smoking: Y Handicap Access: N Payment: C, P, T, V, M

Magen's Bay

HEAVENLY SPENT
Open: year-round

Rates: deluxe
Minimum Stay: one week

What better ambience for a tropical retreat than a bit of Polynesian splendor? Heavenly Spent's colorful island styling adorns its spacious interior and many outside living areas. All three of the bedrooms boast adjoining baths and two open onto private patios built directly into the rocks. The movie library offers more than 400 films for your viewing pleasure. The delightful living and dining area opens onto an observation deck and a sun deck with a pool and a hot tub. This is also a great place to enjoy dinner or an evening cocktail, as the views of the open waters are superb. Contact: Wimco, 28 Pelham St., Newport, RI 02840. Call 1-800-932-3222 (in Rhode Island, 401-849-8012). Ref. MA-HEA.

Children: N Pets: N Smoking: Y Handicap Access: N Payment: C, P, T, A

Magen's Bay

ISLAND FANTASY
Open: year-round

Rates: expensive-deluxe
Minimum Stay: one week

Have you always dreamed of an elegantly furnished home with a full complement of creature comforts and modern amenities, all enjoying an incredibly beautiful setting on a tropical shore? If so, this could be your island fantasy come true. The private pool invites you to spend at least one golden afternoon soaking up the sun and splashing in the water. Each of the three sumptuous bedrooms has its own full bathroom en suite, and the modern kitchen is excellently equipped. Views of the ocean will delight you in every room—you may even spot some of the friendly cetaceans who winter here. Contact: Villa Holidays, 13100 Wayzata Blvd., Suite 150, Minneapolis, MN 55343. Call 1-800-328-6262 (in Minnesota, 612-591-0076).

Children: Y Pets: N Smoking: Y Handicap Access: N Payment: C, P, T, V, M

Magen's Bay

MAGEN'S POINT RESORT HOTEL
Open: year-round

Rates: inexpensive-deluxe
Minimum Stay: three nights

Magen's Bay Beach is considered by some to be one of the most beautiful beaches in the world—decide for yourself during your stay at this delightful resort. The studio, one- and two-bedroom apartments are tastefully furnished and feature air-conditioning, maid service and color TV. Enjoy the chef's creations at the poolside Green Parrot Restaurant or prepare a tropical feast of your own in the convenient kitchenette. The pool is surrounded by tropical rock garden with a sparkling waterfall. There's a tennis pro available to help you with your forehand and scuba instructors to introduce you to the wonders of the deep; you can also enjoy golf at the Mahogany Run course or swimming, sailing and snorkeling at the beach. Contact: Bob Jones, Magen's Point Resort Hotel, Magen's Rd., St. Thomas, USVI 00802. Call 1-800-524-2031 (in St. Thomas, 809-775-5500).

Children: Y Pets: N Smoking: Y Handicap Access: N Payment: C, T, A, V, M

Magen's Bay

MAISON BIJOU   *Rates: deluxe*
Open: year-round   *Minimum Stay: one week*

This opulent jewel is found on the cool northern shore of the island and enjoys exquisite views of the Caribbean. Italian marble graces the floors, staircases and fireplaces; cathedral ceilings, brass chandeliers and French doors are among the other elegant details. Each of the four bedrooms in the main house has its own cable TV and a private phone; the master suite boasts a private balcony, double sinks and showerheads and a marble Jacuzzi. There is also a charming cottage for up to four more guests. The elegant pool is surrounded by a sunny patio, which enjoys unobstructed views of the wild blue seas. Contact: Rent A Home International, 7200 34th Ave. N.W., Seattle, WA 98117. Call 206-545-6963.

Children: Y Pets: N Smoking: Y Handicap Access: N Payment: C, P, T, V, M

Magen's Bay

MIRAMAR   *Rates: deluxe*
Open: year-round   *Minimum Stay: one week*

Beautiful Magen's Bay Beach lies below Miramar, and the mysterious uninhabited island of Hans Lollick can be seen in the distance. French doors in every room of the first floor display this view and open onto the covered galleries and spacious decks. The main part of the house includes a spacious living room, dining room, bedroom with a sitting room and kitchen; the festive decor blends Caribbean color and Mexican tile. On the other side of the pool, there is a very private guest house with two more bedrooms. Maid service is included and creature comforts such as cable TV and a stereo with CD player abound. Contact: Nancy Anderson or Donajen Farrar, McLaughlin Anderson Vacations, 100 Blackbeard's Hill, St. Thomas, USVI 00802. Call 1-800-537-6246 (in St. Thomas, 809-776-0635).

Children: Y Pets: N Smoking: Y Handicap Access: N Payment: C, P, T

Magen's Bay

NIRVANA   *Rates: deluxe*
Open: year-round   *Minimum Stay: one week*

Dreamlike transcendence may indeed be yours at Nirvana, an elegant villa set among delicate palms. The decor features room after room of cool white and pale hues, creating a sense of serenity and spaciousness. The two larger of the three bedrooms have their own cable TVs and another cable TV, VCR and stereo with CD player are found in the entertainment center in the living room. The large eat-in kitchen is well equipped with a dishwasher and a microwave. There is a charming alfresco dining veranda out by the tiled pool, which is surrounded by a large sun deck. From here there are sumptuous views of the Virgin Islands stretching out like a string of jewels set in the aquamarine sea. Contact: Nancy Anderson or Donajen Farrar, McLaughlin Anderson Vacations, 100 Blackbeard's Hill, St. Thomas, USVI 00802. Call 1-800-537-6246 (in St. Thomas, 809-776-0635).

Children: Y   Pets: N   Smoking: Y   Handicap Access: N   Payment: C, P, T

Magen's Bay
PETERBORG-BY-THE-SEA   *Rates: expensive-deluxe*
Open: year-round   *Minimum Stay: one week*

Set amid tropical trees and luxuriant blossoms on the very shore of Magen's Bay, this two-bedroom apartment offers luxury and seclusion only steps away from the crystal-blue waters of the sea. Out on the private veranda or down below on the spacious sun deck, you can soak up the glorious Caribbean sun while listening to the soothing song of the waves; if you get a bit too warm, why not jump right into the water from the magnificent boulders that line the shore here? In the evening, the sight of the dazzling sunset reflecting off the calm water is simply breathtaking. To complete the fantasy, a car is included in the package so you can more easily explore this emerald isle. Contact: Nancy Anderson or Donajen Farrar, McLaughlin Anderson Vacations, 100 Blackbeard's Hill, St. Thomas, USVI 00802. Call 1-800-537-6246 (in St. Thomas, 809-776-0635).

Children: N   Pets: N   Smoking: Y   Handicap Access: N   Payment: C, P, T

Magen's Bay
SAND DOLLAR   *Rates: deluxe*
Open: year-round   *Minimum Stay: one week*

The long, balustraded gallery with its rustic ceiling and gentle archways overlooking a deep blue harbor may tempt you to imagine yourself somewhere on the Mediterranean. But the lush tropical landscaping, splendid white sands and warm island smiles will convince you that this must be the Caribbean. This villa features gracious appointments and air conditioning in all three of the bedrooms. Outside there is a private beach, a lovely pool and a pavilion for dining or just passing the time. Contact: Villa Holidays, 13100 Wayzata Blvd., Suite 150, Minneapolis, MN 55343. Call 1-800-328-6262 (in Minnesota, 612-591-0076).

Children: Y Pets: N Smoking: Y Handicap Access: N Payment: C, P, T, V, M

Magen's Bay
SEACLIFF   *Rates: deluxe*
Open: year-round   *Minimum Stay: one week*

A charming pathway of several decks adorned with wild orchids, palms trees and frangipani leads you to the delightful entryway of Seacliff. The full-length windows in every room capitalize on the spectacular views of the cliffs, the neighboring islands and the Atlantic afforded by Seacliff's position on Picara Point. White tile floors reflect the glorious sunshine that streams in through these windows and the furnishings are a blend of tasteful wicker pieces and fine antiques. Two of the three bedrooms (all with en suite baths) and the cathedral-ceilinged living and dining area open directly onto the upper sun deck, which runs the full length of the house. Steps from here lead down to the lovely swimming pool. Contact: Vacation Home Rentals Worldwide, 235 Kensington Ave., Norwood, NJ 07648. Call 1-800-633-3284 (in New Jersey, 201-767-9393). Ref. ST103.

Children: N   Pets: N   Smoking: Y   Handicap Access: N   Payment: C, P, T

Magen's Bay

SERENDIPITY   *Rates: deluxe*
Open: year-round   *Minimum Stay: one week*

You arrive at this tranquil retreat only after wending your way along the dramatic coastline of the island's cool northern shore. Gorgeous views of both the sparkling waters and the green expanse of the neighboring Mahogany Run Golf Course are to be enjoyed from many large picture windows and the wraparound deck. All four of the spacious bedrooms have private baths and the living room is stylishly furnished with tropical-inspired prints and pale tile. Outside there is a charming ornamental waterfall that flows directly into the lovely pool. Contact: Wimco, 28 Pelham St., Newport, RI 02840. Call 1-800-932-3222 (in Rhode Island, 401-849-8012). Ref. MA-SER.

Children: Y   Pets: N   Smoking: Y   Handicap Access: N   Payment: C, P, T, A

Magen's Bay

SUNSET   *Rates: deluxe*
Open: year-round   *Minimum Stay: one week*

From this secluded position near Magen's Bay, there are lovely views of both the northern and western coasts of the island. And you'll want to spend at least one evening out on the spacious deck with a pina colada in hand, watching the dazzling sunset. The accommodations here are roomy and comfortable, with three bedrooms and a den to stretch out and relax in. The house also boasts lush tropical gardens to stroll through; a lovely pool where you can swim; and a hot tub to soak in after a day of water sports, golf or tennis at some of the nearby facilities. Contact: Villa Holidays, 13100 Wayzata Blvd., Suite 150, Minneapolis, MN 55343. Call 1-800-328-6262 (in Minnesota, 612-591-0076).

Children: Y   Pets: N   Smoking: Y   Handicap Access: N   Payment: C, P, T, V, M

Magen's Bay

TANQUERAY VILLA   *Rates: expensive*
Open: year-round   *Minimum Stay: one week*

Golfers will be delighted by this villa, which overlooks the magnificent grounds of the Mahogany Run Golf Course and the blue sea beyond. The very generous sun deck is a marvelous place to relax after playing a couple of holes; the quiet residential neighborhood will make you feel less like a tourist and more like one of the lucky few who call this island home. Inside are two comfy bedrooms, roomy living areas and a well-equipped kitchen. In addition to golf, there's tennis, sailing, snorkeling and scuba diving for the active crowd; more sedate types may prefer just to bask in the sun, wade in the warm waters and enjoy the delectable local cuisine. Contact: Villa Holidays, 13100 Wayzata Blvd., Suite 150, Minneapolis, MN 55343. Call 1-800-328-6262 (in Minnesota, 612-591-0076).

Children: Y Pets: N Smoking: Y Handicap Access: N Payment: C, P, T, V, M

Magen's Bay

THE HERITAGE MANOR   *Rates: budget-moderate*
Open: year-round   *Minimum Stay: three nights*

Combining the privacy and intimacy of a house with the amenities of a modern hotel, The Heritage Manor offers bed-and-breakfast accommodations for discerning travelers. The interior is charmingly decorated with rich tile floors, leafy green plants, contemporary furniture and interesting objets d'art. The pleasant bedrooms are air-conditioned and feature convenient refrigerators for chilling a bottle of wine to be enjoyed later out on the balcony. A one-bedroom unit offers its own kitchen. The manor has its own swimming pool or you can go to the nearby beach for your daily fix of salt water and water sports activities. Contact: Diane Goh, The Heritage Manor, P.O. Box 90, St. Thomas, USVI 00804. Call 1-800-828-0757 (in St. Thomas, 809-774-3003).

Children: N Pets: N Smoking: Y Handicap Access: N Payment: C, T, A, V, M

Magen's Bay

THE TREE HOUSE   *Rates: inexpensive-moderate*
Open: year-round   *Minimum Stay: one week*

This studio cottage is tucked away in an excellent neighborhood on St. Thomas's northern coast. Exposed-beam ceilings, cheerful prints, rattan furniture and leafy green plants adorn the interior. Outside there's a delightful veranda where you can sip morning coffee or evening cocktails while watching the ever-changing view of the sea. Maid service is provided once a week. The shops and restaurants in town are only a few minutes away, as are the creamy sands and warm waters of famous Magen's Bay Beach. Contact: Villa Holidays, 13100 Wayzata Blvd., Suite 150, Minneapolis, MN 55343. Call 1-800-328-6262 (in Minnesota, 612-591-0076).

Children: Y Pets: N Smoking: Y Handicap Access: N Payment: C, P, T, V, M

Magen's Bay

VILLA KALLACHAI   *Rates: deluxe*
Open: year-round   *Minimum Stay: one week*

From its hillside perch on the cool northern side of the island, this sumptuous residence enjoys unparalleled views of Magen's Bay. A wall of glass doors opens to the sunny terrace; whether you're inside or out, you can watch ships glide by on the azure waters or contemplate the expanse of white beaches and green hills beyond. Three bedrooms, a large kitchen and a TV room are also found in this impressive house. The exclusive neighborhood ensures complete tranquillity and the private pool promises total relaxation. Contact: Villa Holidays, 13100 Wayzata Blvd., Suite 150, Minneapolis, MN 55343. Call 1-800-328-6262 (in Minnesota, 612-591-0076).

Children: Y Pets: N Smoking: Y Handicap Access: N Payment: C, P, T, V, M

Magen's Bay

VILLA MAREA *Rates: deluxe*
Open: year-round *Minimum Stay: one week*

Occupying a coveted position high in a secluded, private cove, this dramatic villa enjoys fabulous views of the surf below and neighboring St. John and the British Virgin Islands. A series of French doors opens onto this panorama, which can also be enjoyed from the splendid pool and patio. Inside you'll find Mexican tile throughout, a stunning granite kitchen and magnificent marble baths. These luxurious accommodations include three large bedrooms, all with excellent views. Tennis, golf and a variety of water sports can be found in the neighborhood. Contact: Villa Holidays, 13100 Wayzata Blvd., Suite 150, Minneapolis, MN 55343. Call 1-800-328-6262 (in Minnesota, 612-591-0076).

Children: Y Pets: N Smoking: Y Handicap Access: N Payment: C, P, T, V, M

Mandahl

DAYBREAK *Rates: expensive-deluxe*
Open: year-round *Minimum Stay: one week*

Charming rattan furniture and friendly houseplants create a feeling of warmth and informality, while stunning white tiles and glittering mirrors add sophisticated glamour to this luxurious two-bedroom condominium. The views of the ocean from the sunny balcony are lovely and the entire residence is air-conditioned. The complex has its own large swimming pool and a plethora of sports facilities are at hand. Venture a bit beyond your own doorstep and you'll be delighted by the glistening beaches and quaint shops of the neighborhood. Contact: Villa Holidays, 13100 Wayzata Blvd., Suite 150, Minneapolis, MN 55343. Call 1-800-328-6262 (in Minnesota, 612-591-0076).

Children: Y Pets: N Smoking: Y Handicap Access: N Payment: C, P, T, V, M

Mandahl

SEASCAPE *Rates: deluxe*
Open: year-round *Minimum Stay: one week*

Ideal for friends who enjoy vacationing together but still value their privacy, this unusual home is really a compound comprised of three separate structures. The main part of the house includes a spacious split-level living and dining area, which also serves as a bedroom; the other two-bedroom suites are connected to this by charming walkways. All three are elegantly furnished in wicker and earth tones, and all are surrounded by decking with magnificent views of the neighboring islands. Golf and tennis are available nearby and the property has its own delightful swimming pool. Contact: Villa Holidays, 13100 Wayzata Blvd., Suite 150, Minneapolis, MN 55343. Call 1-800-328-6262 (in Minnesota, 612-591-0076).

Children: Y Pets: N Smoking: Y Handicap Access: N Payment: C, P, T, V, M

Mandahl

THE BIRD HOUSE   *Rates: moderate*
Open: year-round   *Minimum Stay: one week*

From the private terrace of this house, there are lovely views across the glittering waters of Pillsbury Sound to the green hills of St. John and the open seas beyond. One half of a duplex, this holiday residence has a separate entryway, its own charming garden and a pleasant patio where guests often enjoy meals while recounting the exploits of the day. Water enthusiasts may choose between the lovely pool shared with the owner and the gentle warm waters at nearby Pineapple Beach. Contact: Wimco, 28 Pelham St., Newport, RI 02840. Call 1-800-932-3222 (in Rhode Island, 401-849-8012). Ref. MA-BRD.

Children: Y Pets: N Smoking: Y Handicap Access: N Payment: C, P, T, A

Mandahl

TRANQUILITY   *Rates: deluxe*
Open: year-round   *Minimum Stay: one week*

This recently completed villa has been designed with every vacationer's dream holiday in mind. Each of the three-bedroom suites is handsomely appointed with rich Brazilian mahogany and features a pedestal-mounted bed, a Jacuzzi and a steam bath. The dining room offers splendid ocean views from every seat and there are two elegantly furnished sitting rooms to relax in. The true splendor of Tranquility is perhaps best appreciated outside, as you splash in the pool or sit under an umbrella on the flagstone patio, over whose gently curving balustrade you may view the tops of delicate palm fronds and the endless blue waters of the Caribbean. Contact: Nancy Anderson or Donajen Farrar, McLaughlin Anderson Vacations, 100 Blackbeard's Hill, St. Thomas, U.S. Virgin Islands 00802. Call 1-800-537-6246 (in St. Thomas, 809-776-0635).

Children: Y Pets: N Smoking: Y Handicap Access: N Payment: C, P, T

Mandahl

ZOOK HOUSE   *Rates: moderate*
Open: year-round   *Minimum Stay: one week*

A quiet locale, beautiful views of the water and glittering St. John and comfortable furnishings are among the main attractions of this cozy two-bedroom home. Numerous picture windows let the golden sun inside and louvers open to catch a bit more of the cooling trade winds. The use of an automobile is also included, so you'll be free to explore a bit off the beaten track: The hidden coves, verdant valleys, charming villages with narrow streets and the venerable legacy of the island's plantation past are all within easy reach. Contact: Villa

Holidays, 13100 Wayzata Blvd., Suite 150, Minneapolis, MN 55343. Call 1-800-328-6262 (in Minnesota, 612-591-0076).
Children: Y Pets: N Smoking: Y Handicap Access: N Payment: C, P, T, V, M

North Shore

HARMONY HOUSE   *Rates: deluxe*
Open: year-round   *Minimum Stay: one week*
This exquisite three-bedroom villa on the north side features considerable living space, excellent furnishings and delightful views. A fireplace ornamented by an elegant mirror is found in the lovely living and dining room, whose pale walls and large windows fill the space with light. The enormous gourmet kitchen boasts another dining area for informal dining or you can enjoy your meals out on the patio, which flanks a 40-foot pool with underwater lights and a Jacuzzi. More outdoor living space is found on the large covered veranda and there's also a large yard for afternoon frolicking. Modern amenities include a cable TV, stereo, barbecue and washer and dryer. A full-time housekeeper and cook are available. Contact: Villa Holidays, 13100 Wayzata Blvd., Suite 150, Minneapolis, MN 55343. Call 1-800-328-6262 (in Minnesota, 612-591-0076).
Children: Y Pets: N Smoking: Y Handicap Access: N Payment: C, P, T, V, M

Peterborg

EAGLE'S NEST   *Rates: deluxe*
Open: year-round   *Minimum Stay: one week*
Set on a cliffside perch above the Caribbean, this elegant villa has a private pool where you can sun in seclusion on the fully furnished wooden deck. Dine outside under the stars at the table for four, and watch the ships go by. Swim in the azure sea by day and dive or snorkel around a reef. Go windsurfing or rent scooters in town to explore this magnificent island. You can cook at home in the modern kitchen, or arrange for a full staff to care for you. This comfortably furnished villa has plump cushions on modern rattan furniture, inviting you to curl up with a book at night before sleeping to the sounds of the sea in four lovely bedrooms. Contact: LaCure Villas, 11661 San Vicente Blvd., Suite 1010, Los Angeles, CA 90049. Call 800-387-2715/ 2720.
Children: Y   Pets: N   Smoking: Y   Handicap Access: N   Payment: All

Peterborg

GAZEBO VILLA   *Rates: deluxe*
Open: year-round   *Minimum Stay: one week*
Sun yourself all day on the virtually private white beach, and snorkel, swim and dive in the azure waters of the Caribbean right outside your door. This beautiful three-bedroom, three-bath air-conditioned villa is situated on meticulously landscaped property and features a private pool surrounded by a wooden deck, plus a corner gazebo where you can take a break from the sun. The interior of this home is furnished in cool white wicker covered with pastel cushions. This perfect spot

enjoys spectacular views of the hills and the sea. You can arrange to have a full staff on hand if desired. Contact: LaCure Villas, 11661 San Vicente Blvd., Suite 1010, Los Angeles, CA 90049. Call 800-387-2715/2720.

Children: Y   Pets: N   Smoking: Y   Handicap Access: N   Payment: All

Peterborg

TRADEWINDS   *Rates: deluxe*
Open: year-round   *Minimum Stay: one week*

This spectacular contemporary home constructed of cedar and stone offers complete privacy and panoramic views of the Caribbean. Swim laps in a pool exquisitely set into a wooden deck overlooking the water, or run down to the white sand beach for all manner of water sports. Three bedrooms and three and a half baths welcome you at bedtime, and the spacious living areas are furnished in cool, contemporary wicker. For the ultimate in luxury, call ahead and arrange for a staff to serve you. Any way you take it, this is a vacation spot to relieve all your cares. Contact: LaCure Villas, 11661 San Vicente Blvd., Suite 1010, Los Angeles, CA 90049. Call 800-387-2715/2720.

Children: Y   Pets: N   Smoking: Y   Handicap Access: N   Payment: All

Red Hook

RED HOOK MOUNTAIN APARTMENTS   *Rates: budget-expensive*
Open: year-round   *Minimum Stay: none*

Cooling trade winds caress these mountainside apartments, which offer tranquillity and carefree hospitality only a few miles from bustling Charlotte Amalie. Each comfortable apartment has a fully equipped kitchen and a private deck or screened porch with charming island views. There is also a large common deck with lounges for sunbathing and a complete outdoor kitchen just right for grilling up the daily catch. Perfect for those who ask nothing but sun, surf and sand in the ideal vacation, Red Hook Mountain Apartments are also convenient to the recreational amenities and lively entertainments of the larger resorts. Contact: R. Fulton, Red Hook Mountain Apartments, P.O. Box 9139, St. Thomas, USVI 00801. Call 809-775-6111.

Children: Y   Pets: N   Smoking: Y   Handicap Access: N   Payment: C, T

Red Hook

SAPPHIRE VILLAGE   *Rates: inexpensive-expensive*
Open: year-round   *Minimum Stay: three nights*

Found on the lively eastern end of the island, this delightful condo village combines tasteful accommodations with modern convenience. Both the studio and one-bedroom residences have separate living and dining rooms, dressing rooms and fully equipped kitchens; additional amenities include air conditioning and cable TV. The spacious decks enjoy spectacular views and they are comfortably furnished for your dining and entertaining pleasure. Two large pools, a convivial restaurant and a bar comprise the recreational facilities of the village. The nearby beach is a favorite of swimmers, snorkelers and sun worshippers alike; deep-sea fishing and other water sports are available nearby. Contact: Barbara Shuett, Sapphire Village, Anchorage Route 6, No. 8, St. Thomas, USVI 00802. Call 1-800-524-2038 (in St. Thomas, 809-775-6220).

Children: **Y**   Pets: **N**   Smoking: **Y**   Handicap Access: **N**   Payment: All

Red Hook

SEAWARD   *Rates: deluxe*
Open: year-round   *Minimum Stay: one week*

If the lure of smooth blue waters and ever-changing vistas proves too strong for the seafarer in you, why not consider this graceful 49-foot motor yacht? Whether you take a skipper along or sail it yourself, you'll be richly rewarded with unparalleled views, a unique knowledge of the cays and coves and the lullaby of gently lapping waves soothing you to sleep at night. Luxurious accommodations are provided in the four double staterooms and a saloon that sleeps two more mariners. And what cruise would be complete without a galley fully stocked with delicious food and potent potables? Contact: Villa Holidays, 13100 Wayzata Blvd., Suite 150, Minneapolis, MN 55343. Call 1-800-328-6262 (in Minnesota, 612-591-0076).

Children: **Y** Pets: **N** Smoking: **Y** Handicap Access: **N** Payment: C, P, T, V, M

Red Hook

SERENISSIMA   *Rates: deluxe*
Open: year-round   *Minimum Stay: one week*

This sophisticated Italian-style villa is a splendid abode for groups of friends, family reunions or anyone who wants to vacation in luxurious style. The king-sized master suite boasts two separate bathrooms and private balcony for sipping your morning cappuccino. There are four more bedrooms and bathrooms here, in addition to the spacious main living areas of the house. Outside is a delightfully colonnaded veranda, which overlooks not only the graceful pool and patio but the blue waters and green isles beyond. Contact: Wimco, 28 Pelham St., Newport, RI 02840. Call 1-800-932-3222 (in Rhode Island, 401-849-8012). Ref. AC-SER.

Children: **Y** Pets: **N** Smoking: **Y** Handicap Access: **N** Payment: C, P, T, A

Red Hook

TREETOP VILLA   *Rates: moderate-deluxe*
Open: year-round   *Minimum Stay: one week*

This villa handsomely blends the legacy of St. Thomas's Danish past with a hint of exotic East Indian styling. Terra-cotta tile floors, gracefully arched windows and handsome louvered doors adorn the interior, which includes two luxurious master suites and a spacious living and dining area. From this latter room you can walk out onto the sizable covered deck, which boasts ravishing views of the aquamarine bay and the lush islands a bit further out. Shopping, water sports and more shopping are generally the favored pursuits in St. Thomas, but the island is also home to a varied and vibrant artistic tradition, one which encompasses both Camille Pissaro (the founder of French Impressionism) and the colorful folk-inspired works being produced today. Contact: Wimco, 28 Pelham St., Newport, RI 02840. Call 1-800-932-3222 (in Rhode Island, 401-849-8012). Ref. AC-TOP.

Children: Y Pets: N Smoking: Y Handicap Access: N* Payment: C, P, T, A

St. Thomas Harbor

HARBOR LIGHTS *Rates: deluxe*
Open: year-round *Minimum Stay: one week*

This elegantly appointed three-bedroom home offers tranquil surroundings and fantastic views from its perch above St. Thomas Harbor. Modern amenities inside include air conditioning, cable TV and a VCR, an open bar and even a telescope for a bit of star-gazing. Outside, a refreshing swim in the pool can be followed by a soothing soak in the hot tub, while your beloved grills up a bit of the daily catch on the poolside grill. As you dine out on the terrace, you'll be dazzled by the twinkling lights of the harbor below, truly a beautiful sight. Contact: Nancy Anderson or Donajen Farrar, McLaughlin Anderson Vacations, 100 Blackbeard's Hill, St. Thomas, USVI 00802. Call 1-800-537-6246 (in St. Thomas, 809-776-0635).

Children: Y Pets: N Smoking: Y Handicap Access: N Payment: C, P, T

St. Thomas Harbor

WOUK ESTATE *Rates: deluxe*
Open: year-round *Minimum Stay: one week*

Surrounded by more than an acre of lush grounds and perched high on a hillside above St. Thomas Harbor, this enormous home, formerly owned by Herman Wouk, offers the epitome of luxurious island living. You can enjoy excellent views of the harbor and neighboring islands from the sun porch or deck or follow a flight of stairs down to the magnificent swimming pool, which enjoys equally charming vistas. The spacious interior is adorned with blue bit stone, marble and wood parquet; there are four generous bedrooms as well as plenty of living space. Although its splendid situation ensures tranquillity and seclusion, the town and beach are scarcely two minutes away. Contact: Villa Holidays, 13100 Wayzata Blvd., Suite 150, Minneapolis, MN 55343. Call 1-800-328-6262 (in Minnesota, 612-591-0076).

Children: Y Pets: N Smoking: Y Handicap Access: N Payment: C, P, T, V, M

Tutu Bay

SIGN OF THE GRIFFIN *Rates: inexpensive-moderate*
Open: year-round *Minimum Stay: none*

These one- and two-bedroom resort homes are tastefully furnished and include fully equipped kitchens; cable TV and maid service round out the creature comforts. From your own private balcony you can relish views of the rugged cliffs and aquamarine waters of Tutu Bay, the delightful neighboring islands and the wild blue Atlantic waters beyond. Sailing, scuba diving, snorkeling and tennis can be enjoyed at the nearby resorts and excellent golfing awaits enthusiasts at the Mahogany Run course next door. Despite the complex's secluded location on the quiet northern shore, the charming houses, winding streets and delightful duty-free shops of Charlotte Amalie are only 10 minutes away. Contact: Bill Jowers, Sign of the Griffin, P.O. Box 11668, St. Thomas, USVI 00801. Call 809-775-1715.

Children: Y   Pets: N   Smoking: Y   Handicap Access: N   Payment: C, P, T

Vessup Bay

CABRITE CONDOMINIUMS   *Rates: moderate-expensive*
Open: year-round   *Minimum Stay: one week*

Magnificent sunrises and equally romantic twilights await you here on the eastern end of this blessed isle. Sliding glass doors in each of these studio condos open onto a lovely sun terrace where you can watch the morning bloom into pink and gold or bask in the midday sunshine. Set right on the edge of an inviting pebble beach, they are also ideal for those who crave the sound of the surf. Guests share the use of a swimming pool and a tennis court, and there's also a superb restaurant on the grounds. Other beaches and the bustle of town are just a few minutes away. Contact: Villa Holidays, 13100 Wayzata Blvd., Suite 150, Minneapolis, MN 55343. Call 1-800-328-6262 (in Minnesota, 612-591-0076).

Children: Y Pets: N Smoking: Y Handicap Access: N Payment: C, P, T, V, M

Vessup Bay

EASTERN SHORE   *Rates: deluxe*
Open: year-round   *Minimum Stay: one week*

This sprawling four-bedroom contemporary house on the bustling eastern end of the island will delight you with its charming views and plush amenities. The living and dining area features high ceilings, tasteful furnishings and two walls of picture windows. This room opens onto the tiled sun deck and large pool and shares with them a panorama of the bustling harbor, green hillsides and open waters beyond. A pleasant stroll will bring you to Vessup Beach and water sports aplenty, while restaurants and nightspots are right around the corner. Contact: Villa Holidays, 13100 Wayzata Blvd., Suite 150, Minneapolis, MN 55343. Call 1-800-328-6262 (in Minnesota, 612-591-0076).

Children: Y Pets: N Smoking: Y Handicap Access: N Payment: C, P, T, V, M

Vessup Bay

EASTWIND   *Rates: inexpensive-moderate*
Open: year-round   *Minimum Stay: one week*

Tucked away in a quiet residential neighborhood on the far eastern end of the island, this impeccably maintained one-bedroom condo is a delightful retreat for up to four guests. From your balcony you can watch the palms swaying in the breeze as you sip a frozen daiquiri after a day of shopping in Charlotte Amalie. Early risers will be richly rewarded if they stroll down to the soft sands of Vessup Beach to watch the glorious sunrise over the neighboring islands. A variety of water sports can be enjoyed in the area and just a bit to the north, the unique underwater observatory at Coral World brings the wonders of the marine realm amazingly close. Contact: Wimco, 28 Pelham St., Newport, RI 02840. Call 1-800-932-3222 (in Rhode Island, 401-849-8012). Ref. MA-EAS.

Children: Y Pets: N Smoking: Y Handicap Access: N Payment: C, P, T, A

Vessup Bay

FIVE GABLES   *Rates: deluxe*
Open: year-round   *Minimum Stay: one week*

The balustraded terraces, gently curving archways and handsome landscaping of this multi-level house lend it an air of easy elegance. The interior features cool tile floors and informal rattan furniture in the main living areas and three generous bedrooms. Charming stairways lead down to the gracious pool, where you can splash or sun at your leisure. Entertaining and private relaxation are made all the more convenient by the poolside wet bar and barbecue. A short drive will bring you to marinas and the yacht club, not to mention the exquisite beaches for which this island is so loved. Contact: Wimco, 28 Pelham St., Newport, RI 02840. Call 1-800-932-3222 (in Rhode Island, 401-849-8012). Ref. BB-FRA.

Children: Y Pets: N Smoking: Y Handicap Access: N Payment: C, P, T, A

Vessup Bay

ISLAND VIEW   *Rates: deluxe*
Open: year-round   *Minimum Stay: one week*

This four-bedroom, four-bath home in St. Thomas overlooks Red Hook Harbor and offers sweeping views of the Caribbean and the neighboring islands. Relax in the wicker furniture in the living and dining areas, both of which have large glass doors opening onto the terrace, where you can dive into the private pool. Sun in the lounge chairs after you swim or go snorkeling, diving, windsurfing, or boating. Rent a bike or scooter in town and explore the island, then shop in quaint stores and duty-free shops. You can even arrange for a full staff to wait on you from head to toe. Contact: LaCure Villas, 11661 San Vicente Blvd., Suite 1010, Los Angeles, CA 90049. Call 800-387-2715/2720.

Children: Y Pets: N Smoking: Y Handicap Access: N Payment: All

Vessup Bay

POINT CONDOMINIUMS   *Rates: inexpensive-deluxe*
Open: year-round   *Minimum Stay: one week*

Found on the popular eastern end of the island, these condos are fabulous bases for active vacations or lazy holidays. The complex resembles a residential neighborhood rather than a tourist resort due to the well-planned layout. The beach is only a few minutes away, and there's a delightful new restaurant located right on the premises. The two-bedroom units feature a full kitchen and a large living room opening through sliding glass doors to a bi-level sun deck with lovely views and fine furnishings. Modern amenities include a washer and dryer and a stereo. The one-bedroom units have a kitchenette and a porch with barbecue that faces the harbor. Both boast color TV and ceiling fans. Contact: Vacation Home Rentals Worldwide, 235 Kensington Ave., Norwood, NJ 07648. Call 1-800-633-3284 (in New Jersey, 201-767-9393). Ref. ST101, ST102.

Children: Y   Pets: N   Smoking: Y   Handicap Access: N   Payment: C, P, T

Water Island

MURRAY HOUSE   *Rates: moderate-expensive*
Open: year-round   *Minimum Stay: one week*

Water Island is a completely private tropical islet found at the opening of Charlotte Amalie Bay. The car that's included with this lovely home means you'll be able to explore this secluded wonderland at your leisure. The house itself includes three bedrooms—two of them quite large—and a spacious living and dining area. This latter area opens onto a generous patio, where you can enjoy stunning views of the Caribbean Sea and neighboring islands. Nearby are the silky sands and warm waters of Honeymoon Beach and the excitement of Charlotte Amalie is only a ferry ride away. Contact: Rent A Home International, 7200 34th Ave. N.W., Seattle, WA 98117. Call 206-545-6963.

Children: Y Pets: N Smoking: Y Handicap Access: N Payment: C, P, T, V, M

Water Island

PELICAN POINT BREEZE VILLA   *Rates: deluxe*
Open: year-round   *Minimum Stay: one week*

Every room in this light-filled house enjoys delightful ocean views and opens through a sliding glass door onto the spacious covered balcony. Located on tranquil Water Island, just a few minutes by ferry from St. Thomas, this pretty home offers three bedrooms and three baths for up to four guests. Modern amenities abound, from the appliances in the gourmet kitchen, to the stereo and TV, to the use of a car for exploring the island. A charming pathway lined with unusual plants leads you down to warm private waters, ideal for snorkeling, fishing, swimming or just splashing about. Contact: Villa Holidays, 13100 Wayzata Blvd., Suite 150, Minneapolis, MN 55343. Call 1-800-328-6262 (in Minnesota, 612-591-0076).

Children: Y Pets: N Smoking: Y Handicap Access: N Payment: C, P, T, V, M

Water Island

PINEAPPLE VILLAGE   *Rates: moderate-expensive*
Open: year-round   *Minimum Stay: one week*

Ideal for those who want to be near all the action but removed from the crowds, lovely Pineapple Village is found in a secluded corner of one of the island's most luxurious resorts. Just a few steps away are several large swimming pools, a health club, restaurants, shops, and hotel amenities, all at your disposal. Of course, the delightfully warm waters at the beach await nearby as well. The units vary in size (so groups of almost any number can easily be accommodated) but they all enjoy pleasant furnishings and lovely garden patios. Contact: Villa

Holidays, 13100 Wayzata Blvd., Suite 150, Minneapolis, MN 55343.
Call 1-800-328-6262 (in Minnesota, 612-591-0076).

Children: Y Pets: N Smoking: Y Handicap Access: N Payment: C, P, T, V, M

Water Island

REEF TERRACES

Rates: inexpensive-moderate

Open: year-round

Minimum Stay: one week

If even the mellow pace of life in St. Thomas seems too hectic for you,
consider this lovely complex tucked away on the "private" Virgin isle
of Water Island. The studios at Reef Terraces feature complete kitchens and spacious terraces that are almost as large as the entire apartment. You'll want to spend some time out here, since the views of the
Caribbean from this hillside location are stunning. A short walk will
bring you to a delightful palm-lined beach. And seclusion doesn't have
to mean isolation: The excitement and bustle of St. Thomas is only
five minutes away by ferry. Contact: Rent A Home International, 7200
34th Ave. N.W., Seattle, WA 98117. Call 206-545-6963.

Children: Y Pets: N Smoking: Y Handicap Access: N Payment: C, P, T, V, M

Caribbean Tourist Offices

ANGUILLA
  Tourist Information
  271 Main Street
  Northport, NY 11721
  212-869-0402
  800-553-4939

ANTIGUA & BARBUDA
  Tourist Board
  610 Fifth Avenue
  New York, NY 10020
  212-541-4117

ARUBA
  Tourist Authority
  521 Fifth Avenue
  New York, NY 10017
  212-246-3030

BAHAMAS
  Tourist Office
  150 East 52nd Street
  New York, NY 10022
  212-758-2777

  875 North Michigan Avenue
  Chicago, IL 60611
  312-787-8203

  3450 Wilshire Boulevard
  Los Angeles, CA 90010
  213-385-0033

BARBADOS
  Board of Tourism
  800 Second Avenue
  New York, NY 10017
  212-986-6516

  3440 Wilshire Boulevard
  Los Angeles, CA 90010
  213-380-2198

BERMUDA
  Department of Tourism
  310 Madison Avenue
  New York, NY 10017
  212-818-9800

BONAIRE
  Tourist Office
  275 Seventh Avenue
  New York, NY 10001
  212-242-7707

BRITISH VIRGIN ISLANDS
  Tourist Board
  370 Lexington Avenue
  New York, NY 10017
  212-696-0400
  800-835-8530

  1686 Union Street
  San Francisco, CA 94123
  415-775-0344

CAYMAN ISLANDS
  Department of Tourism
  420 Lexington Avenue
  New York, NY 10170
  212-682-5582

  980 North Michigan Avenue
  Chicago, IL 60611
  312-944-5602

  3440 Wilshire Boulevard
  Los Angeles, CA 90010
  213-738-1968

CURACAO
  Tourist Board
  400 Madison Avenue
  New York, NY 10017
  212-751-8266

DOMINICAN REPUBLIC
  Tourist Office
  485 Madison Avenue
  New York, NY 10022
  212-826-0750

FRENCH WEST INDIES
(Guadeloupe, Martinique, St.
Barthelemy, St. Martin)
  Tourist Board
  610 Fifth Avenue
  New York, NY 10020
  212-757-1125

French West Indies (*cont.*)
2305 Cedars Spring Road
Dallas, TX 75201
214-720-4010

1 Hallidie Plaza #250
San Francisco, CA 94102
415-986-4174

GRENADA
Tourist Board
141 East 44th Street
New York, NY 10017
212-687-9554

JAMAICA
Tourist Board
866 Second Avenue
New York, NY 10017
212-688-7650

36 South Wabash Avenue
Chicago, IL 60603
312-346-1546

3440 Wilshire Boulevard
Los Angeles, CA 90010
213-384-1123

MONTSERRAT
Tourist Board
P.O. Box 7, Plymouth
Montserrat, West Indies
809-491-2230

PUERTO RICO
Tourism Company
575 Fifth Avenue
New York, NY 10017
212-599-6262

9733 Marquette Avenue
Chicago, IL 60617
312-221-3733

3575 West Cahuenga Boulevard
Los Angeles, CA 90068
213-874-5991

SABA & ST. EUSTATIUS
Tourist Office
271 Main Street
Northport, NY 11768
212-936-0050

ST. KITTS & NEVIS
Tourist Board
414 East 75th Street
New York, NY 10021
212-535-1234

ST. LUCIA
Tourist Board
820 Second Avenue
New York, NY 10017
212-867-2950

ST. MAARTEN
Tourist Board
275 Seventh Avenue
New York, NY 10001
212-989-0000

ST. VINCENT
Tourist Office
801 Second Avenue
New York, NY 10017
212-687-4981
800-696-9611

TRINIDAD & TOBAGO
Tourist Board
118-35 Queens Boulevard
Forest Hills, NY 11375
718-575-3909

TURKS & CAICOS
Tourist Board
271 Main Street
Northport, NY 11768
516-261-9600
800-441-4419

U.S. VIRGIN ISLANDS
(St. Croix, St. John, St. Thomas)
Division of Tourism
1270 Avenue of the Americas
New York, NY 10020
212-582-4520

122 South Michigan Avenue
Chicago, IL 60603
312-461-0180

3460 Wilshire Boulevard
Los Angeles, CA 90010
213-739-0138